The Princess of Convenient Plot Devices

Characters 2

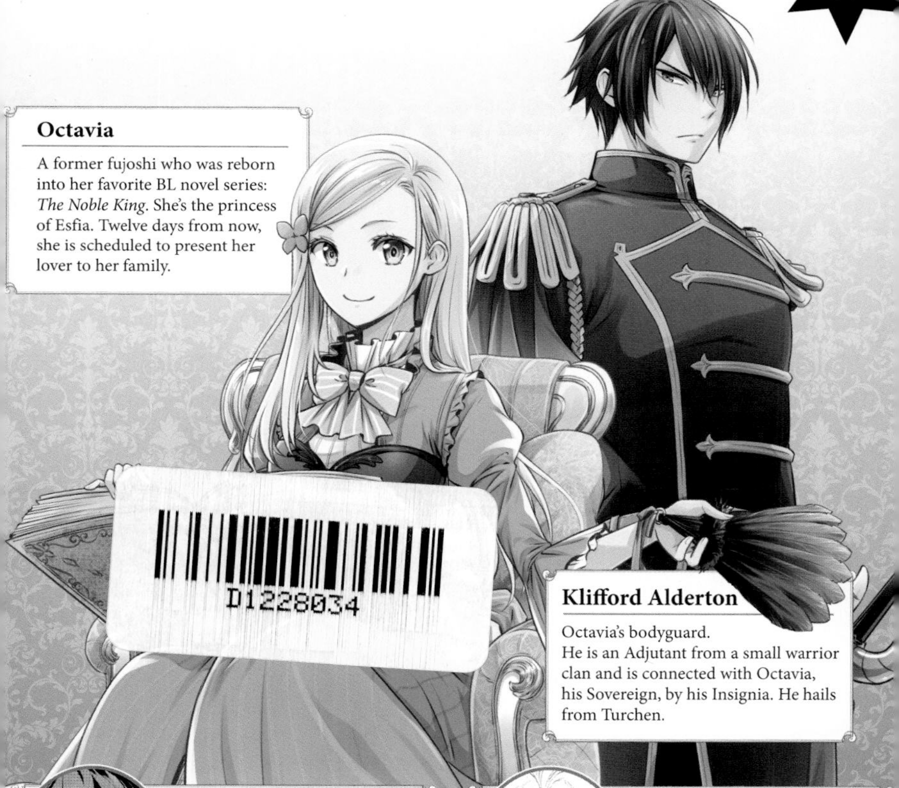

Octavia

A former fujoshi who was reborn into her favorite BL novel series: *The Noble King*. She's the princess of Esfia. Twelve days from now, she is scheduled to present her lover to her family.

Klifford Alderton

Octavia's bodyguard.
He is an Adjutant from a small warrior clan and is connected with Octavia, his Sovereign, by his Insignia. He hails from Turchen.

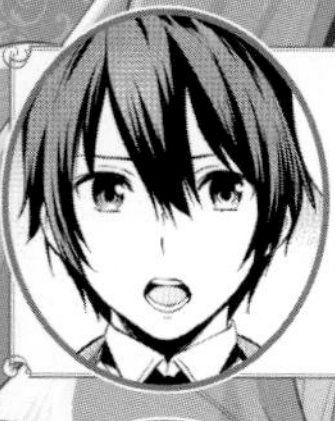

Sil Burks

The protagonist of *The Noble King* and Sirius's lover. Somebody wants him dead. His past holds a dark secret...

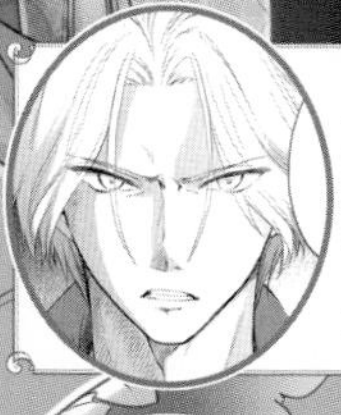

Sirius

The first prince of Esfia and the future king. He's seeking out the ringleader targeting Sil. Mysteriously, he's missing part of his childhood memories.

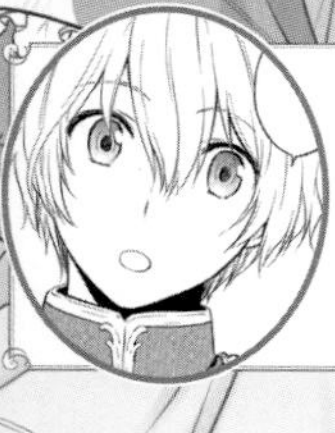

Alexis

The second prince of Esfia. Octavia's baby brother and confidant. He's currently away on a secret mission.

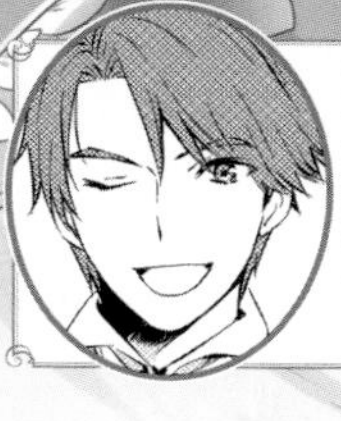

Derek Nightfellow

The son of Duke Nightfellow. Friend and ride-or-die ally of Sirius and Sil. He picked on Octavia when they were kids.

contents

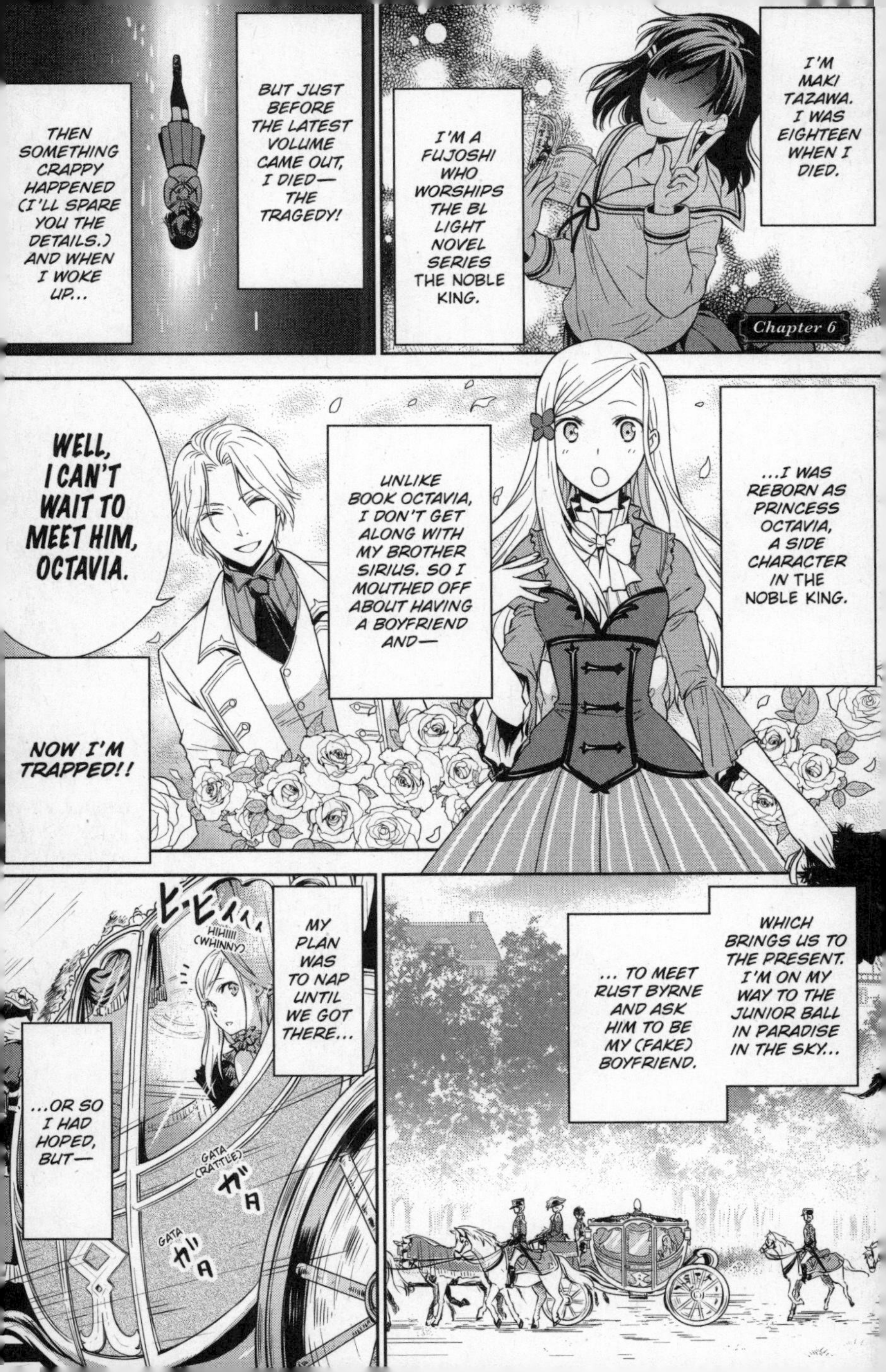

Chapter 6
I'M MAKI TAZAWA. I WAS EIGHTEEN WHEN I DIED.
I'M A FUJOSHI WHO WORSHIPS THE BL LIGHT NOVEL SERIES THE NOBLE KING.
BUT JUST BEFORE THE LATEST VOLUME CAME OUT, I DIED—THE TRAGEDY!
THEN SOMETHING CRAPPY HAPPENED (I'LL SPARE YOU THE DETAILS.) AND WHEN I WOKE UP...
...I WAS REBORN AS PRINCESS OCTAVIA, A SIDE CHARACTER IN THE NOBLE KING.
UNLIKE BOOK OCTAVIA, I DON'T GET ALONG WITH MY BROTHER SIRIUS. SO I MOUTHED OFF ABOUT HAVING A BOYFRIEND AND—
WELL, I CAN'T WAIT TO MEET HIM, OCTAVIA.
NOW I'M TRAPPED!!
WHICH BRINGS US TO THE PRESENT. I'M ON MY WAY TO THE JUNIOR BALL IN PARADISE IN THE SKY...
... TO MEET RUST BYRNE AND ASK HIM TO BE MY (FAKE) BOYFRIEND.
MY PLAN WAS TO NAP UNTIL WE GOT THERE...
HIHIIII (WHINNY)
...OR SO I HAD HOPED, BUT—
GATA (RATTLE)
GATA

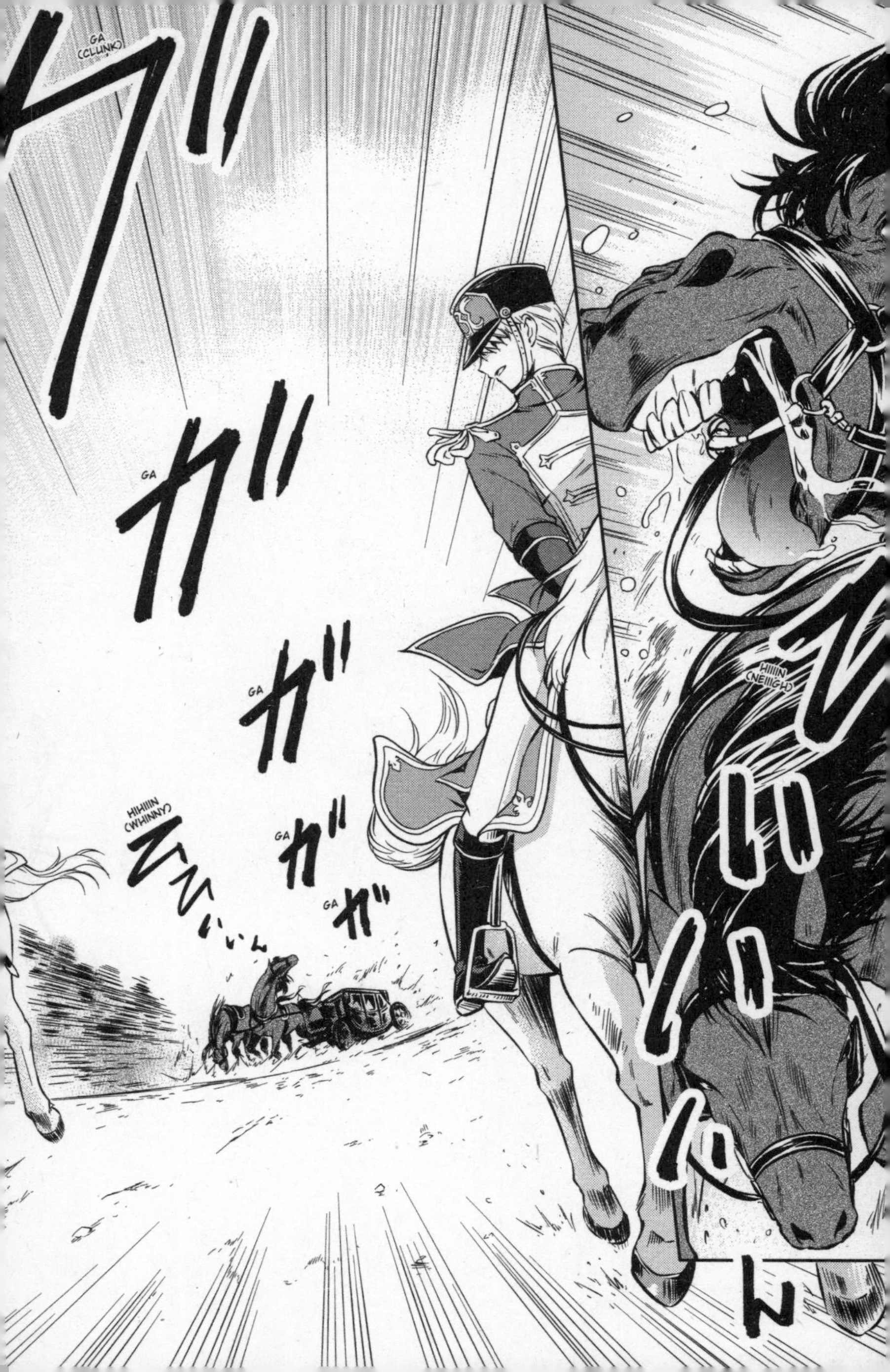
HIIIIN (NEIIIGH)
GA (CLUNK)
GA
GA
GA
GA
HIHIIIN (WHINNY)

To be continued...

The Princess of Convenient Plot Devices

2

Kazusa Yoneda

Original Story
Mamecyoro

Character Design
Mitsuya Fuji

Translation
Sarah Moon

Lettering
Phil Christie

WATASHI WA GOTSUGOSHUGI NA KAIKETSUTANTO NO OJO DEARU Vol. 2
©Kazusa Yoneda 2020
©Mamecyoro, Mitsuya Fuji 2020
First published in Japan in 2020 by KADOKAWA CORPORATION, Tokyo.
English translation rights arranged with KADOKAWA CORPORATION, Tokyo, through TUTTLE-MORI AGENCY, INC., Tokyo.

Yen Press
150 West 30th Street, 19th Floor
New York, NY 10001

✦ Visit us at yenpress.com
✦ facebook.com/yenpress
✦ twitter.com/yenpress
✦ yenpress.tumblr.com
✦ instagram.com/yenpress

First Yen Press Edition: June 2023
Edited by Yen Press Editorial: Emily Gikas, Riley Pearsall
Designed by Yen Press Design: Andy Swist

Yen Press is an imprint of Yen Press, LLC.
The Yen Press name and logo are trademarks of Yen Press, LLC.

Library of Congress Control Number: 2022947769

ISBNs: 978-1-9753-4876-2 (paperback)
        978-1-9753-4877-9 (ebook)

10 9 8 7 6 5 4 3 2 1

LSC-C

Printed in the United States of America

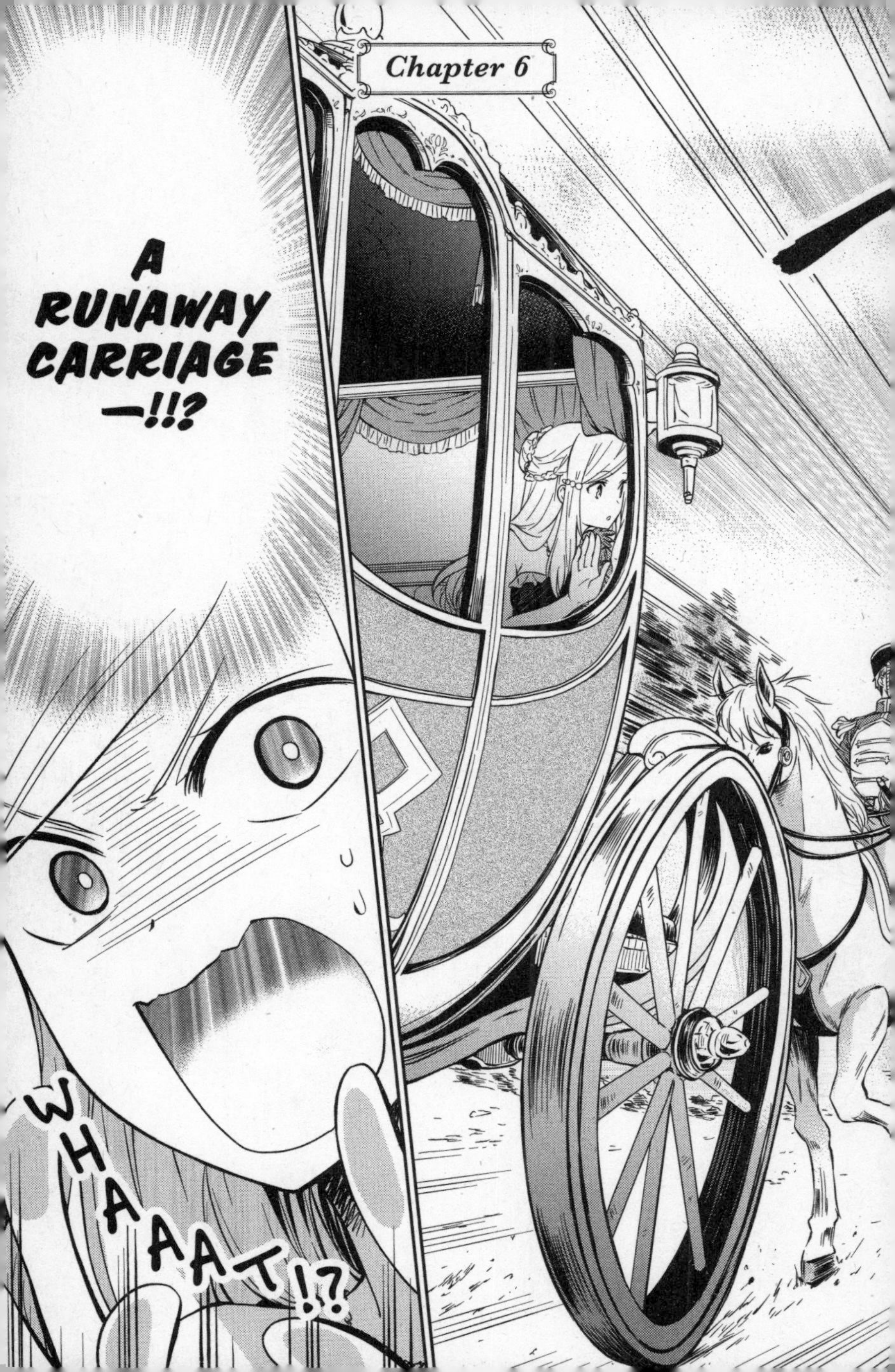
Chapter 6
A RUNAWAY CARRIAGE —!!?
WHAAAAT!?

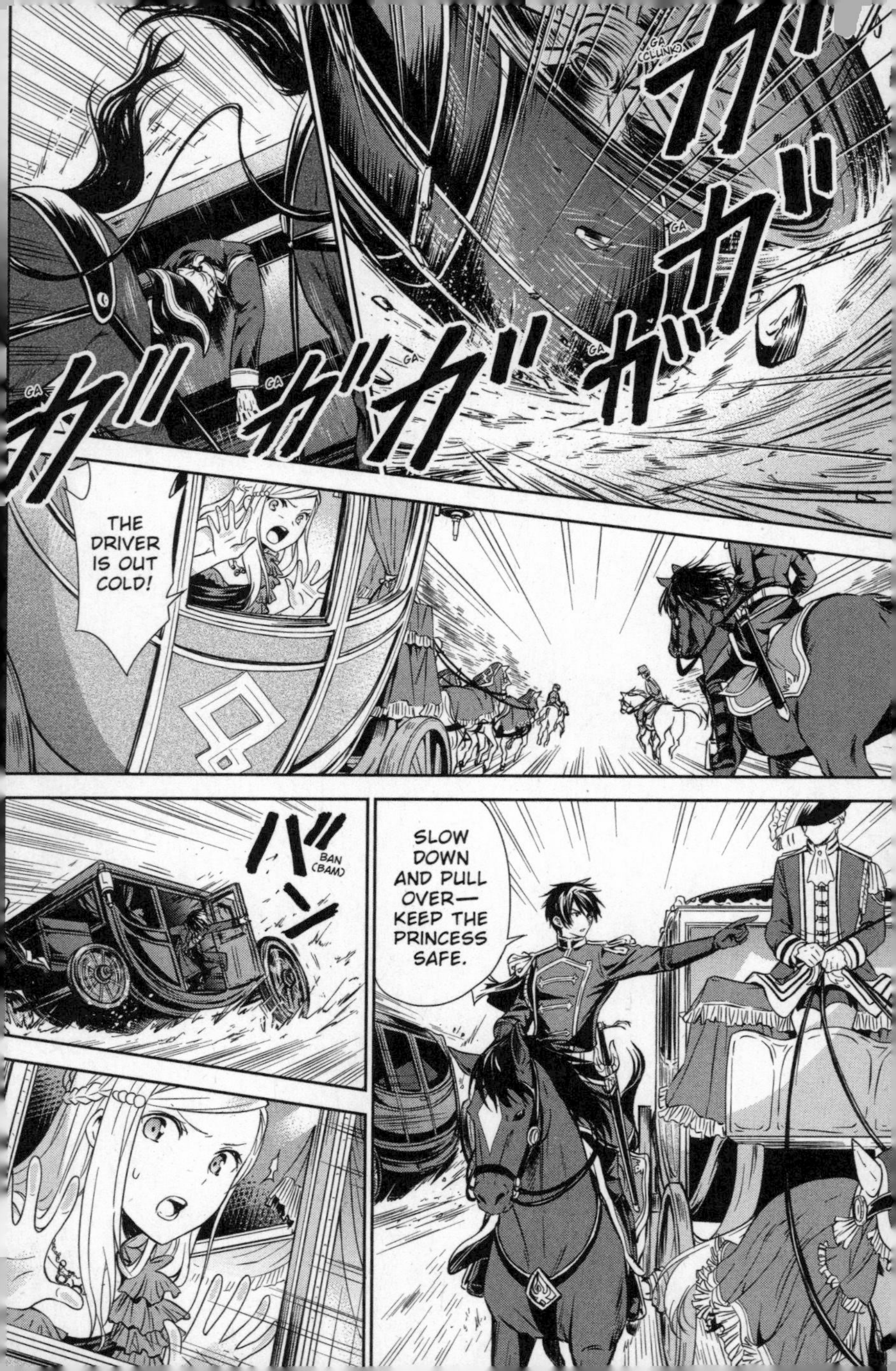
GA (CLUNK)
GA
GA
GA
GA
GA
THE DRIVER IS OUT COLD!
SLOW DOWN AND PULL OVER— KEEP THE PRINCESS SAFE.
BAN (BAM)

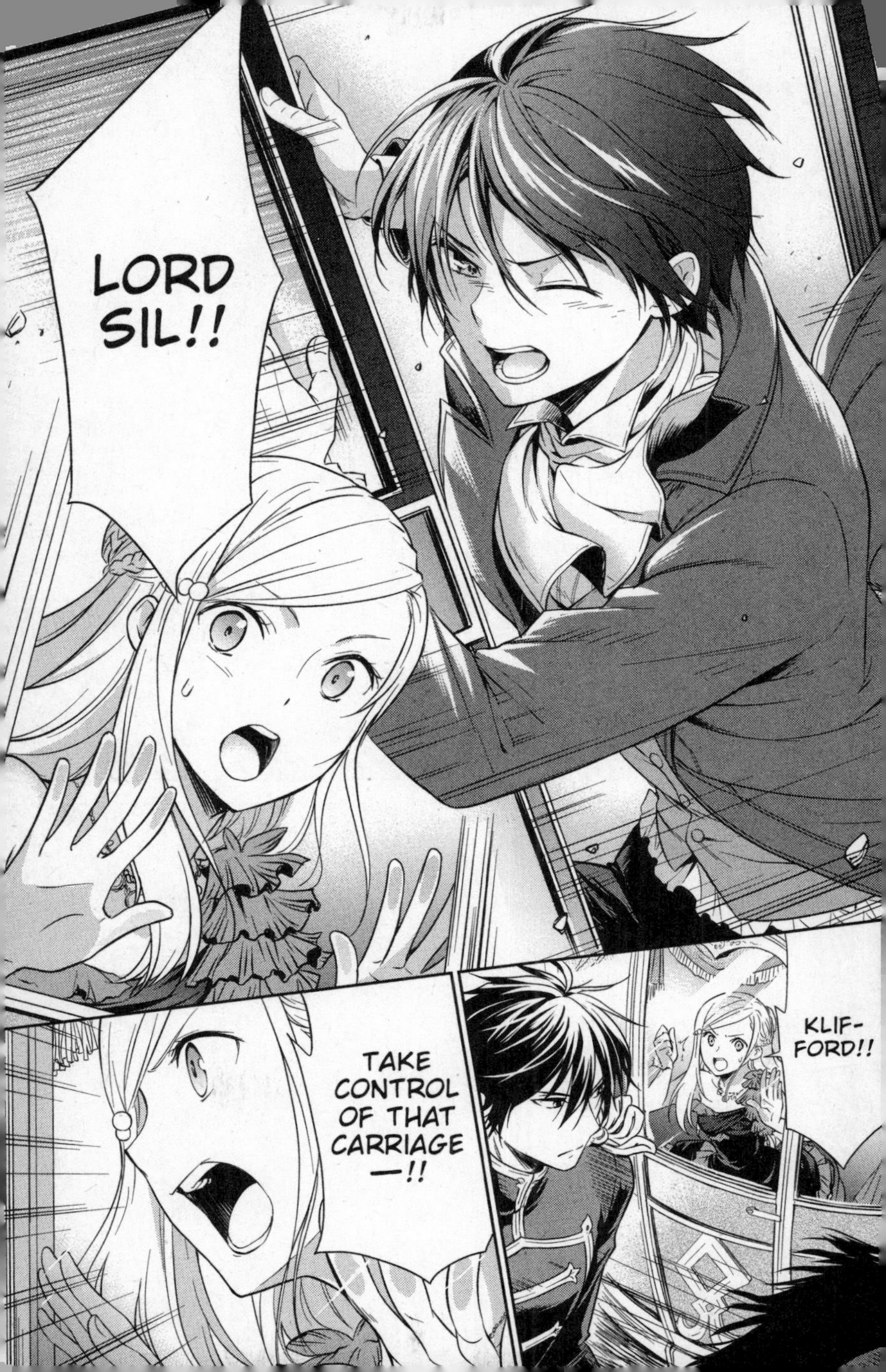
LORD SIL!!
KLIF-FORD!!
TAKE CONTROL OF THAT CARRIAGE —!!

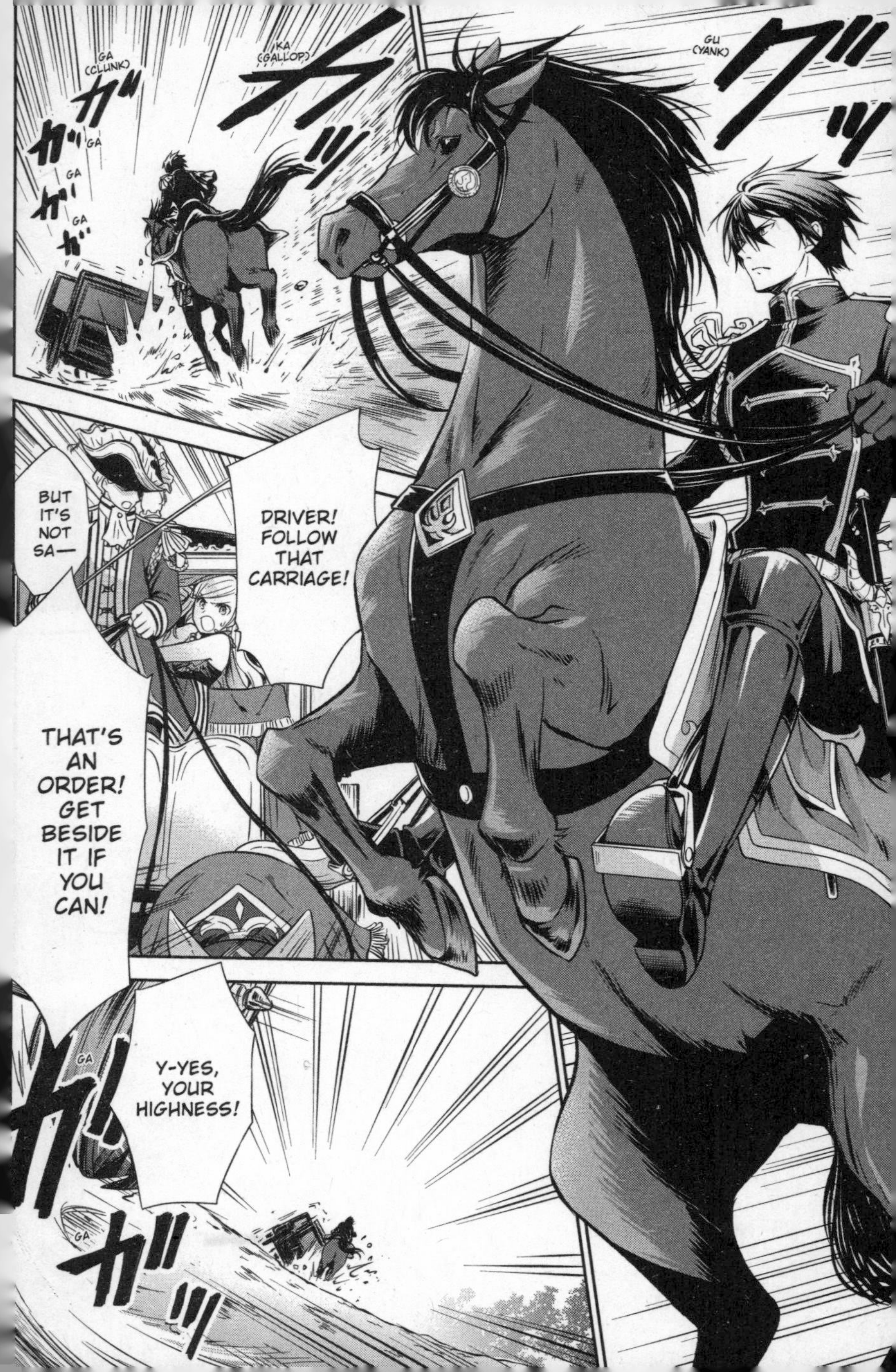
GU (YANK)
KA (GALLOP)
GA (CLUNK)
GA
GA
GA
DRIVER! FOLLOW THAT CARRIAGE!
BUT IT'S NOT SA—
THAT'S AN ORDER! GET BESIDE IT IF YOU CAN!
Y-YES, YOUR HIGHNESS!
GA
GA

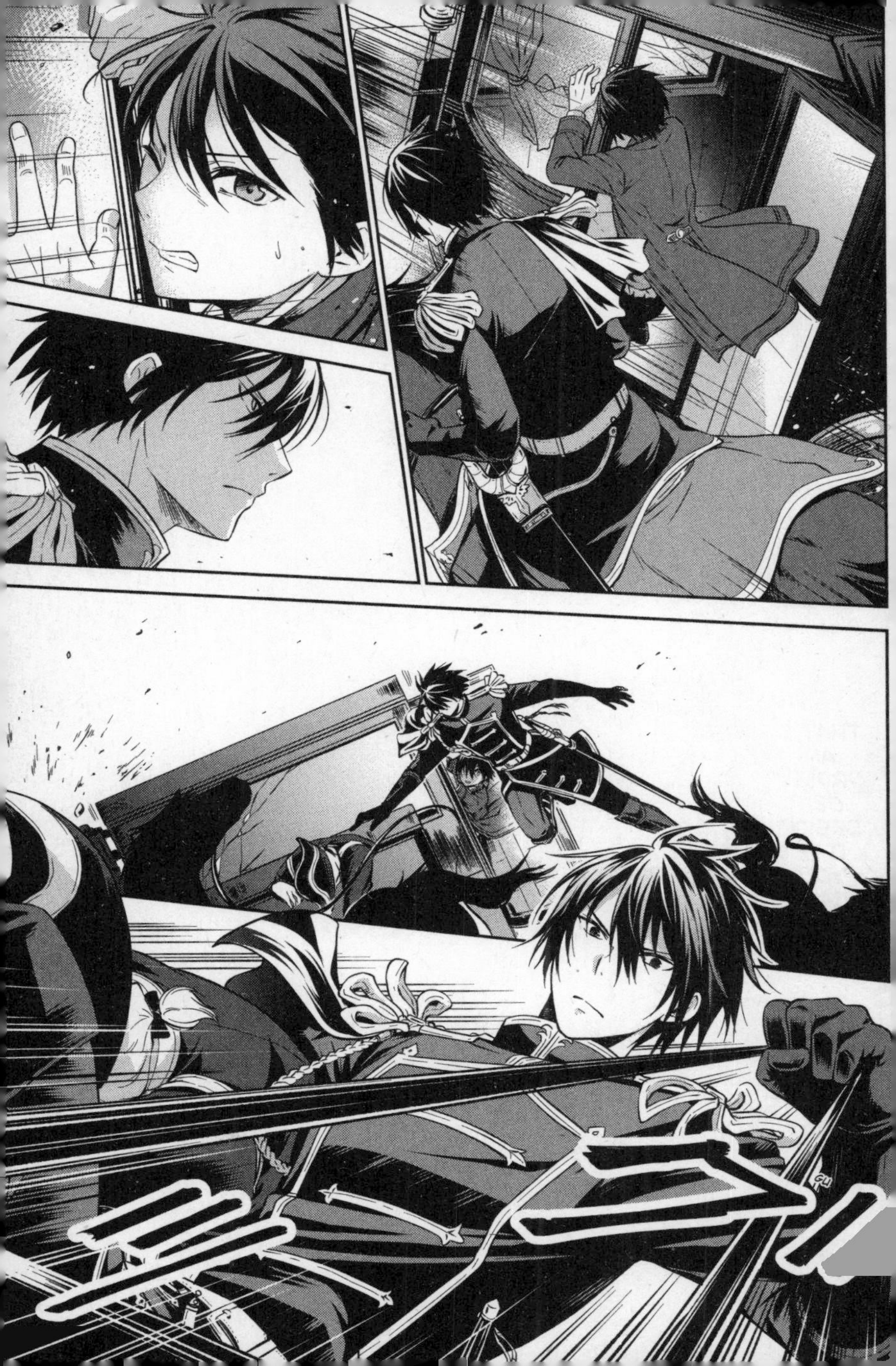
GU

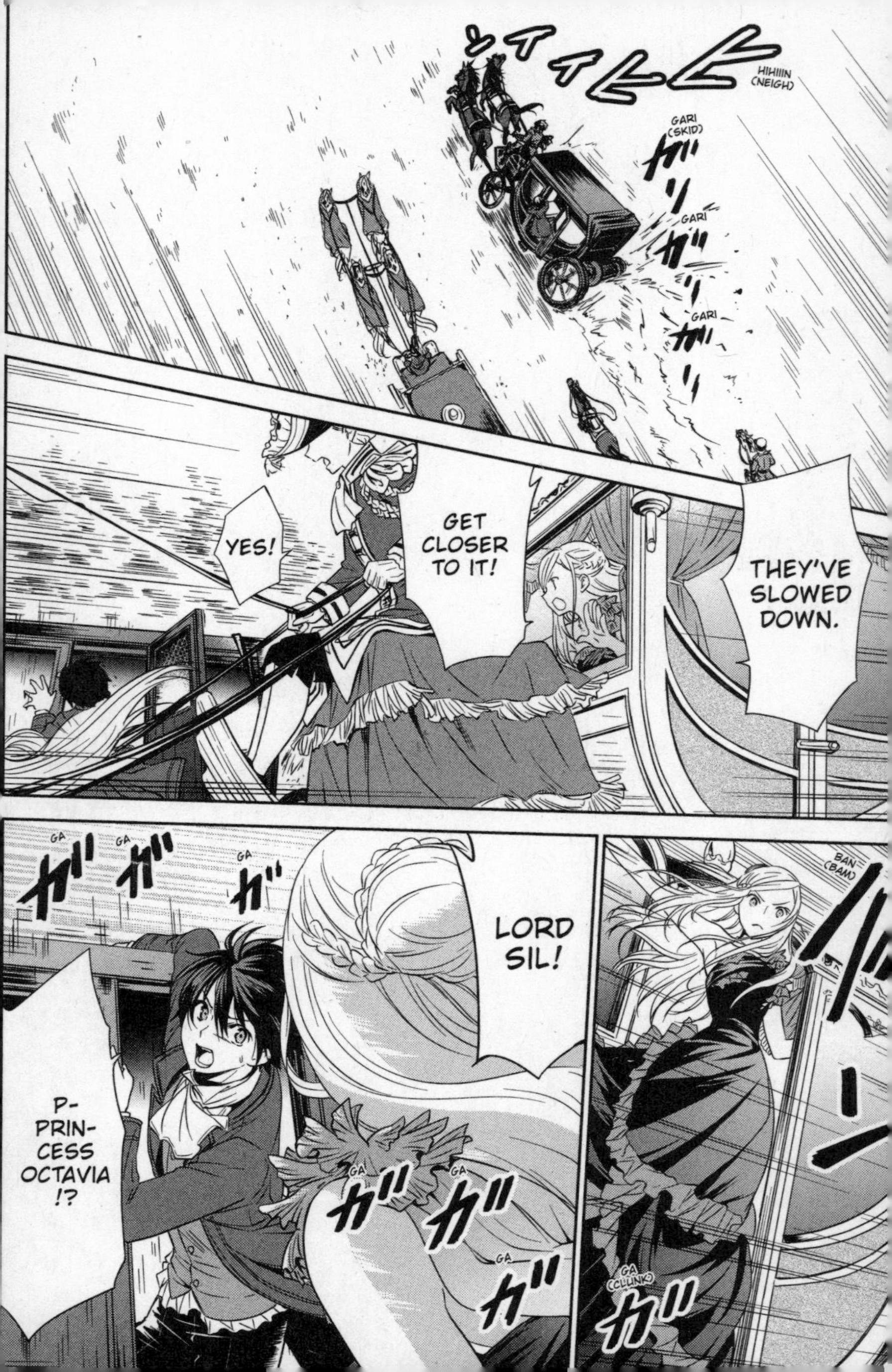
HIHIIIN (NEIGH)
GARI (SKID)
GARI
GARI
THEY'VE SLOWED DOWN.
GET CLOSER TO IT!
YES!
BAN (BAM)
GA (CLUNK)
LORD SIL!
GA
GA
GA
GA
GA
GA
P-PRINCESS OCTAVIA!?

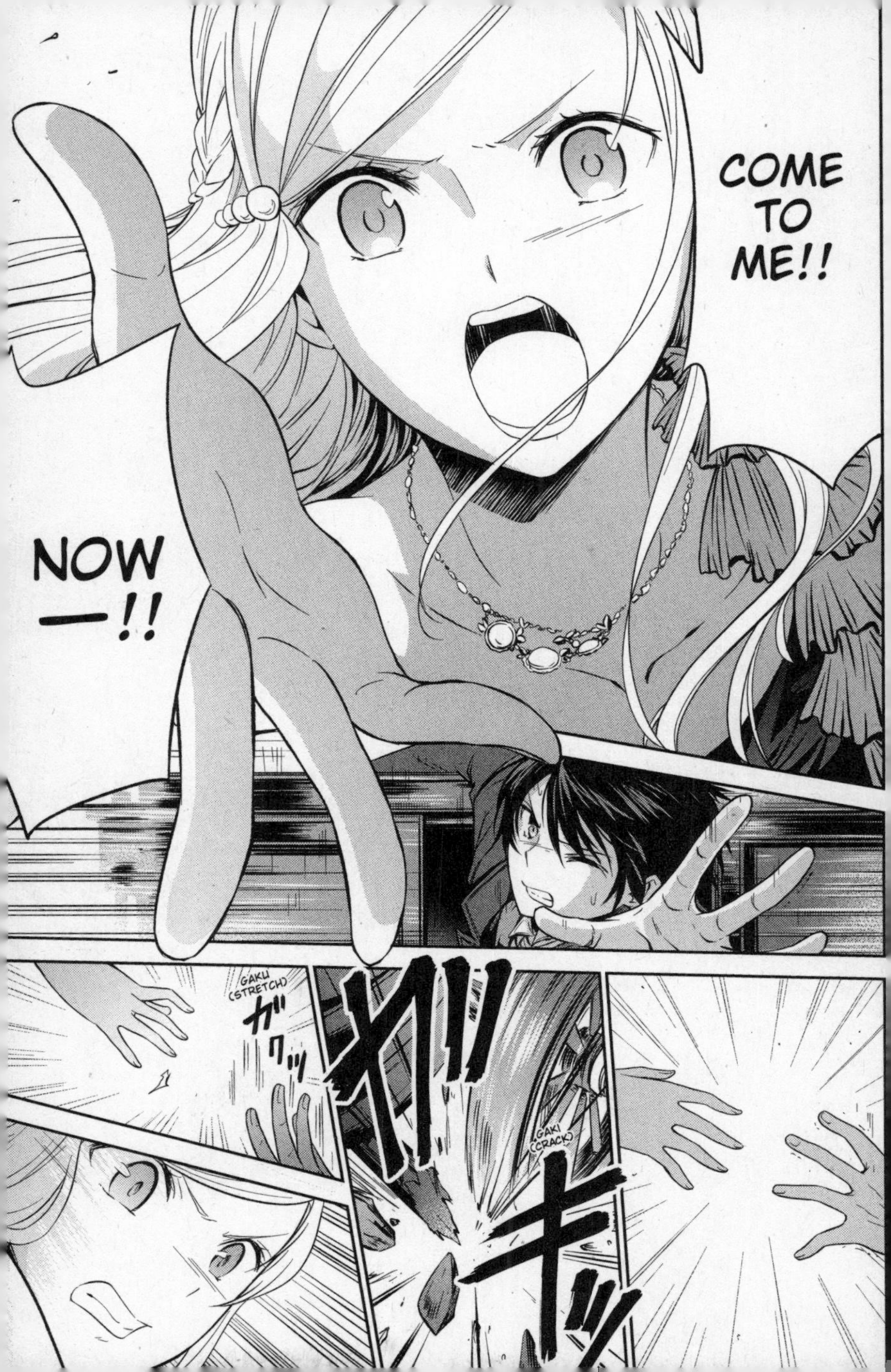
COME TO ME!!
NOW—!!
GAKI (CRACK)
GAKU (STRETCH)

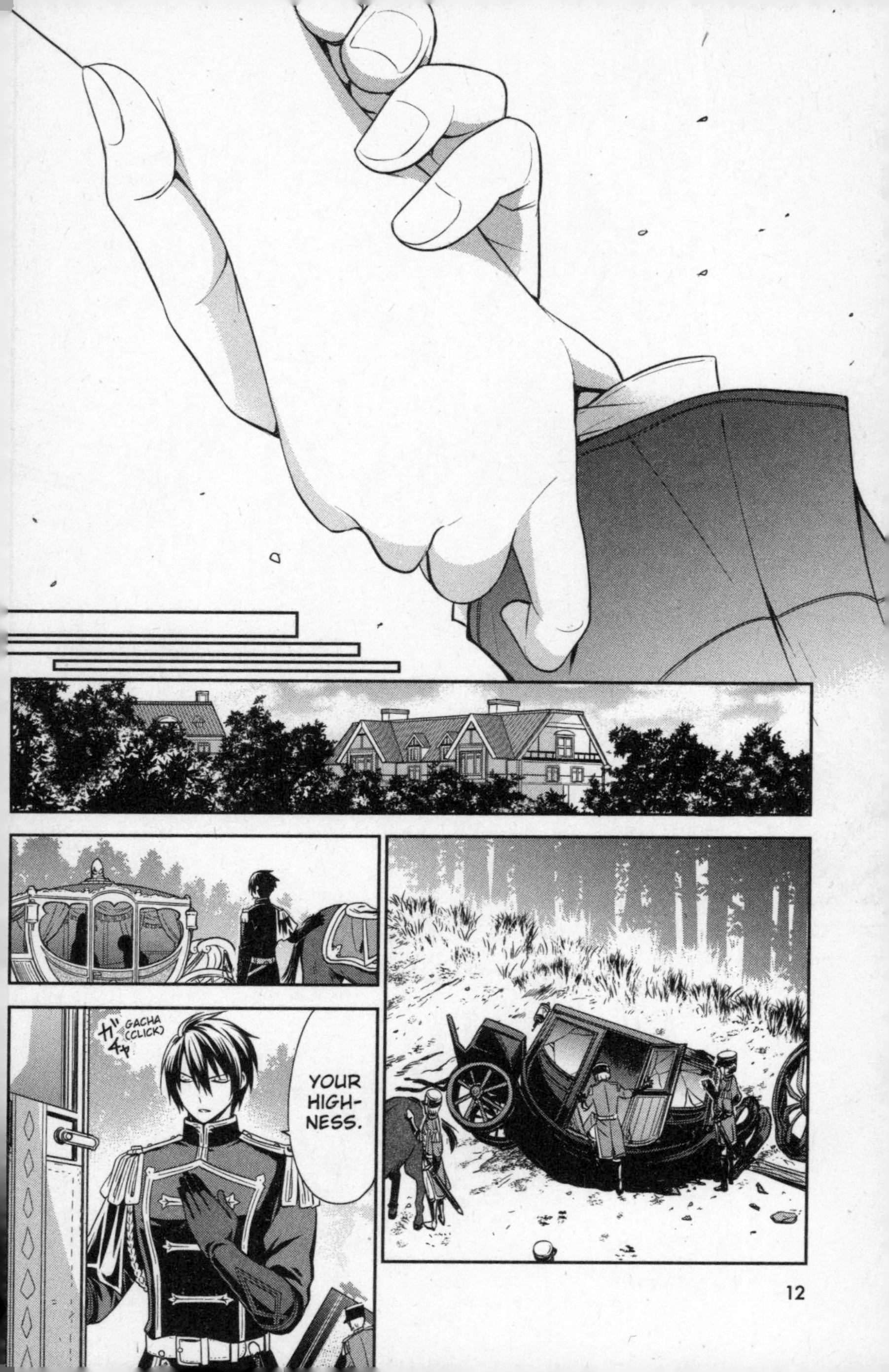
ガチャ GACHA (CLICK)
YOUR HIGH-NESS.

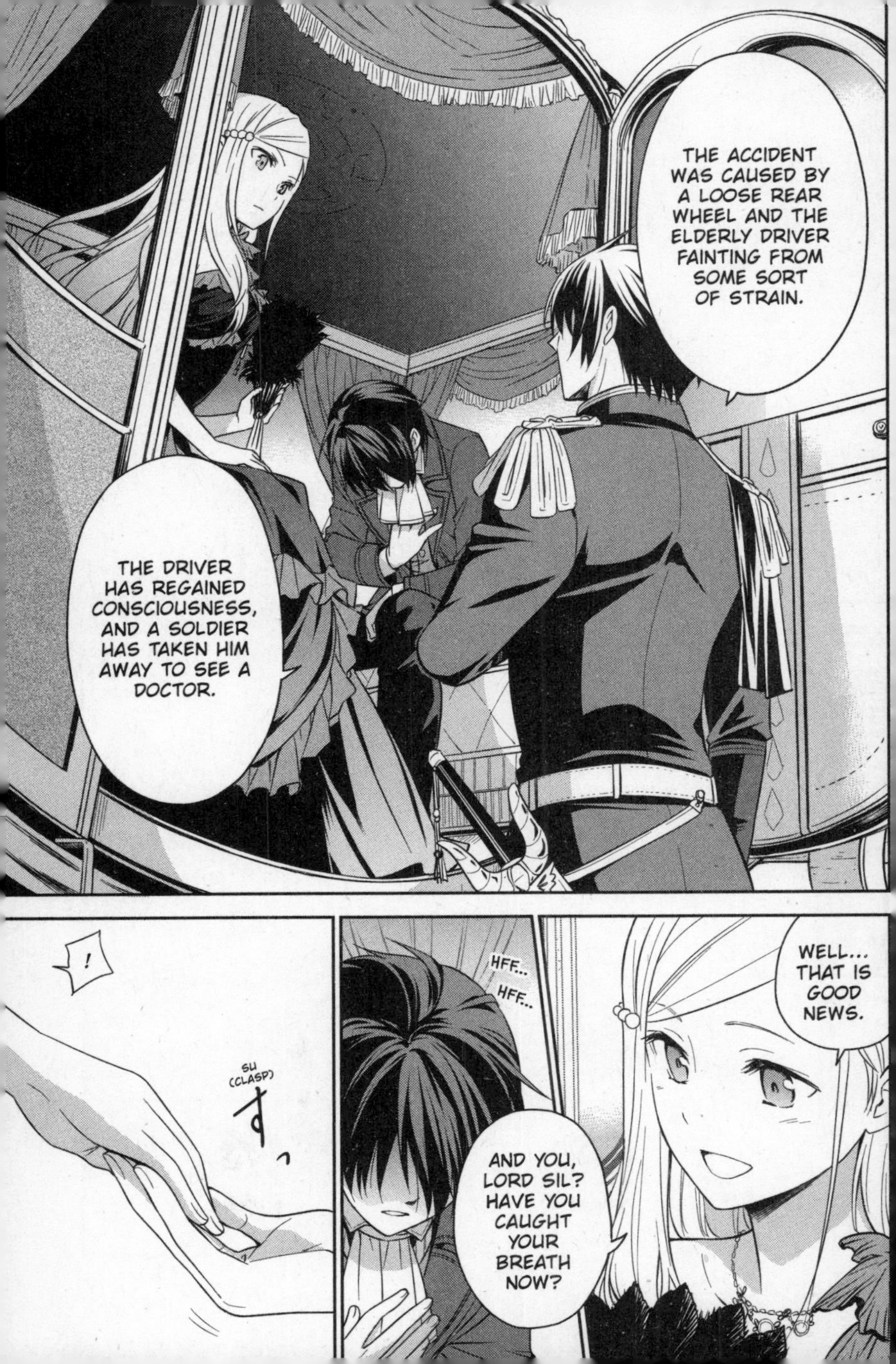
THE ACCIDENT WAS CAUSED BY A LOOSE REAR WHEEL AND THE ELDERLY DRIVER FAINTING FROM SOME SORT OF STRAIN.
THE DRIVER HAS REGAINED CONSCIOUSNESS, AND A SOLDIER HAS TAKEN HIM AWAY TO SEE A DOCTOR.
WELL... THAT IS GOOD NEWS.
HFF... HFF...
AND YOU, LORD SIL? HAVE YOU CAUGHT YOUR BREATH NOW?
!
SU (CLASP)

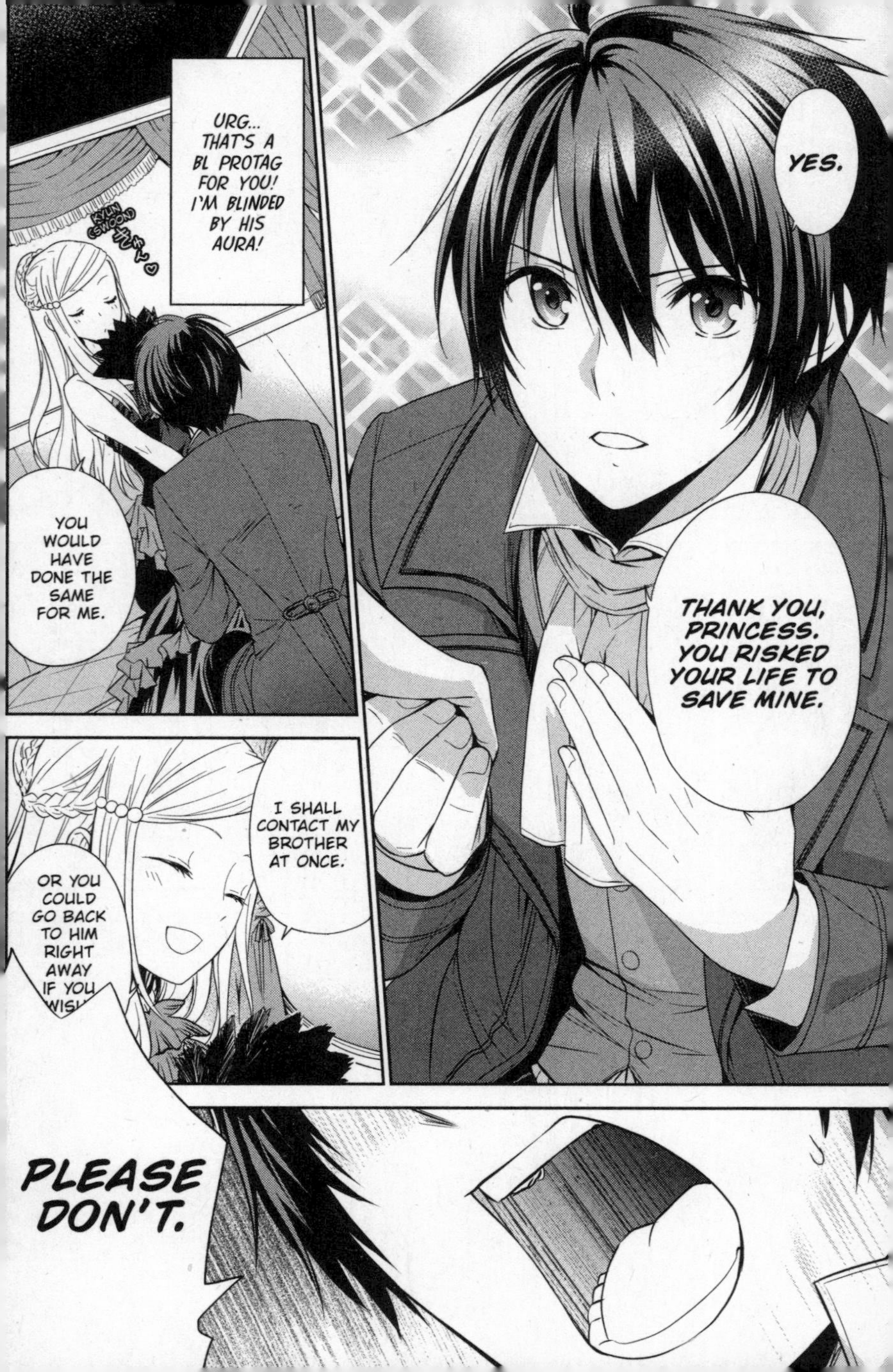
YES.
THANK YOU, PRINCESS. YOU RISKED YOUR LIFE TO SAVE MINE.
URG... THAT'S A BL PROTAG FOR YOU! I'M BLINDED BY HIS AURA!
KYUN (SWOON)
YOU WOULD HAVE DONE THE SAME FOR ME.
I SHALL CONTACT MY BROTHER AT ONCE.
OR YOU COULD GO BACK TO HIM RIGHT AWAY IF YOU WISH.
PLEASE DON'T.

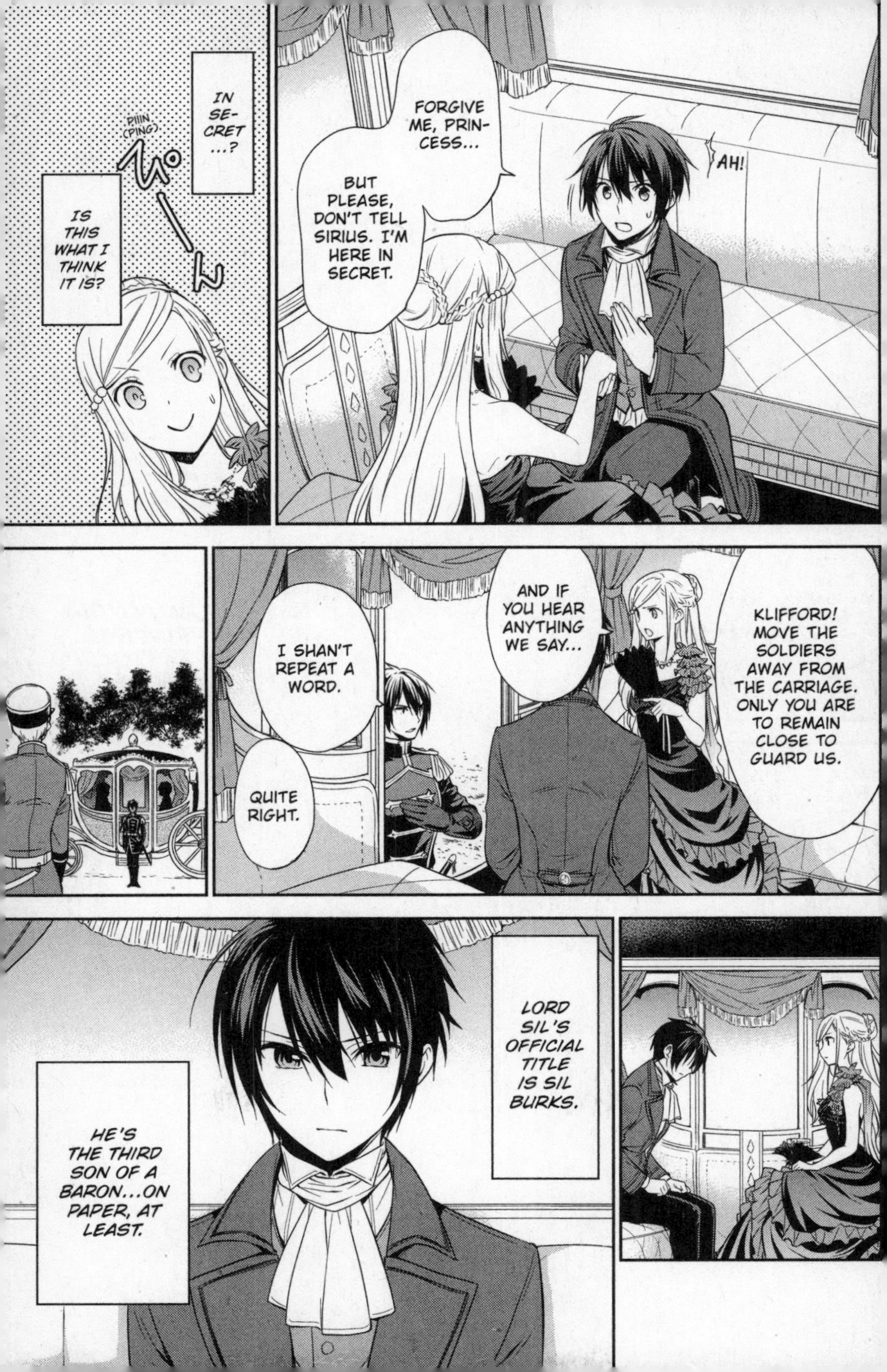
AH!
FORGIVE ME, PRINCESS...
BUT PLEASE, DON'T TELL SIRIUS. I'M HERE IN SECRET.
IN SECRET...?
PIIIN (PING)
IS THIS WHAT I THINK IT IS?
KLIFFORD! MOVE THE SOLDIERS AWAY FROM THE CARRIAGE. ONLY YOU ARE TO REMAIN CLOSE TO GUARD US.
AND IF YOU HEAR ANYTHING WE SAY...
I SHAN'T REPEAT A WORD.
QUITE RIGHT.
LORD SIL'S OFFICIAL TITLE IS SIL BURKS.
HE'S THE THIRD SON OF A BARON...ON PAPER, AT LEAST.

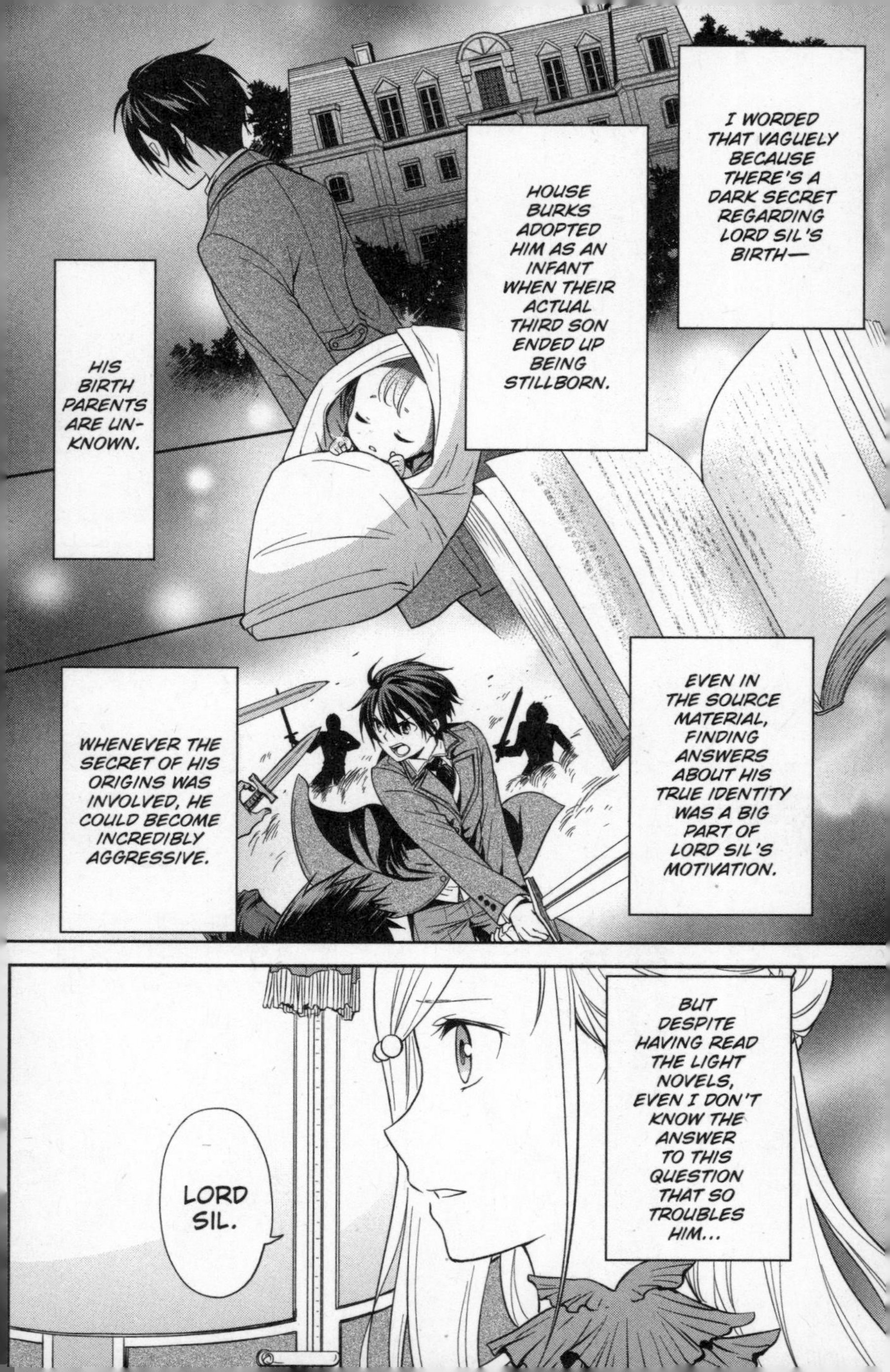
I WORDED THAT VAGUELY BECAUSE THERE'S A DARK SECRET REGARDING LORD SIL'S BIRTH—
HOUSE BURKS ADOPTED HIM AS AN INFANT WHEN THEIR ACTUAL THIRD SON ENDED UP BEING STILLBORN.
HIS BIRTH PARENTS ARE UN-KNOWN.
EVEN IN THE SOURCE MATERIAL, FINDING ANSWERS ABOUT HIS TRUE IDENTITY WAS A BIG PART OF LORD SIL'S MOTIVATION.
WHENEVER THE SECRET OF HIS ORIGINS WAS INVOLVED, HE COULD BECOME INCREDIBLY AGGRESSIVE.
BUT DESPITE HAVING READ THE LIGHT NOVELS, EVEN I DON'T KNOW THE ANSWER TO THIS QUESTION THAT SO TROUBLES HIM...
LORD SIL.

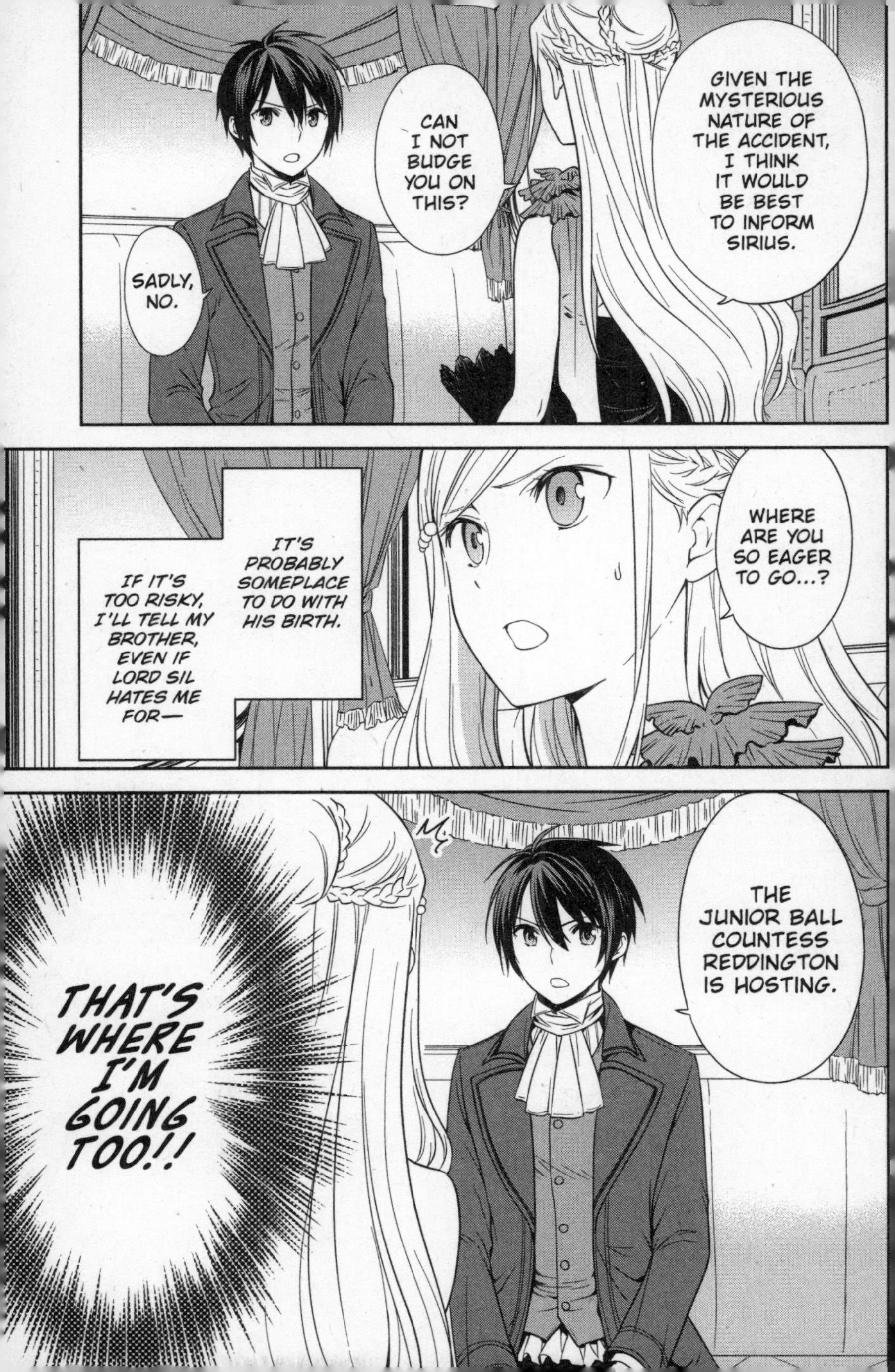
GIVEN THE MYSTERIOUS NATURE OF THE ACCIDENT, I THINK IT WOULD BE BEST TO INFORM SIRIUS.
CAN I NOT BUDGE YOU ON THIS?
SADLY, NO.
WHERE ARE YOU SO EAGER TO GO...?
IT'S PROBABLY SOMEPLACE TO DO WITH HIS BIRTH.
IF IT'S TOO RISKY, I'LL TELL MY BROTHER, EVEN IF LORD SIL HATES ME FOR—
THE JUNIOR BALL COUNTESS REDDINGTON IS HOSTING.
THAT'S WHERE I'M GOING TOO!!

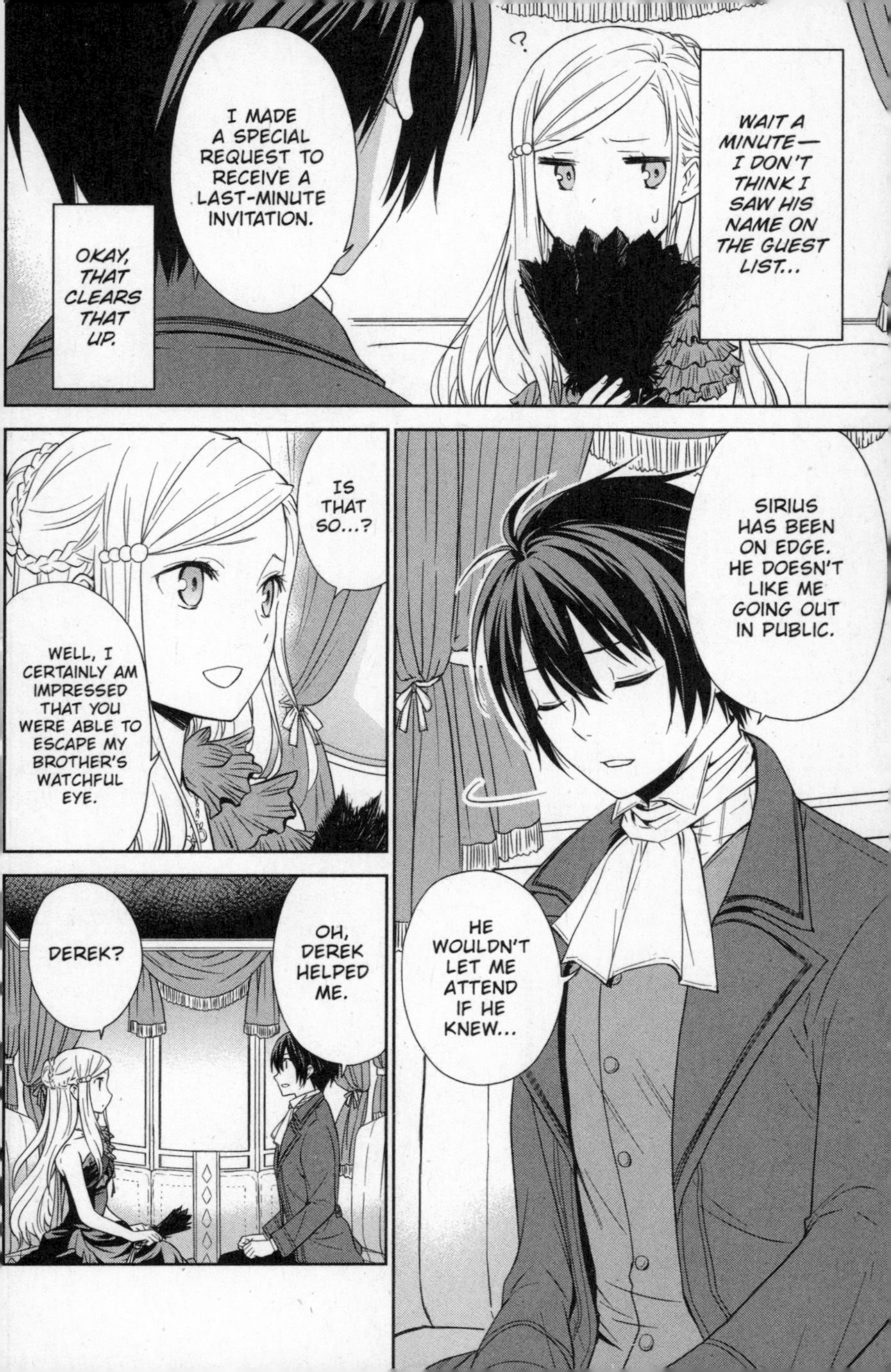
WAIT A MINUTE— I DON'T THINK I SAW HIS NAME ON THE GUEST LIST...
I MADE A SPECIAL REQUEST TO RECEIVE A LAST-MINUTE INVITATION.
OKAY, THAT CLEARS THAT UP.
SIRIUS HAS BEEN ON EDGE. HE DOESN'T LIKE ME GOING OUT IN PUBLIC.
HE WOULDN'T LET ME ATTEND IF HE KNEW...
IS THAT SO...?
WELL, I CERTAINLY AM IMPRESSED THAT YOU WERE ABLE TO ESCAPE MY BROTHER'S WATCHFUL EYE.
DEREK?
OH, DEREK HELPED ME.

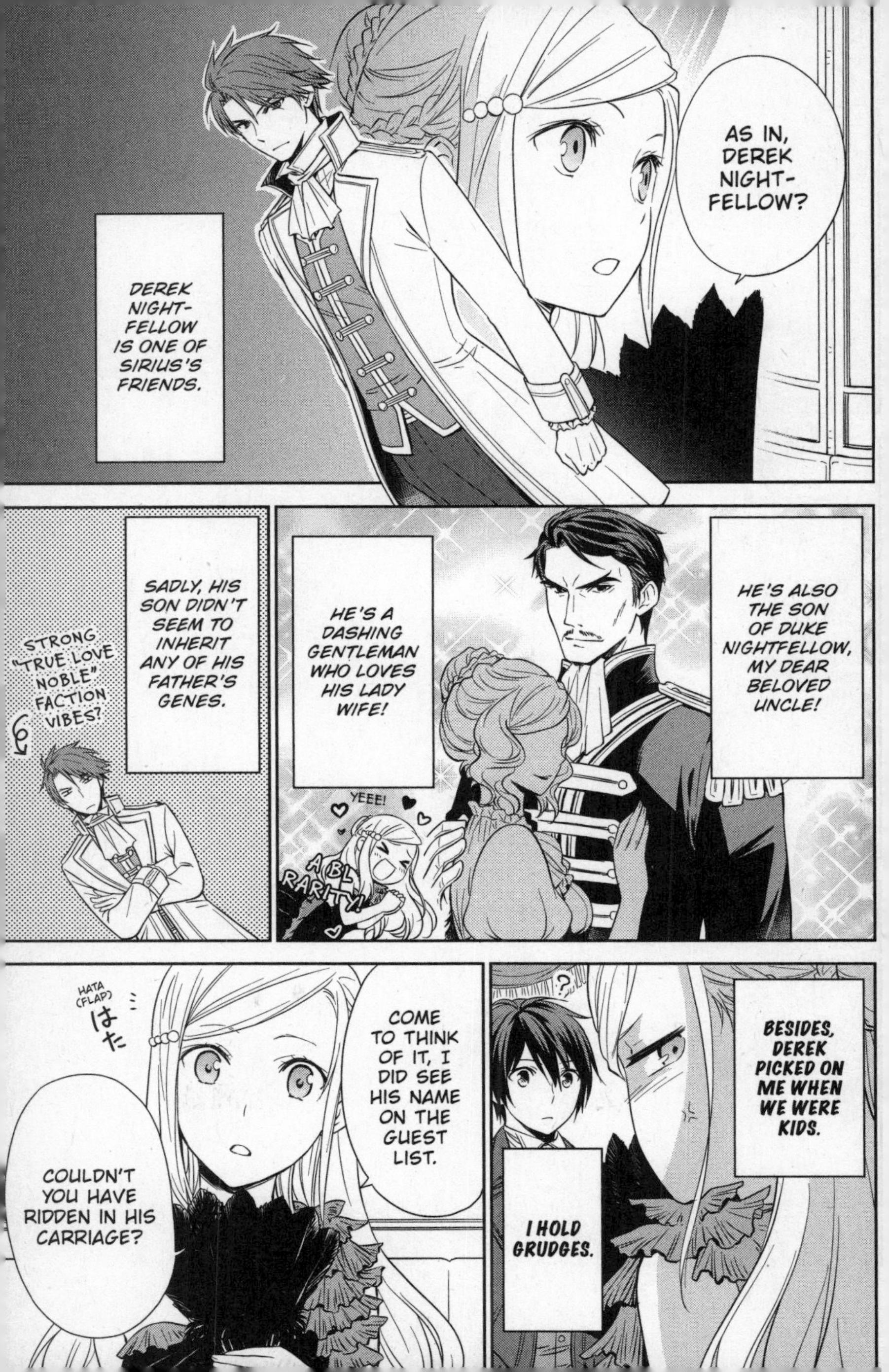
AS IN, DEREK NIGHT-FELLOW?
DEREK NIGHT-FELLOW IS ONE OF SIRIUS'S FRIENDS.
HE'S ALSO THE SON OF DUKE NIGHTFELLOW, MY DEAR BELOVED UNCLE!
HE'S A DASHING GENTLEMAN WHO LOVES HIS LADY WIFE!
YEEE!
A BL RARITY!
SADLY, HIS SON DIDN'T SEEM TO INHERIT ANY OF HIS FATHER'S GENES.
STRONG "TRUE LOVE NOBLE" FACTION VIBES?
BESIDES, DEREK PICKED ON ME WHEN WE WERE KIDS.
?
I HOLD GRUDGES.
COME TO THINK OF IT, I DID SEE HIS NAME ON THE GUEST LIST.
HATA (FLAP)
はた
COULDN'T YOU HAVE RIDDEN IN HIS CARRIAGE?

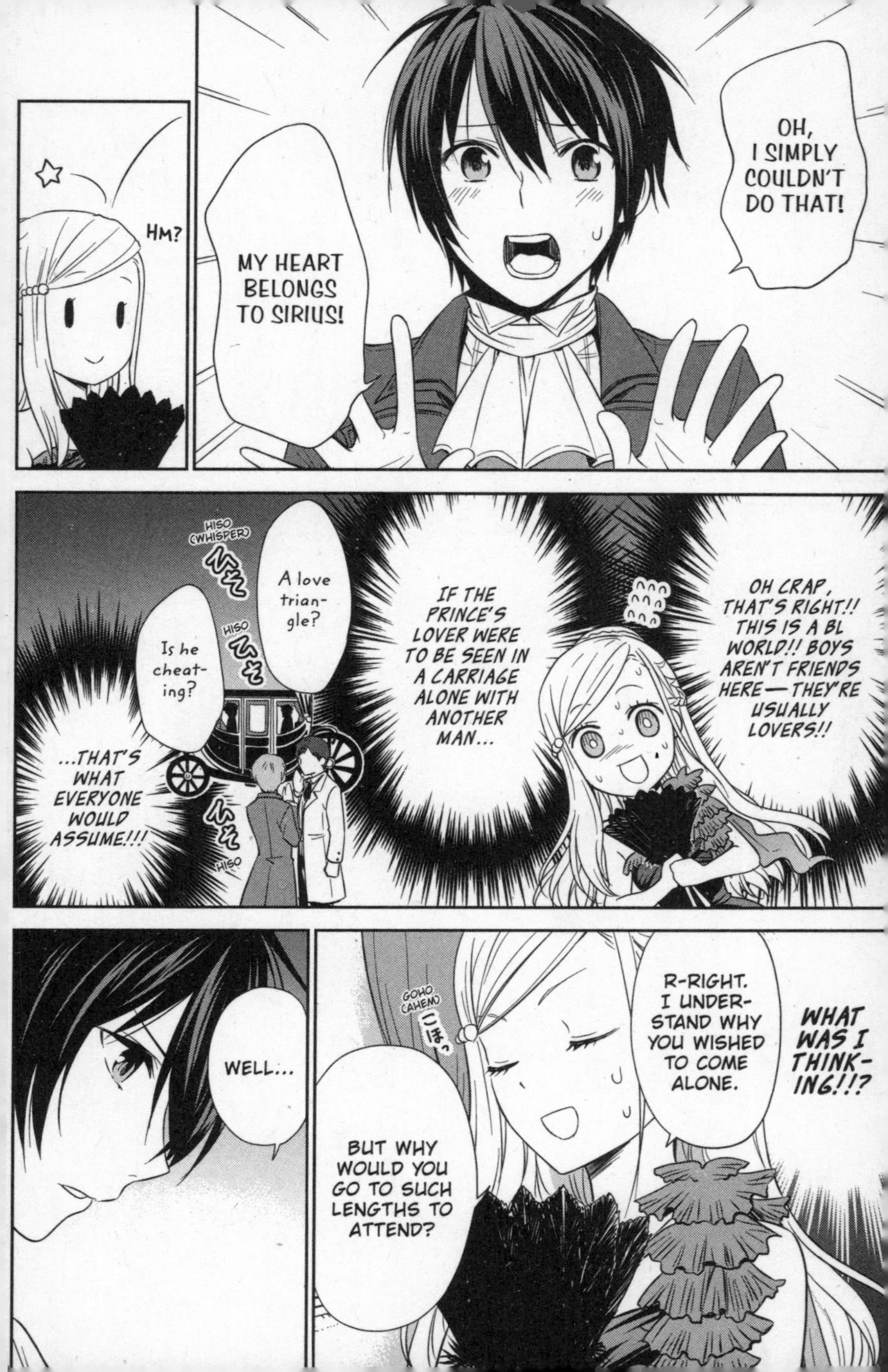
OH, I SIMPLY COULDN'T DO THAT!
MY HEART BELONGS TO SIRIUS!
HM?
OH CRAP, THAT'S RIGHT!! THIS IS A BL WORLD!! BOYS AREN'T FRIENDS HERE—THEY'RE USUALLY LOVERS!!
IF THE PRINCE'S LOVER WERE TO BE SEEN IN A CARRIAGE ALONE WITH ANOTHER MAN...
A love triangle?
HISO (WHISPER)
HISO
Is he cheating?
HISO
...THAT'S WHAT EVERYONE WOULD ASSUME!!!
WHAT WAS I THINKING!!?
R-RIGHT. I UNDERSTAND WHY YOU WISHED TO COME ALONE.
GOHO (AHEM)
BUT WHY WOULD YOU GO TO SUCH LENGTHS TO ATTEND?
WELL...

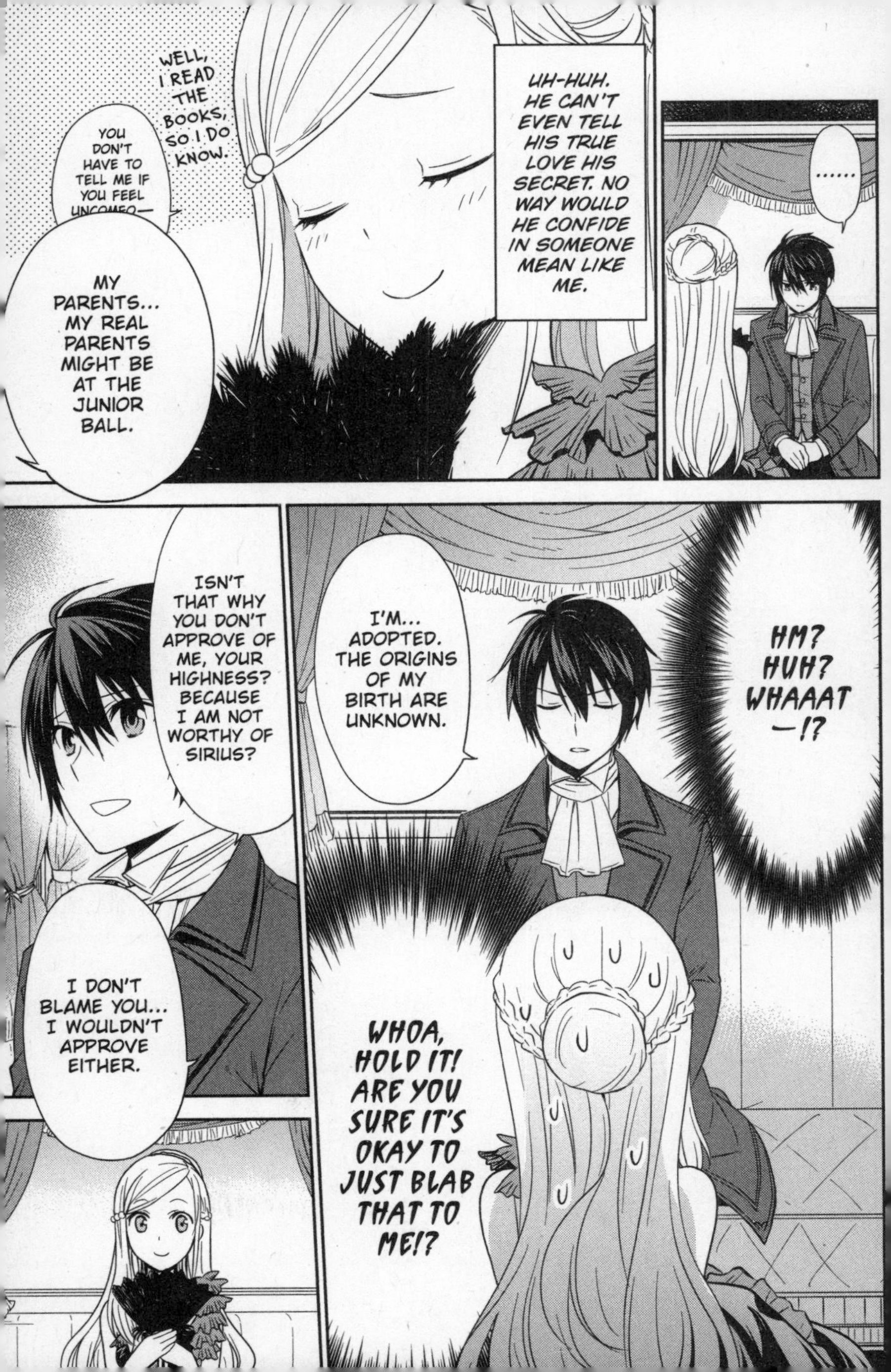
......
UH-HUH. HE CAN'T EVEN TELL HIS TRUE LOVE HIS SECRET. NO WAY WOULD HE CONFIDE IN SOMEONE MEAN LIKE ME.
WELL, I READ THE BOOKS, SO I DO KNOW.
YOU DON'T HAVE TO TELL ME IF YOU FEEL UNCOMFO—
MY PARENTS... MY REAL PARENTS MIGHT BE AT THE JUNIOR BALL.
I'M... ADOPTED. THE ORIGINS OF MY BIRTH ARE UNKNOWN.
HM? HUH? WHAAAT—!?
WHOA, HOLD IT! ARE YOU SURE IT'S OKAY TO JUST BLAB THAT TO ME!?
ISN'T THAT WHY YOU DON'T APPROVE OF ME, YOUR HIGHNESS? BECAUSE I AM NOT WORTHY OF SIRIUS?
I DON'T BLAME YOU... I WOULDN'T APPROVE EITHER.

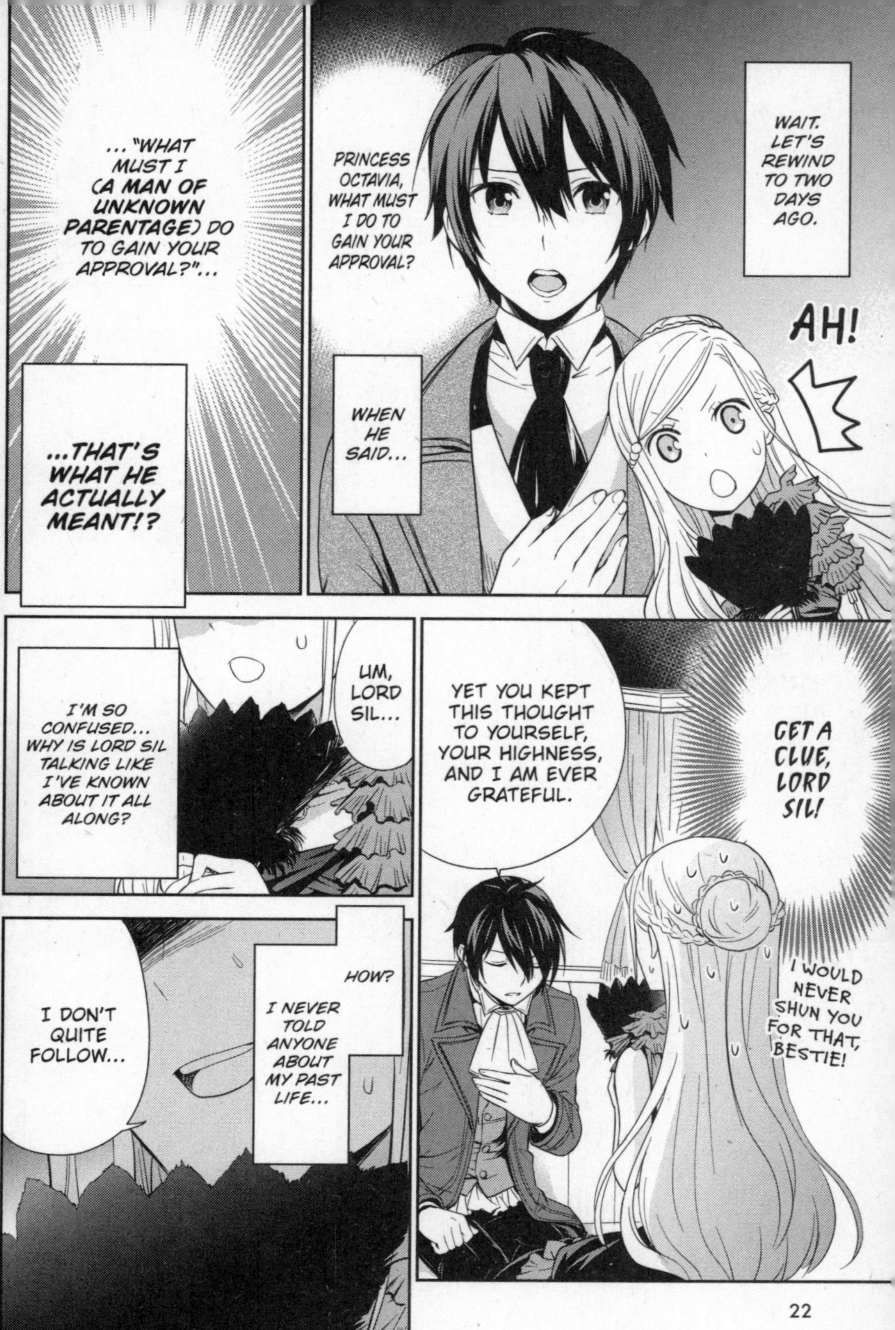
WAIT. LET'S REWIND TO TWO DAYS AGO.
AH!
PRINCESS OCTAVIA, WHAT MUST I DO TO GAIN YOUR APPROVAL?
WHEN HE SAID...
..."WHAT MUST I (A MAN OF UNKNOWN PARENTAGE) DO TO GAIN YOUR APPROVAL?"...
...THAT'S WHAT HE ACTUALLY MEANT!?
GET A CLUE, LORD SIL!
YET YOU KEPT THIS THOUGHT TO YOURSELF, YOUR HIGHNESS, AND I AM EVER GRATEFUL.
I WOULD NEVER SHUN YOU FOR THAT, BESTIE!
UM, LORD SIL...
I'M SO CONFUSED... WHY IS LORD SIL TALKING LIKE I'VE KNOWN ABOUT IT ALL ALONG?
HOW?
I NEVER TOLD ANYONE ABOUT MY PAST LIFE...
I DON'T QUITE FOLLOW...

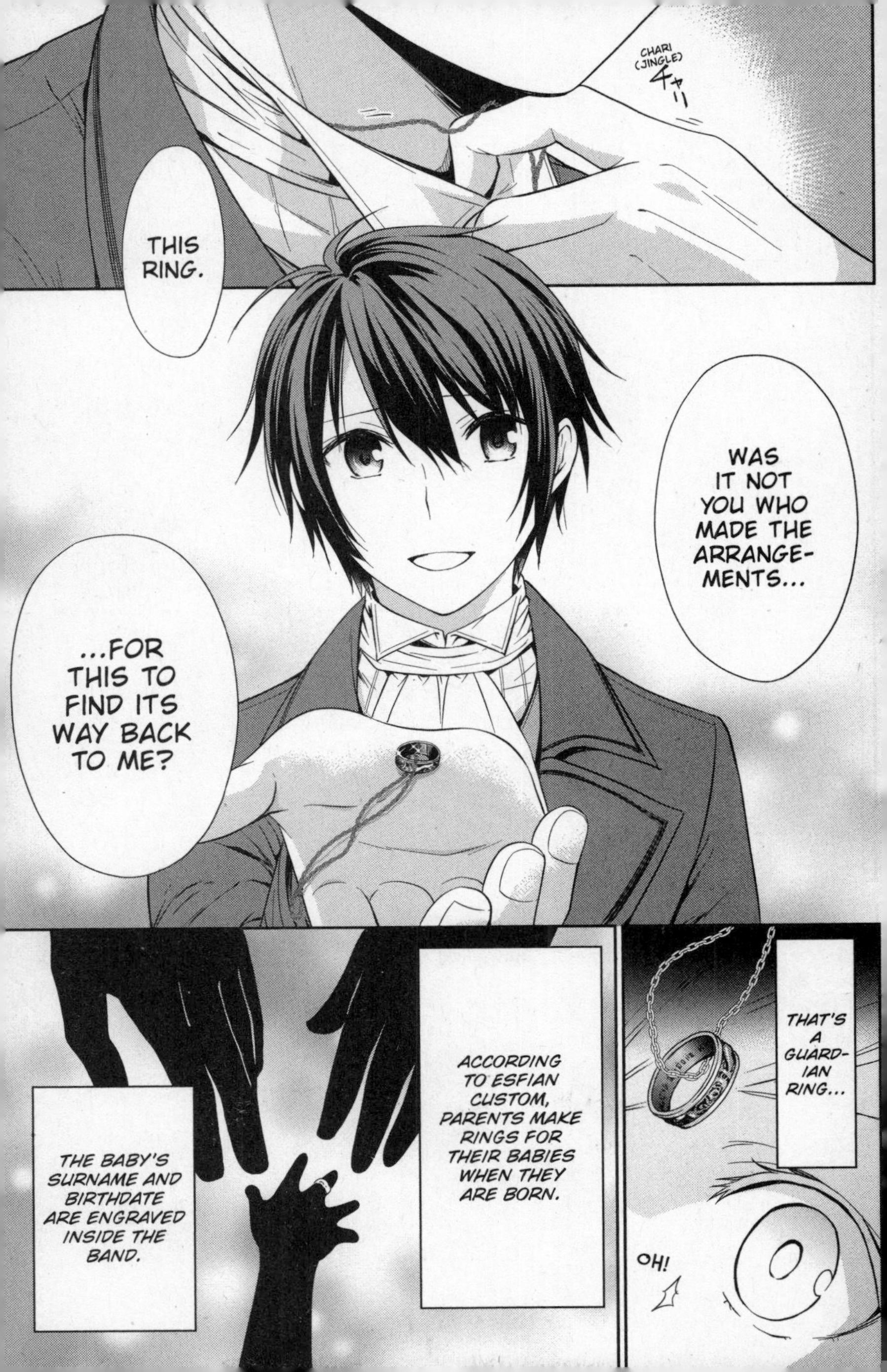
CHARI (JINGLE)
THIS RING.
WAS IT NOT YOU WHO MADE THE ARRANGE-MENTS...
...FOR THIS TO FIND ITS WAY BACK TO ME?
THAT'S A GUARD-IAN RING...
OH!
ACCORDING TO ESFIAN CUSTOM, PARENTS MAKE RINGS FOR THEIR BABIES WHEN THEY ARE BORN.
THE BABY'S SURNAME AND BIRTHDATE ARE ENGRAVED INSIDE THE BAND.

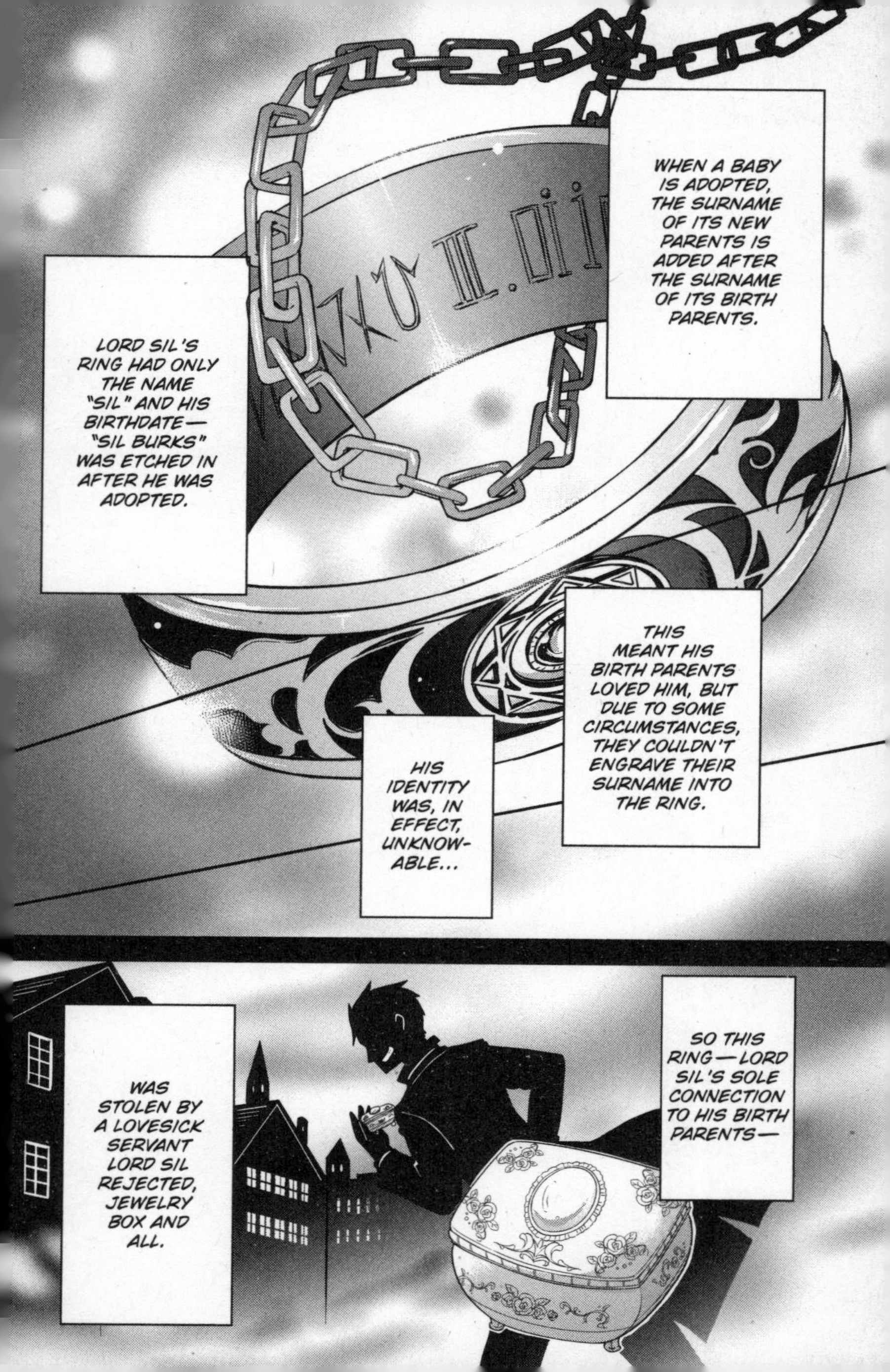
WHEN A BABY IS ADOPTED, THE SURNAME OF ITS NEW PARENTS IS ADDED AFTER THE SURNAME OF ITS BIRTH PARENTS.
LORD SIL'S RING HAD ONLY THE NAME "SIL" AND HIS BIRTHDATE— "SIL BURKS" WAS ETCHED IN AFTER HE WAS ADOPTED.
THIS MEANT HIS BIRTH PARENTS LOVED HIM, BUT DUE TO SOME CIRCUMSTANCES, THEY COULDN'T ENGRAVE THEIR SURNAME INTO THE RING.
HIS IDENTITY WAS, IN EFFECT, UNKNOW-ABLE...
SO THIS RING—LORD SIL'S SOLE CONNECTION TO HIS BIRTH PARENTS—
WAS STOLEN BY A LOVESICK SERVANT LORD SIL REJECTED, JEWELRY BOX AND ALL.

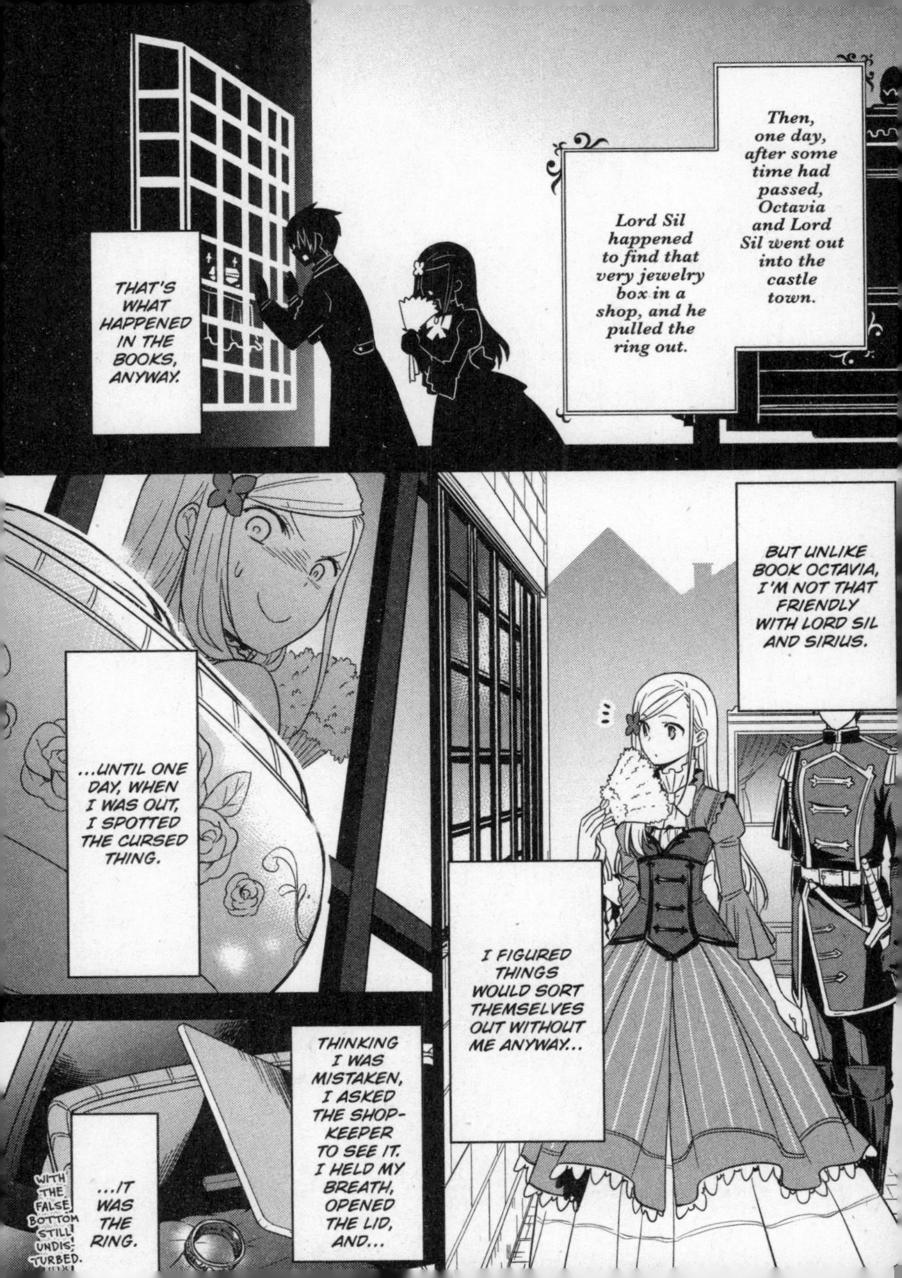
Then, one day, after some time had passed, Octavia and Lord Sil went out into the castle town.
Lord Sil happened to find that very jewelry box in a shop, and he pulled the ring out.
THAT'S WHAT HAPPENED IN THE BOOKS, ANYWAY.
BUT UNLIKE BOOK OCTAVIA, I'M NOT THAT FRIENDLY WITH LORD SIL AND SIRIUS.
...
I FIGURED THINGS WOULD SORT THEMSELVES OUT WITHOUT ME ANYWAY...
...UNTIL ONE DAY, WHEN I WAS OUT, I SPOTTED THE CURSED THING.
THINKING I WAS MISTAKEN, I ASKED THE SHOP-KEEPER TO SEE IT. I HELD MY BREATH, OPENED THE LID, AND...
...IT WAS THE RING.
WITH THE FALSE BOTTOM STILL UNDIS-TURBED.

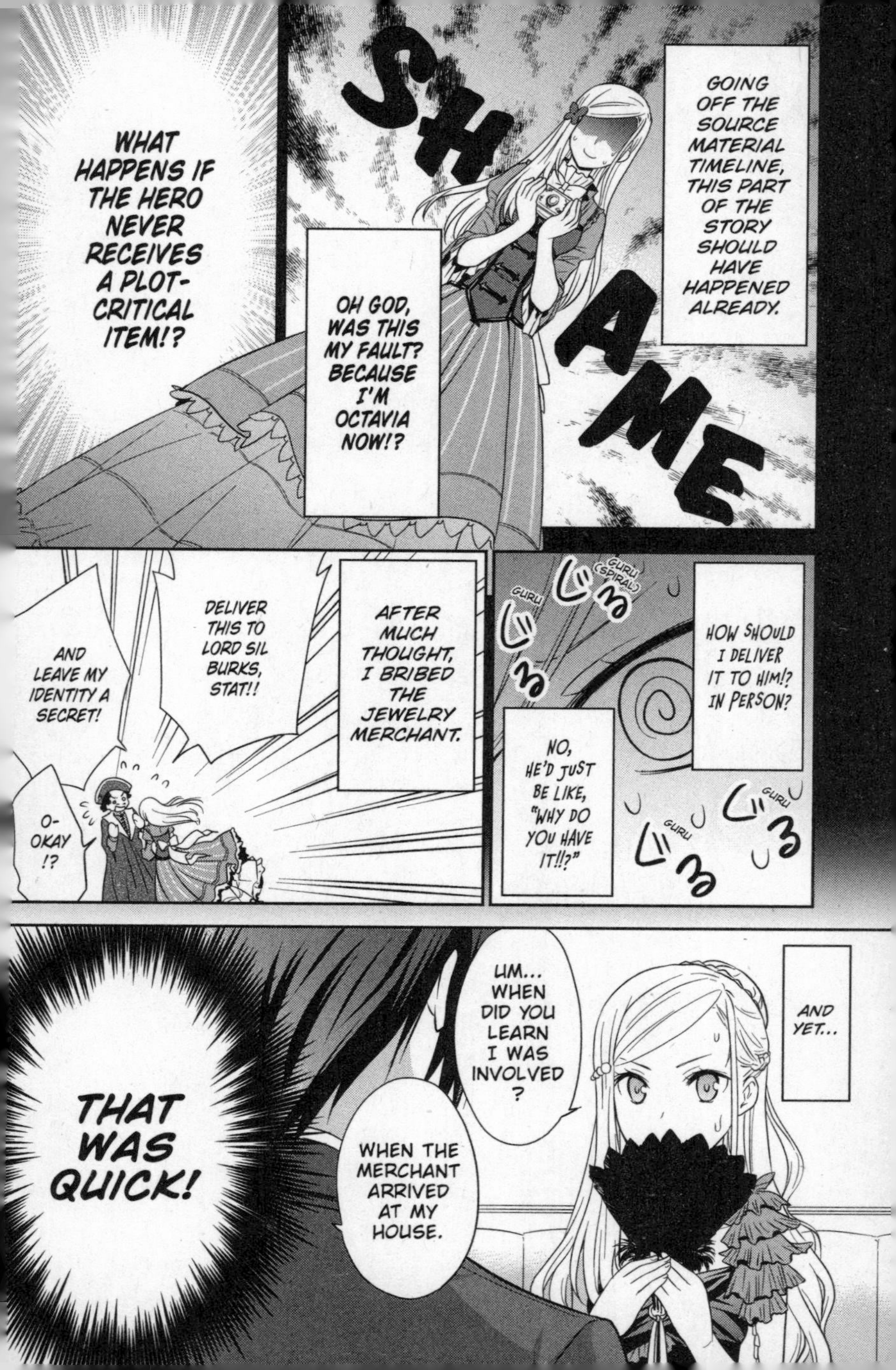
GOING OFF THE SOURCE MATERIAL TIMELINE, THIS PART OF THE STORY SHOULD HAVE HAPPENED ALREADY.
SHAME
OH GOD, WAS THIS MY FAULT? BECAUSE I'M OCTAVIA NOW!?
WHAT HAPPENS IF THE HERO NEVER RECEIVES A PLOT-CRITICAL ITEM!?
HOW SHOULD I DELIVER IT TO HIM!? IN PERSON?
GURU (SPIRAL)
GURU
NO, HE'D JUST BE LIKE, "WHY DO YOU HAVE IT!!?"
GURU
GURU
AFTER MUCH THOUGHT, I BRIBED THE JEWELRY MERCHANT.
DELIVER THIS TO LORD SIL BURKS, STAT!!
AND LEAVE MY IDENTITY A SECRET!
O-OKAY!?
AND YET...
UM... WHEN DID YOU LEARN I WAS INVOLVED?
WHEN THE MERCHANT ARRIVED AT MY HOUSE.
THAT WAS QUICK!

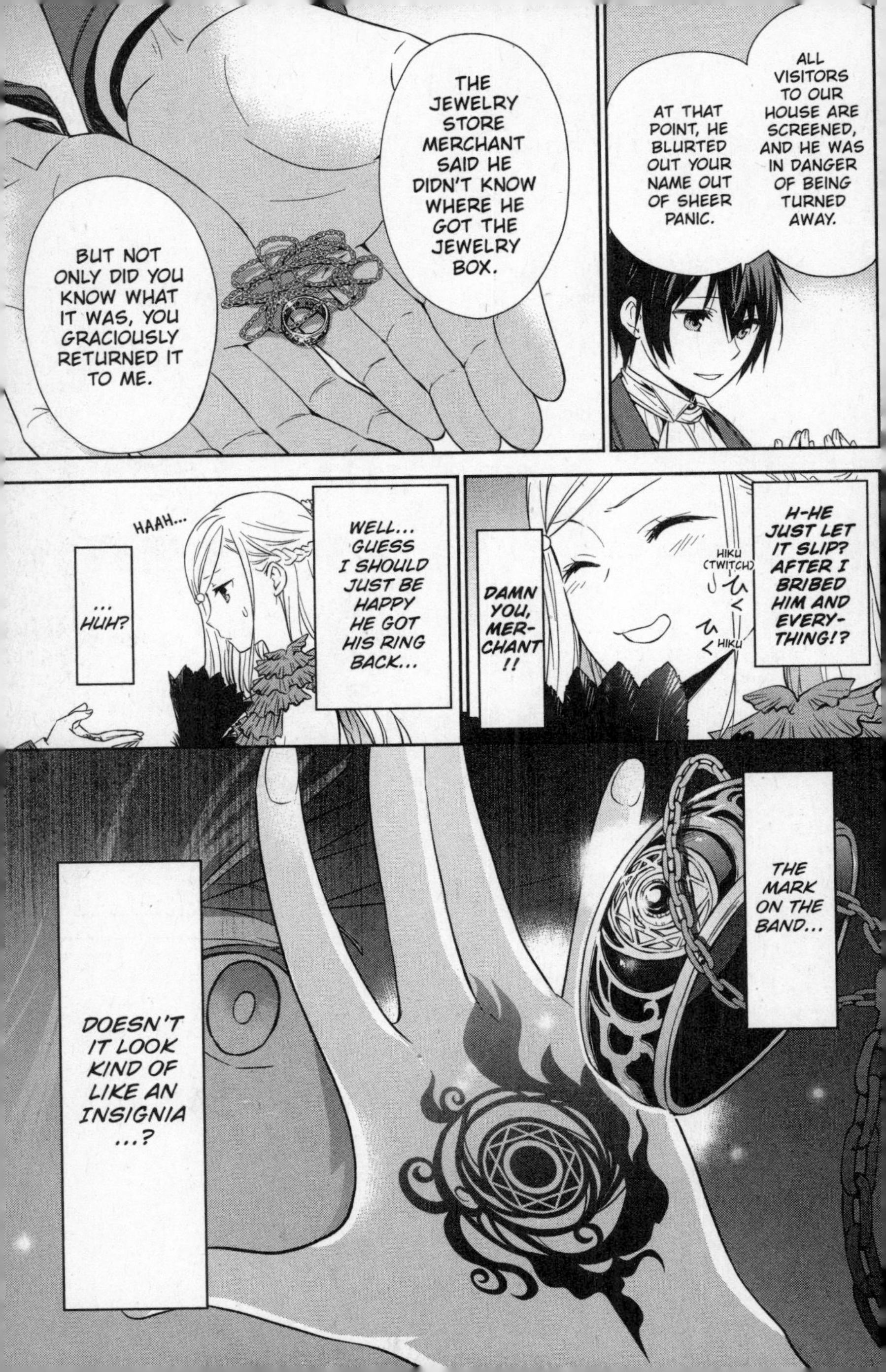
ALL VISITORS TO OUR HOUSE ARE SCREENED, AND HE WAS IN DANGER OF BEING TURNED AWAY.
AT THAT POINT, HE BLURTED OUT YOUR NAME OUT OF SHEER PANIC.
THE JEWELRY STORE MERCHANT SAID HE DIDN'T KNOW WHERE HE GOT THE JEWELRY BOX.
BUT NOT ONLY DID YOU KNOW WHAT IT WAS, YOU GRACIOUSLY RETURNED IT TO ME.
H-HE JUST LET IT SLIP? AFTER I BRIBED HIM AND EVERY-THING!?
HIKU (TWITCH)
HIKU
DAMN YOU, MER-CHANT!!
WELL... GUESS I SHOULD JUST BE HAPPY HE GOT HIS RING BACK...
... HUH?
HAAAH...
THE MARK ON THE BAND...
DOESN'T IT LOOK KIND OF LIKE AN INSIGNIA ...?

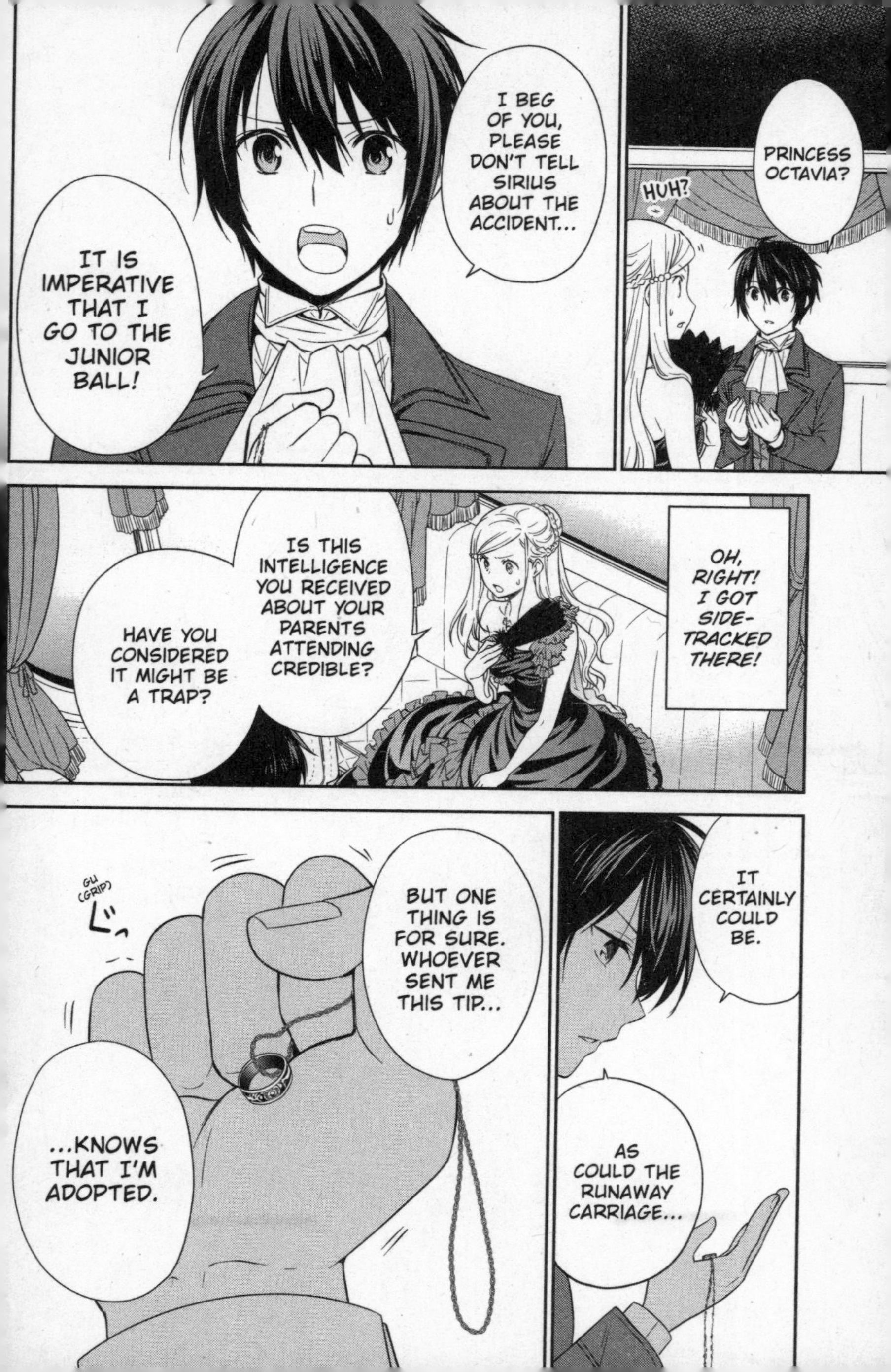
PRINCESS OCTAVIA?
HUH?
I BEG OF YOU, PLEASE DON'T TELL SIRIUS ABOUT THE ACCIDENT...
IT IS IMPERATIVE THAT I GO TO THE JUNIOR BALL!
OH, RIGHT! I GOT SIDE-TRACKED THERE!
IS THIS INTELLIGENCE YOU RECEIVED ABOUT YOUR PARENTS ATTENDING CREDIBLE?
HAVE YOU CONSIDERED IT MIGHT BE A TRAP?
IT CERTAINLY COULD BE.
AS COULD THE RUNAWAY CARRIAGE...
BUT ONE THING IS FOR SURE. WHOEVER SENT ME THIS TIP...
GU (GRIP)
...KNOWS THAT I'M ADOPTED.

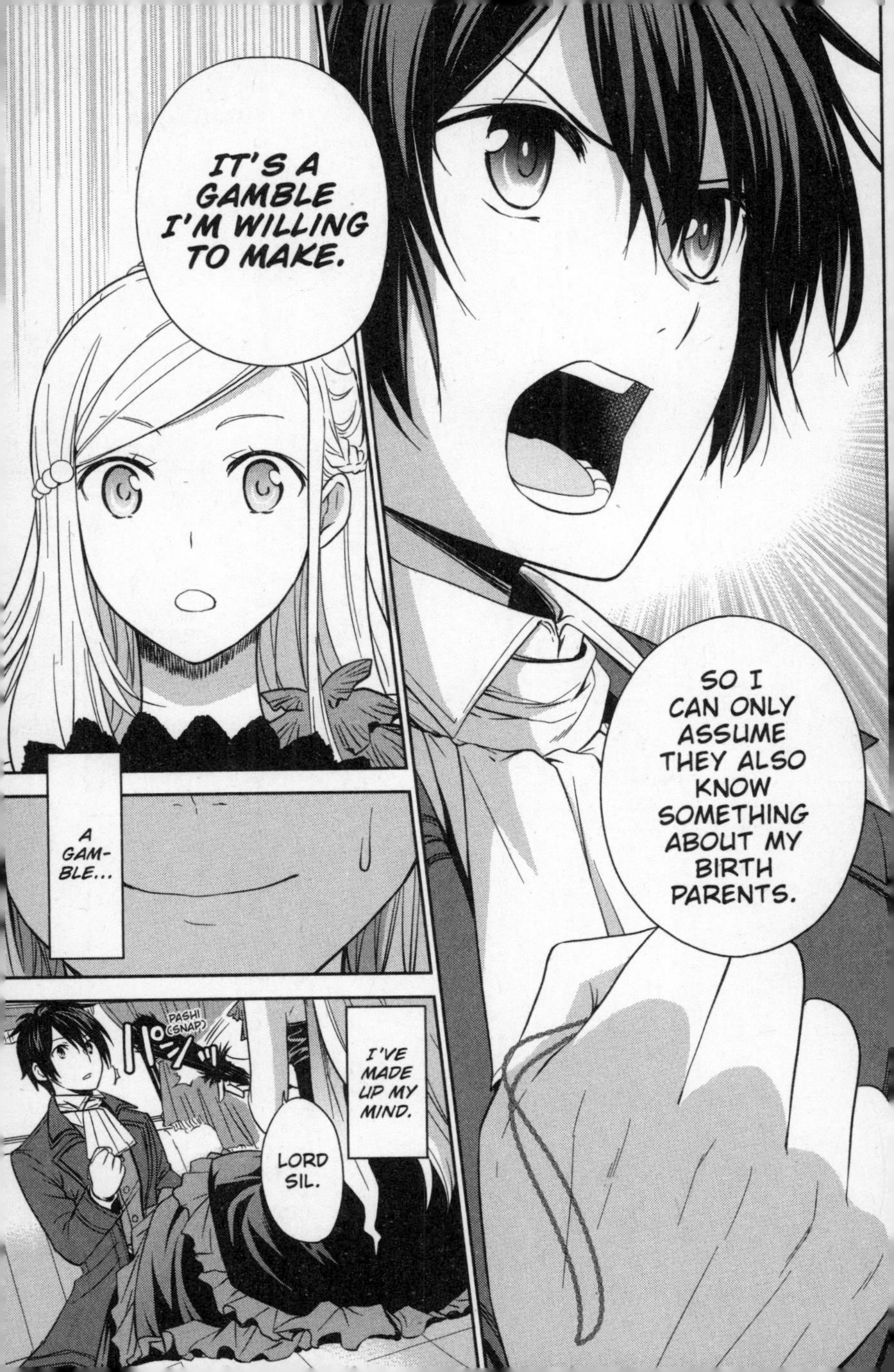
SO I CAN ONLY ASSUME THEY ALSO KNOW SOMETHING ABOUT MY BIRTH PARENTS.
IT'S A GAMBLE I'M WILLING TO MAKE.
A GAMBLE...
PASHI (SNAP)
I'VE MADE UP MY MIND.
LORD SIL.

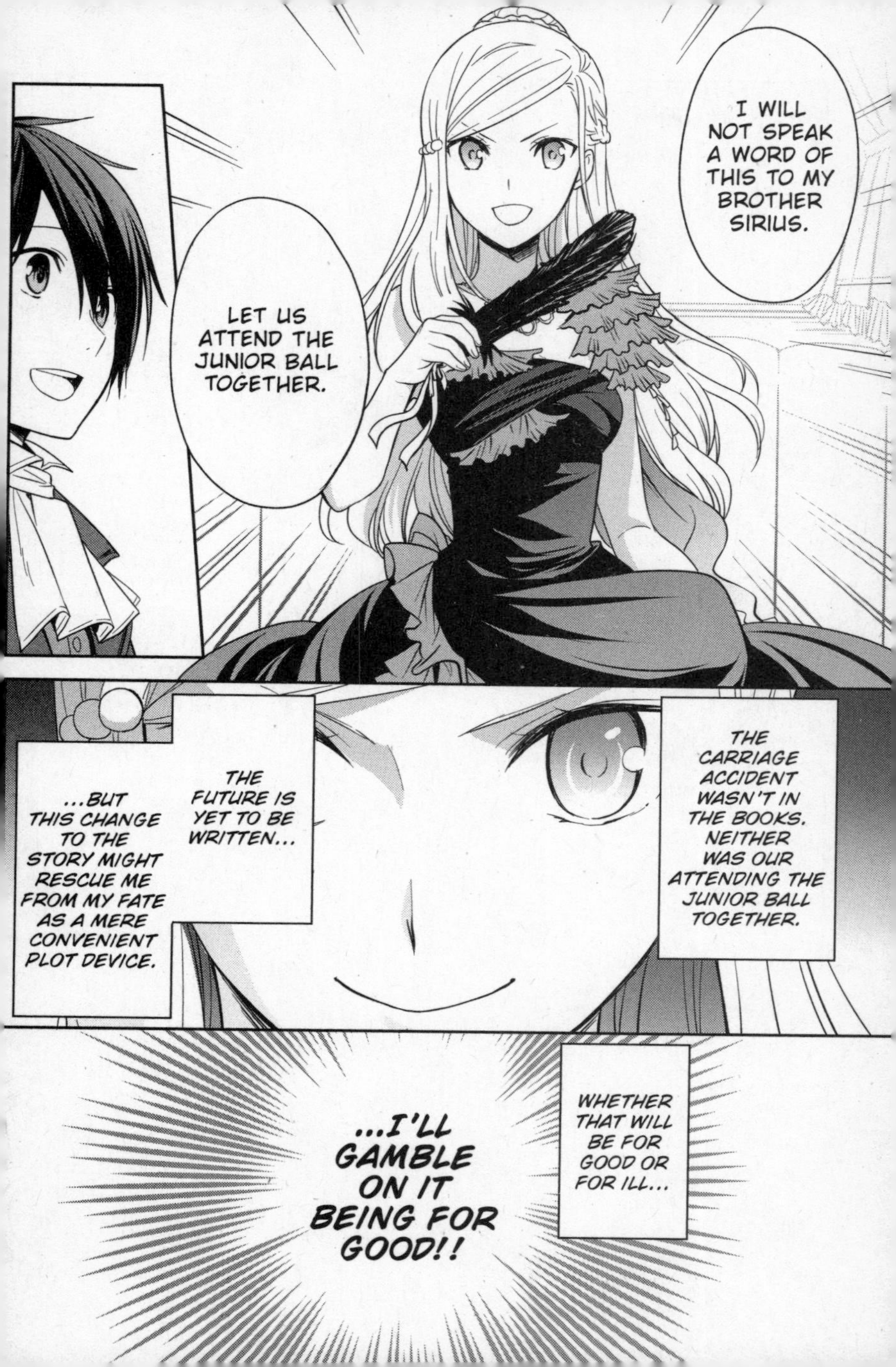
I WILL NOT SPEAK A WORD OF THIS TO MY BROTHER SIRIUS.
LET US ATTEND THE JUNIOR BALL TOGETHER.
THE CARRIAGE ACCIDENT WASN'T IN THE BOOKS. NEITHER WAS OUR ATTENDING THE JUNIOR BALL TOGETHER.
THE FUTURE IS YET TO BE WRITTEN...
...BUT THIS CHANGE TO THE STORY MIGHT RESCUE ME FROM MY FATE AS A MERE CONVENIENT PLOT DEVICE.
WHETHER THAT WILL BE FOR GOOD OR FOR ILL...
...I'LL GAMBLE ON IT BEING FOR GOOD!!

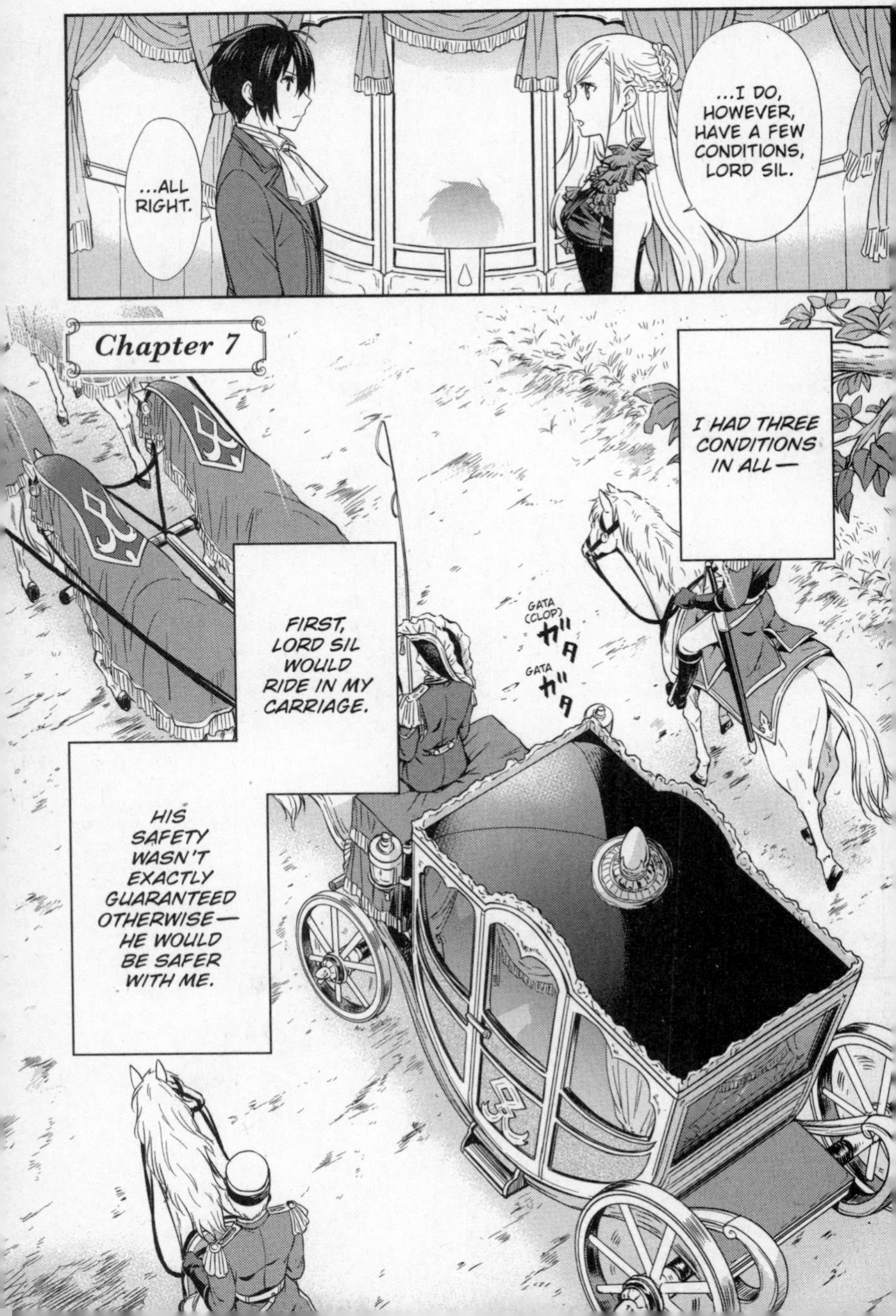
...I DO, HOWEVER, HAVE A FEW CONDITIONS, LORD SIL.
...ALL RIGHT.
Chapter 7
I HAD THREE CONDITIONS IN ALL—
GATA (CLOP)
GATA
FIRST, LORD SIL WOULD RIDE IN MY CARRIAGE.
HIS SAFETY WASN'T EXACTLY GUARANTEED OTHERWISE—HE WOULD BE SAFER WITH ME.

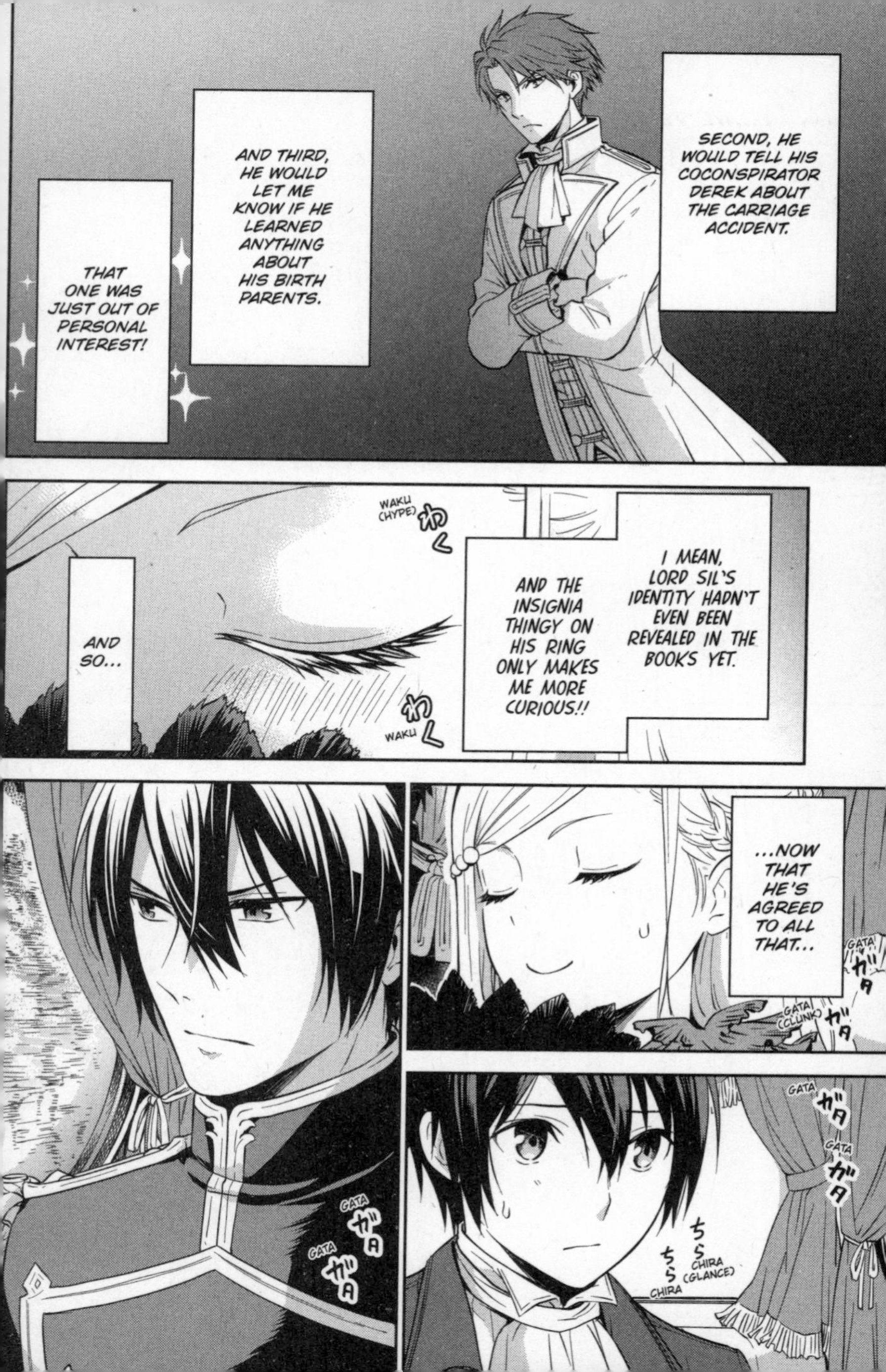
SECOND, HE WOULD TELL HIS COCONSPIRATOR DEREK ABOUT THE CARRIAGE ACCIDENT.
AND THIRD, HE WOULD LET ME KNOW IF HE LEARNED ANYTHING ABOUT HIS BIRTH PARENTS.
THAT ONE WAS JUST OUT OF PERSONAL INTEREST!
I MEAN, LORD SIL'S IDENTITY HADN'T EVEN BEEN REVEALED IN THE BOOKS YET.
AND THE INSIGNIA THINGY ON HIS RING ONLY MAKES ME MORE CURIOUS!!
わく
WAKU (HYPE)
わく
WAKU
AND SO...
...NOW THAT HE'S AGREED TO ALL THAT...
ガタ
GATA
ガタ
GATA (CLUNK)
ガタ
GATA
ガタ
GATA
ちら
ちら
CHIRA
CHIRA (GLANCE)
ガタ
GATA
ガタ
GATA

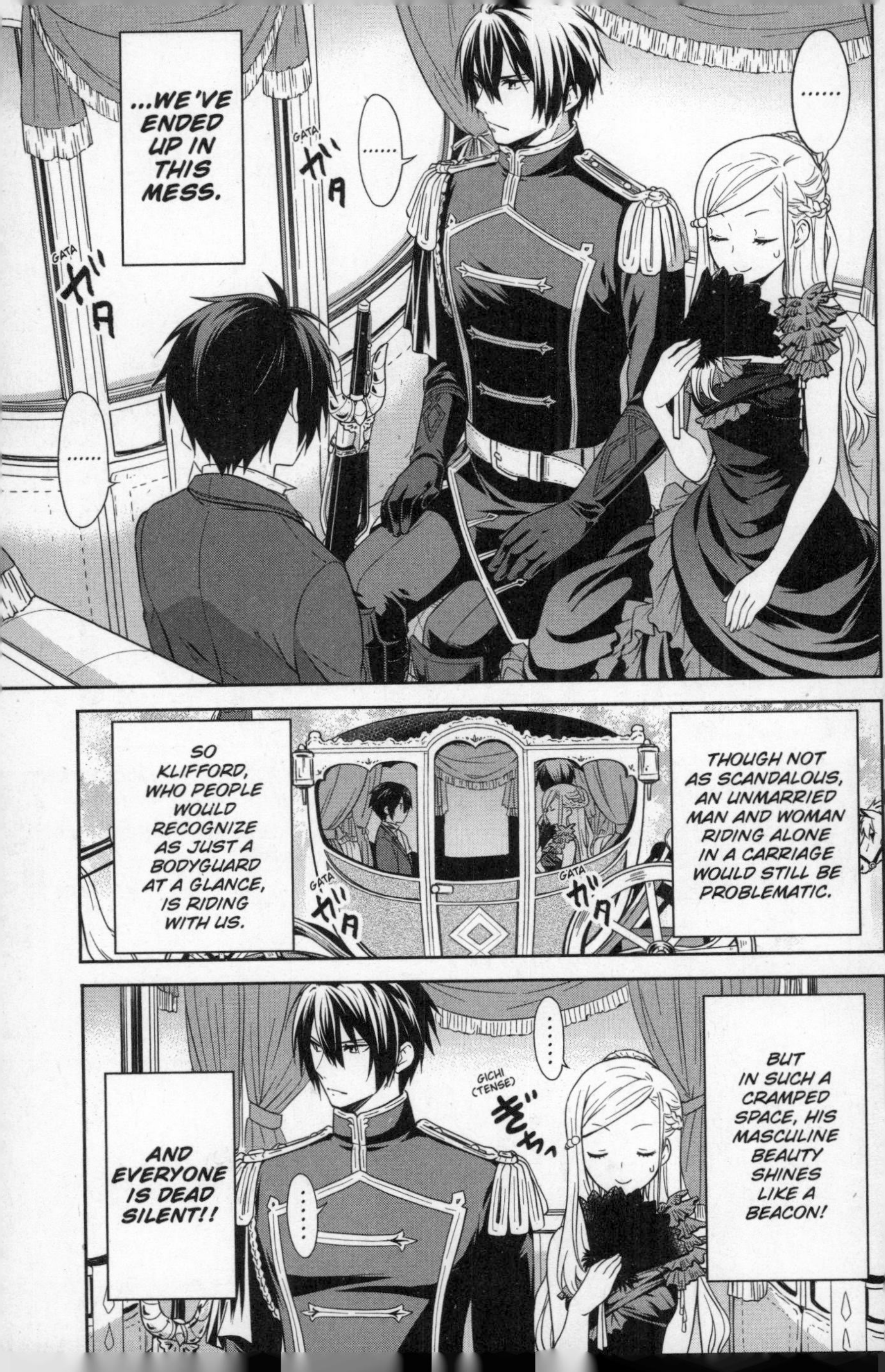
......
...WE'VE ENDED UP IN THIS MESS.
GATA
......
GATA
......
THOUGH NOT AS SCANDALOUS, AN UNMARRIED MAN AND WOMAN RIDING ALONE IN A CARRIAGE WOULD STILL BE PROBLEMATIC.
GATA
GATA
SO KLIFFORD, WHO PEOPLE WOULD RECOGNIZE AS JUST A BODYGUARD AT A GLANCE, IS RIDING WITH US.
BUT IN SUCH A CRAMPED SPACE, HIS MASCULINE BEAUTY SHINES LIKE A BEACON!
......
GICHI (TENSE)
......
AND EVERYONE IS DEAD SILENT!!

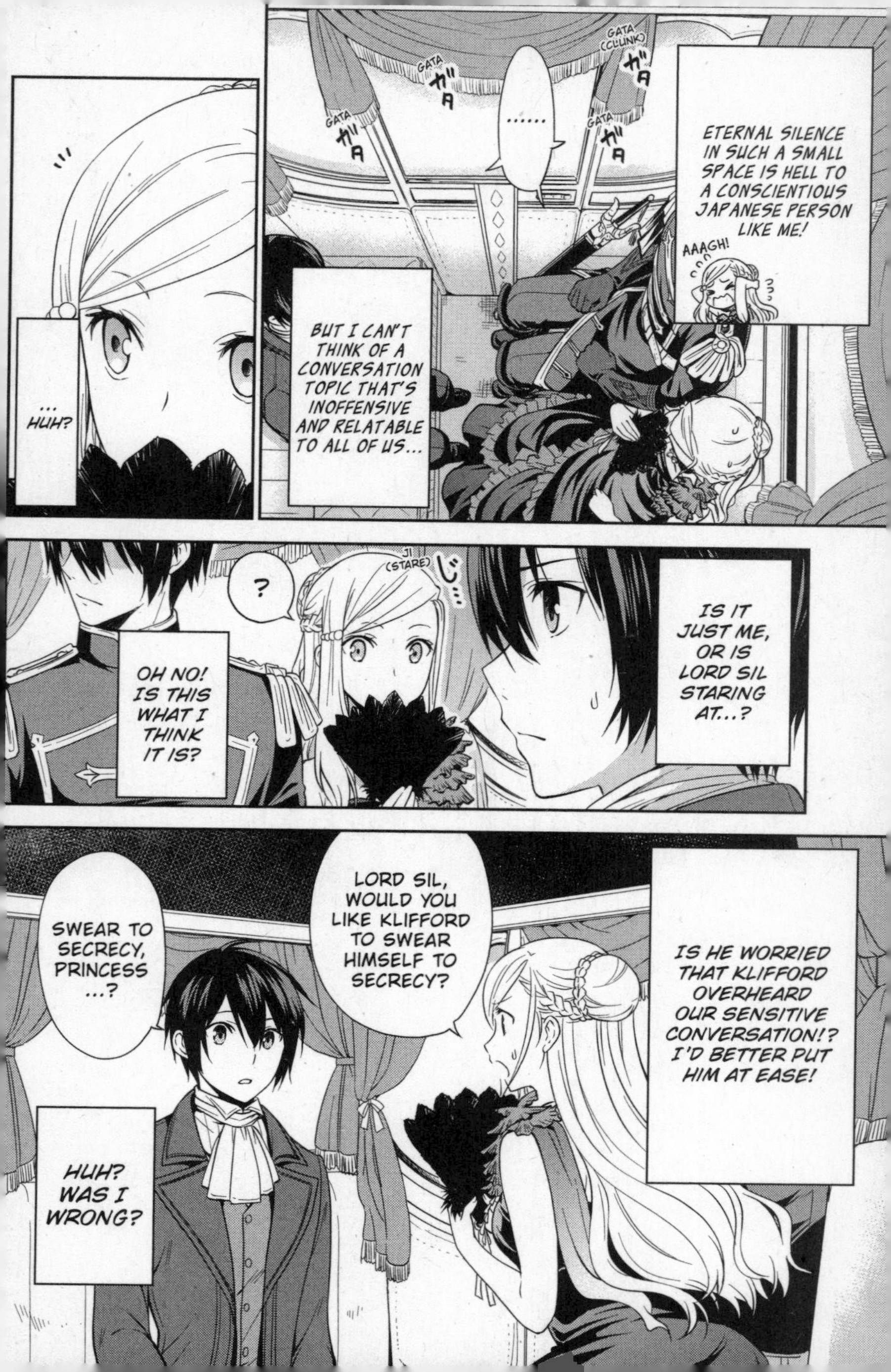
ETERNAL SILENCE IN SUCH A SMALL SPACE IS HELL TO A CONSCIENTIOUS JAPANESE PERSON LIKE ME!
AAAGH!
GATA (CLUNK)
GATA
GATA
......
BUT I CAN'T THINK OF A CONVERSATION TOPIC THAT'S INOFFENSIVE AND RELATABLE TO ALL OF US...
...HUH?
IS IT JUST ME, OR IS LORD SIL STARING AT...?
JI (STARE)
?
OH NO! IS THIS WHAT I THINK IT IS?
IS HE WORRIED THAT KLIFFORD OVERHEARD OUR SENSITIVE CONVERSATION!? I'D BETTER PUT HIM AT EASE!
LORD SIL, WOULD YOU LIKE KLIFFORD TO SWEAR HIMSELF TO SECRECY?
SWEAR TO SECRECY, PRINCESS ...?
HUH? WAS I WRONG?

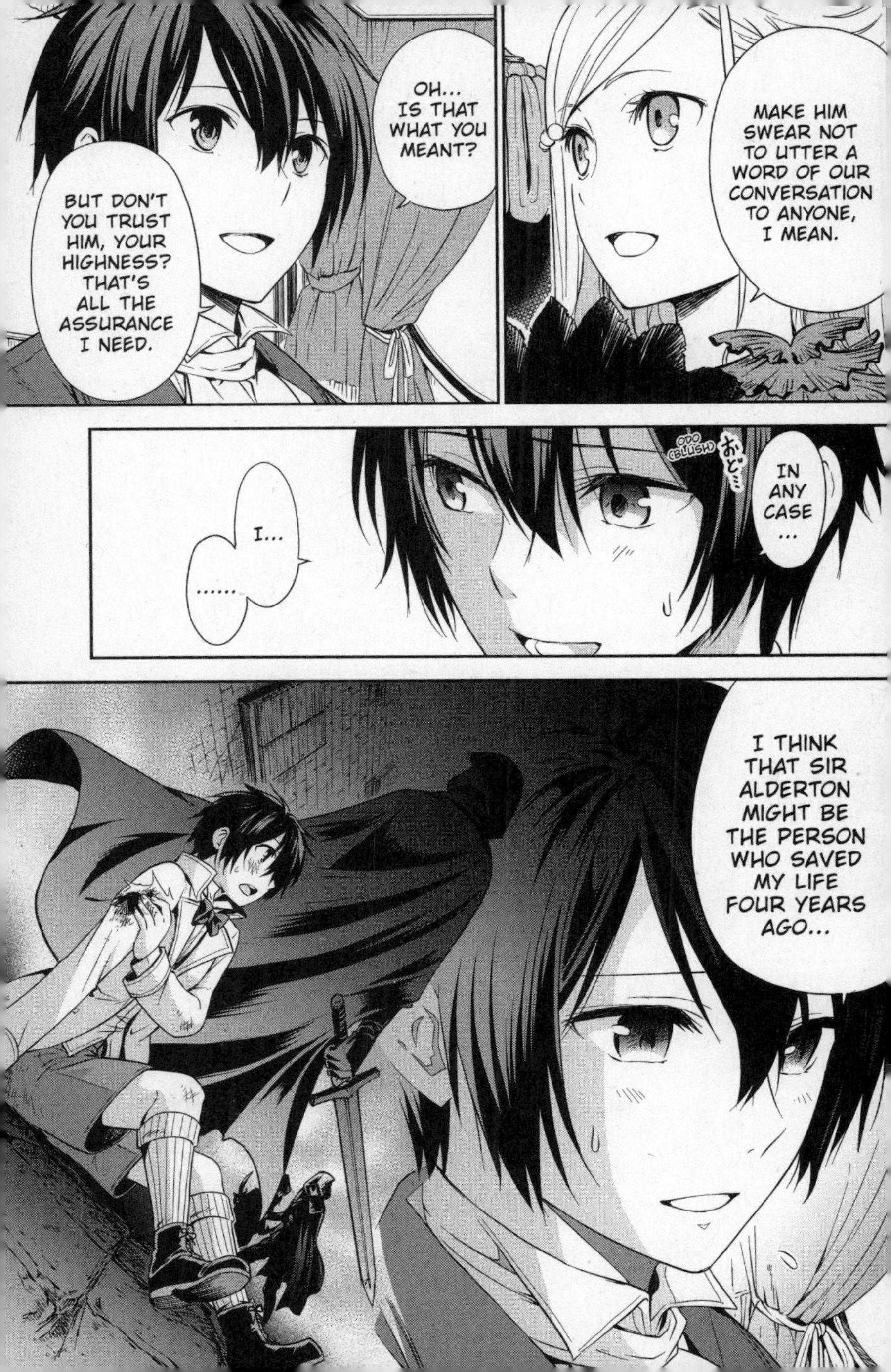
MAKE HIM SWEAR NOT TO UTTER A WORD OF OUR CONVERSATION TO ANYONE, I MEAN.
OH... IS THAT WHAT YOU MEANT?
BUT DON'T YOU TRUST HIM, YOUR HIGHNESS? THAT'S ALL THE ASSURANCE I NEED.
IN ANY CASE...
ODO (BLUSH)
I... ......
I THINK THAT SIR ALDERTON MIGHT BE THE PERSON WHO SAVED MY LIFE FOUR YEARS AGO...

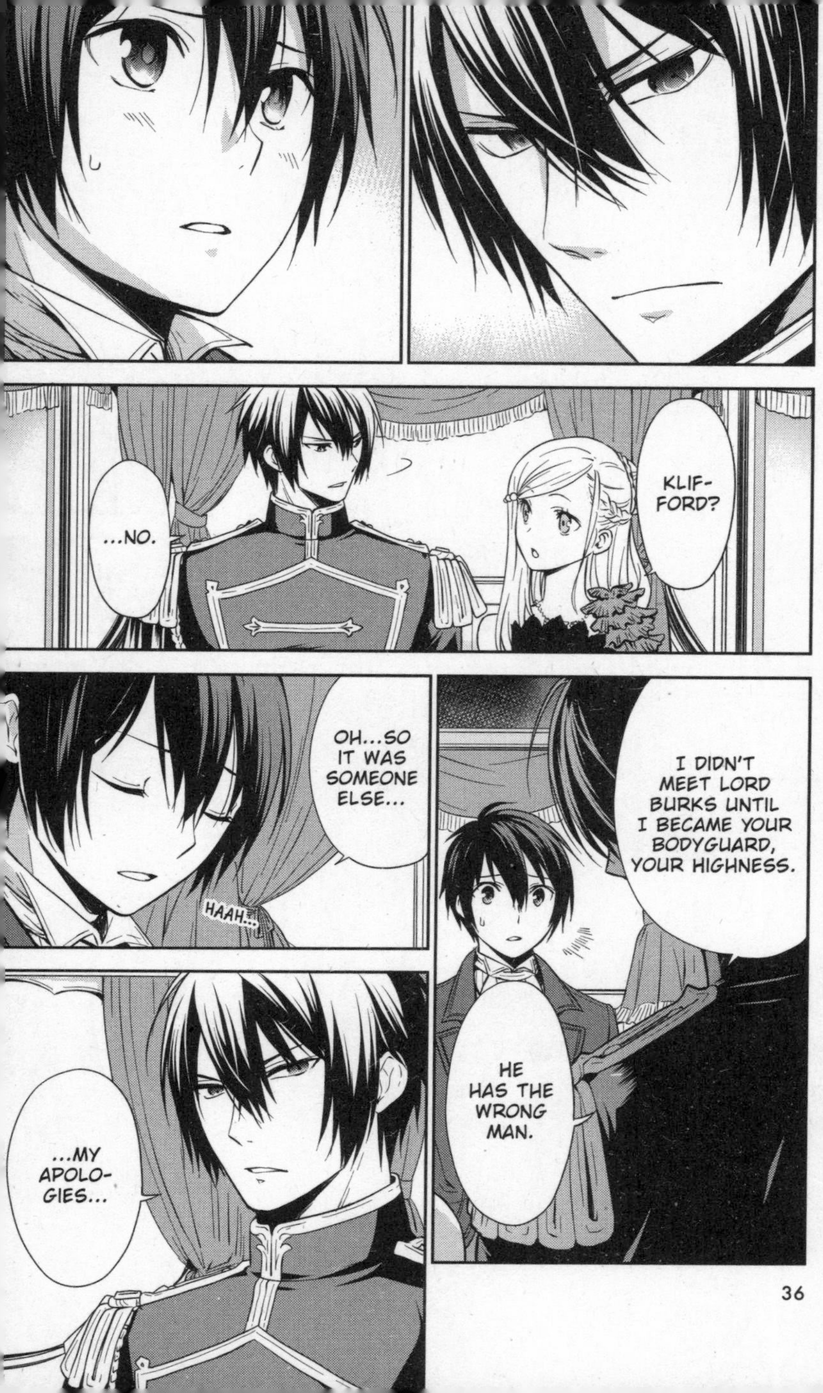
KLIF-FORD?
...NO.
I DIDN'T MEET LORD BURKS UNTIL I BECAME YOUR BODYGUARD, YOUR HIGHNESS.
OH...SO IT WAS SOMEONE ELSE...
HAAH...
HE HAS THE WRONG MAN.
...MY APOLO-GIES...

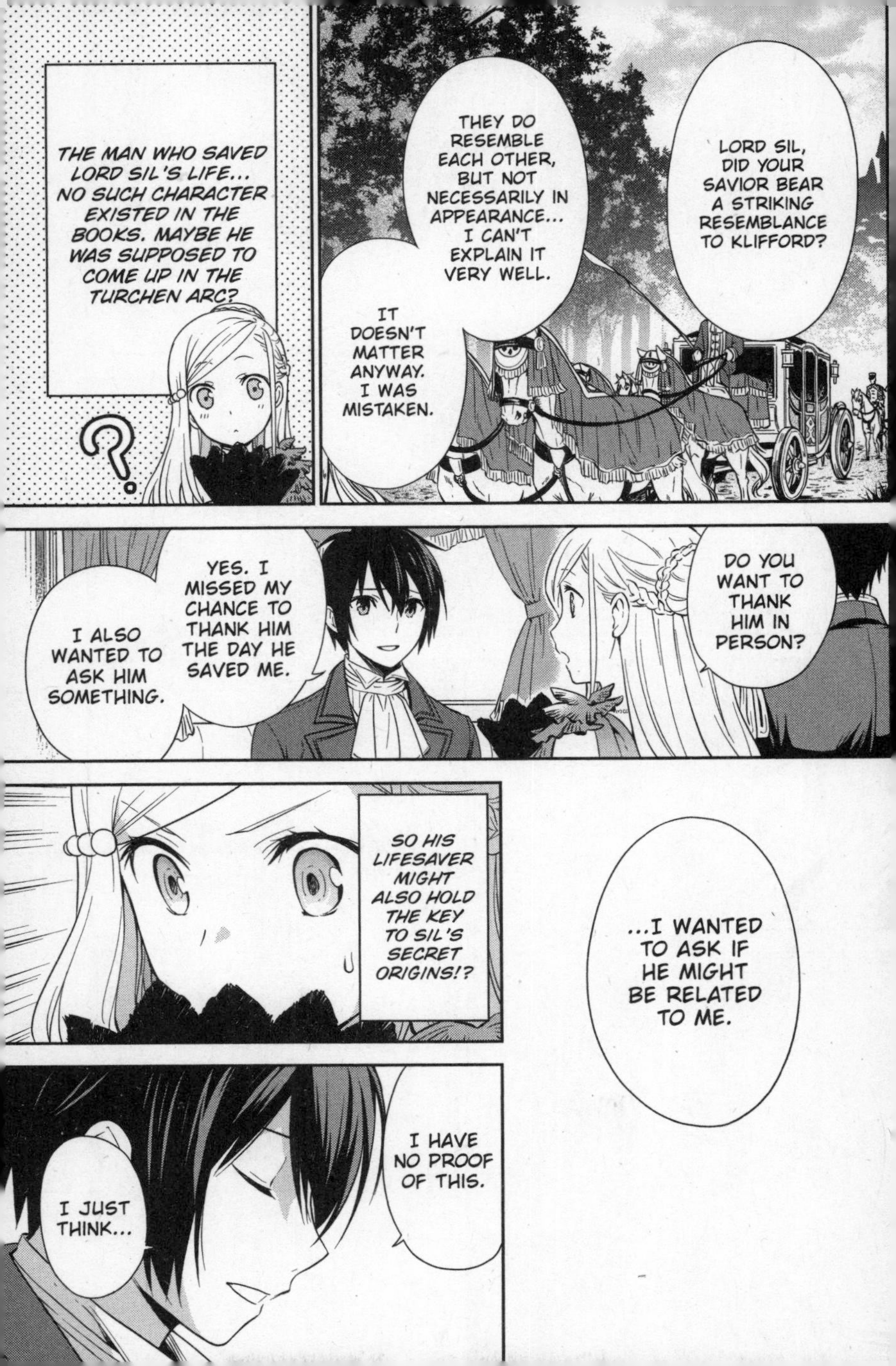
LORD SIL, DID YOUR SAVIOR BEAR A STRIKING RESEMBLANCE TO KLIFFORD?
THEY DO RESEMBLE EACH OTHER, BUT NOT NECESSARILY IN APPEARANCE... I CAN'T EXPLAIN IT VERY WELL.
IT DOESN'T MATTER ANYWAY. I WAS MISTAKEN.
THE MAN WHO SAVED LORD SIL'S LIFE... NO SUCH CHARACTER EXISTED IN THE BOOKS. MAYBE HE WAS SUPPOSED TO COME UP IN THE TURCHEN ARC?
?
DO YOU WANT TO THANK HIM IN PERSON?
YES. I MISSED MY CHANCE TO THANK HIM THE DAY HE SAVED ME.
I ALSO WANTED TO ASK HIM SOMETHING.
...I WANTED TO ASK IF HE MIGHT BE RELATED TO ME.
SO HIS LIFESAVER MIGHT ALSO HOLD THE KEY TO SIL'S SECRET ORIGINS!?
I HAVE NO PROOF OF THIS.
I JUST THINK...

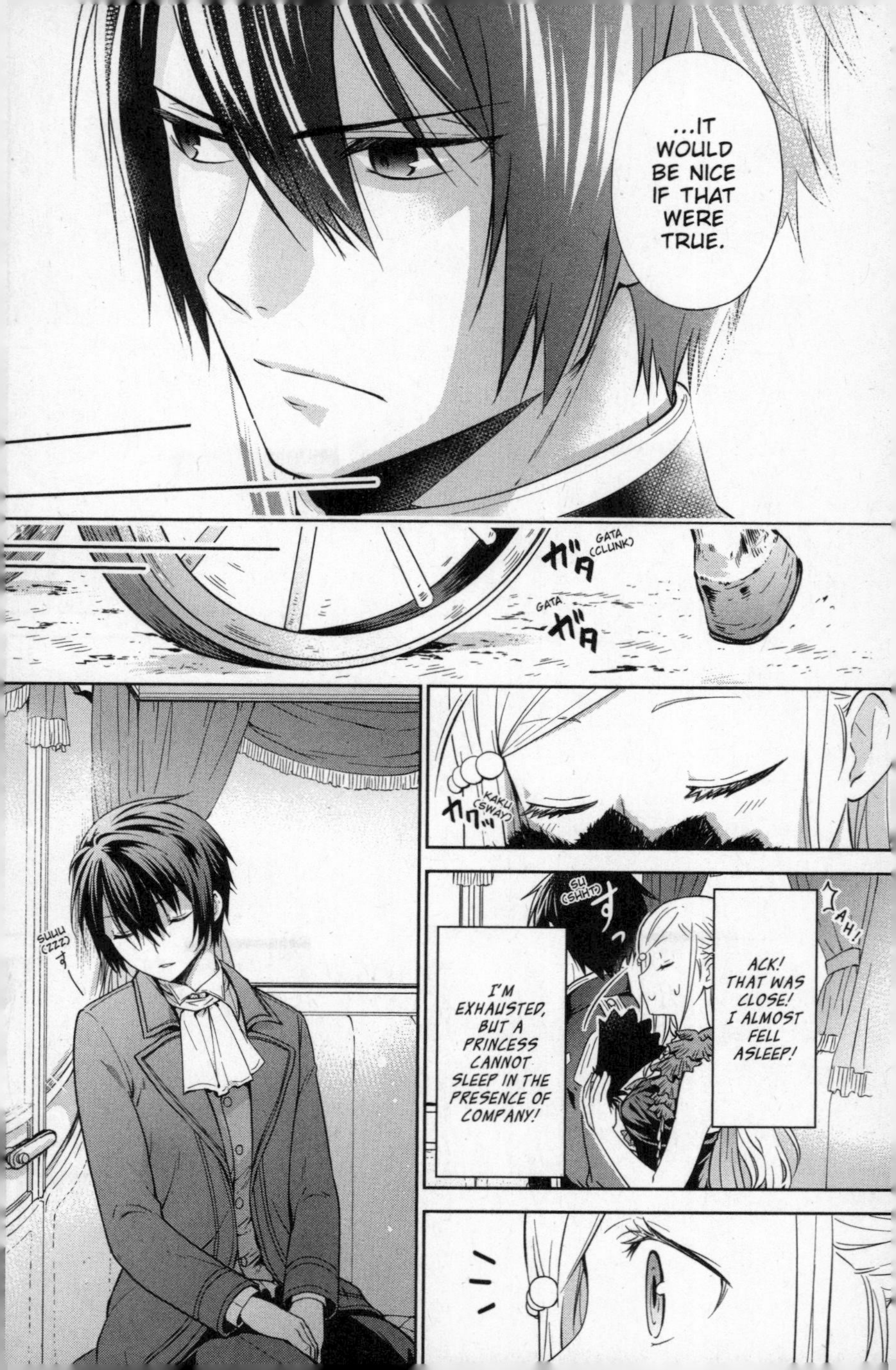
...IT WOULD BE NICE IF THAT WERE TRUE.
GATA (CLUNK)
GATA
KAKU (SWAY)
AH!
ACK! THAT WAS CLOSE! I ALMOST FELL ASLEEP!
SU (SHHT)
I'M EXHAUSTED, BUT A PRINCESS CANNOT SLEEP IN THE PRESENCE OF COMPANY!
SUUU (ZZZ)

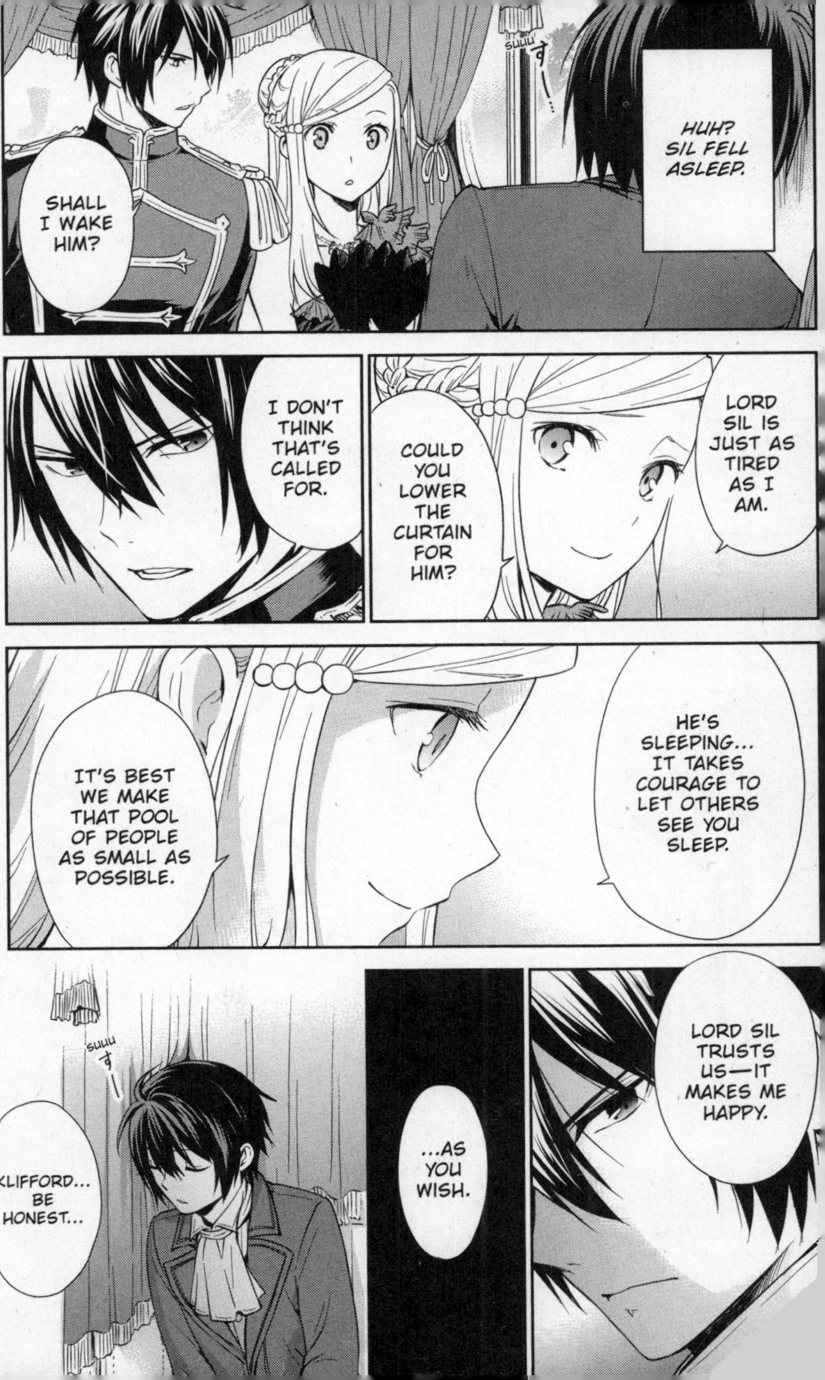
HUH? SIL FELL ASLEEP.
SUUU
SHALL I WAKE HIM?
LORD SIL IS JUST AS TIRED AS I AM.
COULD YOU LOWER THE CURTAIN FOR HIM?
I DON'T THINK THAT'S CALLED FOR.
HE'S SLEEPING... IT TAKES COURAGE TO LET OTHERS SEE YOU SLEEP.
IT'S BEST WE MAKE THAT POOL OF PEOPLE AS SMALL AS POSSIBLE.
LORD SIL TRUSTS US—IT MAKES ME HAPPY.
...AS YOU WISH.
SUUU
KLIFFORD... BE HONEST...

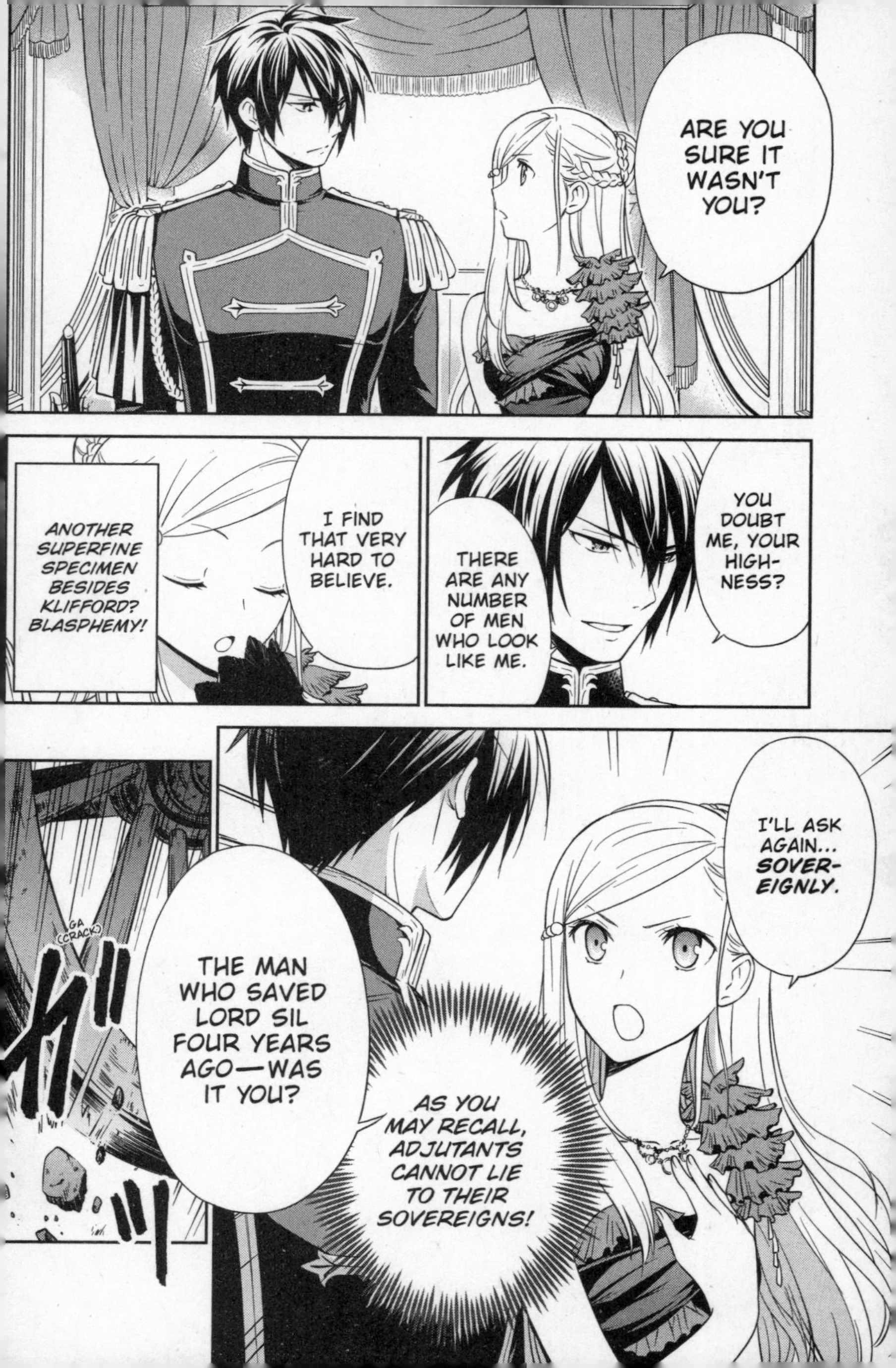
ARE YOU SURE IT WASN'T YOU?
YOU DOUBT ME, YOUR HIGH-NESS?
THERE ARE ANY NUMBER OF MEN WHO LOOK LIKE ME.
I FIND THAT VERY HARD TO BELIEVE.
ANOTHER SUPERFINE SPECIMEN BESIDES KLIFFORD? BLASPHEMY!
I'LL ASK AGAIN... SOVER-EIGNLY.
THE MAN WHO SAVED LORD SIL FOUR YEARS AGO—WAS IT YOU?
AS YOU MAY RECALL, ADJUTANTS CANNOT LIE TO THEIR SOVEREIGNS!
GA (CRACK)

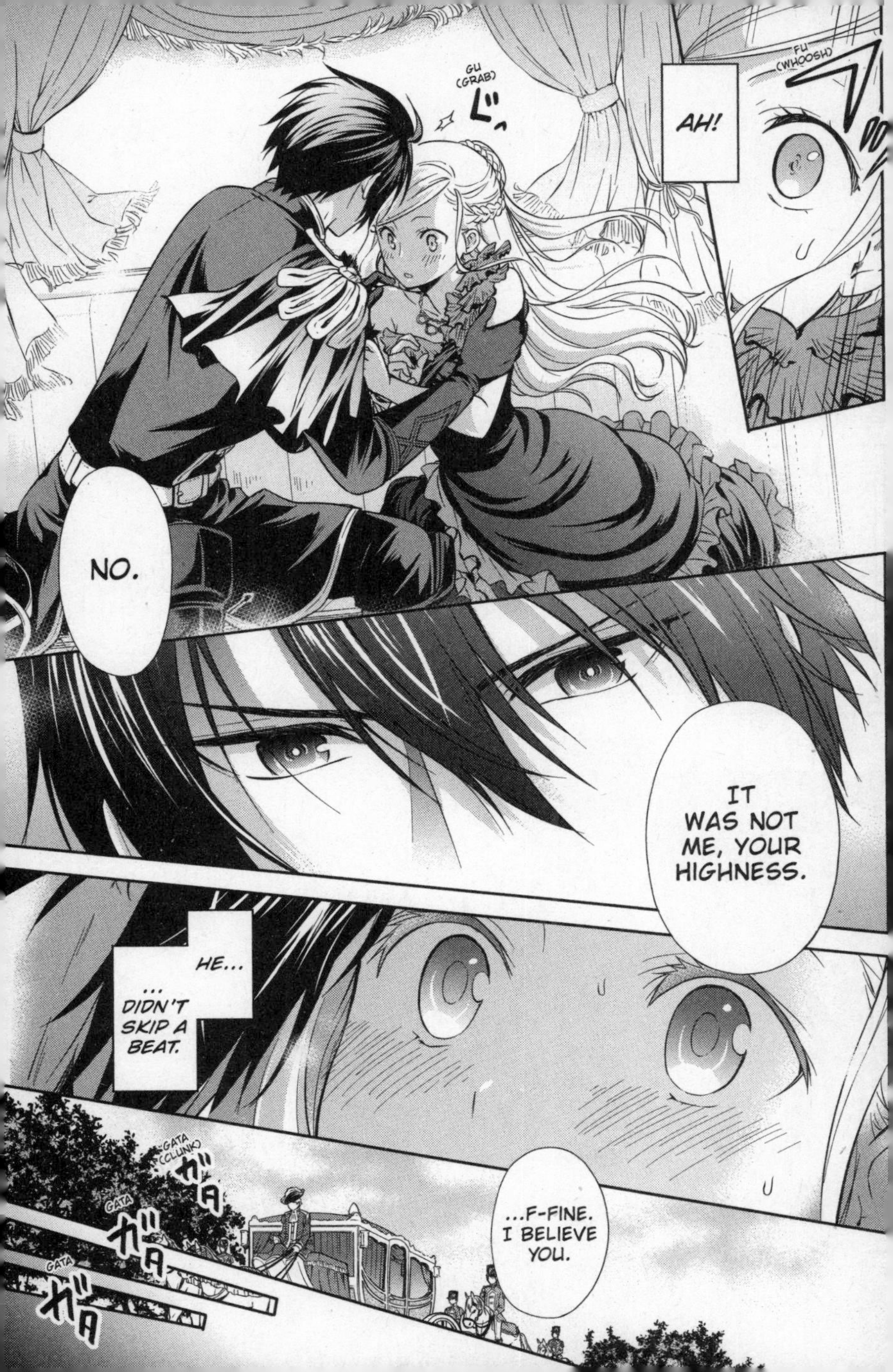
FU (WHOOSH)
AH!
GU (GRAB)
NO.
IT WAS NOT ME, YOUR HIGHNESS.
HE...
... DIDN'T SKIP A BEAT.
...F-FINE. I BELIEVE YOU.
GATA (CLUNK)
GATA
GATA

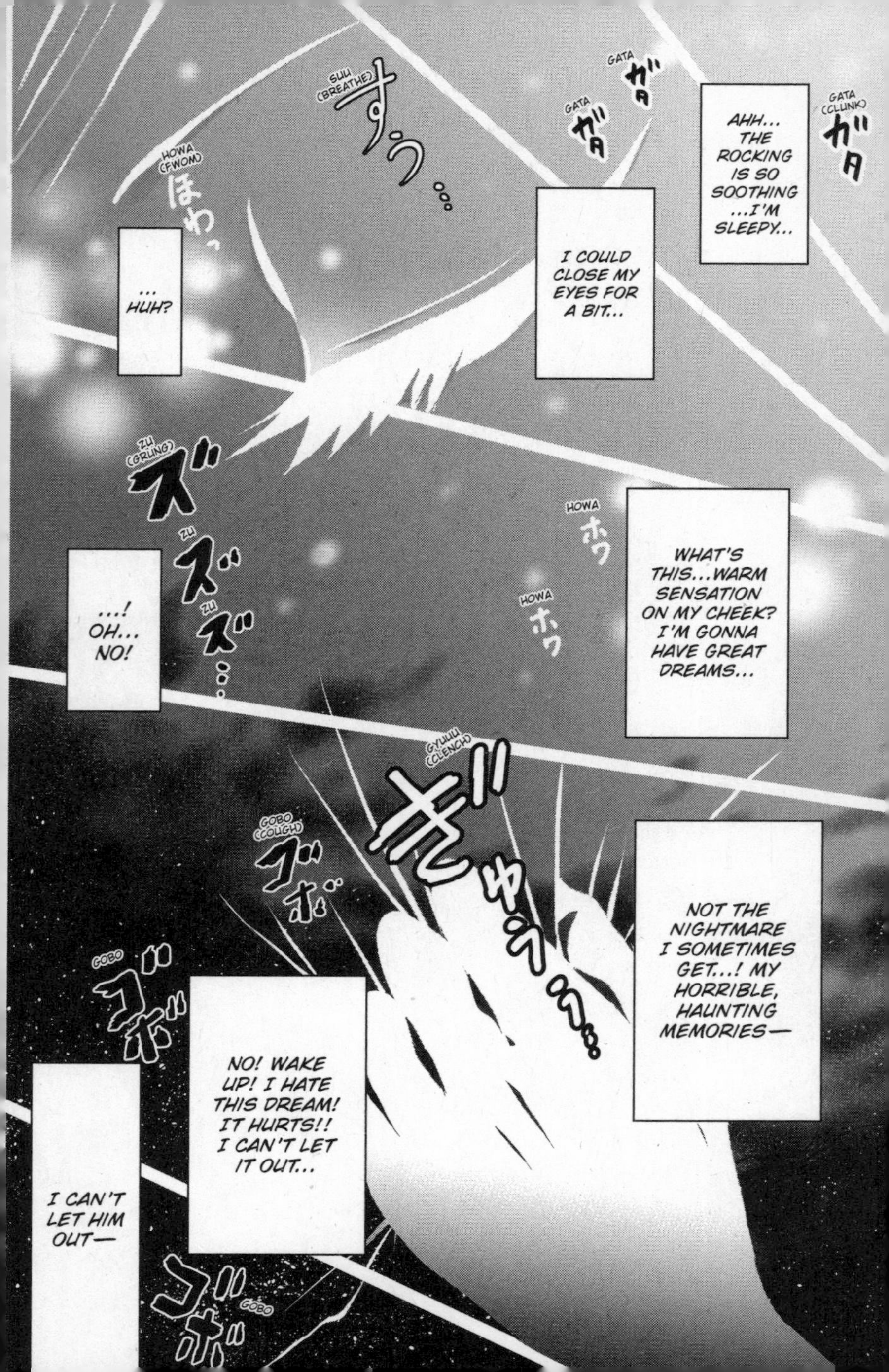
GATA (CLUNK)
AHH... THE ROCKING IS SO SOOTHING ...I'M SLEEPY...
GATA
GATA
I COULD CLOSE MY EYES FOR A BIT...
SUU (BREATHE)
HOWA (FWOM)
... HUH?
WHAT'S THIS...WARM SENSATION ON MY CHEEK? I'M GONNA HAVE GREAT DREAMS...
HOWA
HOWA
ZU (GRUNG)
ZU
ZU
...! OH... NO!
GYUUU (CLENCH)
NOT THE NIGHTMARE I SOMETIMES GET...! MY HORRIBLE, HAUNTING MEMORIES—
GOBO (COUGH)
NO! WAKE UP! I HATE THIS DREAM! IT HURTS!! I CAN'T LET IT OUT...
GOBO
I CAN'T LET HIM OUT—
GOBO

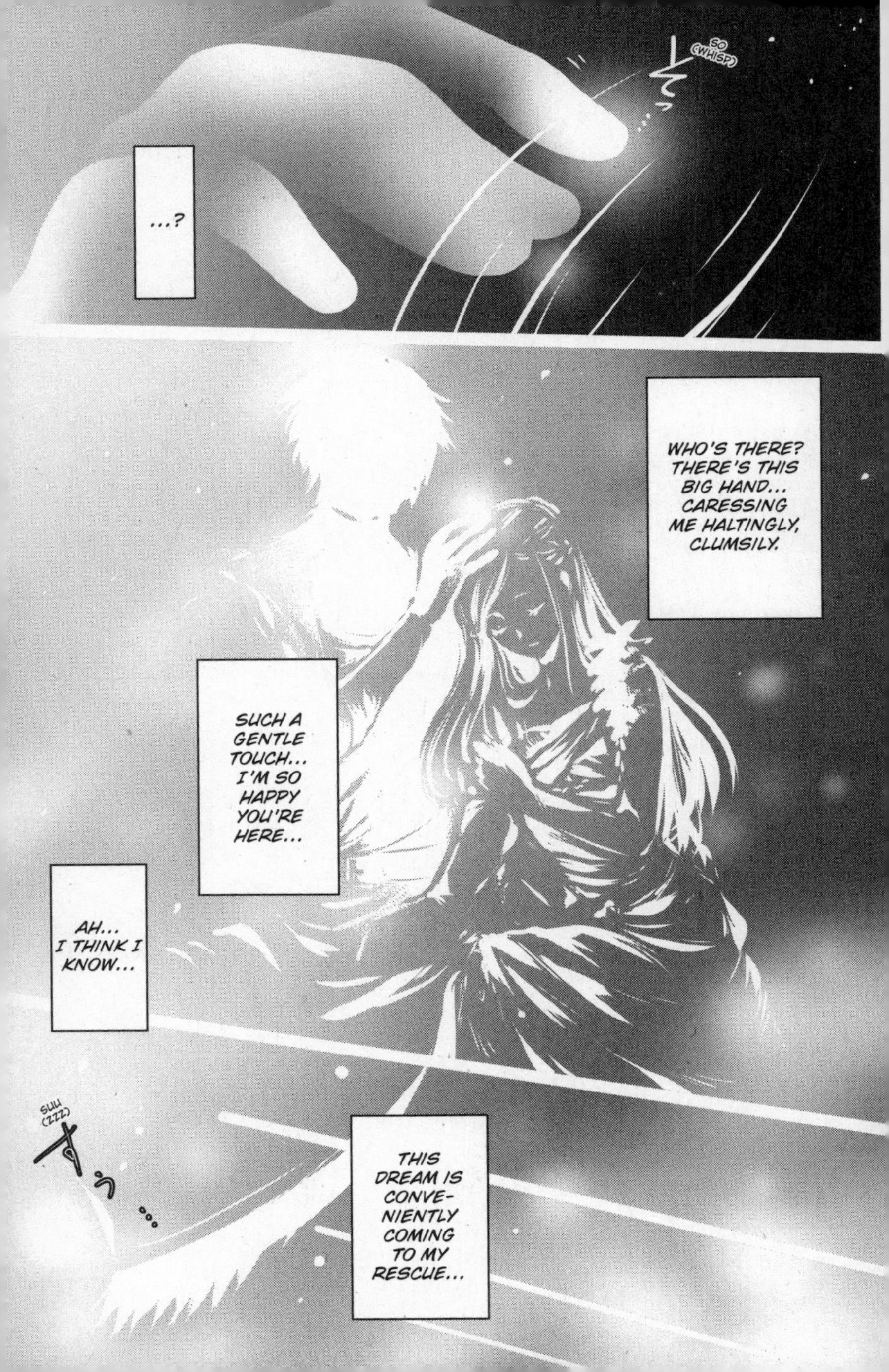
SO (WHISP)
...?
WHO'S THERE? THERE'S THIS BIG HAND... CARESSING ME HALTINGLY, CLUMSILY.
SUCH A GENTLE TOUCH... I'M SO HAPPY YOU'RE HERE...
AH... I THINK I KNOW...
THIS DREAM IS CONVE-NIENTLY COMING TO MY RESCUE...
SUU (ZZZ)

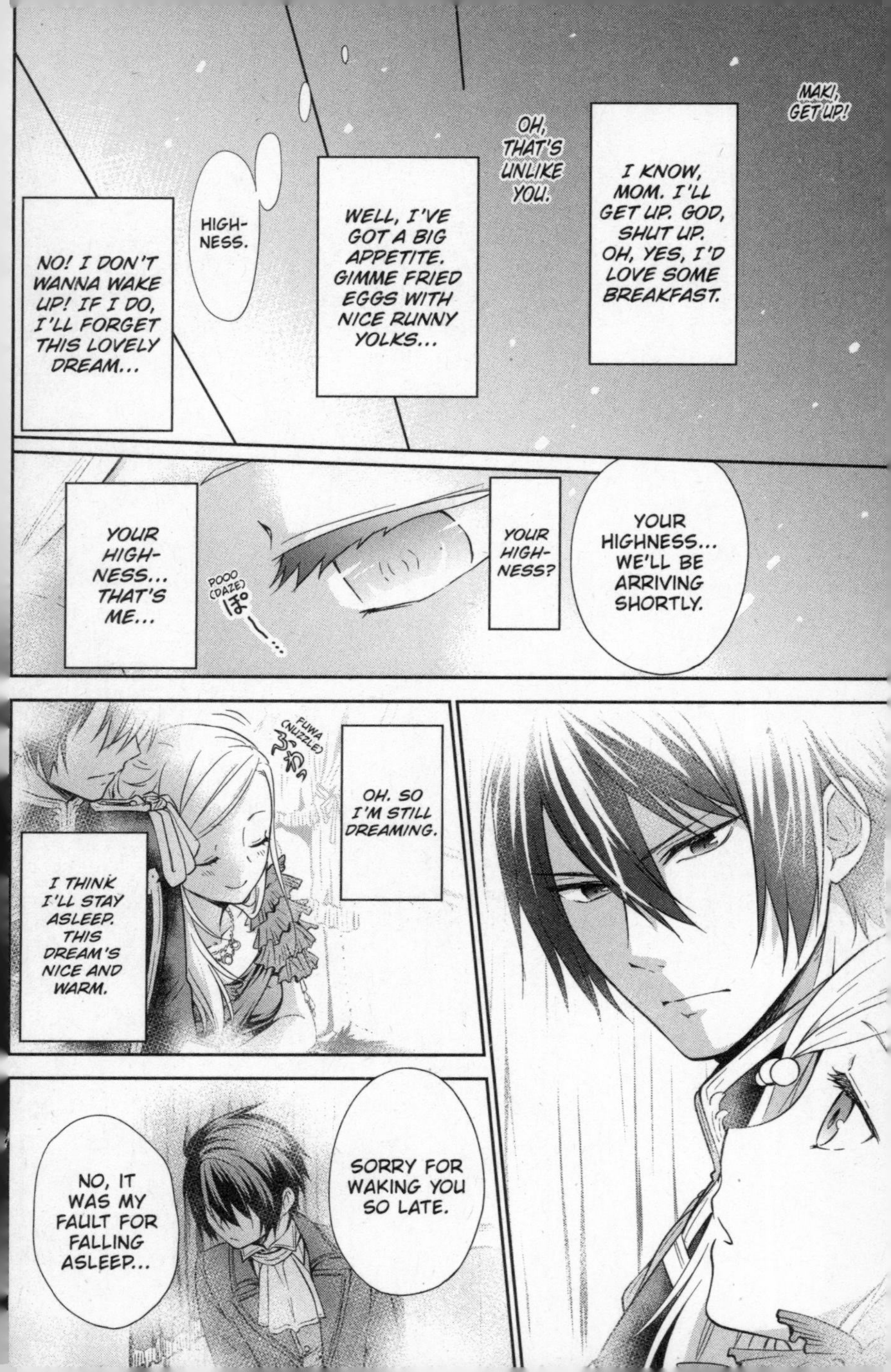
MAKI, GET UP!
I KNOW, MOM. I'LL GET UP. GOD, SHUT UP. OH, YES, I'D LOVE SOME BREAKFAST.
OH, THAT'S UNLIKE YOU.
WELL, I'VE GOT A BIG APPETITE. GIMME FRIED EGGS WITH NICE RUNNY YOLKS...
HIGH-NESS.
NO! I DON'T WANNA WAKE UP! IF I DO, I'LL FORGET THIS LOVELY DREAM...
YOUR HIGHNESS... WE'LL BE ARRIVING SHORTLY.
YOUR HIGH-NESS?
POOO (DAZE)
YOUR HIGH-NESS... THAT'S ME...
FUWA (NUZZLE)
OH. SO I'M STILL DREAMING.
I THINK I'LL STAY ASLEEP. THIS DREAM'S NICE AND WARM.
SORRY FOR WAKING YOU SO LATE.
NO, IT WAS MY FAULT FOR FALLING ASLEEP...

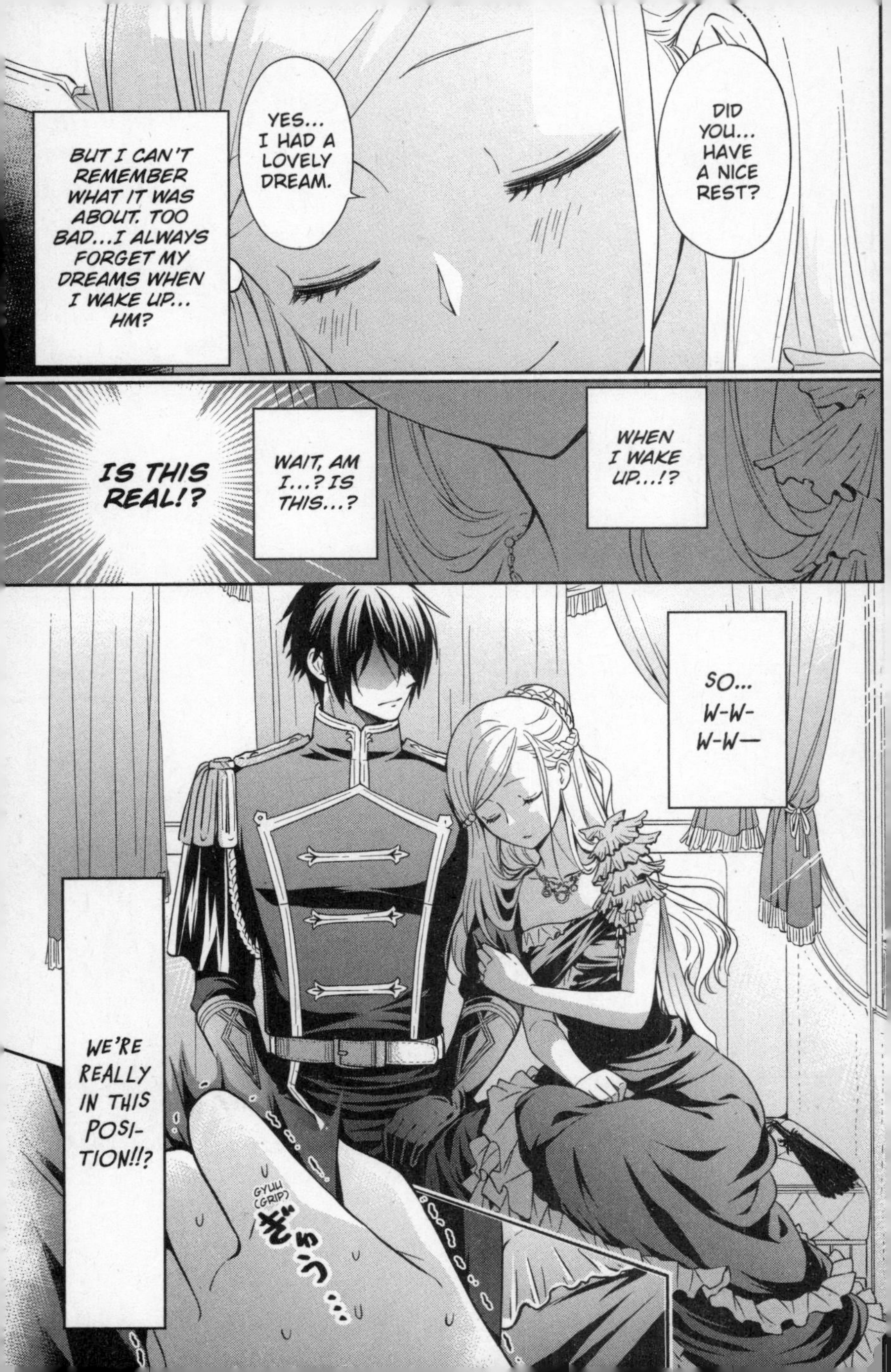
DID YOU... HAVE A NICE REST?
YES... I HAD A LOVELY DREAM.
BUT I CAN'T REMEMBER WHAT IT WAS ABOUT. TOO BAD...I ALWAYS FORGET MY DREAMS WHEN I WAKE UP... HM?
WHEN I WAKE UP...!?
WAIT, AM I...? IS THIS...?
IS THIS REAL!?
SO... W-W-W-W—
GYUU (GRIP)
WE'RE REALLY IN THIS POSI-TION!!?

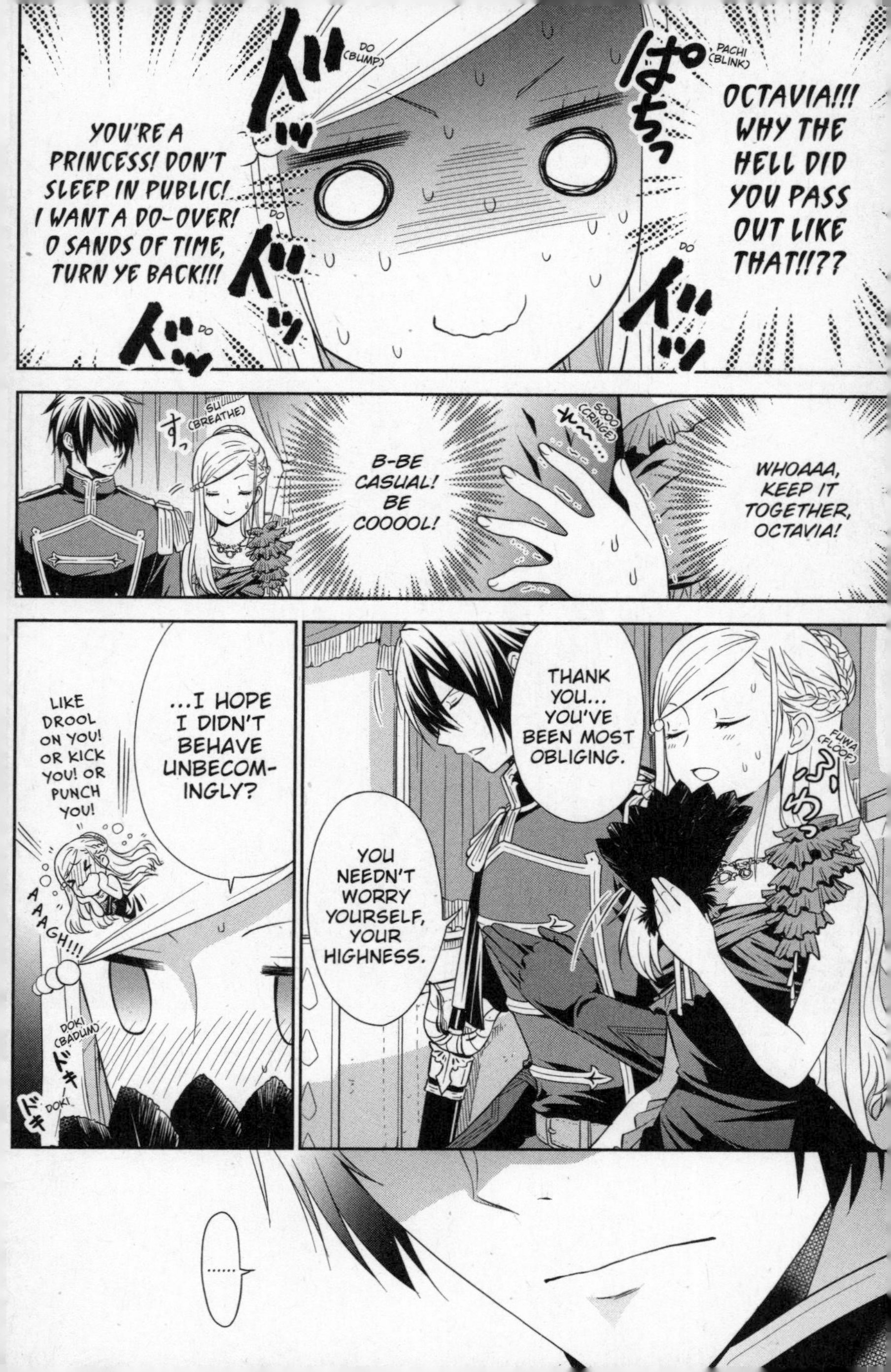
PACHI (BLINK)
OCTAVIA!!! WHY THE HELL DID YOU PASS OUT LIKE THAT!!??
DO (BUMP)
DO
DO
DO
YOU'RE A PRINCESS! DON'T SLEEP IN PUBLIC! I WANT A DO-OVER! O SANDS OF TIME, TURN YE BACK!!!
WHOAAA, KEEP IT TOGETHER, OCTAVIA!
SOOO (CRINGE)
B-BE CASUAL! BE COOOOL!
SU (BREATHE)
FUWA (FLOOF)
THANK YOU... YOU'VE BEEN MOST OBLIGING.
YOU NEEDN'T WORRY YOURSELF, YOUR HIGHNESS.
...I HOPE I DIDN'T BEHAVE UNBECOMINGLY?
LIKE DROOL ON YOU! OR KICK YOU! OR PUNCH YOU!
AAAGH!!!
DOKI (BADUM)
DOKI
......

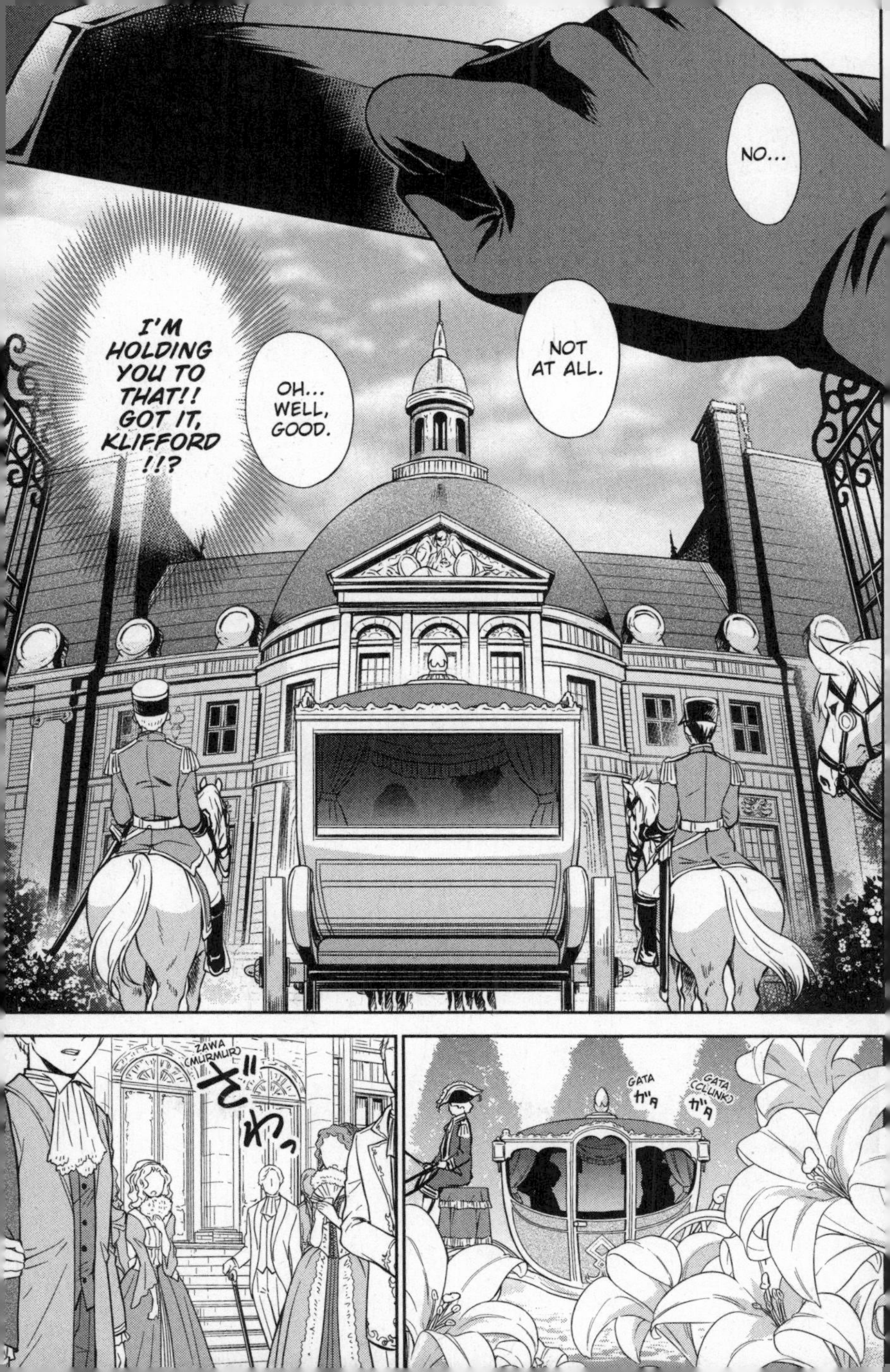
NO...
NOT AT ALL.
OH... WELL, GOOD.
I'M HOLDING YOU TO THAT!! GOT IT, KLIFFORD!!?
GATA (CLUNK) ガタ
GATA ガタ
ZAWA (MURMUR) ざわっ

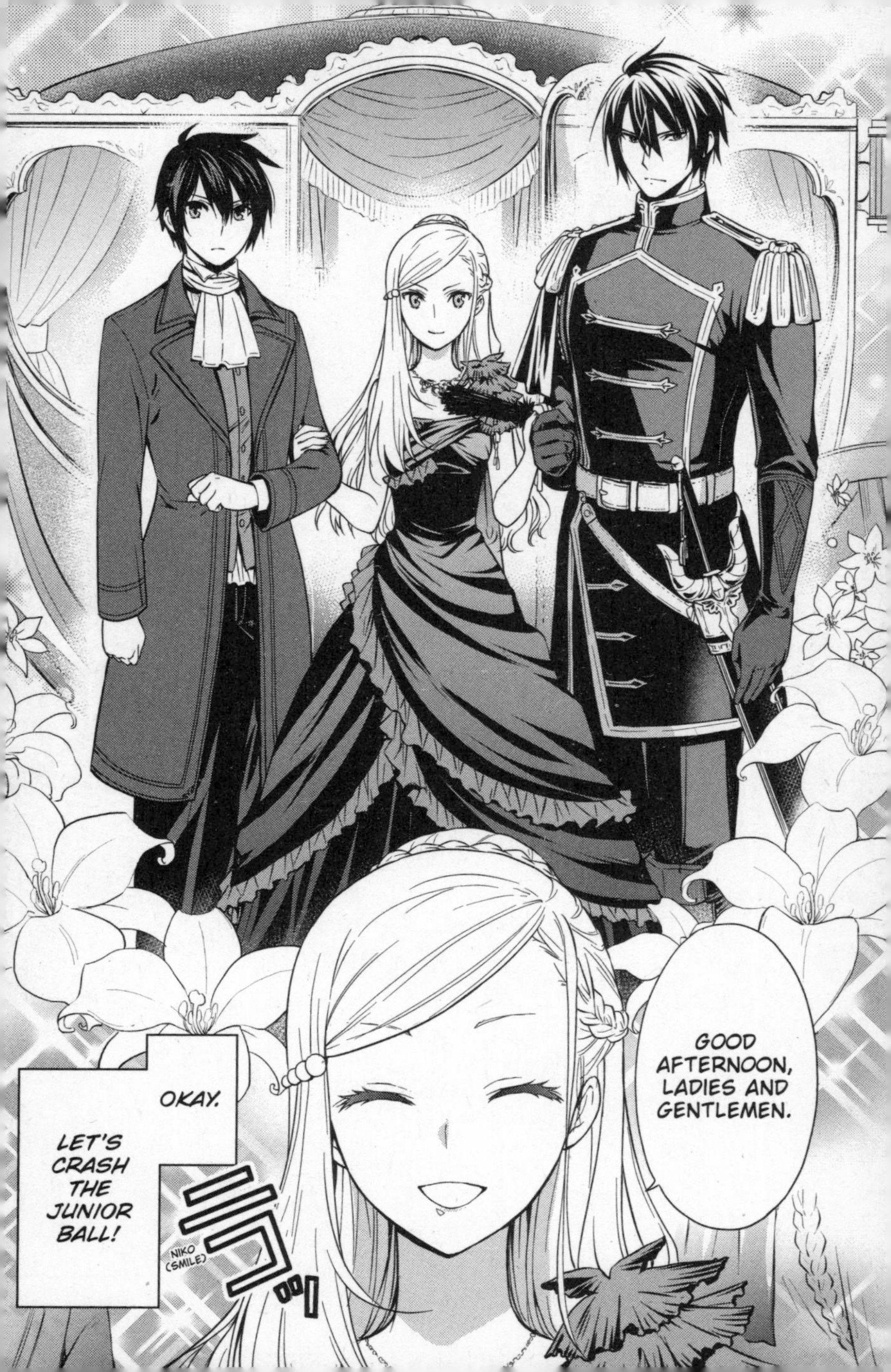
GOOD AFTERNOON, LADIES AND GENTLEMEN.
NIKO (SMILE)
OKAY.
LET'S CRASH THE JUNIOR BALL!

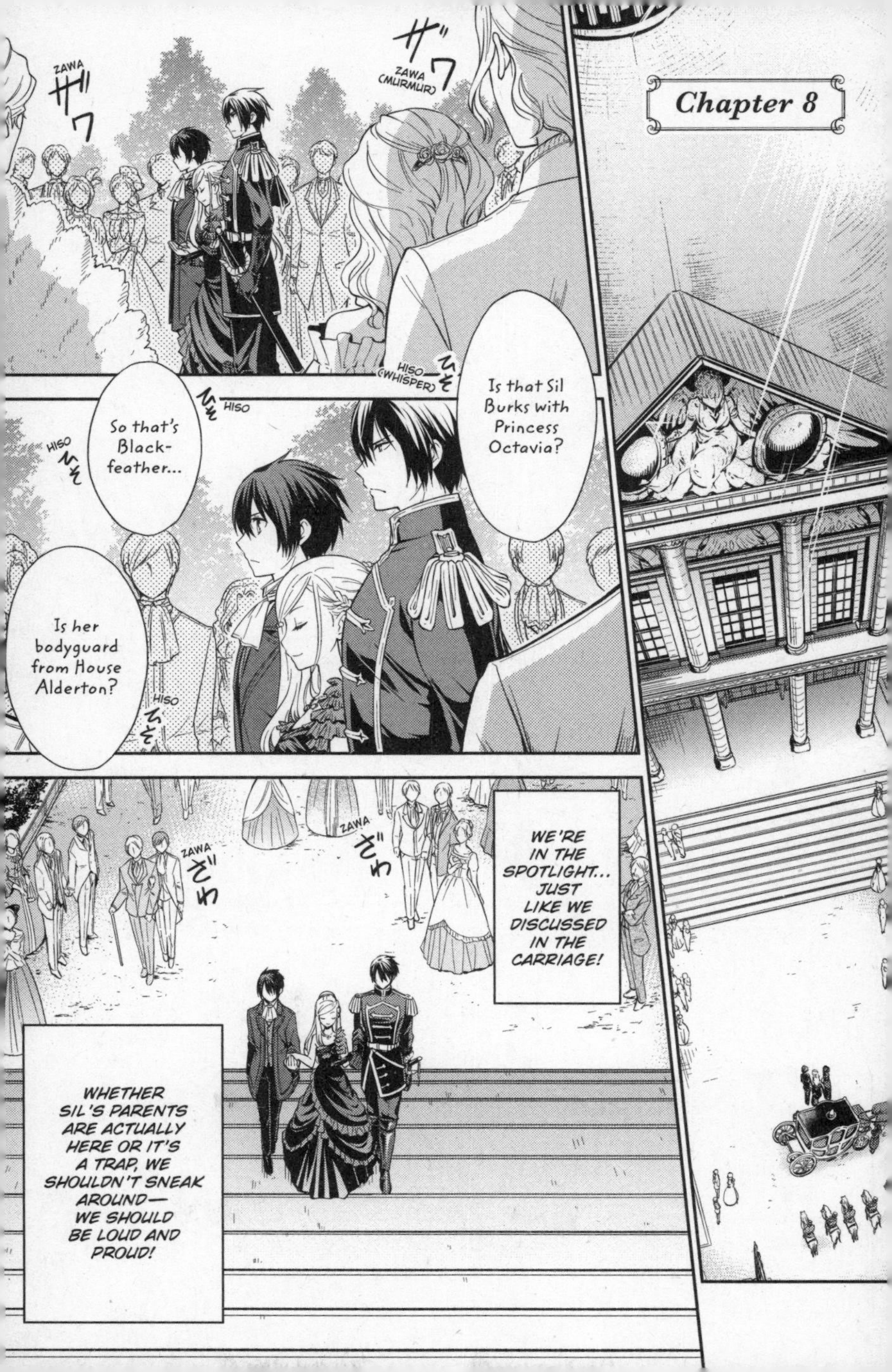

Chapter 8
ZAWA (MURMUR)
ZAWA
HISO (WHISPER)
Is that Sil Burks with Princess Octavia?
HISO
So that's Black-feather...
HISO
Is her bodyguard from House Alderton?
HISO
WE'RE IN THE SPOTLIGHT... JUST LIKE WE DISCUSSED IN THE CARRIAGE!
ZAWA
ZAWA
WHETHER SIL'S PARENTS ARE ACTUALLY HERE OR IT'S A TRAP, WE SHOULDN'T SNEAK AROUND— WE SHOULD BE LOUD AND PROUD!

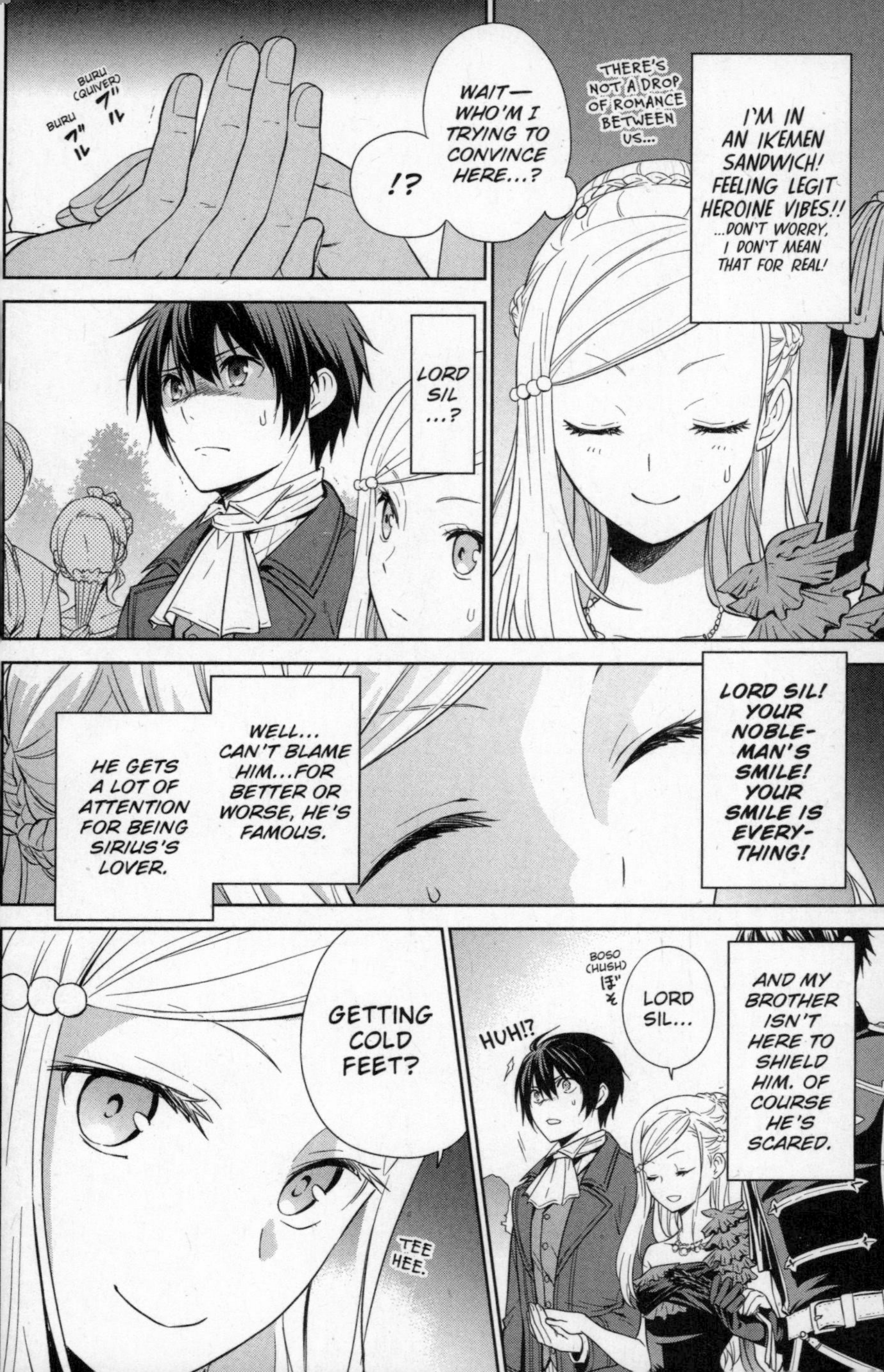
I'M IN AN IKEMEN SANDWICH! FEELING LEGIT HEROINE VIBES!! ...DON'T WORRY, I DON'T MEAN THAT FOR REAL!
THERE'S NOT A DROP OF ROMANCE BETWEEN US...
WAIT— WHO'M I TRYING TO CONVINCE HERE...?
!?
BURU (QUIVER) ブル
BURU ブル
LORD SIL ...?
LORD SIL! YOUR NOBLEMAN'S SMILE! YOUR SMILE IS EVERYTHING!
WELL... CAN'T BLAME HIM...FOR BETTER OR WORSE, HE'S FAMOUS.
HE GETS A LOT OF ATTENTION FOR BEING SIRIUS'S LOVER.
AND MY BROTHER ISN'T HERE TO SHIELD HIM. OF COURSE HE'S SCARED.
BOSO (HUSH) ぼそ
LORD SIL...
HUH!?
GETTING COLD FEET?
TEE HEE.

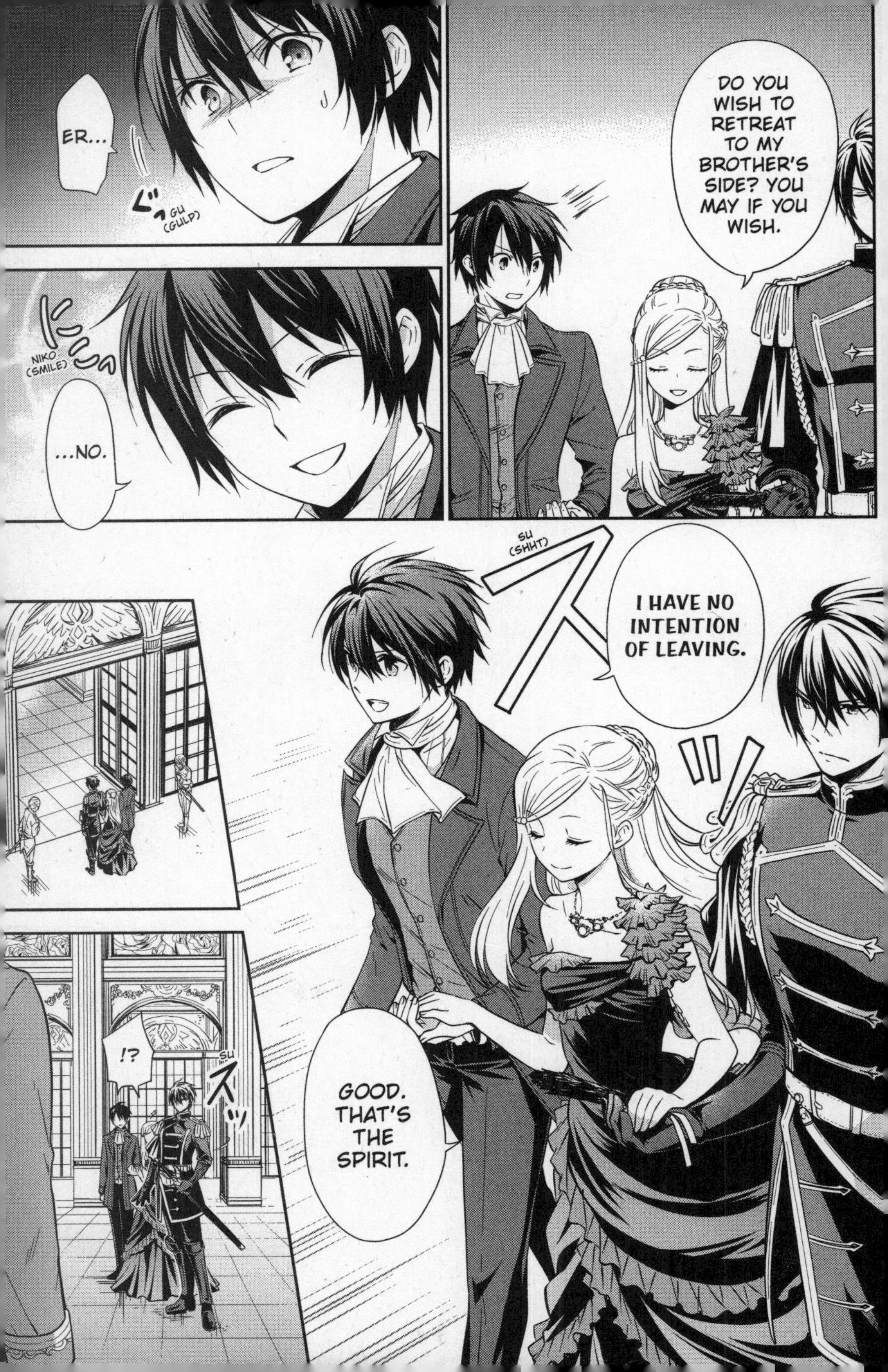
DO YOU WISH TO RETREAT TO MY BROTHER'S SIDE? YOU MAY IF YOU WISH.
ER...
GU (GULP)
NIKO (SMILE)
...NO.
SU (SHHT)
I HAVE NO INTENTION OF LEAVING.
SU
!?
GOOD. THAT'S THE SPIRIT.

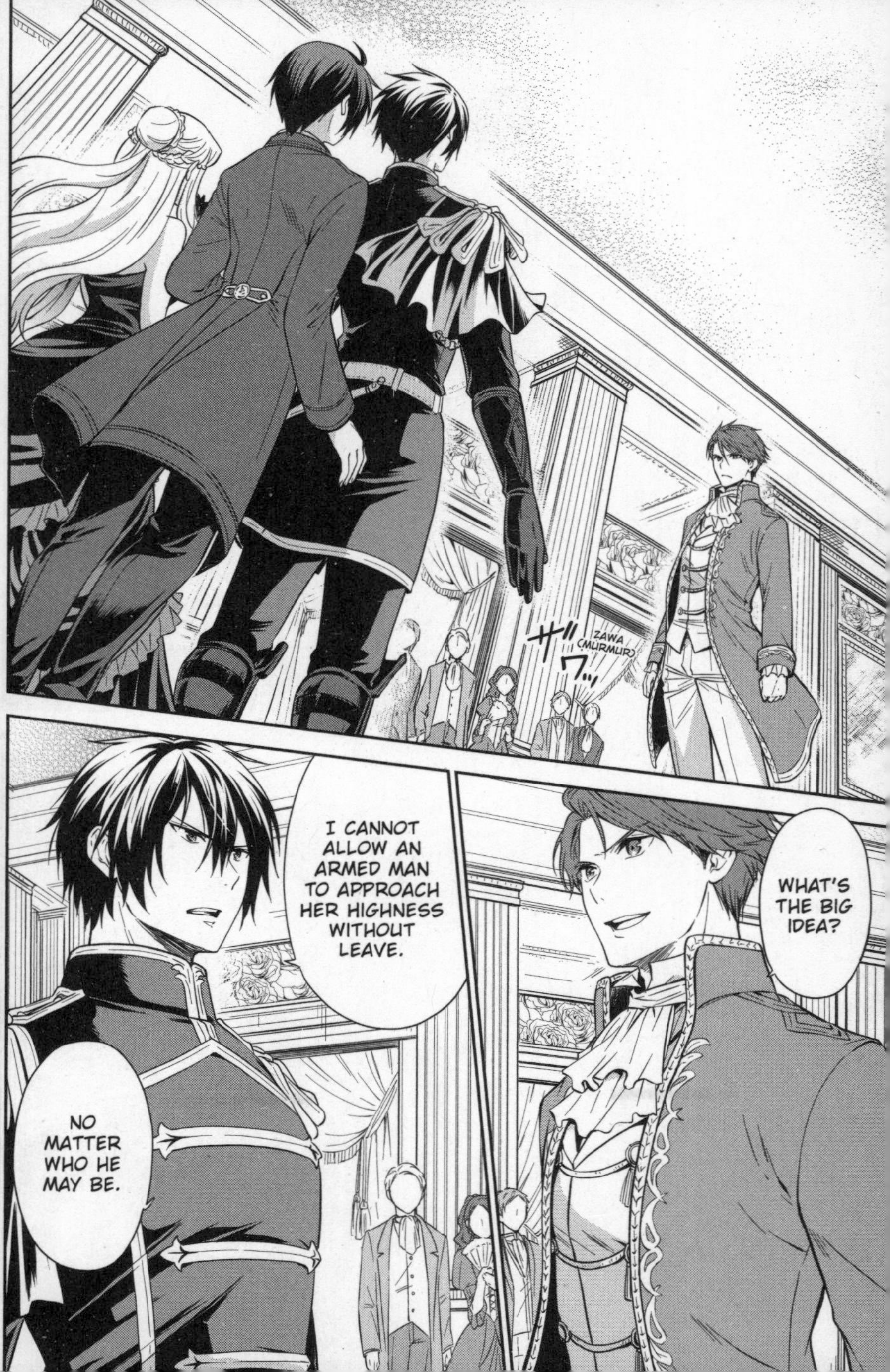
ZAWA (MURMUR)
ザワッ
WHAT'S THE BIG IDEA?
I CANNOT ALLOW AN ARMED MAN TO APPROACH HER HIGHNESS WITHOUT LEAVE.
NO MATTER WHO HE MAY BE.

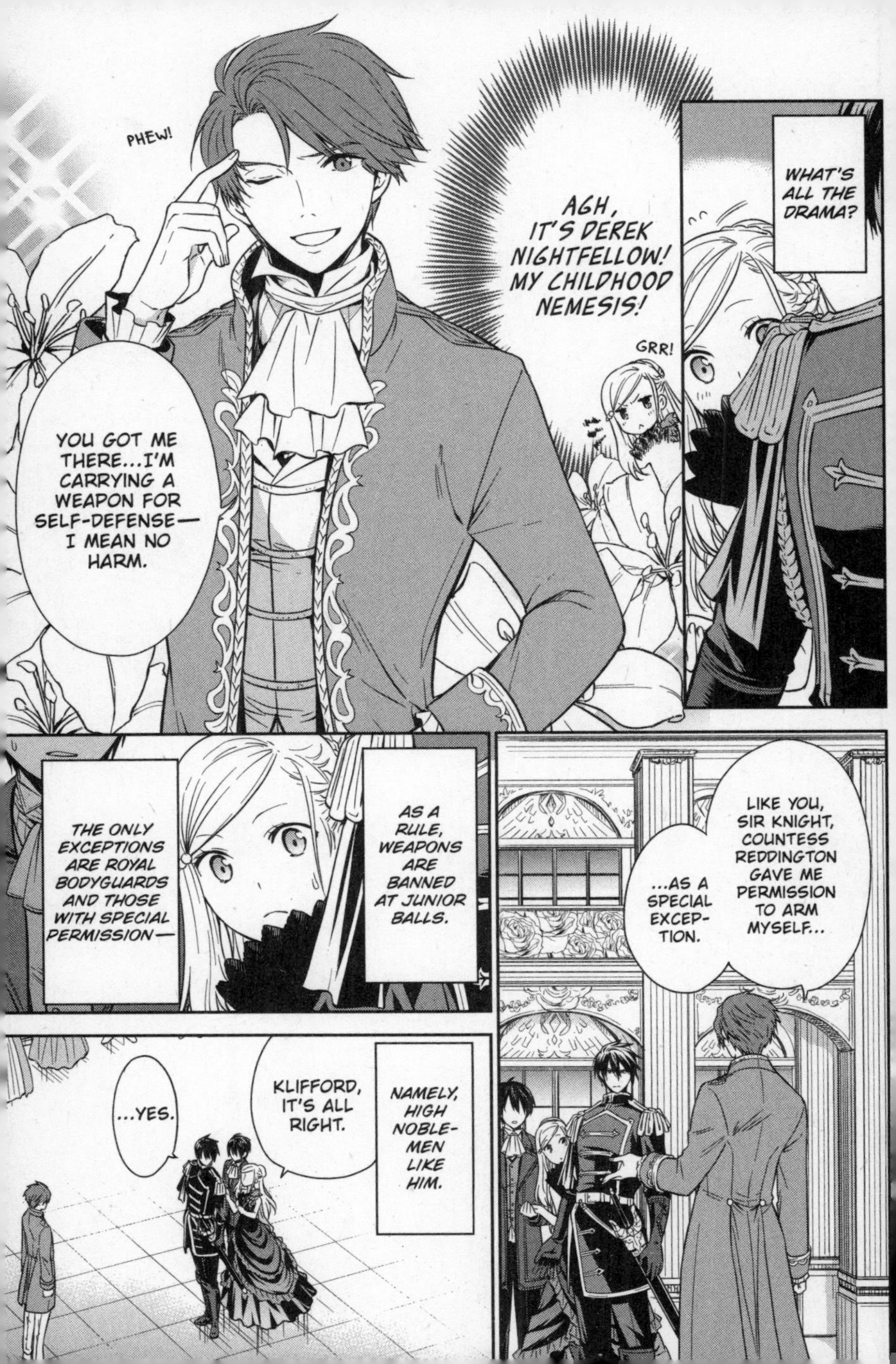
WHAT'S ALL THE DRAMA?
AGH, IT'S DEREK NIGHTFELLOW! MY CHILDHOOD NEMESIS!
GRR!
PHEW!
YOU GOT ME THERE...I'M CARRYING A WEAPON FOR SELF-DEFENSE—I MEAN NO HARM.
LIKE YOU, SIR KNIGHT, COUNTESS REDDINGTON GAVE ME PERMISSION TO ARM MYSELF...
...AS A SPECIAL EXCEP-TION.
AS A RULE, WEAPONS ARE BANNED AT JUNIOR BALLS.
THE ONLY EXCEPTIONS ARE ROYAL BODYGUARDS AND THOSE WITH SPECIAL PERMISSION—
NAMELY, HIGH NOBLE-MEN LIKE HIM.
KLIFFORD, IT'S ALL RIGHT.
...YES.

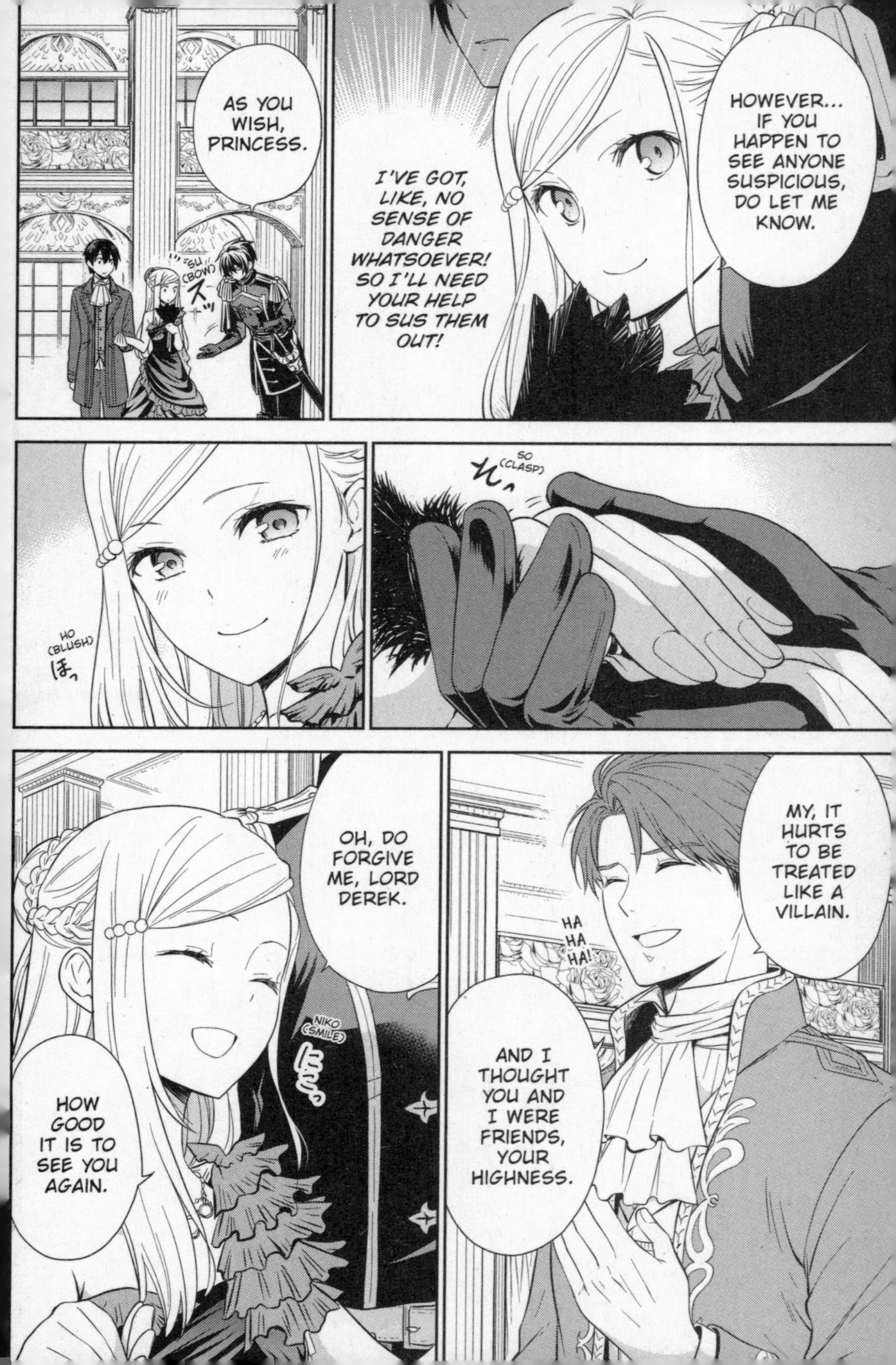
HOWEVER... IF YOU HAPPEN TO SEE ANYONE SUSPICIOUS, DO LET ME KNOW.
I'VE GOT, LIKE, NO SENSE OF DANGER WHATSOEVER! SO I'LL NEED YOUR HELP TO SUS THEM OUT!
AS YOU WISH, PRINCESS.
SU (BOW)
SO (CLASP)
HO (BLUSH)
MY, IT HURTS TO BE TREATED LIKE A VILLAIN.
HA HA HA!
AND I THOUGHT YOU AND I WERE FRIENDS, YOUR HIGHNESS.
OH, DO FORGIVE ME, LORD DEREK.
NIKO (SMILE)
HOW GOOD IT IS TO SEE YOU AGAIN.

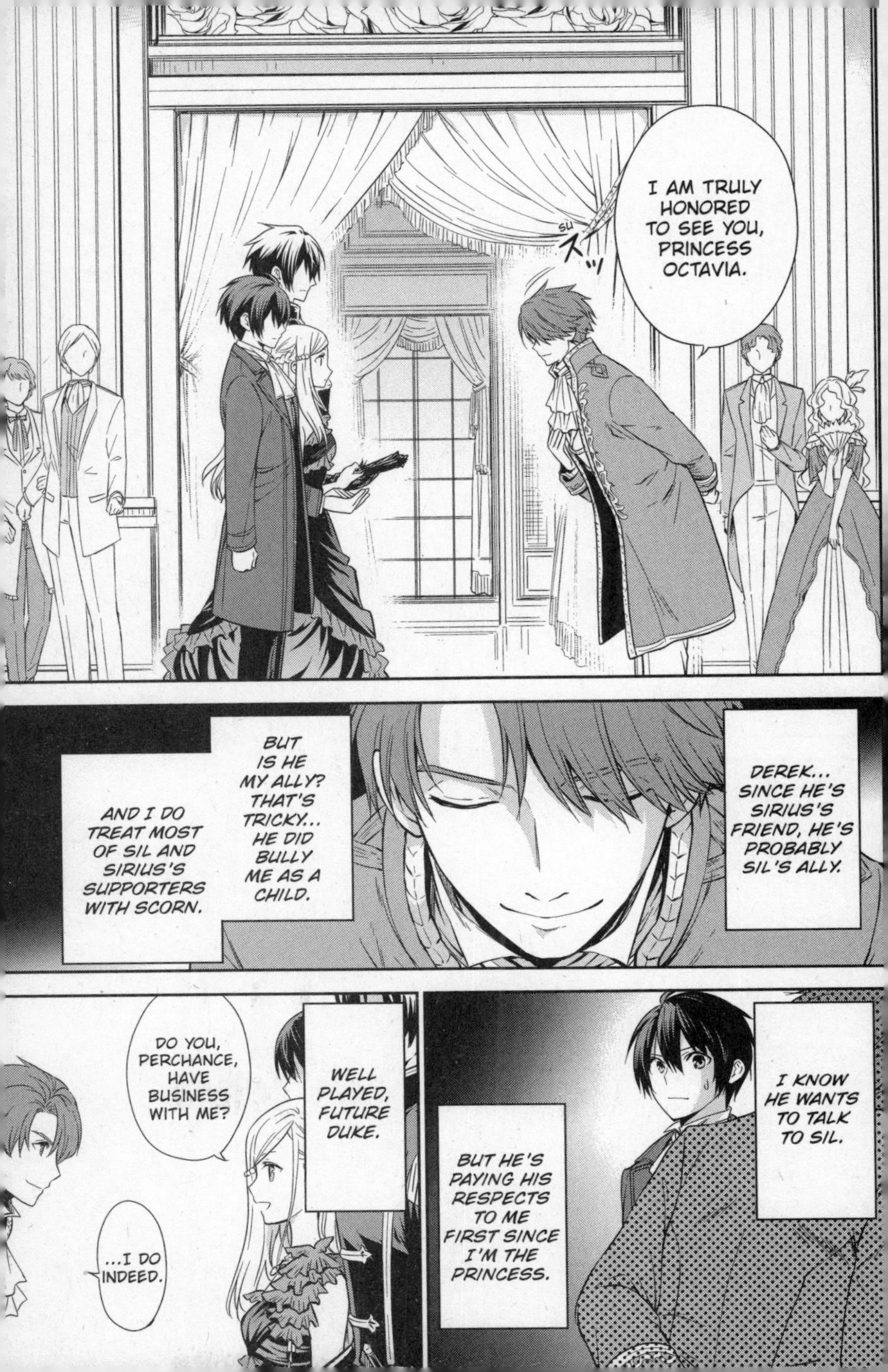
I AM TRULY HONORED TO SEE YOU, PRINCESS OCTAVIA.
SU
DEREK... SINCE HE'S SIRIUS'S FRIEND, HE'S PROBABLY SIL'S ALLY.
BUT IS HE MY ALLY? THAT'S TRICKY... HE DID BULLY ME AS A CHILD.
AND I DO TREAT MOST OF SIL AND SIRIUS'S SUPPORTERS WITH SCORN.
I KNOW HE WANTS TO TALK TO SIL.
BUT HE'S PAYING HIS RESPECTS TO ME FIRST SINCE I'M THE PRINCESS.
WELL PLAYED, FUTURE DUKE.
DO YOU, PERCHANCE, HAVE BUSINESS WITH ME?
...I DO INDEED.

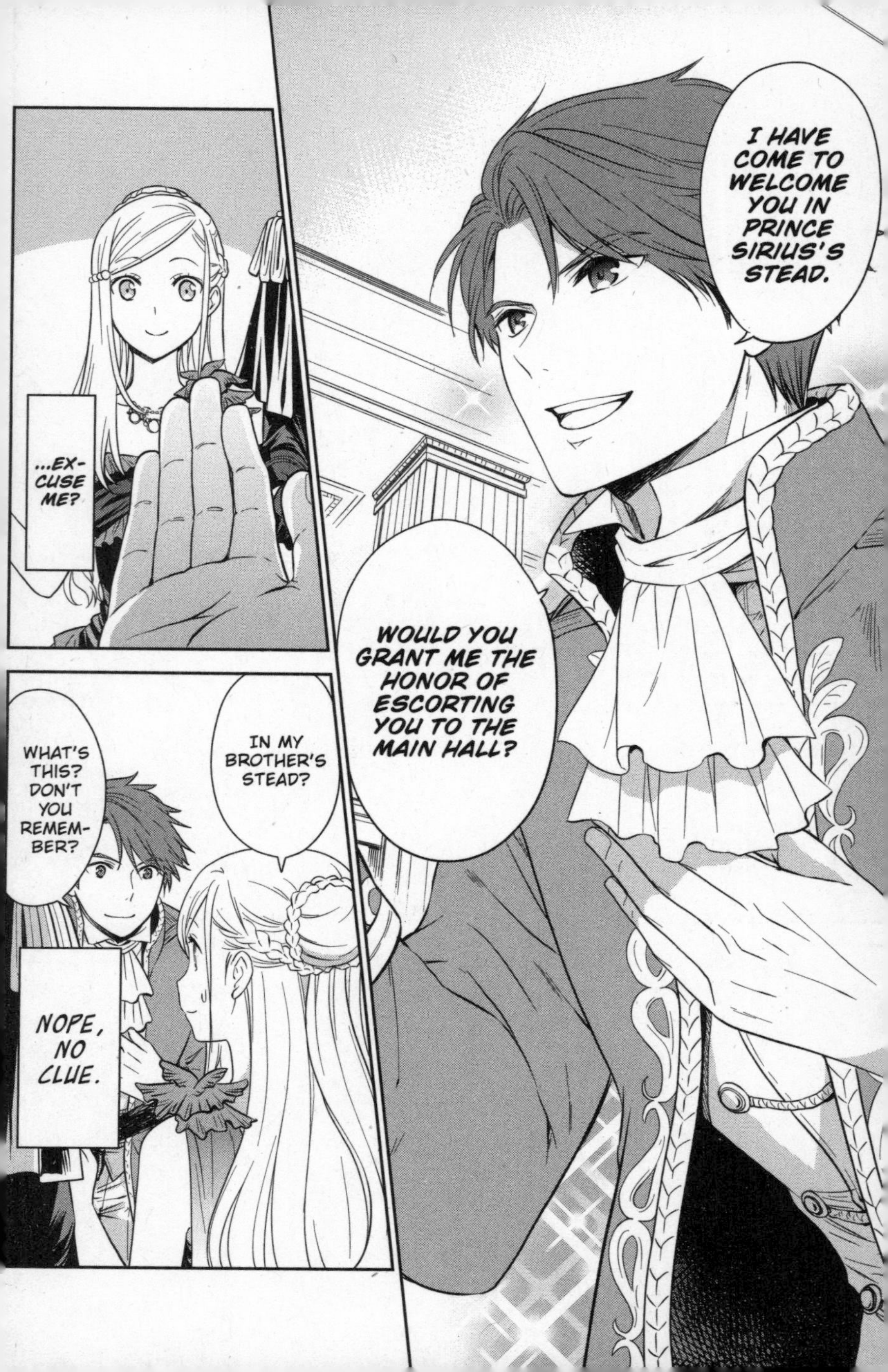
I HAVE COME TO WELCOME YOU IN PRINCE SIRIUS'S STEAD.
WOULD YOU GRANT ME THE HONOR OF ESCORTING YOU TO THE MAIN HALL?
...EX-CUSE ME?
IN MY BROTHER'S STEAD?
WHAT'S THIS? DON'T YOU REMEM-BER?
NOPE, NO CLUE.

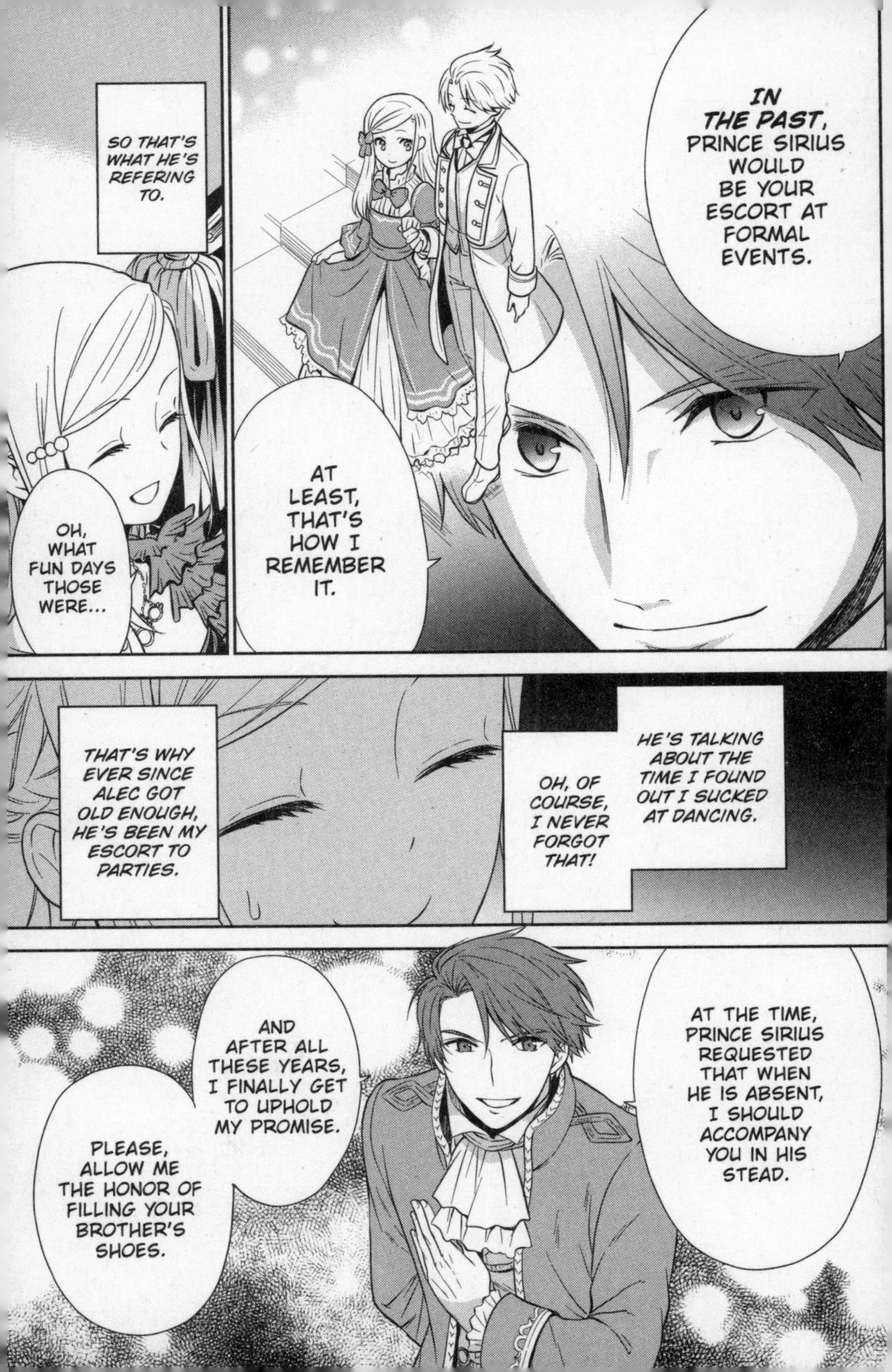
IN THE PAST, PRINCE SIRIUS WOULD BE YOUR ESCORT AT FORMAL EVENTS.
AT LEAST, THAT'S HOW I REMEMBER IT.
SO THAT'S WHAT HE'S REFERING TO.
OH, WHAT FUN DAYS THOSE WERE...
HE'S TALKING ABOUT THE TIME I FOUND OUT I SUCKED AT DANCING.
OH, OF COURSE, I NEVER FORGOT THAT!
THAT'S WHY EVER SINCE ALEC GOT OLD ENOUGH, HE'S BEEN MY ESCORT TO PARTIES.
AT THE TIME, PRINCE SIRIUS REQUESTED THAT WHEN HE IS ABSENT, I SHOULD ACCOMPANY YOU IN HIS STEAD.
AND AFTER ALL THESE YEARS, I FINALLY GET TO UPHOLD MY PROMISE.
PLEASE, ALLOW ME THE HONOR OF FILLING YOUR BROTHER'S SHOES.

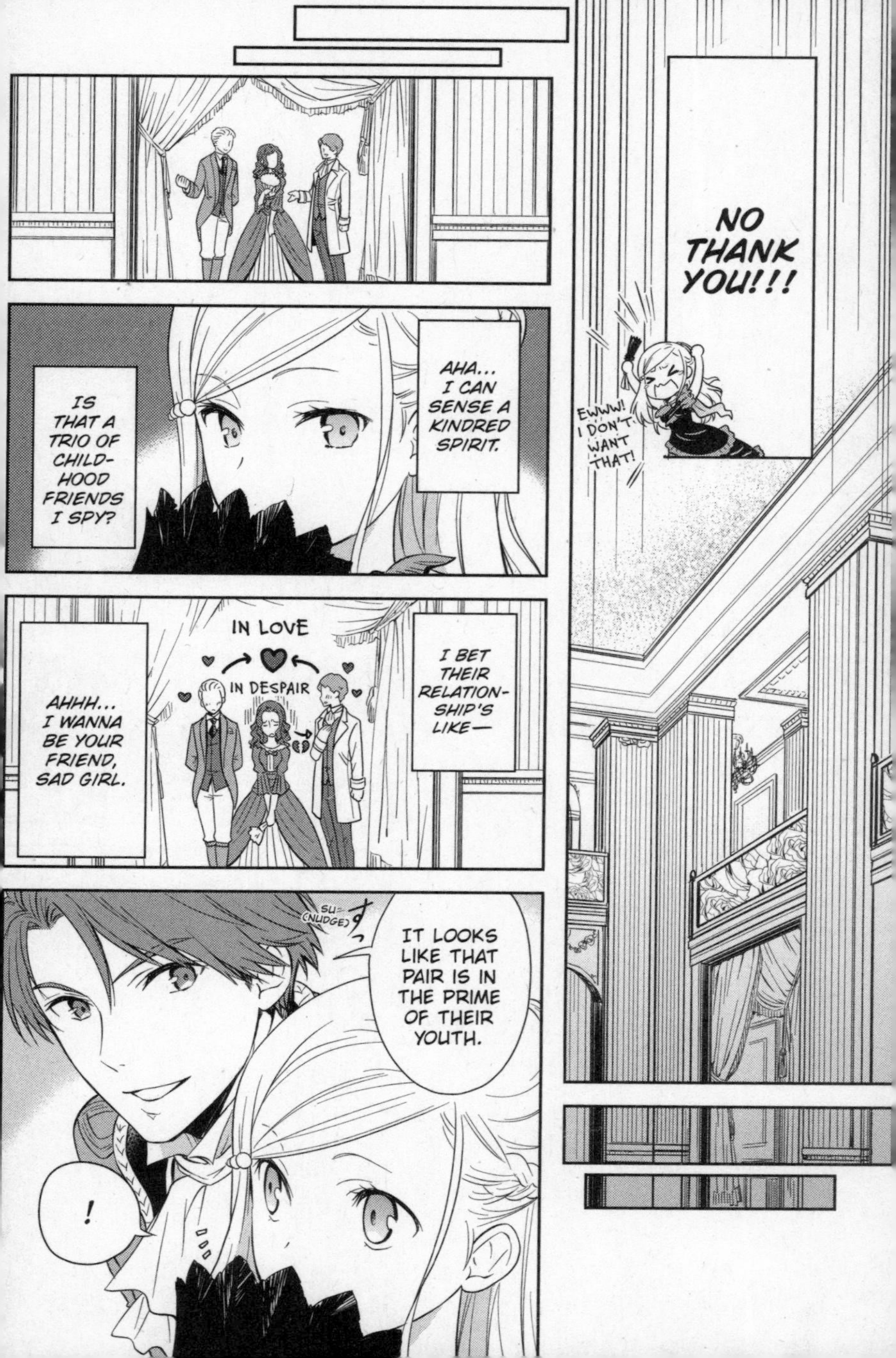
AHA... I CAN SENSE A KINDRED SPIRIT.
IS THAT A TRIO OF CHILD-HOOD FRIENDS I SPY?
I BET THEIR RELATION-SHIP'S LIKE—
IN LOVE
IN DESPAIR
AHHH... I WANNA BE YOUR FRIEND, SAD GIRL.
SU- (NUDGE)
IT LOOKS LIKE THAT PAIR IS IN THE PRIME OF THEIR YOUTH.
!
NO THANK YOU!!!
EWWW! I DON'T WANT THAT!

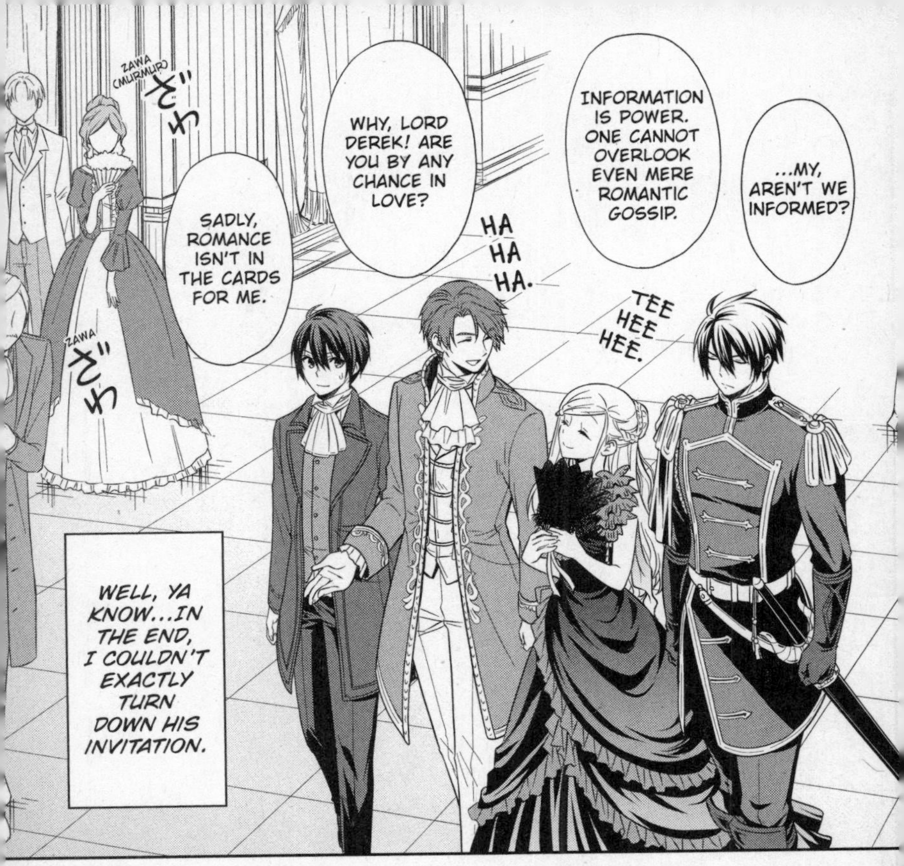
...MY, AREN'T WE INFORMED?
TEE HEE HEE.
INFORMATION IS POWER. ONE CANNOT OVERLOOK EVEN MERE ROMANTIC GOSSIP.
WHY, LORD DEREK! ARE YOU BY ANY CHANCE IN LOVE?
HA HA HA.
SADLY, ROMANCE ISN'T IN THE CARDS FOR ME.
ZAWA (MURMUR) ざわ
ZAWA ざわ
WELL, YA KNOW...IN THE END, I COULDN'T EXACTLY TURN DOWN HIS INVITATION.
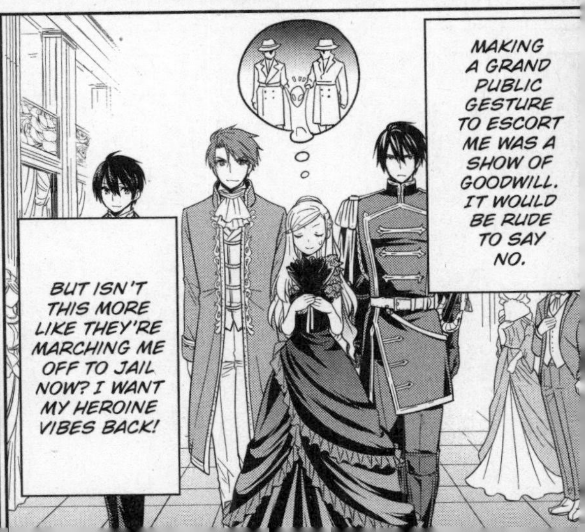
MAKING A GRAND PUBLIC GESTURE TO ESCORT ME WAS A SHOW OF GOODWILL. IT WOULD BE RUDE TO SAY NO.
BUT ISN'T THIS MORE LIKE THEY'RE MARCHING ME OFF TO JAIL NOW? I WANT MY HEROINE VIBES BACK!
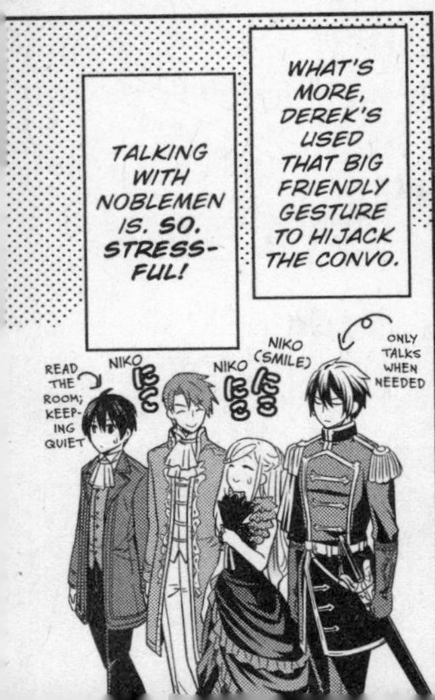
WHAT'S MORE, DEREK'S USED THAT BIG FRIENDLY GESTURE TO HIJACK THE CONVO.
TALKING WITH NOBLEMEN IS. SO. STRESS-FUL!
ONLY TALKS WHEN NEEDED
NIKO (SMILE) にこ
NIKO にこ
NIKO にこ
READ THE ROOM; KEEPING QUIET

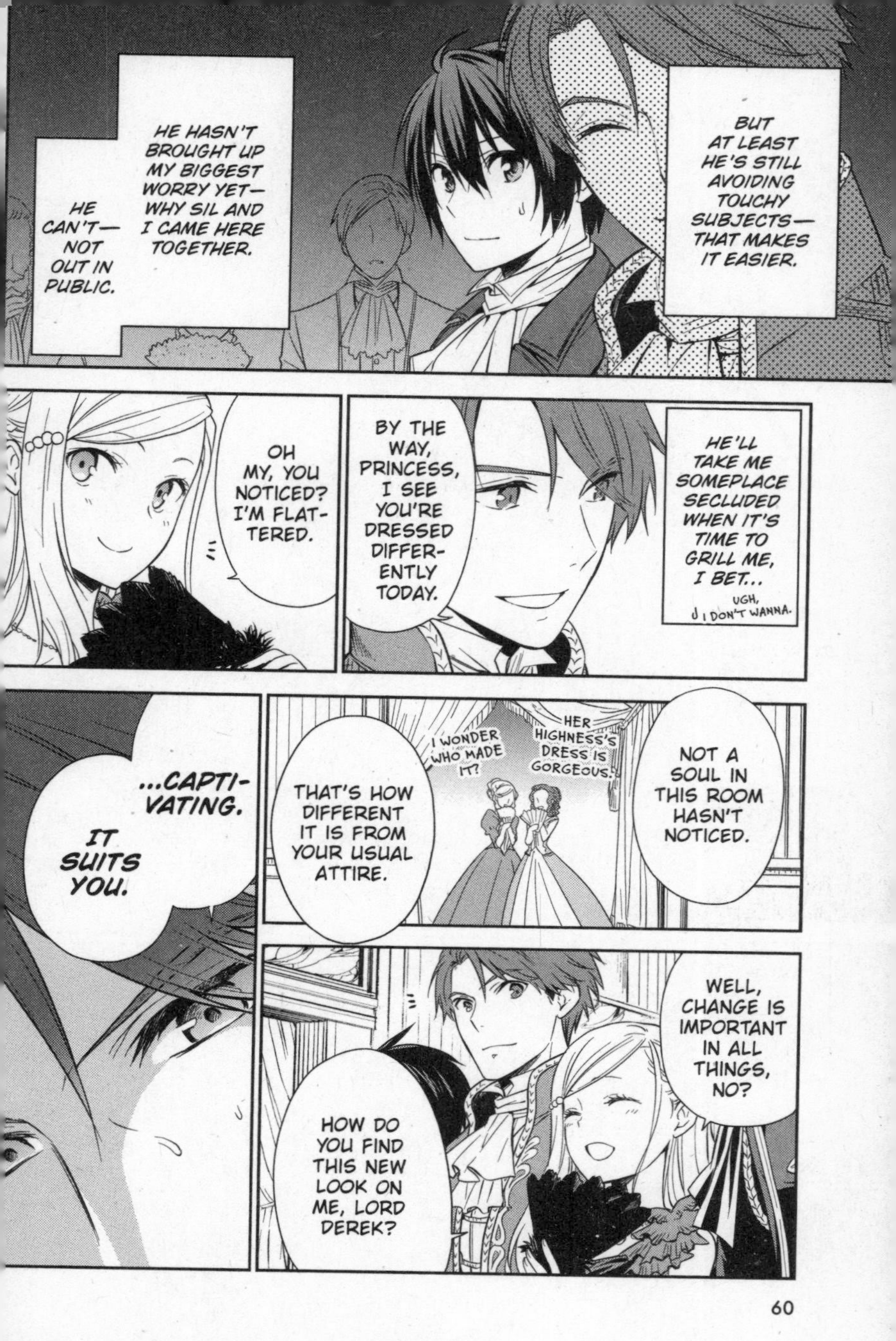
BUT AT LEAST HE'S STILL AVOIDING TOUCHY SUBJECTS—THAT MAKES IT EASIER.
HE HASN'T BROUGHT UP MY BIGGEST WORRY YET—WHY SIL AND I CAME HERE TOGETHER.
HE CAN'T—NOT OUT IN PUBLIC.
HE'LL TAKE ME SOMEPLACE SECLUDED WHEN IT'S TIME TO GRILL ME, I BET...
UGH, I DON'T WANNA.
BY THE WAY, PRINCESS, I SEE YOU'RE DRESSED DIFFERENTLY TODAY.
OH MY, YOU NOTICED? I'M FLATTERED.
NOT A SOUL IN THIS ROOM HASN'T NOTICED.
HER HIGHNESS'S DRESS IS GORGEOUS.
I WONDER WHO MADE IT?
THAT'S HOW DIFFERENT IT IS FROM YOUR USUAL ATTIRE.
WELL, CHANGE IS IMPORTANT IN ALL THINGS, NO?
HOW DO YOU FIND THIS NEW LOOK ON ME, LORD DEREK?
...CAPTIVATING.
IT SUITS YOU.

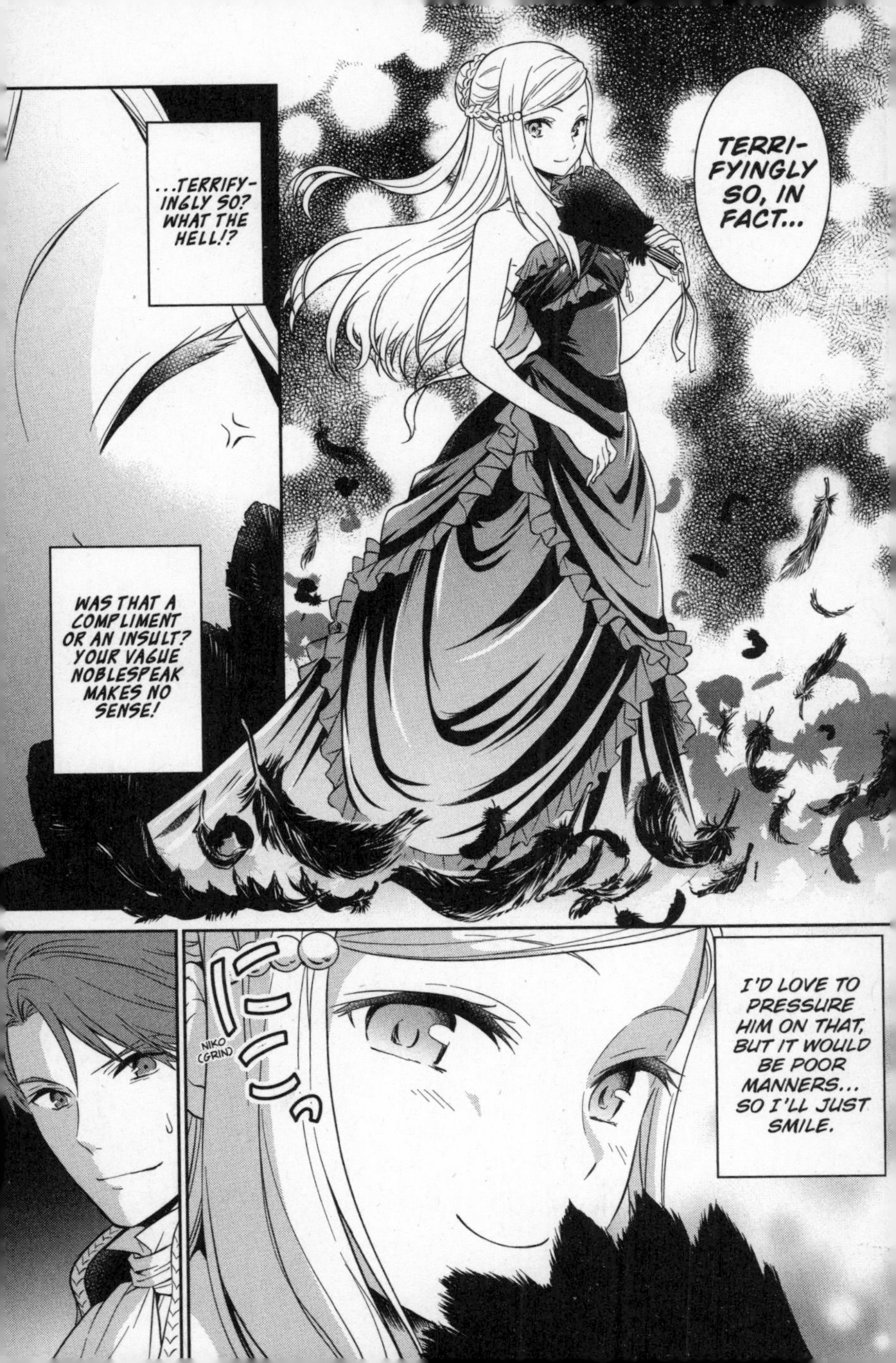
TERRI-FYINGLY SO, IN FACT...
...TERRIFY-INGLY SO? WHAT THE HELL!?
WAS THAT A COMPLIMENT OR AN INSULT? YOUR VAGUE NOBLESPEAK MAKES NO SENSE!
I'D LOVE TO PRESSURE HIM ON THAT, BUT IT WOULD BE POOR MANNERS... SO I'LL JUST SMILE.
NIKO (GRIN)

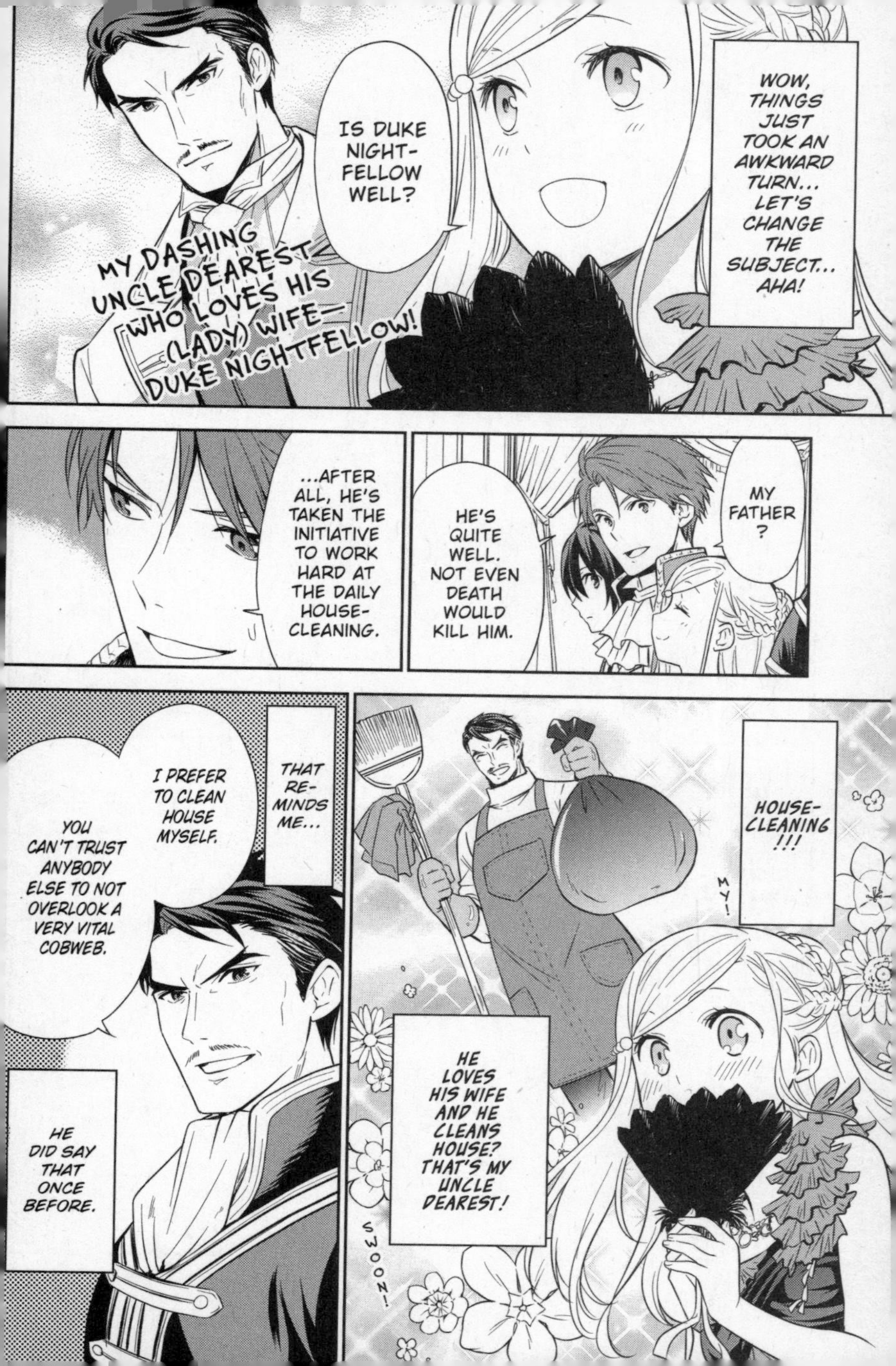
WOW, THINGS JUST TOOK AN AWKWARD TURN... LET'S CHANGE THE SUBJECT... AHA!
IS DUKE NIGHT-FELLOW WELL?
MY DASHING UNCLE DEAREST WHO LOVES HIS (LADY) WIFE—DUKE NIGHTFELLOW!
MY FATHER?
HE'S QUITE WELL. NOT EVEN DEATH WOULD KILL HIM.
...AFTER ALL, HE'S TAKEN THE INITIATIVE TO WORK HARD AT THE DAILY HOUSE-CLEANING.
HOUSE-CLEANING!!!
MY!
HE LOVES HIS WIFE AND HE CLEANS HOUSE? THAT'S MY UNCLE DEAREST!
SWOON!
THAT RE-MINDS ME...
I PREFER TO CLEAN HOUSE MYSELF.
YOU CAN'T TRUST ANYBODY ELSE TO NOT OVERLOOK A VERY VITAL COBWEB.
HE DID SAY THAT ONCE BEFORE.

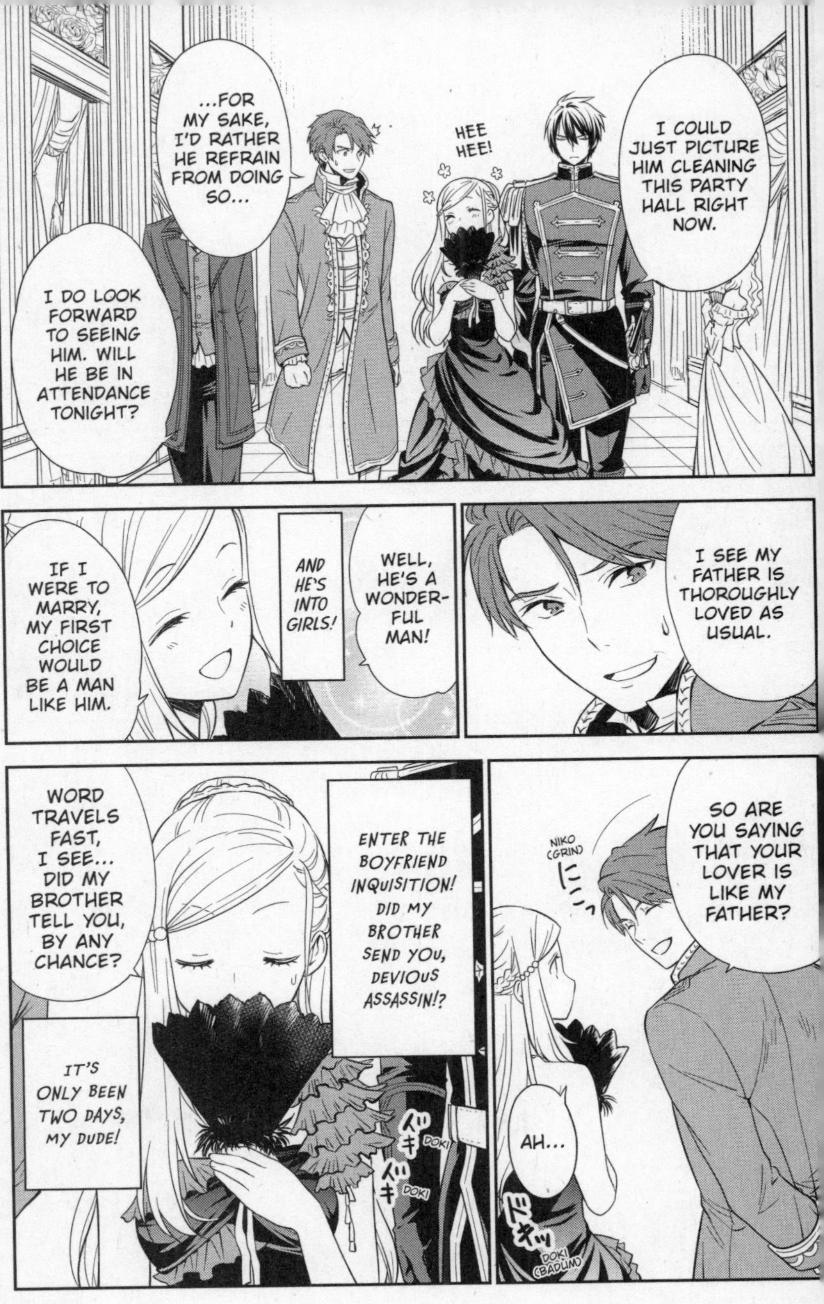
I COULD JUST PICTURE HIM CLEANING THIS PARTY HALL RIGHT NOW.
HEE HEE!
...FOR MY SAKE, I'D RATHER HE REFRAIN FROM DOING SO...
I DO LOOK FORWARD TO SEEING HIM. WILL HE BE IN ATTENDANCE TONIGHT?
I SEE MY FATHER IS THOROUGHLY LOVED AS USUAL.
WELL, HE'S A WONDER-FUL MAN!
AND HE'S INTO GIRLS!
IF I WERE TO MARRY, MY FIRST CHOICE WOULD BE A MAN LIKE HIM.
SO ARE YOU SAYING THAT YOUR LOVER IS LIKE MY FATHER?
NIKO (GRIN)
AH...
DOKI (BADUM)
ENTER THE BOYFRIEND INQUISITION! DID MY BROTHER SEND YOU, DEVIOUS ASSASSIN!?
WORD TRAVELS FAST, I SEE... DID MY BROTHER TELL YOU, BY ANY CHANCE?
DOKI
DOKI
IT'S ONLY BEEN TWO DAYS, MY DUDE!

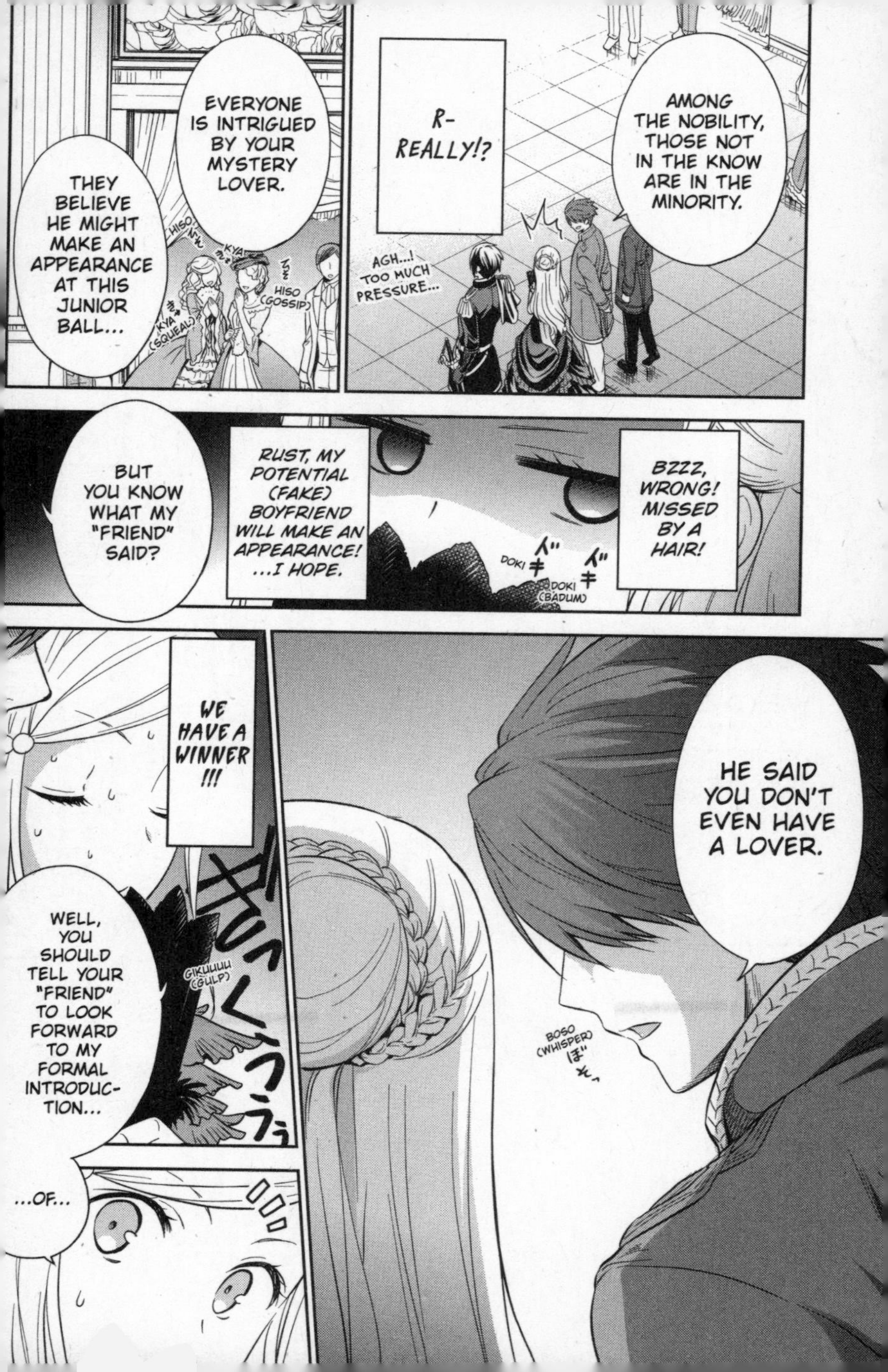
AMONG THE NOBILITY, THOSE NOT IN THE KNOW ARE IN THE MINORITY.
R-REALLY!?
AGH...! TOO MUCH PRESSURE...
EVERYONE IS INTRIGUED BY YOUR MYSTERY LOVER.
THEY BELIEVE HE MIGHT MAKE AN APPEARANCE AT THIS JUNIOR BALL...
HISO (GOSSIP)
KYA (SQUEAL)
BZZZ, WRONG! MISSED BY A HAIR!
DOKI DOKI (BADUM)
RUST, MY POTENTIAL (FAKE) BOYFRIEND WILL MAKE AN APPEARANCE! ...I HOPE.
BUT YOU KNOW WHAT MY "FRIEND" SAID?
HE SAID YOU DON'T EVEN HAVE A LOVER.
BOSO (WHISPER)
WE HAVE A WINNER !!!
GIKUUUU (GULP)
WELL, YOU SHOULD TELL YOUR "FRIEND" TO LOOK FORWARD TO MY FORMAL INTRODUCTION...
...OF...

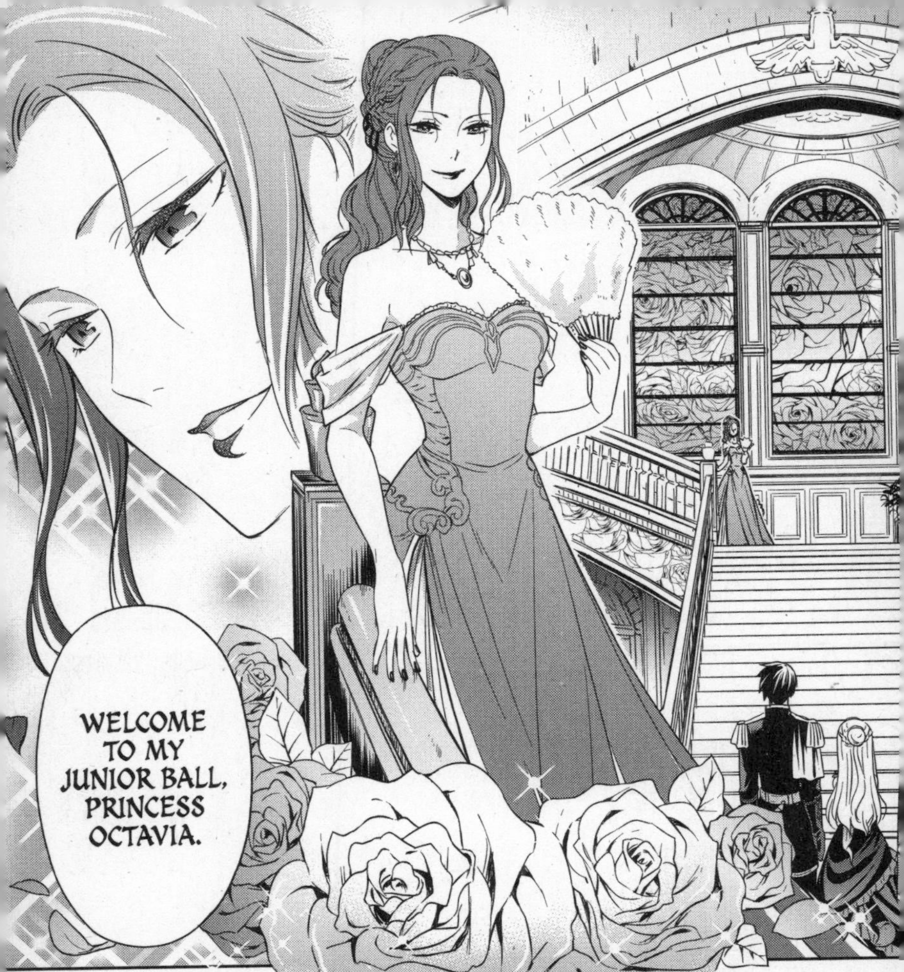
WELCOME TO MY JUNIOR BALL, PRINCESS OCTAVIA.

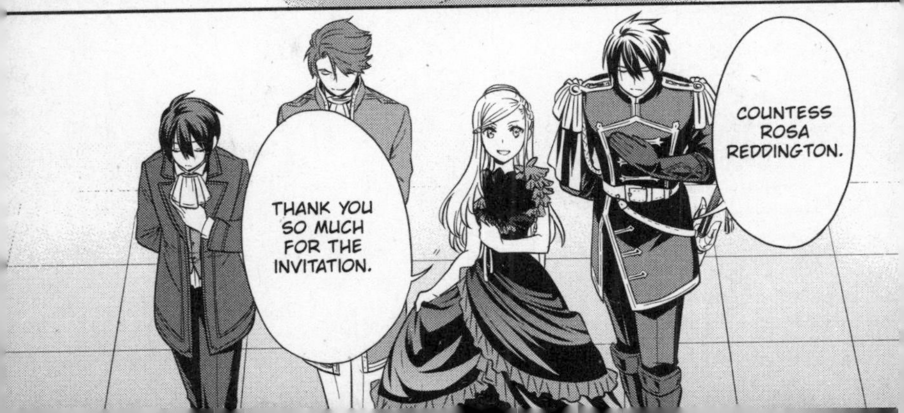
COUNTESS ROSA REDDINGTON.
THANK YOU SO MUCH FOR THE INVITATION.

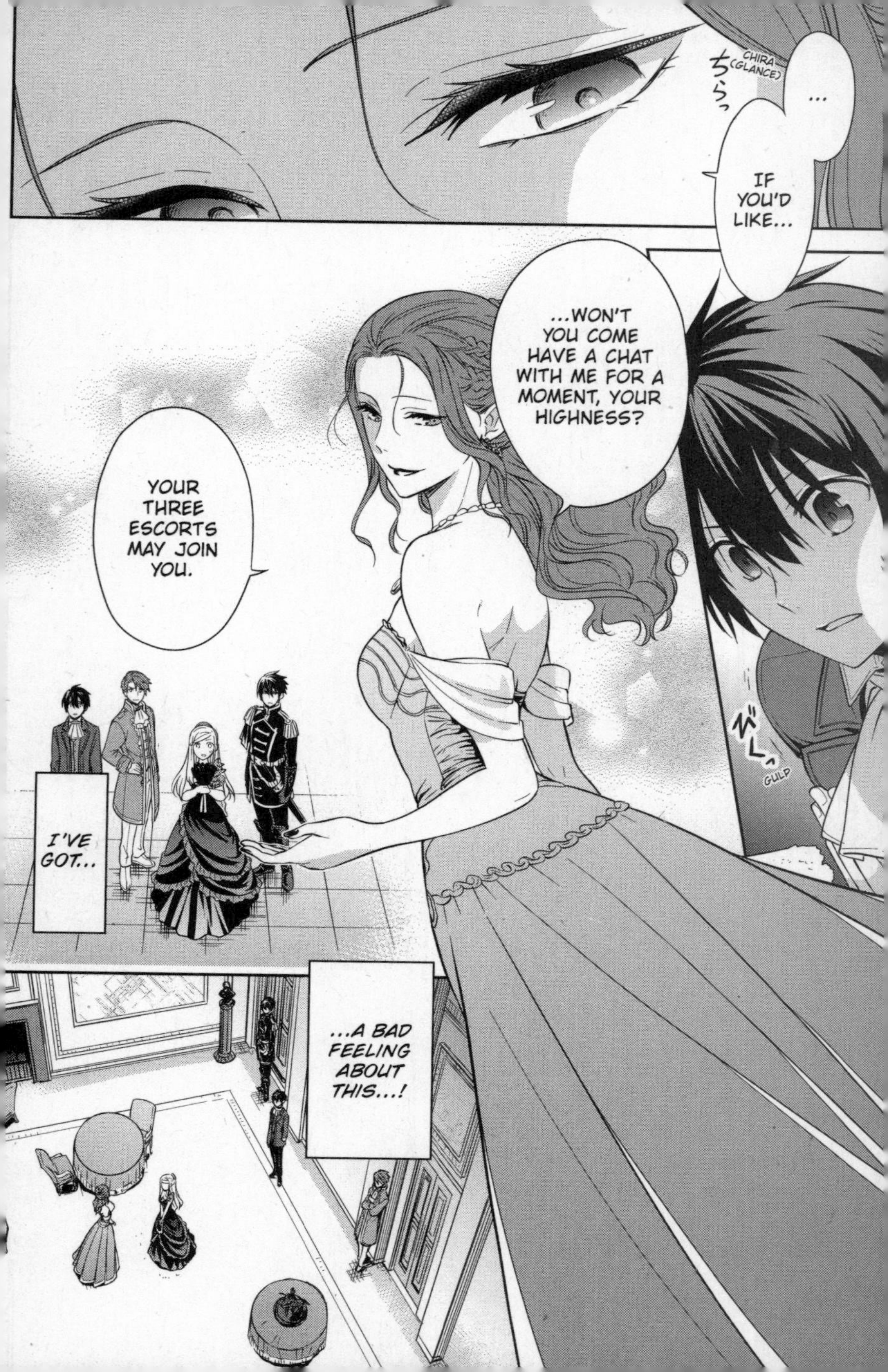
ちらっ
CHIRA (GLANCE)
...
IF YOU'D LIKE...
...WON'T YOU COME HAVE A CHAT WITH ME FOR A MOMENT, YOUR HIGHNESS?
YOUR THREE ESCORTS MAY JOIN YOU.
ゴクッ
GULP
I'VE GOT...
...A BAD FEELING ABOUT THIS...!

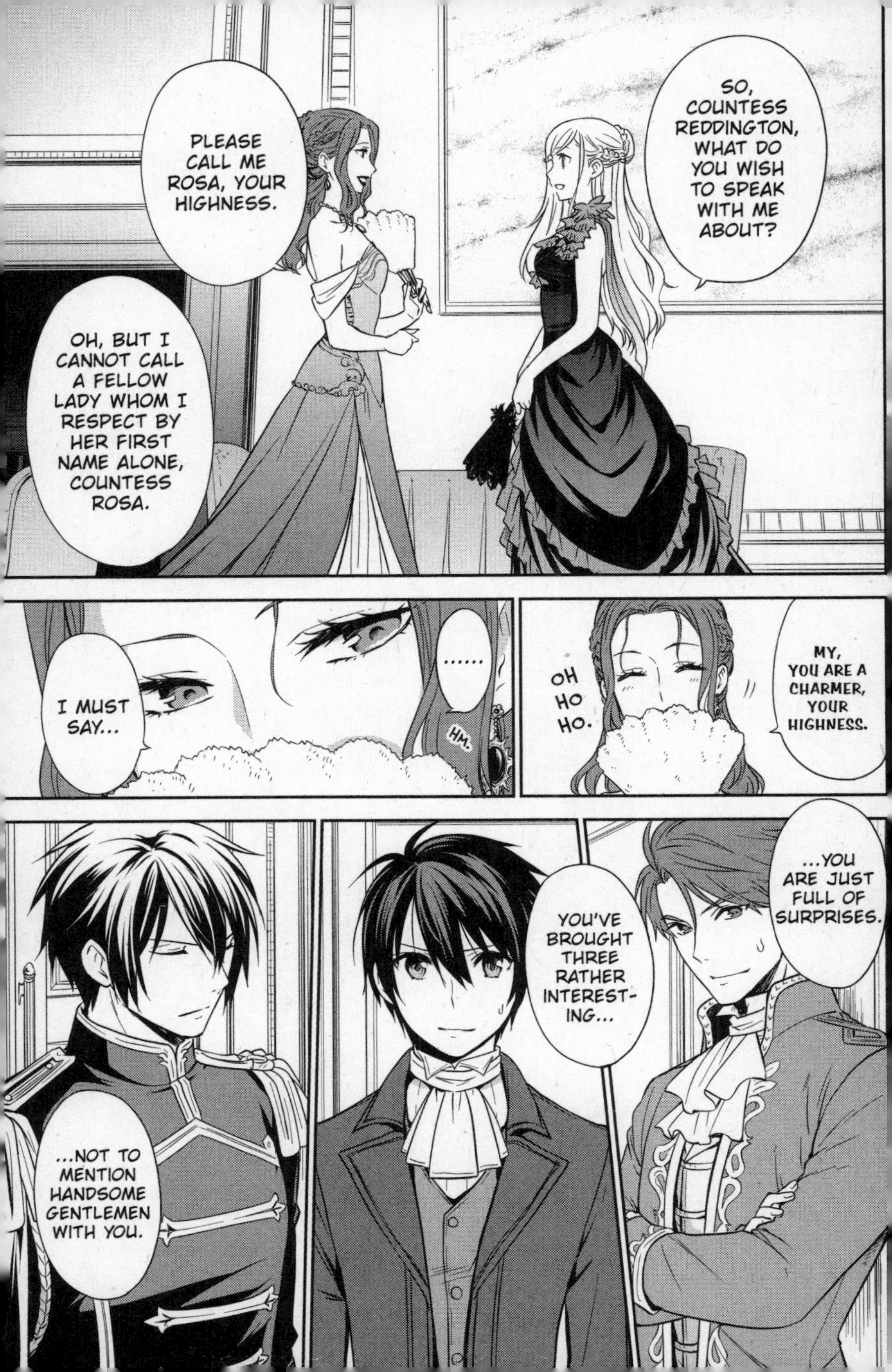
SO, COUNTESS REDDINGTON, WHAT DO YOU WISH TO SPEAK WITH ME ABOUT?
PLEASE CALL ME ROSA, YOUR HIGHNESS.
OH, BUT I CANNOT CALL A FELLOW LADY WHOM I RESPECT BY HER FIRST NAME ALONE, COUNTESS ROSA.
MY, YOU ARE A CHARMER, YOUR HIGHNESS.
OH HO HO.
......
HM.
I MUST SAY...
...YOU ARE JUST FULL OF SURPRISES.
YOU'VE BROUGHT THREE RATHER INTERESTING...
...NOT TO MENTION HANDSOME GENTLEMEN WITH YOU.

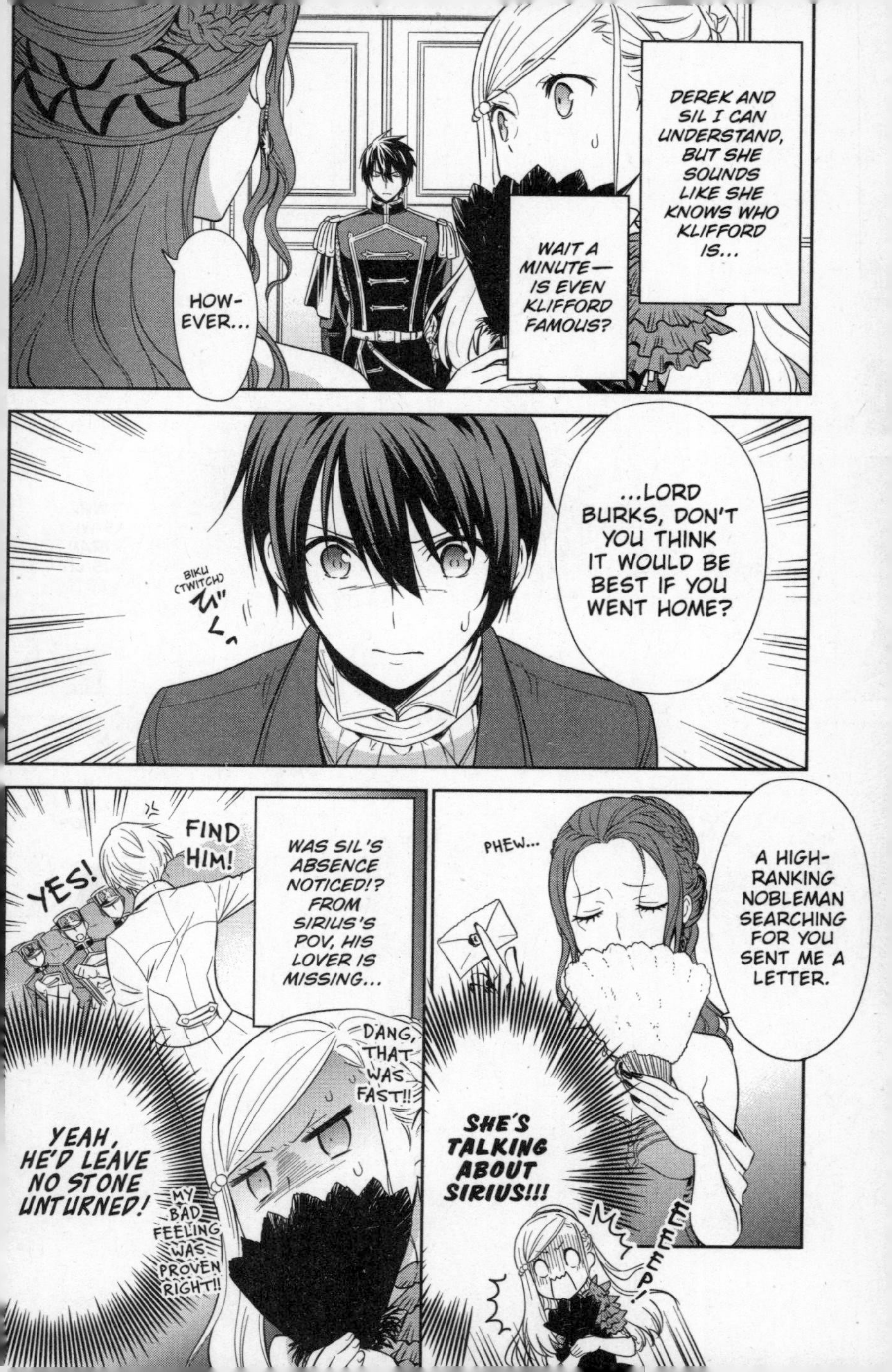
DEREK AND SIL I CAN UNDERSTAND, BUT SHE SOUNDS LIKE SHE KNOWS WHO KLIFFORD IS...
WAIT A MINUTE—IS EVEN KLIFFORD FAMOUS?
HOW-EVER...
...LORD BURKS, DON'T YOU THINK IT WOULD BE BEST IF YOU WENT HOME?
BIKU (TWITCH)
A HIGH-RANKING NOBLEMAN SEARCHING FOR YOU SENT ME A LETTER.
PHEW...
SHE'S TALKING ABOUT SIRIUS!!!
MEEEP!
WAS SIL'S ABSENCE NOTICED!? FROM SIRIUS'S POV, HIS LOVER IS MISSING...
FIND HIM!
YES!
DANG, THAT WAS FAST!!
YEAH, HE'D LEAVE NO STONE UNTURNED!
MY BAD FEELING WAS PROVEN RIGHT!!

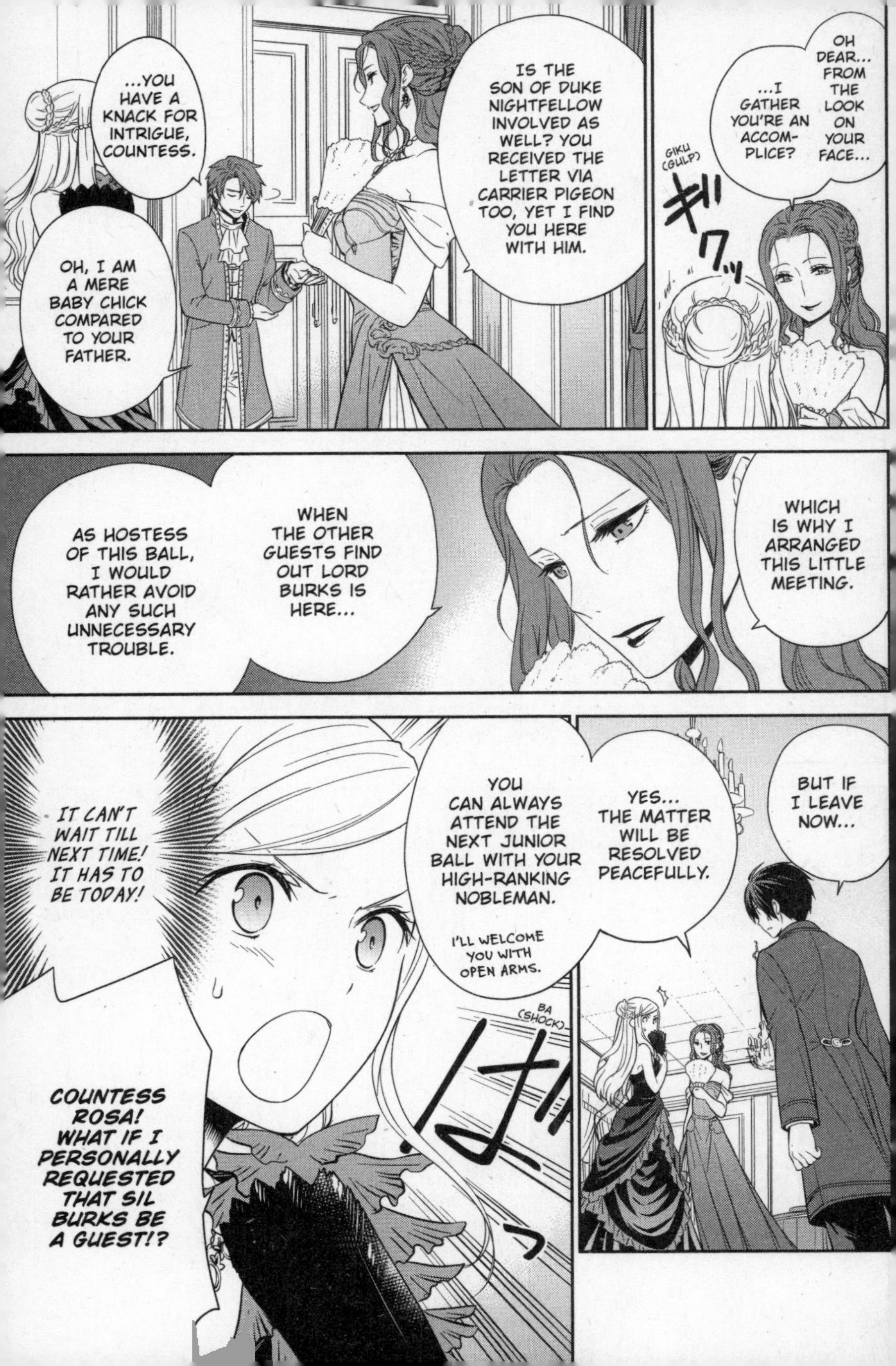
OH DEAR... FROM THE LOOK ON YOUR FACE...
...I GATHER YOU'RE AN ACCOMPLICE?
GIKU (GULP)
IS THE SON OF DUKE NIGHTFELLOW INVOLVED AS WELL? YOU RECEIVED THE LETTER VIA CARRIER PIGEON TOO, YET I FIND YOU HERE WITH HIM.
...YOU HAVE A KNACK FOR INTRIGUE, COUNTESS.
OH, I AM A MERE BABY CHICK COMPARED TO YOUR FATHER.
WHICH IS WHY I ARRANGED THIS LITTLE MEETING.
WHEN THE OTHER GUESTS FIND OUT LORD BURKS IS HERE...
AS HOSTESS OF THIS BALL, I WOULD RATHER AVOID ANY SUCH UNNECESSARY TROUBLE.
BUT IF I LEAVE NOW...
YES... THE MATTER WILL BE RESOLVED PEACEFULLY.
YOU CAN ALWAYS ATTEND THE NEXT JUNIOR BALL WITH YOUR HIGH-RANKING NOBLEMAN.
I'LL WELCOME YOU WITH OPEN ARMS.
BA (SHOCK)
IT CAN'T WAIT TILL NEXT TIME! IT HAS TO BE TODAY!
COUNTESS ROSA! WHAT IF I PERSONALLY REQUESTED THAT SIL BURKS BE A GUEST!?

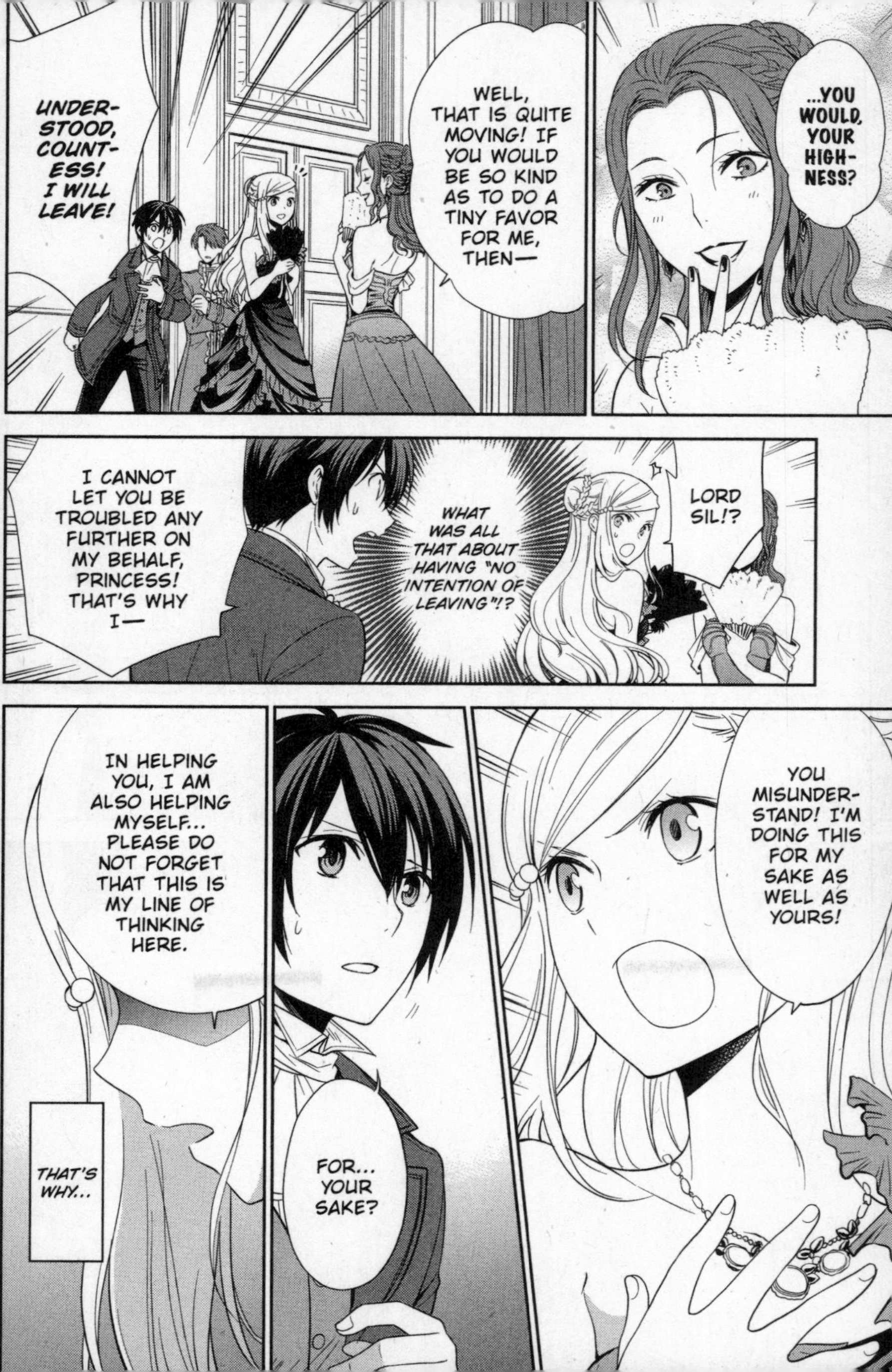
...YOU WOULD, YOUR HIGHNESS?
WELL, THAT IS QUITE MOVING! IF YOU WOULD BE SO KIND AS TO DO A TINY FAVOR FOR ME, THEN—
UNDERSTOOD, COUNTESS! I WILL LEAVE!
LORD SIL!?
WHAT WAS ALL THAT ABOUT HAVING "NO INTENTION OF LEAVING"!?
I CANNOT LET YOU BE TROUBLED ANY FURTHER ON MY BEHALF, PRINCESS! THAT'S WHY I—
YOU MISUNDERSTAND! I'M DOING THIS FOR MY SAKE AS WELL AS YOURS!
FOR... YOUR SAKE?
IN HELPING YOU, I AM ALSO HELPING MYSELF... PLEASE DO NOT FORGET THAT THIS IS MY LINE OF THINKING HERE.
THAT'S WHY...

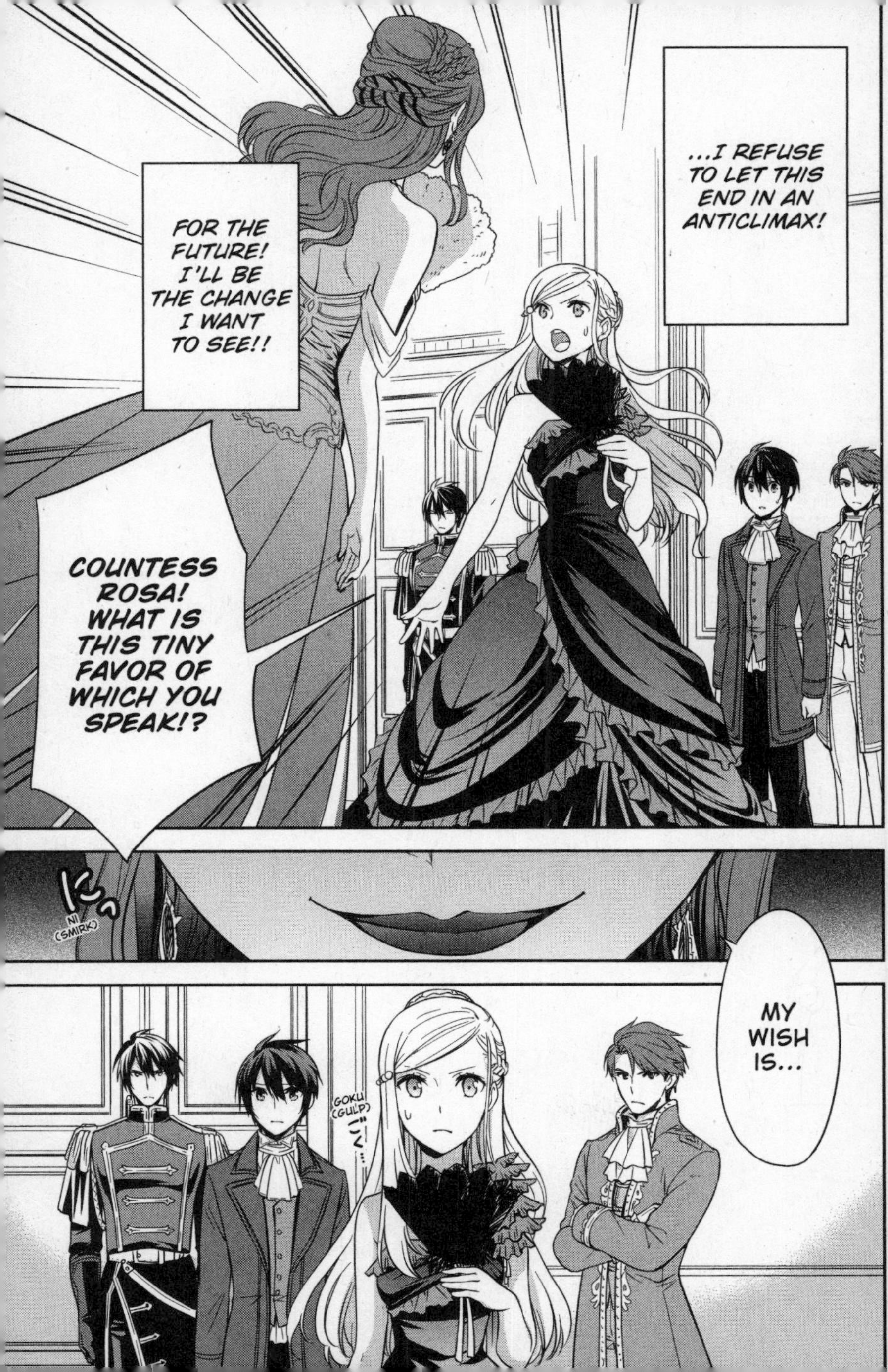
...I REFUSE TO LET THIS END IN AN ANTICLIMAX!
FOR THE FUTURE! I'LL BE THE CHANGE I WANT TO SEE!!
COUNTESS ROSA! WHAT IS THIS TINY FAVOR OF WHICH YOU SPEAK!?
NI (SMIRK)
MY WISH IS...
GOKU (GULP)

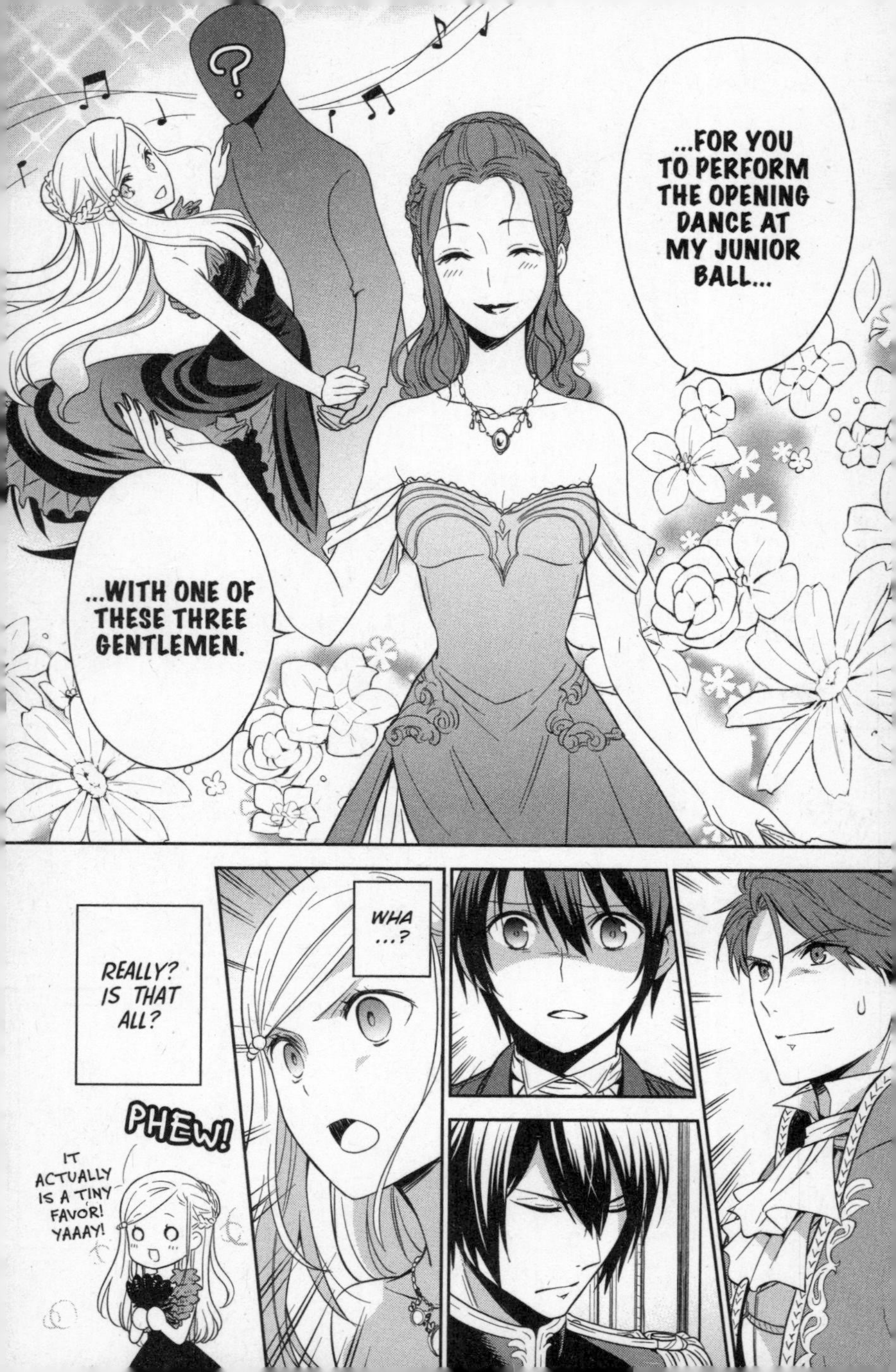

...FOR YOU TO PERFORM THE OPENING DANCE AT MY JUNIOR BALL...
...WITH ONE OF THESE THREE GENTLEMEN.
WHA ...?
REALLY? IS THAT ALL?
PHEW!
IT ACTUALLY IS A TINY FAVOR! YAAAY!

Chapter 9

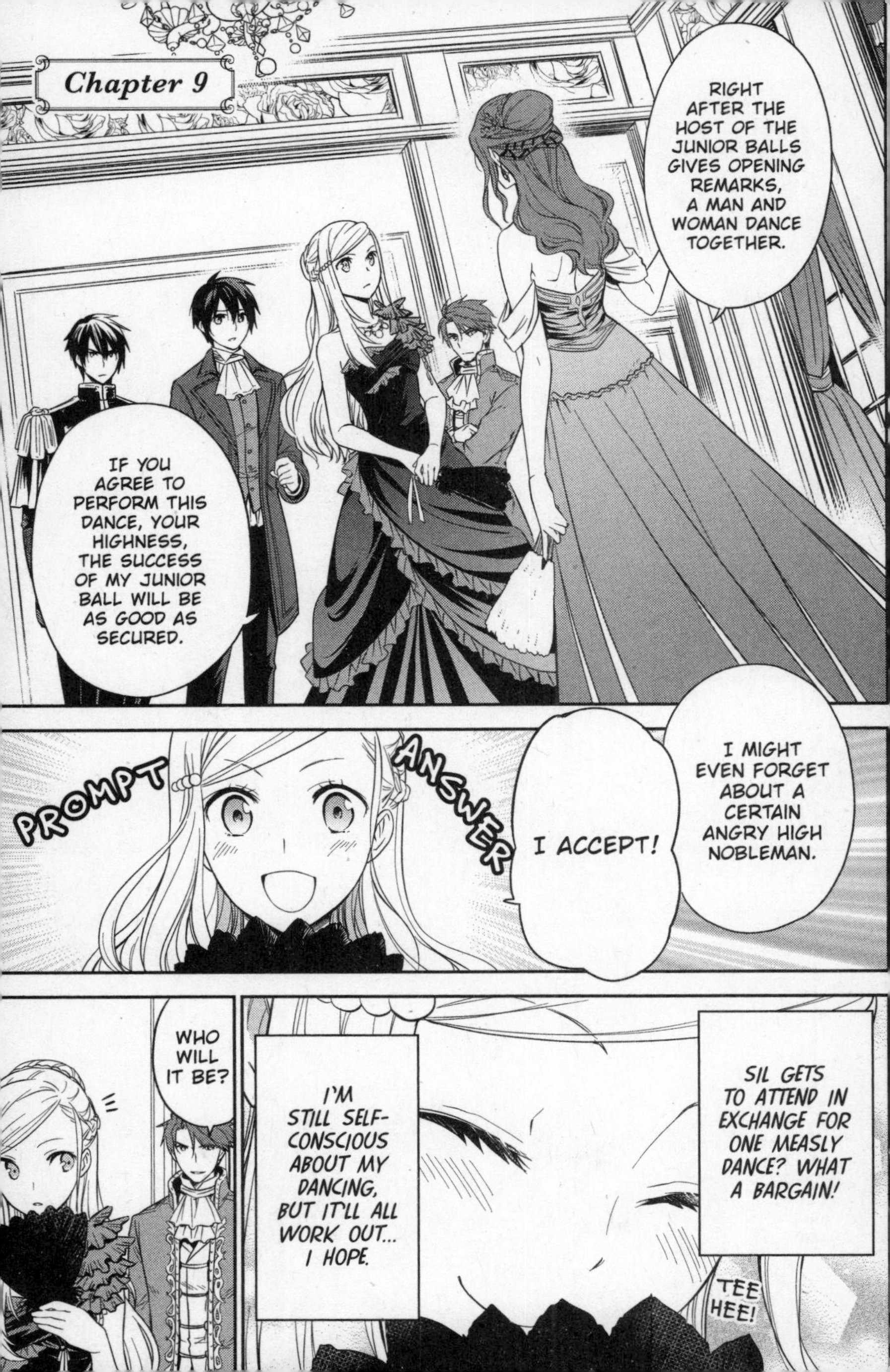

RIGHT AFTER THE HOST OF THE JUNIOR BALLS GIVES OPENING REMARKS, A MAN AND WOMAN DANCE TOGETHER.
IF YOU AGREE TO PERFORM THIS DANCE, YOUR HIGHNESS, THE SUCCESS OF MY JUNIOR BALL WILL BE AS GOOD AS SECURED.
I MIGHT EVEN FORGET ABOUT A CERTAIN ANGRY HIGH NOBLEMAN.
I ACCEPT!
ANSWER
PROMPT
SIL GETS TO ATTEND IN EXCHANGE FOR ONE MEASLY DANCE? WHAT A BARGAIN!
TEE HEE!
I'M STILL SELF-CONSCIOUS ABOUT MY DANCING, BUT IT'LL ALL WORK OUT... I HOPE.
WHO WILL IT BE?

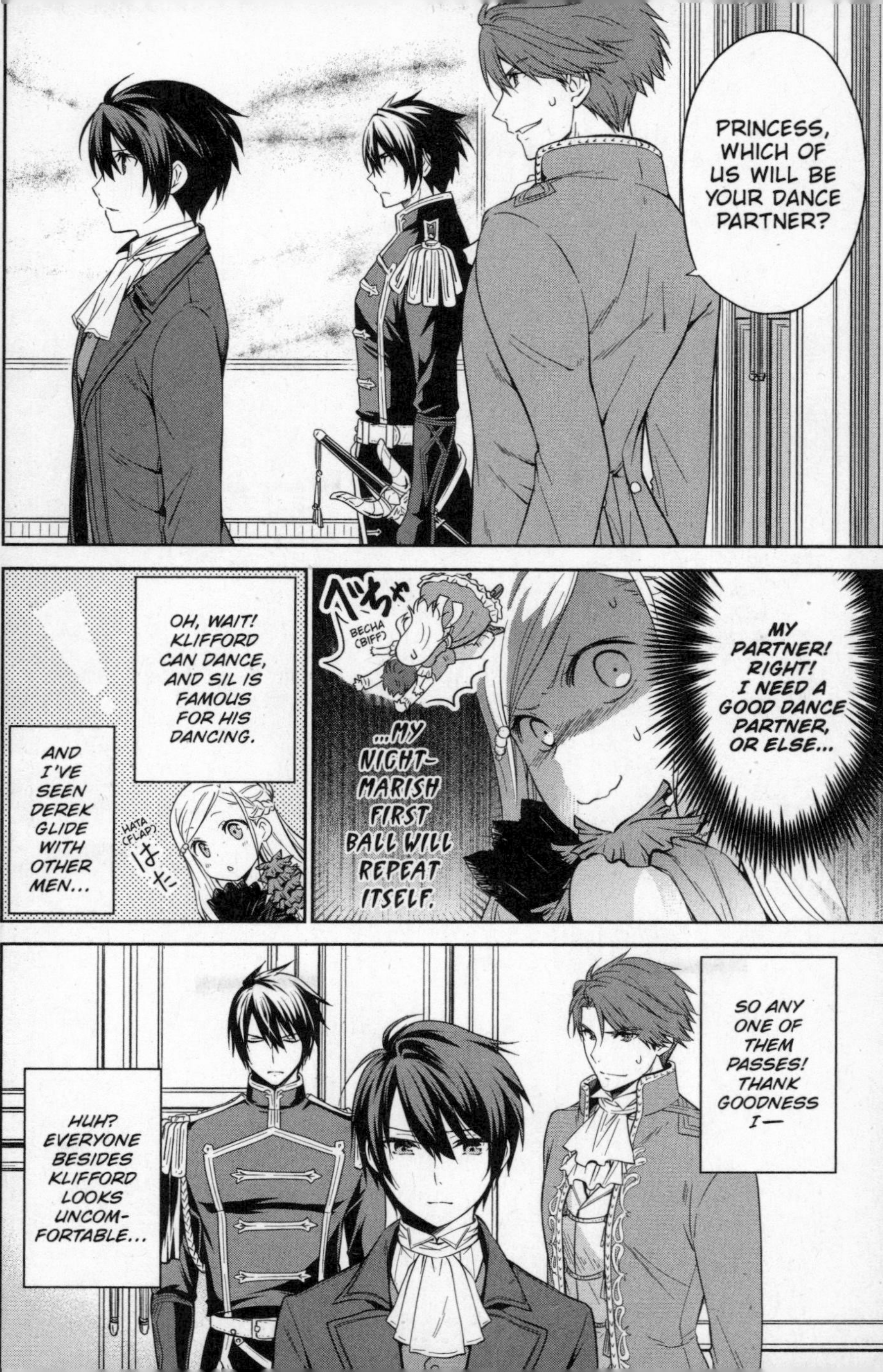
PRINCESS, WHICH OF US WILL BE YOUR DANCE PARTNER?
MY PARTNER! RIGHT! I NEED A GOOD DANCE PARTNER, OR ELSE...
BECHA (BIFF)
...MY NIGHTMARISH FIRST BALL WILL REPEAT ITSELF.
OH, WAIT! KLIFFORD CAN DANCE, AND SIL IS FAMOUS FOR HIS DANCING.
AND I'VE SEEN DEREK GLIDE WITH OTHER MEN...
HATA (FLAP)
SO ANY ONE OF THEM PASSES! THANK GOODNESS I—
HUH? EVERYONE BESIDES KLIFFORD LOOKS UNCOMFORTABLE...

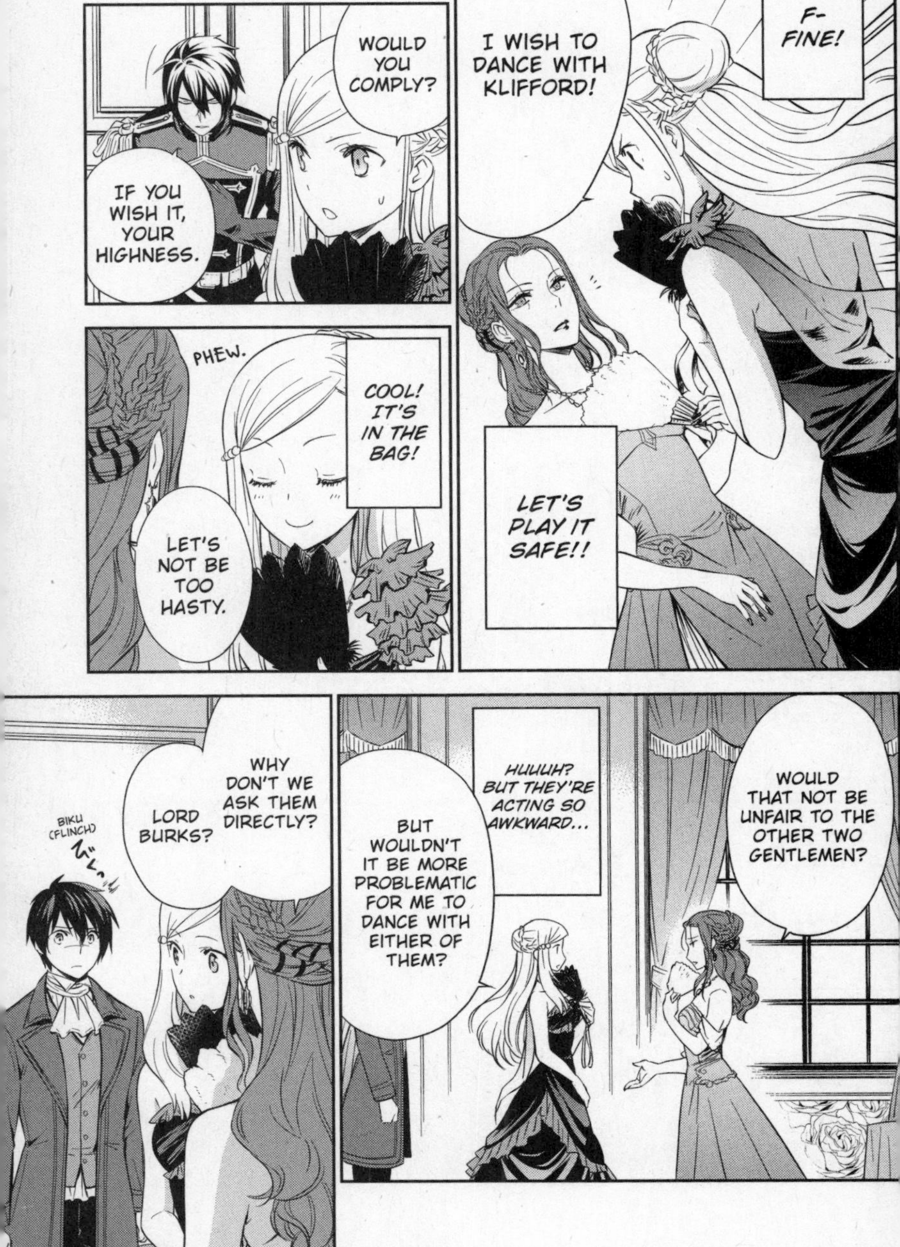
F-FINE!
I WISH TO DANCE WITH KLIFFORD!
LET'S PLAY IT SAFE!!
WOULD YOU COMPLY?
IF YOU WISH IT, YOUR HIGHNESS.
COOL! IT'S IN THE BAG!
PHEW.
LET'S NOT BE TOO HASTY.
WOULD THAT NOT BE UNFAIR TO THE OTHER TWO GENTLEMEN?
HUUUH? BUT THEY'RE ACTING SO AWKWARD...
BUT WOULDN'T IT BE MORE PROBLEMATIC FOR ME TO DANCE WITH EITHER OF THEM?
WHY DON'T WE ASK THEM DIRECTLY?
LORD BURKS?
BIKU (FLINCH)

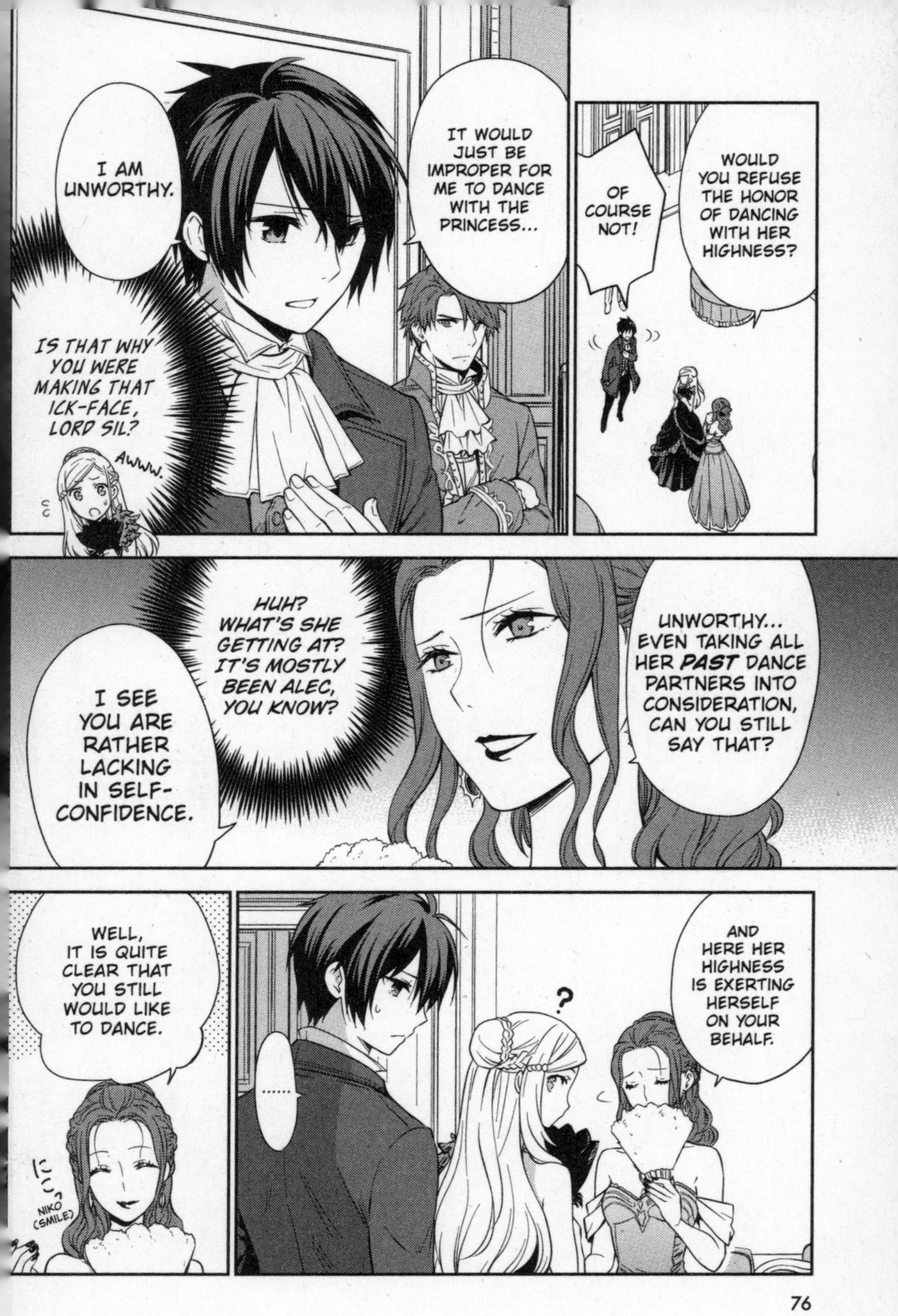

WOULD YOU REFUSE THE HONOR OF DANCING WITH HER HIGHNESS?
OF COURSE NOT!
IT WOULD JUST BE IMPROPER FOR ME TO DANCE WITH THE PRINCESS...
I AM UNWORTHY.
IS THAT WHY YOU WERE MAKING THAT ICK-FACE, LORD SIL?
AWWW.
UNWORTHY... EVEN TAKING ALL HER PAST DANCE PARTNERS INTO CONSIDERATION, CAN YOU STILL SAY THAT?
HUH? WHAT'S SHE GETTING AT? IT'S MOSTLY BEEN ALEC, YOU KNOW?
I SEE YOU ARE RATHER LACKING IN SELF-CONFIDENCE.
AND HERE HER HIGHNESS IS EXERTING HERSELF ON YOUR BEHALF.
?
......
WELL, IT IS QUITE CLEAR THAT YOU STILL WOULD LIKE TO DANCE.
にこっ
NIKO (SMILE)

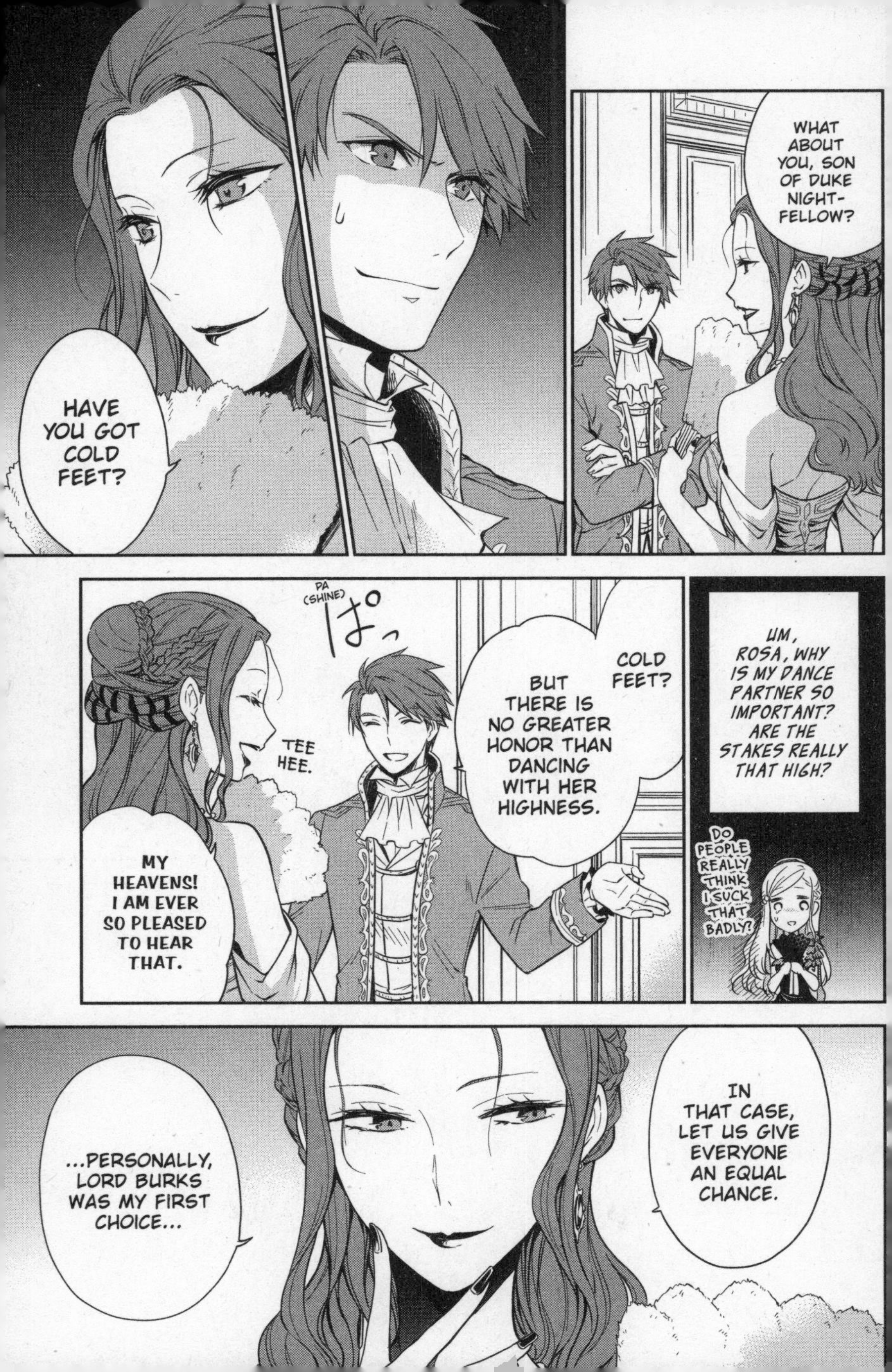
WHAT ABOUT YOU, SON OF DUKE NIGHT-FELLOW?
HAVE YOU GOT COLD FEET?
UM, ROSA, WHY IS MY DANCE PARTNER SO IMPORTANT? ARE THE STAKES REALLY THAT HIGH?
DO PEOPLE REALLY THINK I SUCK THAT BADLY?
COLD FEET?
BUT THERE IS NO GREATER HONOR THAN DANCING WITH HER HIGHNESS.
PA (SHINE)
ぱっ
TEE HEE.
MY HEAVENS! I AM EVER SO PLEASED TO HEAR THAT.
IN THAT CASE, LET US GIVE EVERYONE AN EQUAL CHANCE.
...PERSONALLY, LORD BURKS WAS MY FIRST CHOICE...

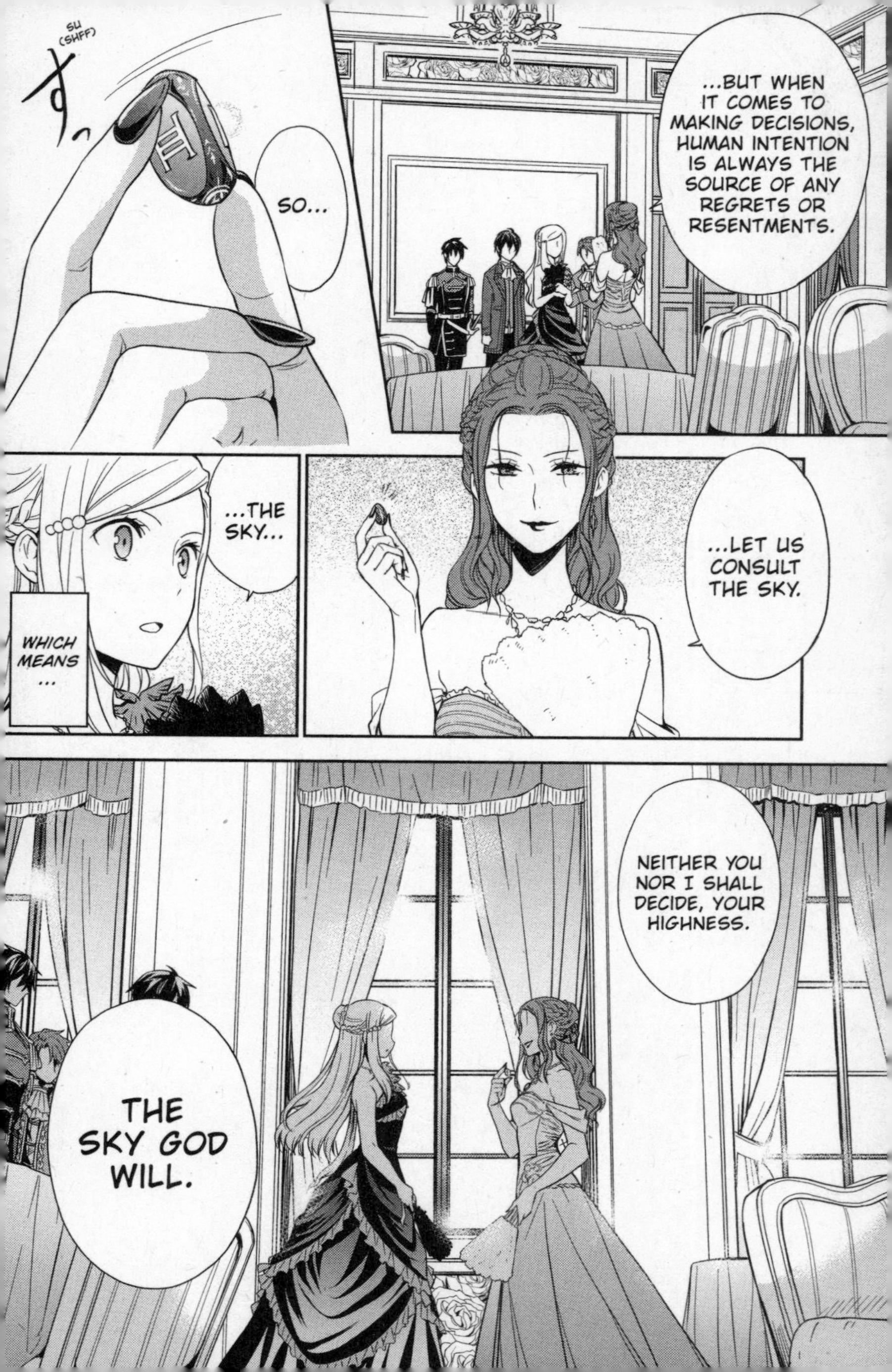
...BUT WHEN IT COMES TO MAKING DECISIONS, HUMAN INTENTION IS ALWAYS THE SOURCE OF ANY REGRETS OR RESENTMENTS.
SO...
す
SU (SHFF)
...LET US CONSULT THE SKY.
...THE SKY...
WHICH MEANS ...
NEITHER YOU NOR I SHALL DECIDE, YOUR HIGHNESS.
THE SKY GOD WILL.

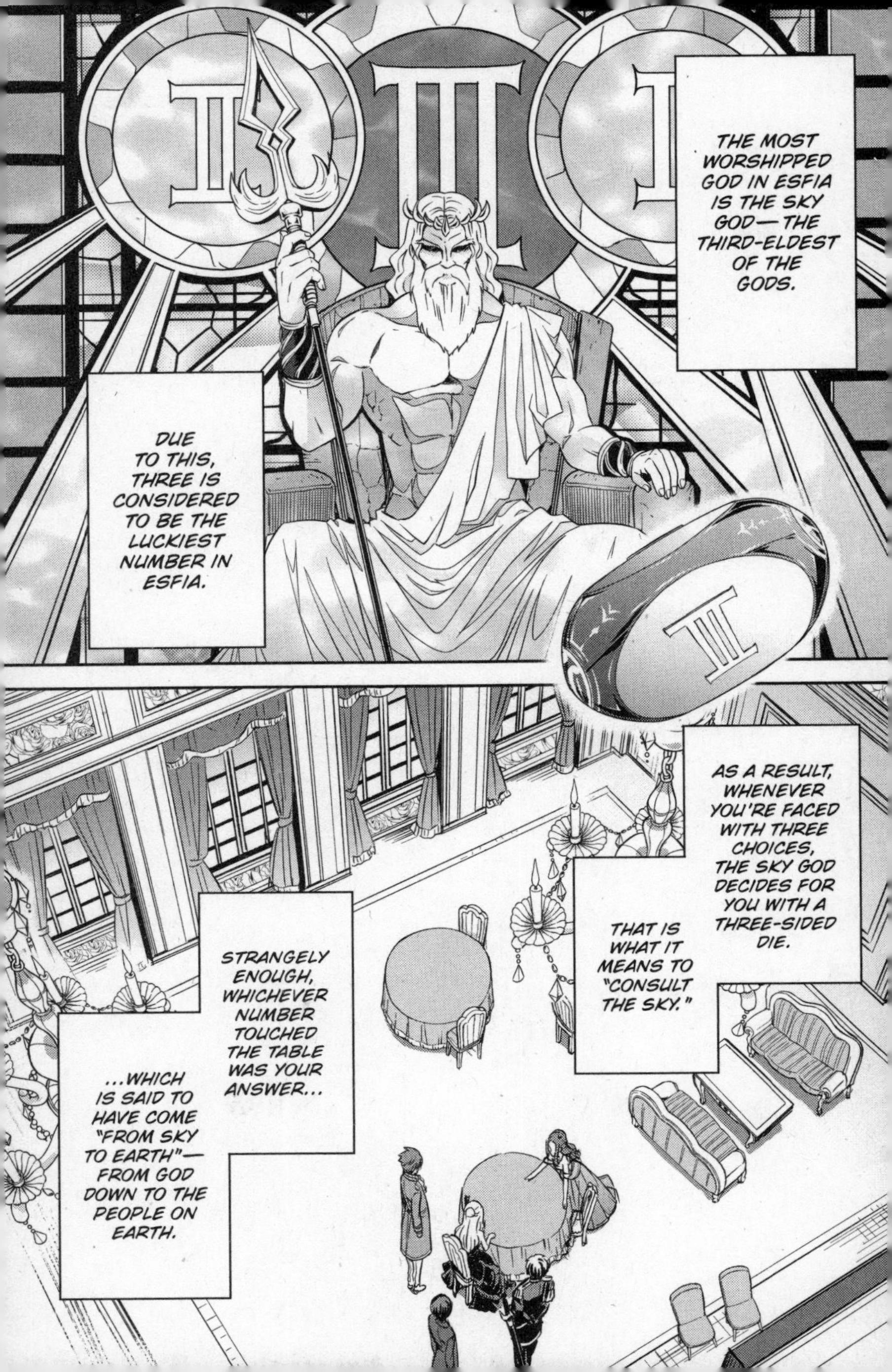
THE MOST WORSHIPPED GOD IN ESFIA IS THE SKY GOD—THE THIRD-ELDEST OF THE GODS.
DUE TO THIS, THREE IS CONSIDERED TO BE THE LUCKIEST NUMBER IN ESFIA.
AS A RESULT, WHENEVER YOU'RE FACED WITH THREE CHOICES, THE SKY GOD DECIDES FOR YOU WITH A THREE-SIDED DIE.
THAT IS WHAT IT MEANS TO "CONSULT THE SKY."
STRANGELY ENOUGH, WHICHEVER NUMBER TOUCHED THE TABLE WAS YOUR ANSWER...
...WHICH IS SAID TO HAVE COME "FROM SKY TO EARTH"—FROM GOD DOWN TO THE PEOPLE ON EARTH.

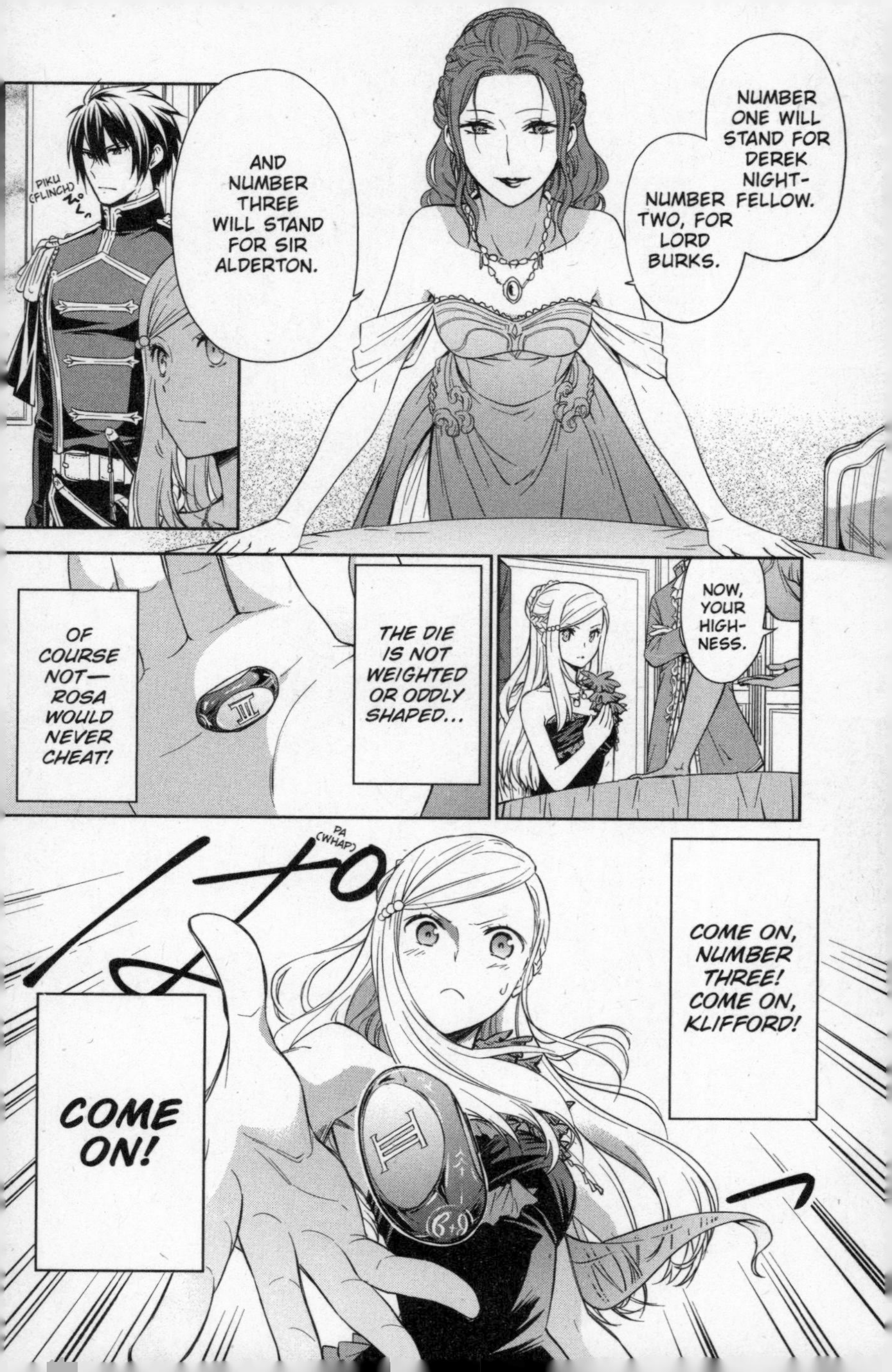
NUMBER ONE WILL STAND FOR DEREK NIGHT-FELLOW.
NUMBER TWO, FOR LORD BURKS.
AND NUMBER THREE WILL STAND FOR SIR ALDERTON.
PIKU (FLINCH)
NOW, YOUR HIGH-NESS.
THE DIE IS NOT WEIGHTED OR ODDLY SHAPED...
OF COURSE NOT— ROSA WOULD NEVER CHEAT!
COME ON, NUMBER THREE! COME ON, KLIFFORD!
PA (WHAP)
COME ON!

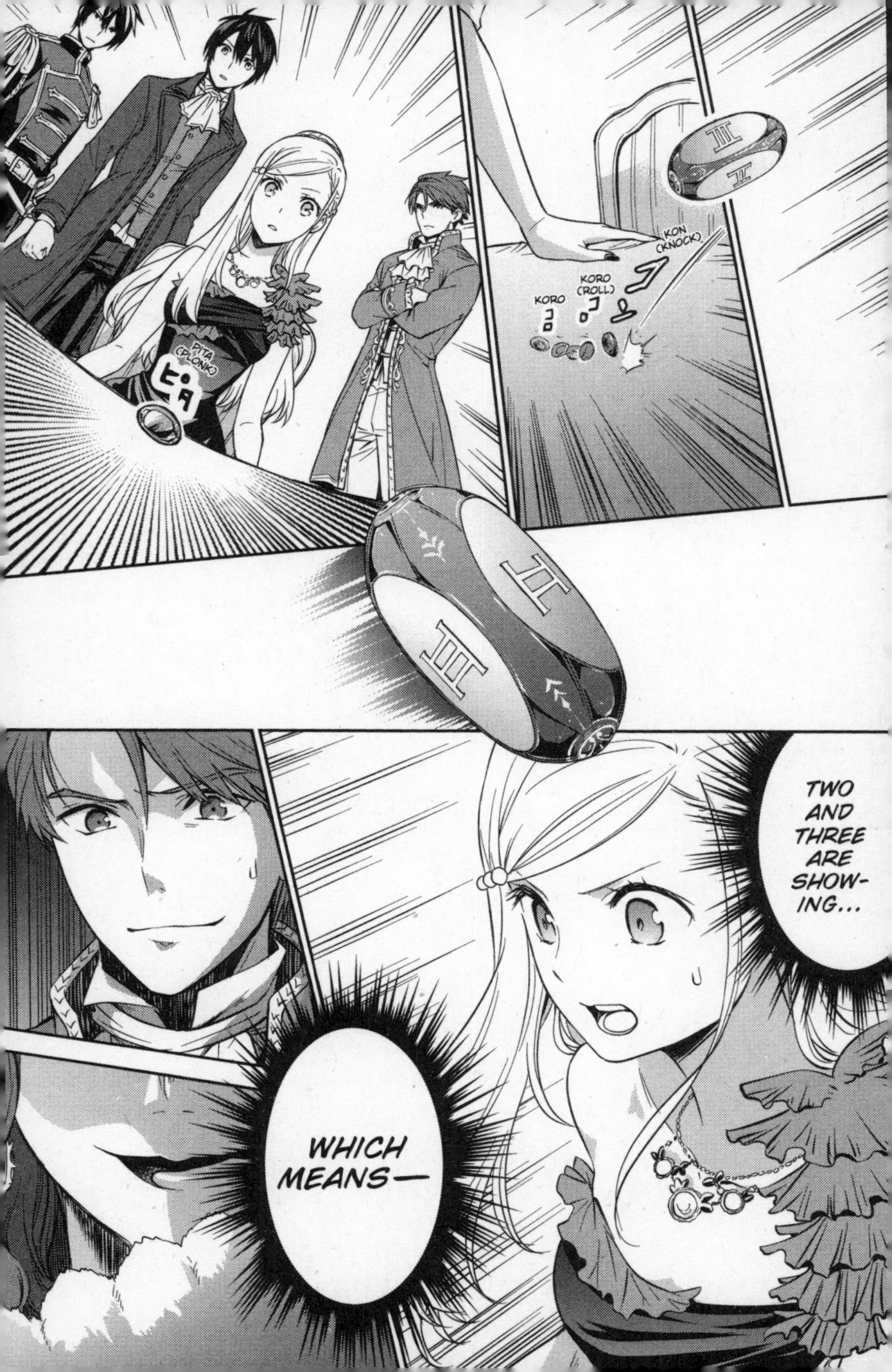
KON (KNOCK)
KORO (ROLL)
KORO
PITA (PLONK)
TWO AND THREE ARE SHOWING...
WHICH MEANS—

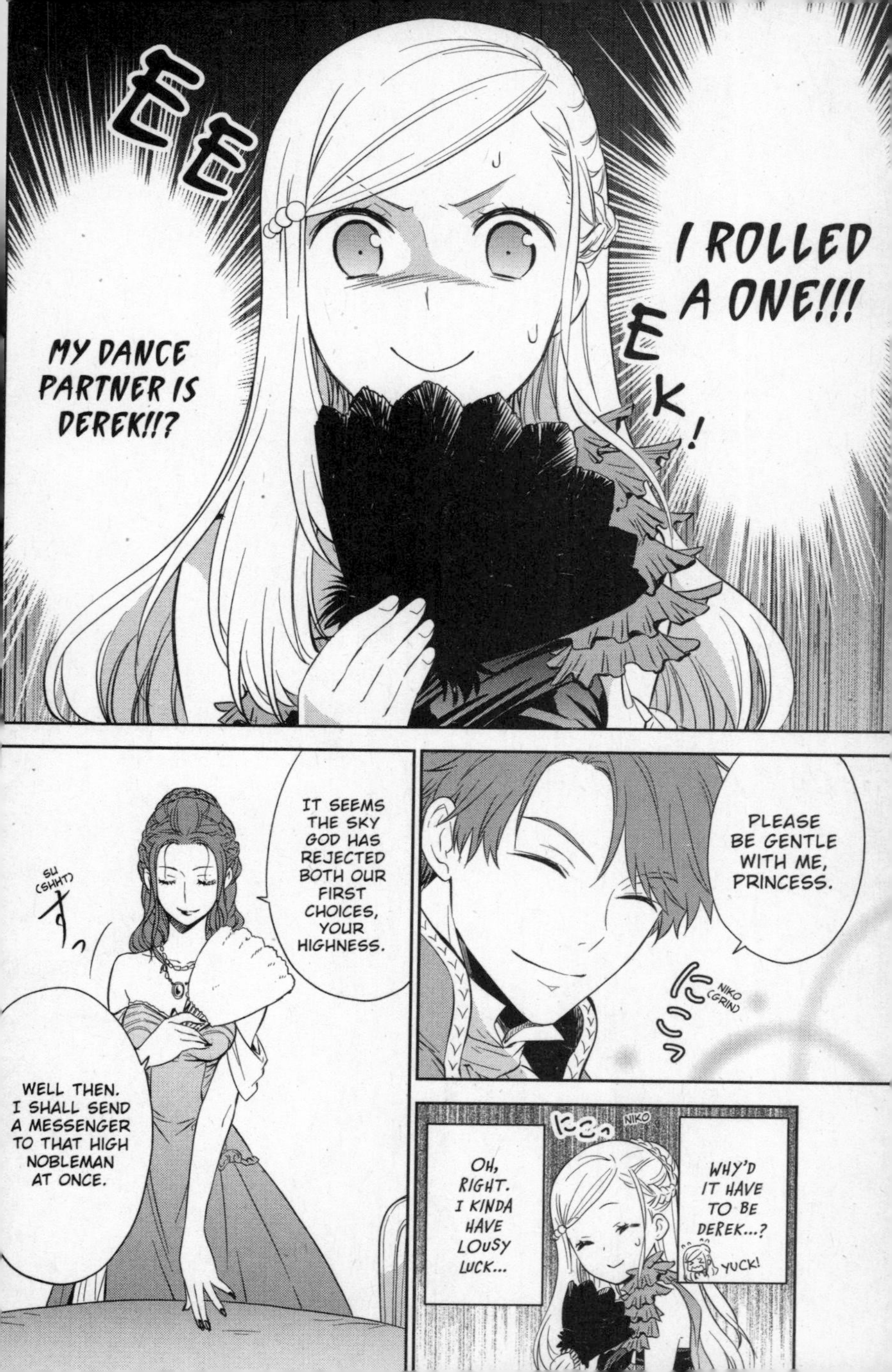
EE
EK!
I ROLLED A ONE!!!
MY DANCE PARTNER IS DEREK!!?
PLEASE BE GENTLE WITH ME, PRINCESS.
NIKO (GRIN)
NIKO
WHY'D IT HAVE TO BE DEREK...?
YUCK!
OH, RIGHT. I KINDA HAVE LOUSY LUCK...
IT SEEMS THE SKY GOD HAS REJECTED BOTH OUR FIRST CHOICES, YOUR HIGHNESS.
SU (SHHT)
WELL THEN. I SHALL SEND A MESSENGER TO THAT HIGH NOBLEMAN AT ONCE.

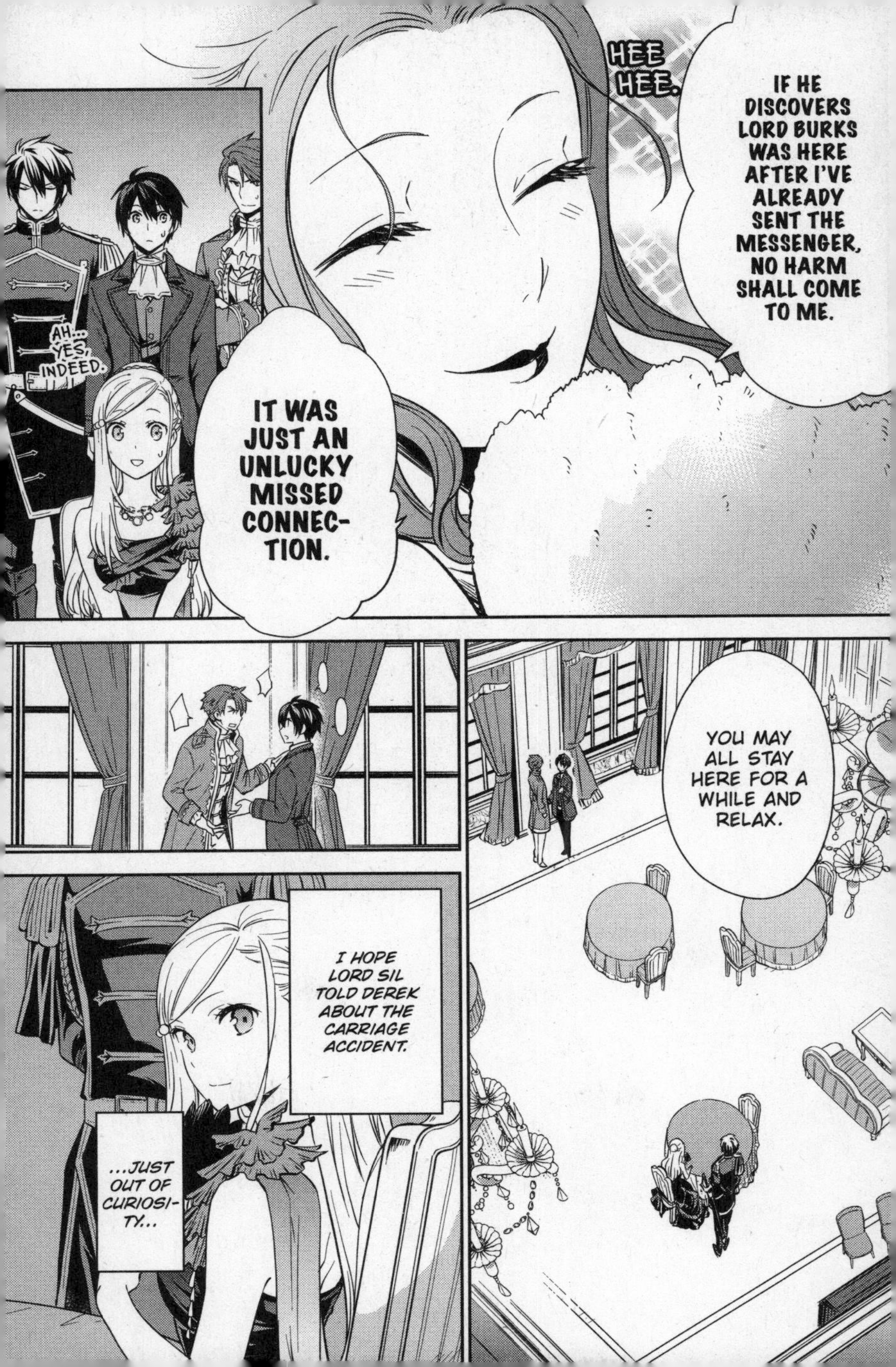
IF HE DISCOVERS LORD BURKS WAS HERE AFTER I'VE ALREADY SENT THE MESSENGER, NO HARM SHALL COME TO ME.
HEE HEE.
IT WAS JUST AN UNLUCKY MISSED CONNECTION.
AH... YES, INDEED.
YOU MAY ALL STAY HERE FOR A WHILE AND RELAX.
I HOPE LORD SIL TOLD DEREK ABOUT THE CARRIAGE ACCIDENT.
...JUST OUT OF CURIOSITY...

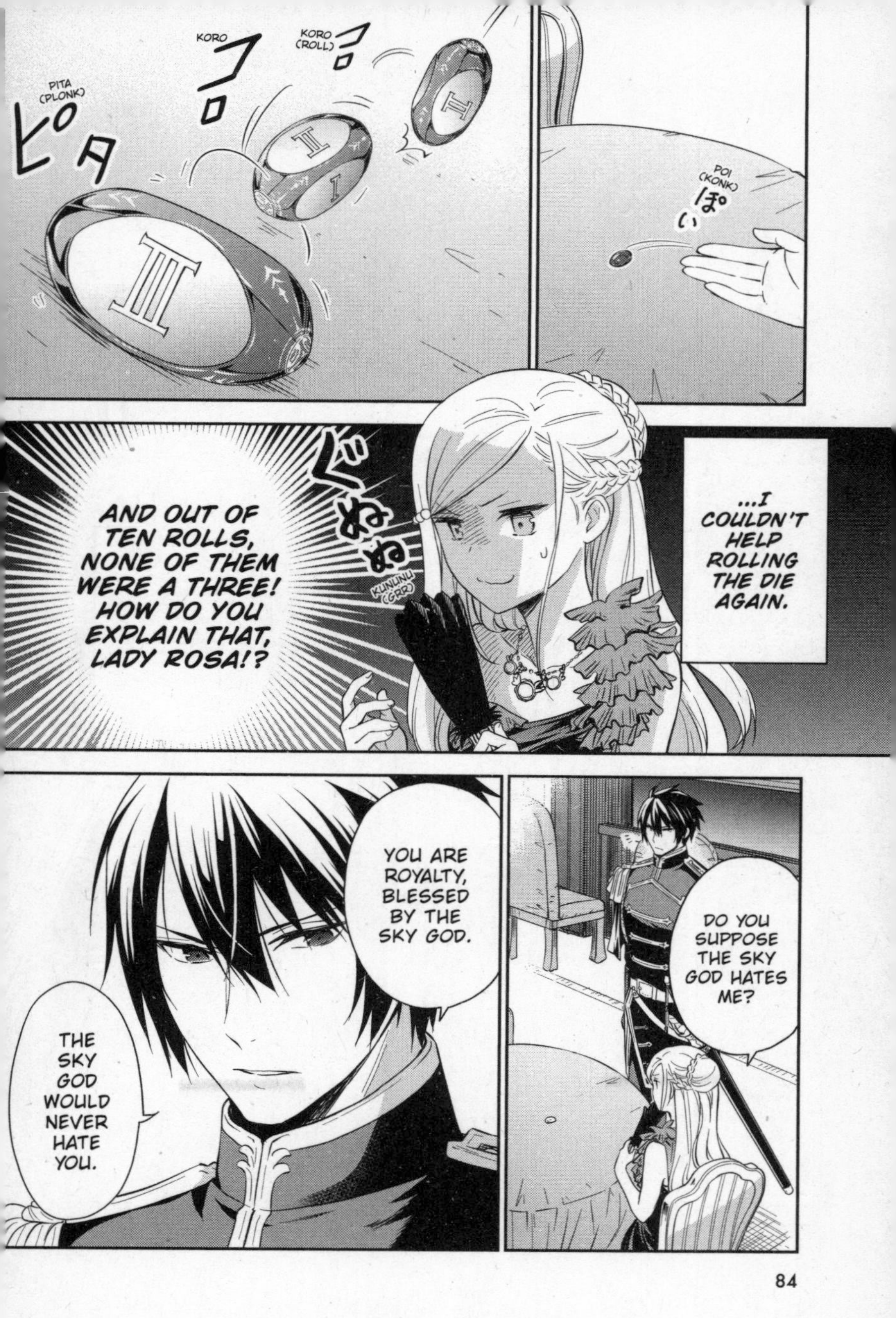
POI (KONK)
ぽい
KORO
コ
KORO (ROLL)
ロ
PITA (PLONK)
ピタ
...I COULDN'T HELP ROLLING THE DIE AGAIN.
KUNUNU (GRR)
ぐぬぬ
AND OUT OF TEN ROLLS, NONE OF THEM WERE A THREE! HOW DO YOU EXPLAIN THAT, LADY ROSA!?
DO YOU SUPPOSE THE SKY GOD HATES ME?
YOU ARE ROYALTY, BLESSED BY THE SKY GOD.
THE SKY GOD WOULD NEVER HATE YOU.

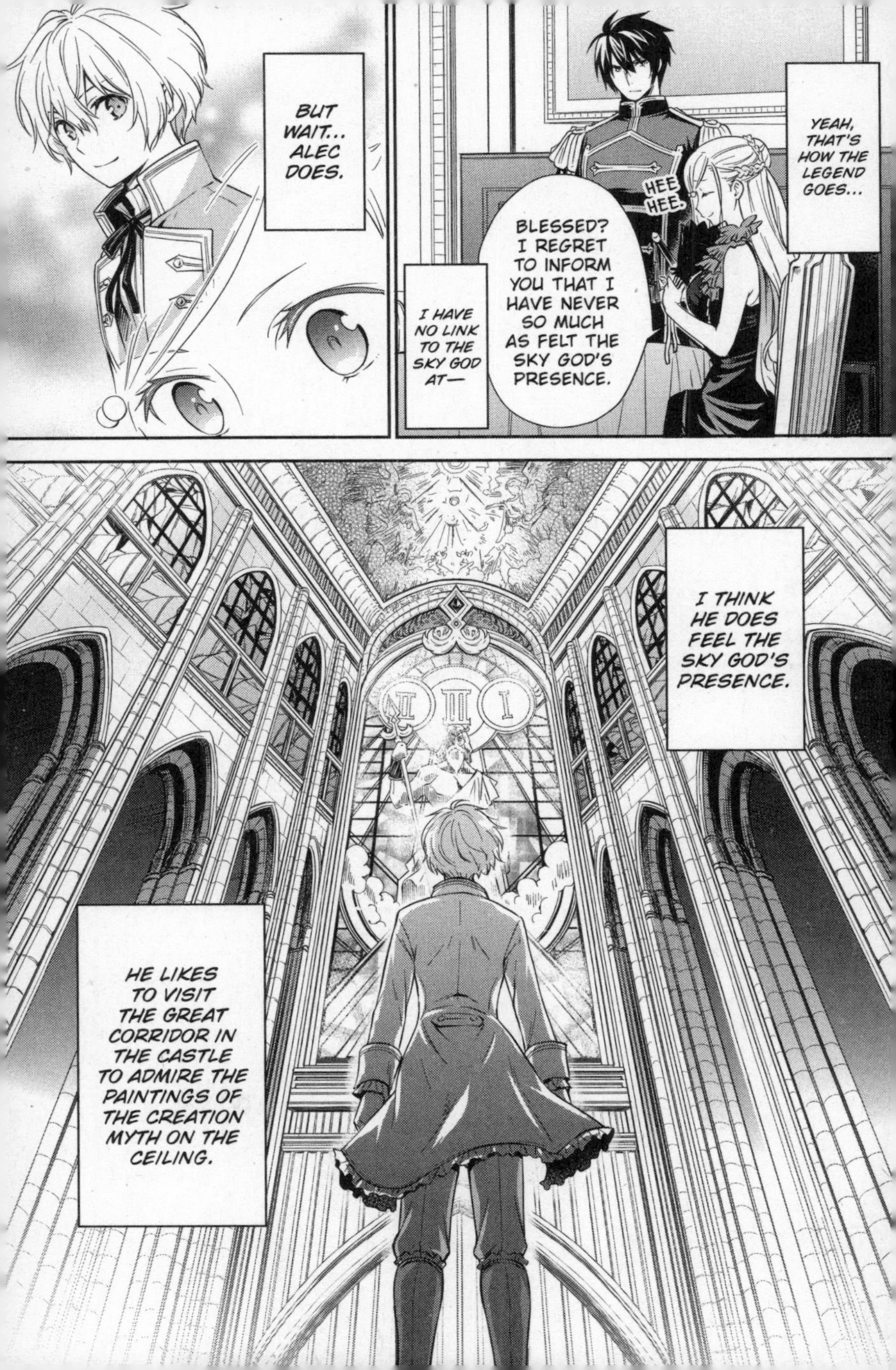
YEAH, THAT'S HOW THE LEGEND GOES...
HEE HEE.
BLESSED? I REGRET TO INFORM YOU THAT I HAVE NEVER SO MUCH AS FELT THE SKY GOD'S PRESENCE.
I HAVE NO LINK TO THE SKY GOD AT—
BUT WAIT... ALEC DOES.
I THINK HE DOES FEEL THE SKY GOD'S PRESENCE.
HE LIKES TO VISIT THE GREAT CORRIDOR IN THE CASTLE TO ADMIRE THE PAINTINGS OF THE CREATION MYTH ON THE CEILING.

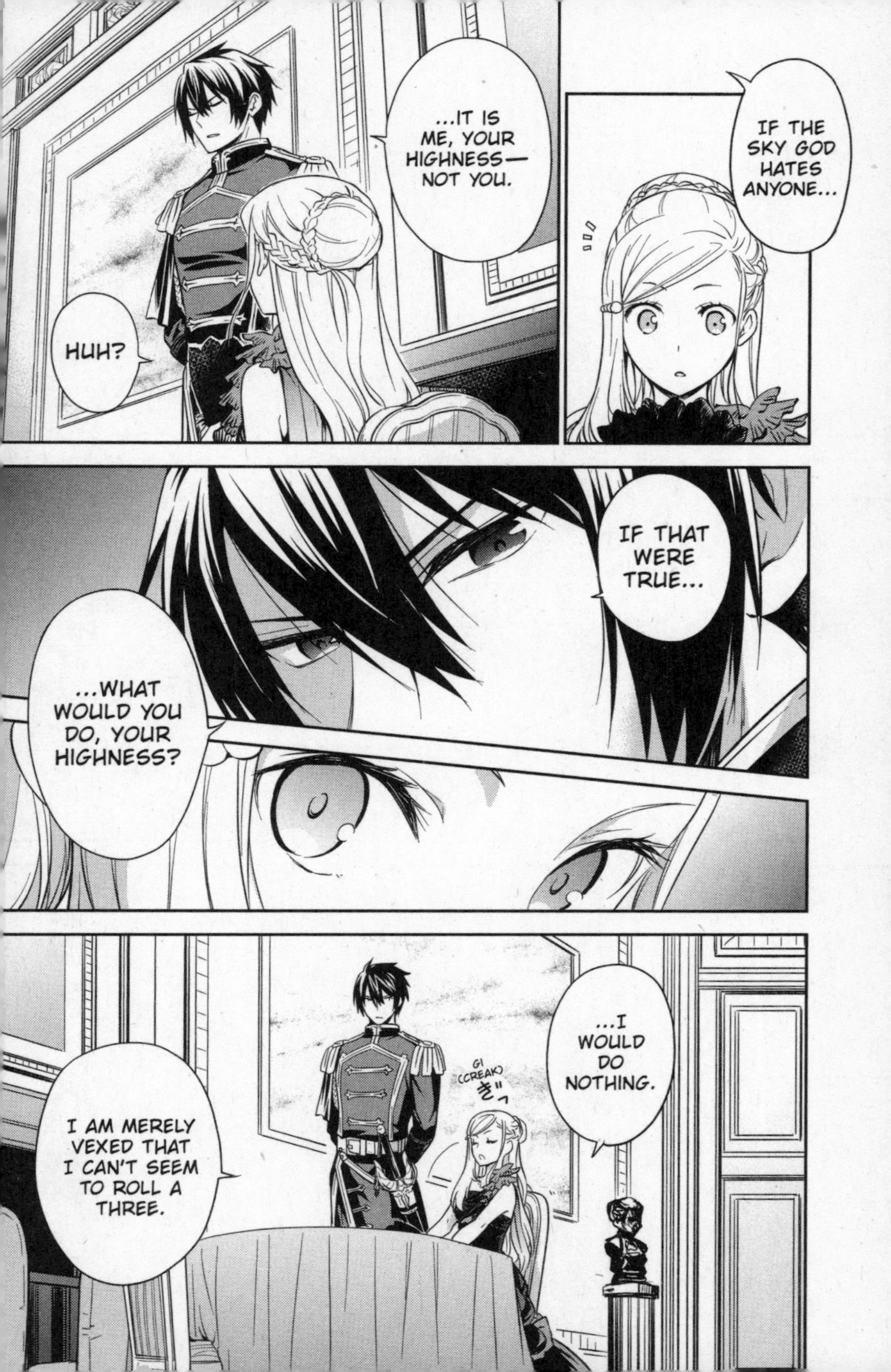
IF THE SKY GOD HATES ANYONE...
...IT IS ME, YOUR HIGHNESS—NOT YOU.
HUH?
IF THAT WERE TRUE...
...WHAT WOULD YOU DO, YOUR HIGHNESS?
...I WOULD DO NOTHING.
GI (CREAK)
ぎっ
I AM MERELY VEXED THAT I CAN'T SEEM TO ROLL A THREE.

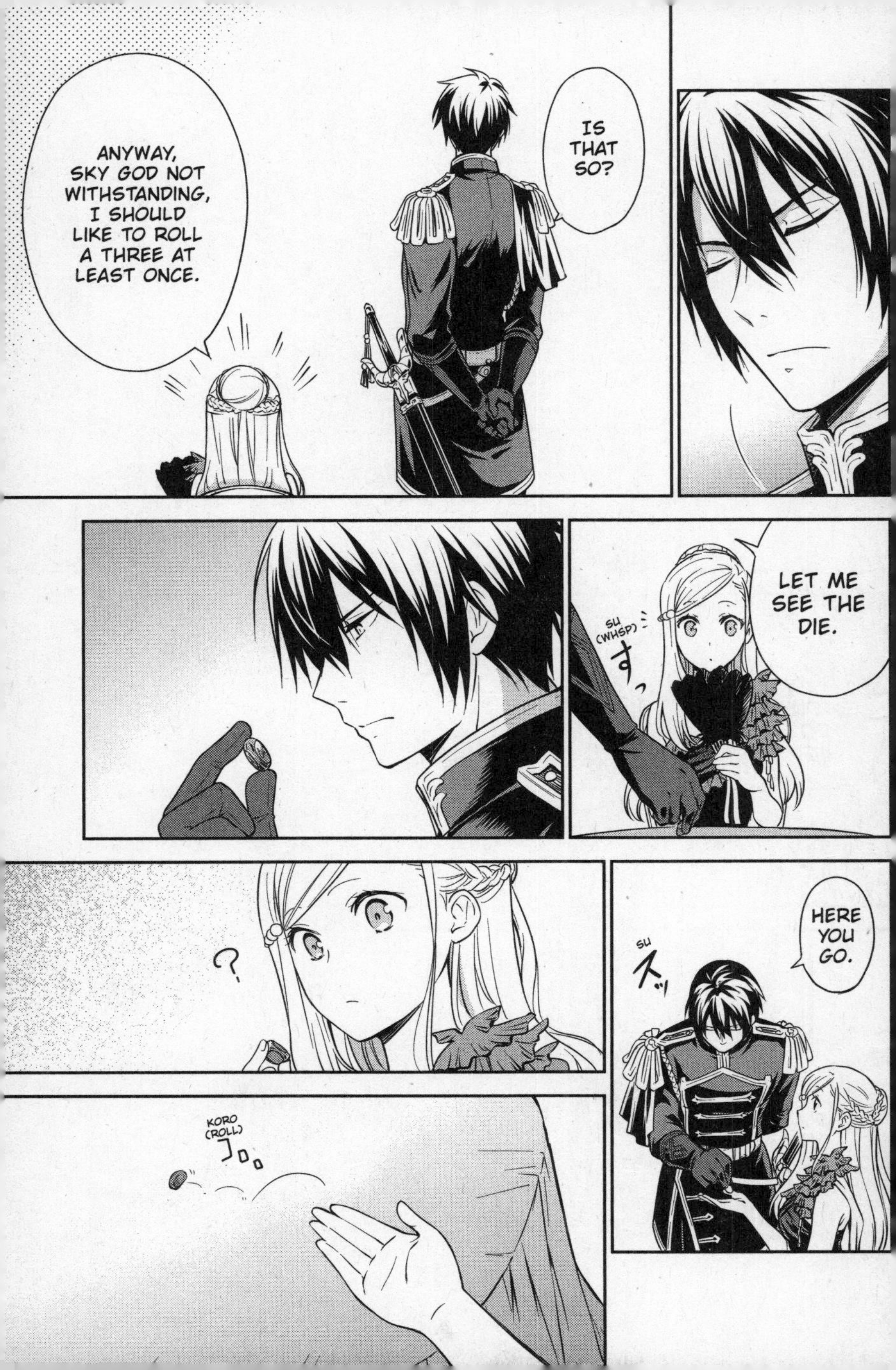
IS THAT SO?
ANYWAY, SKY GOD NOT WITHSTANDING, I SHOULD LIKE TO ROLL A THREE AT LEAST ONCE.
LET ME SEE THE DIE.
SU (WHSP)
HERE YOU GO.
SU
?
KORO (ROLL)

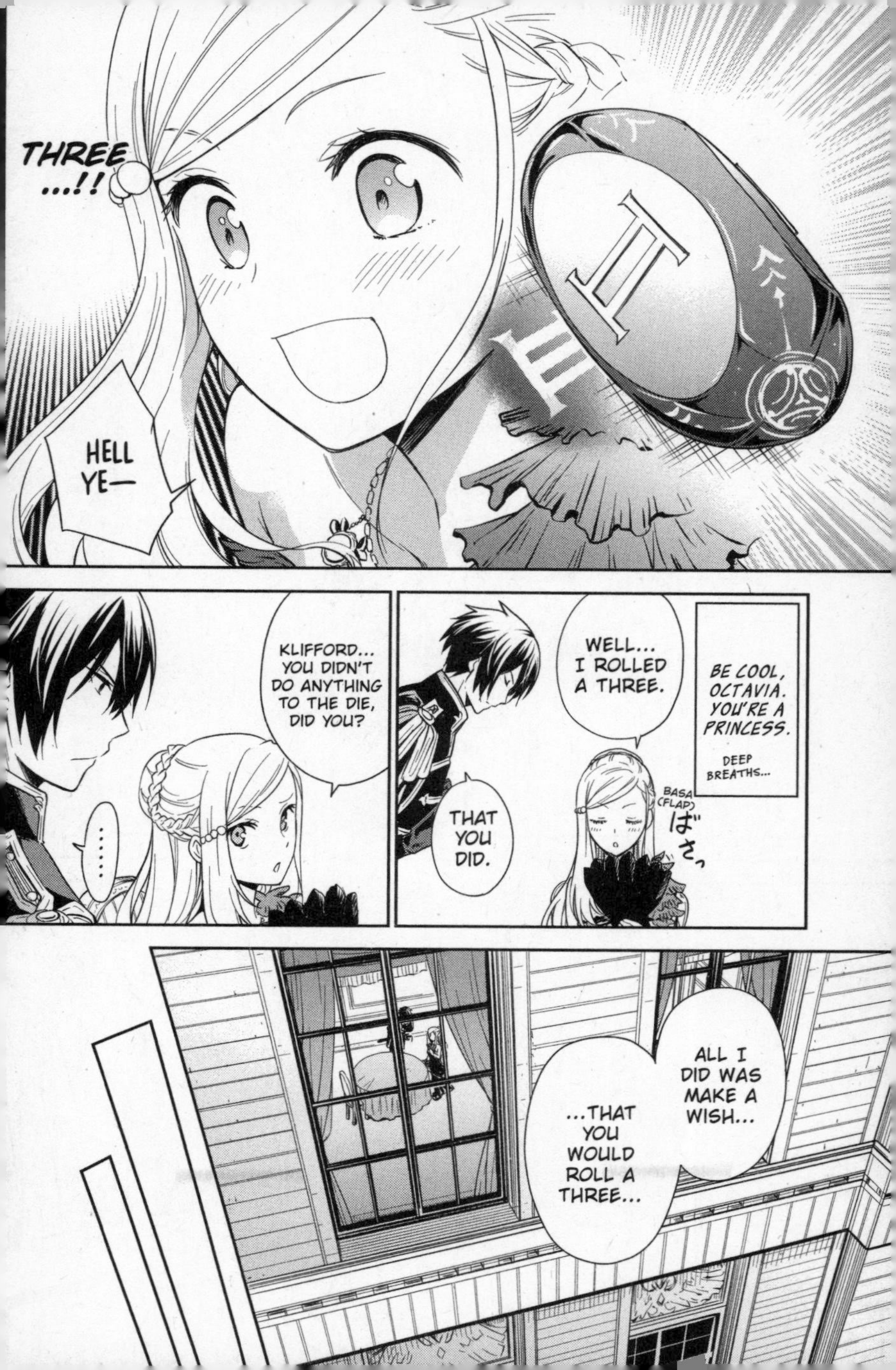
THREE ...!!
HELL YE—
WELL... I ROLLED A THREE.
BE COOL, OCTAVIA. YOU'RE A PRINCESS.
DEEP BREATHS...
BASA (FLAP) ばさっ
THAT YOU DID.
KLIFFORD... YOU DIDN'T DO ANYTHING TO THE DIE, DID YOU?
......
ALL I DID WAS MAKE A WISH...
...THAT YOU WOULD ROLL A THREE...

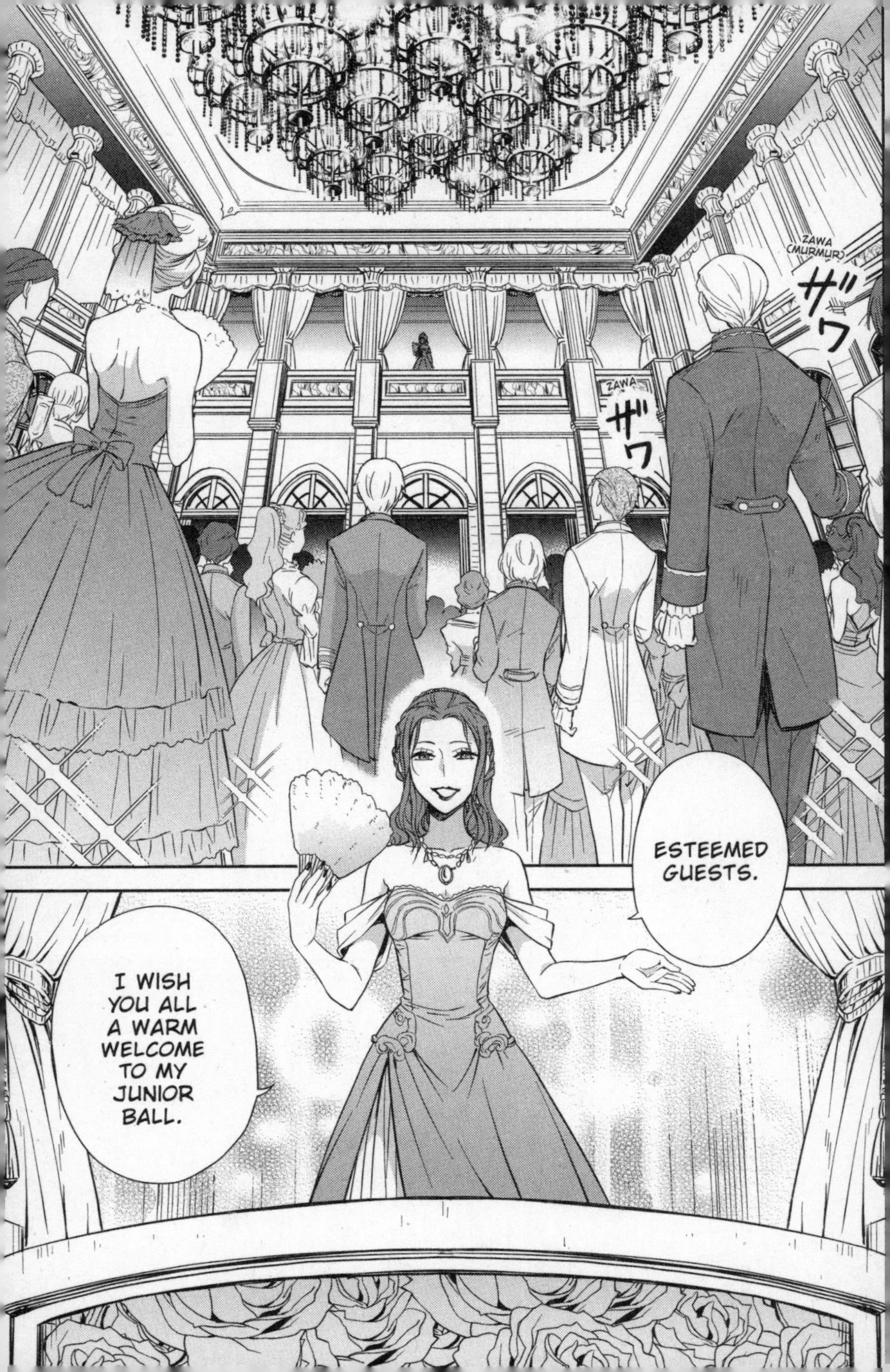
ザワ
ZAWA (MURMUR)
ザワ
ZAWA
ESTEEMED GUESTS.
I WISH YOU ALL A WARM WELCOME TO MY JUNIOR BALL.

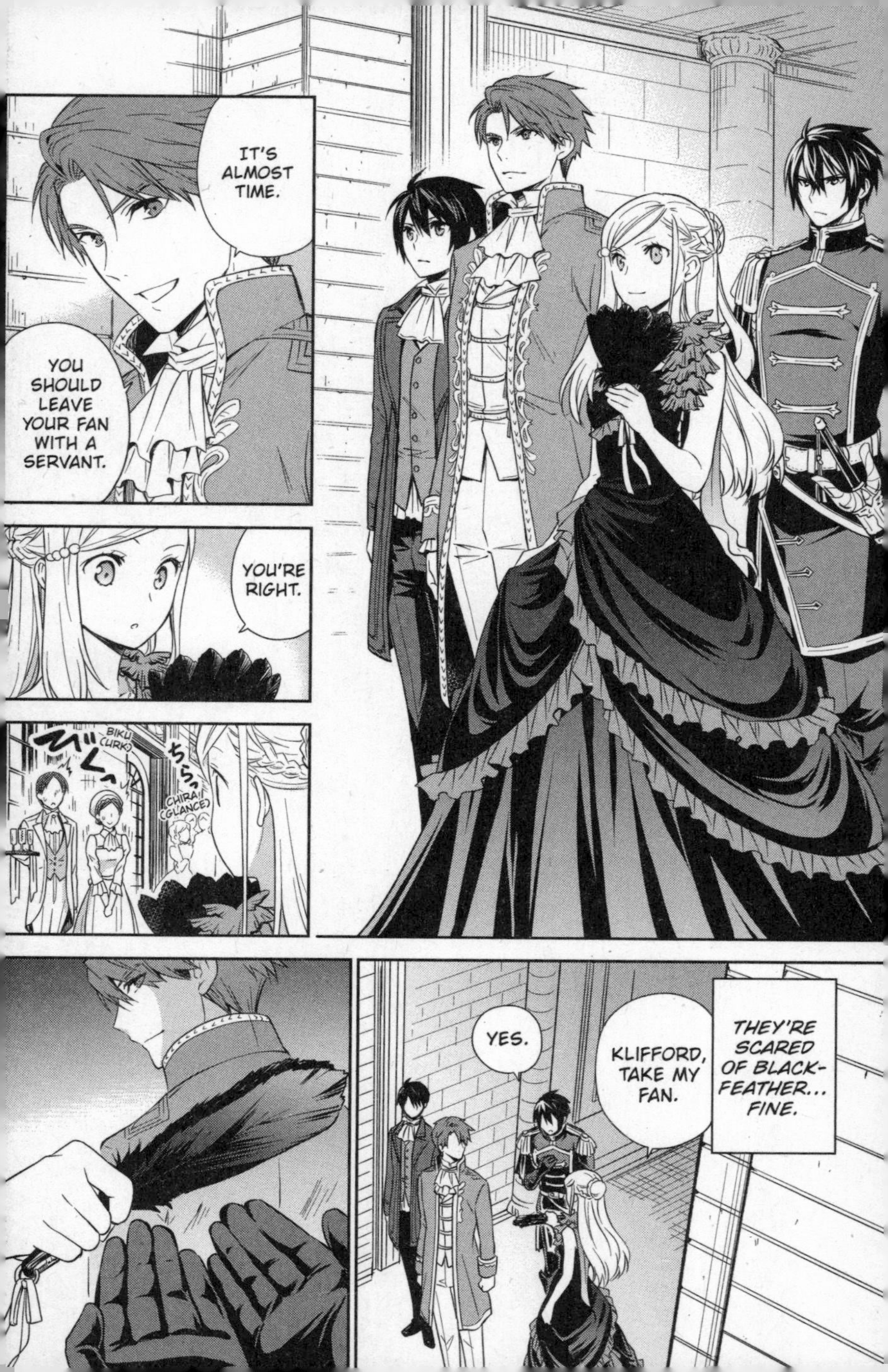
IT'S ALMOST TIME.
YOU SHOULD LEAVE YOUR FAN WITH A SERVANT.
YOU'RE RIGHT.
びくっ
BIKU (URK)
ちらっ
CHIRA (GLANCE)
THEY'RE SCARED OF BLACK-FEATHER... FINE.
KLIFFORD, TAKE MY FAN.
YES.

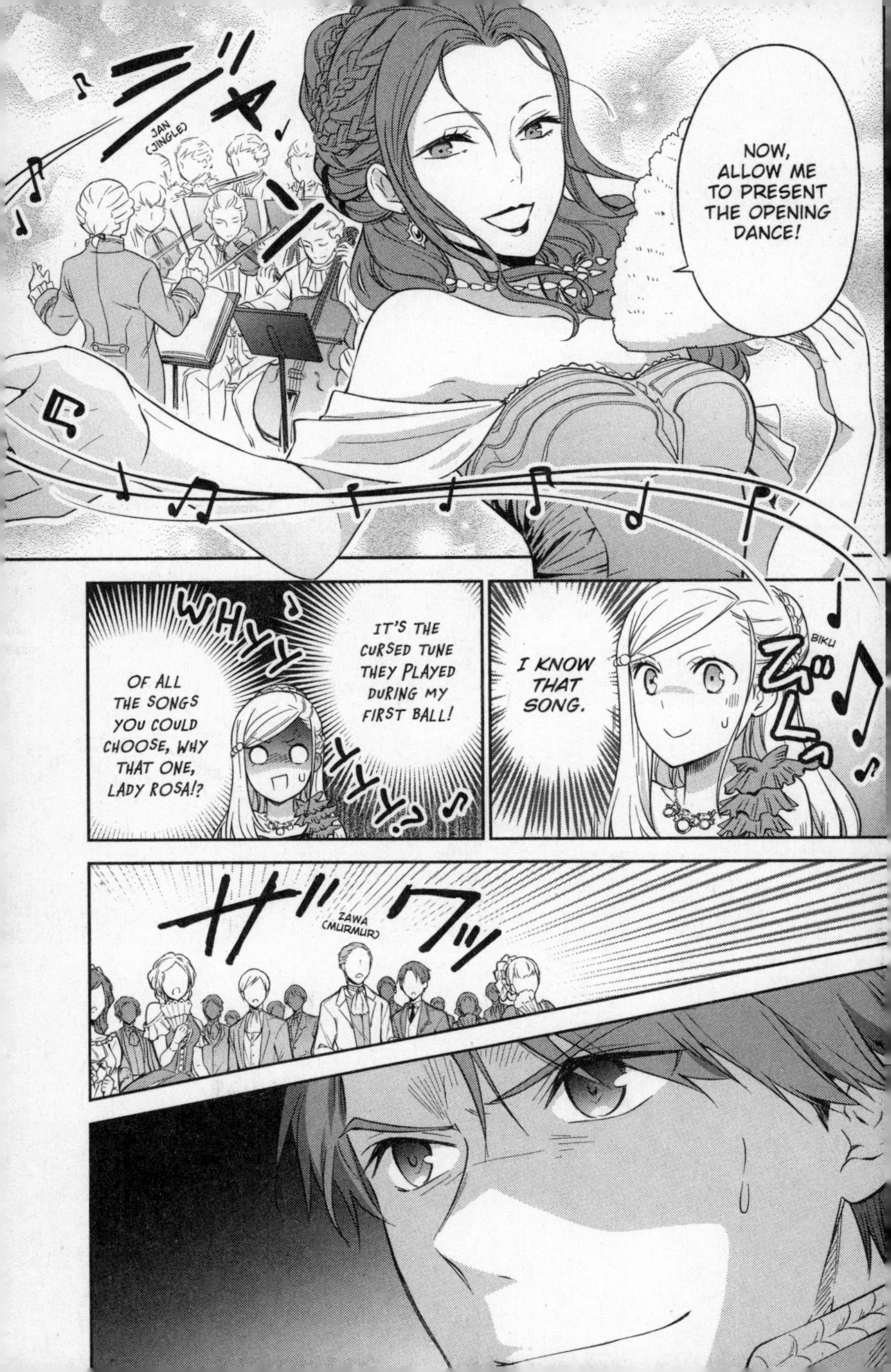
NOW, ALLOW ME TO PRESENT THE OPENING DANCE!
JAN (JINGLE)
BIKU
I KNOW THAT SONG.
IT'S THE CURSED TUNE THEY PLAYED DURING MY FIRST BALL!
OF ALL THE SONGS YOU COULD CHOOSE, WHY THAT ONE, LADY ROSA!?
WHYYYYYY?
ZAWA (MURMUR)

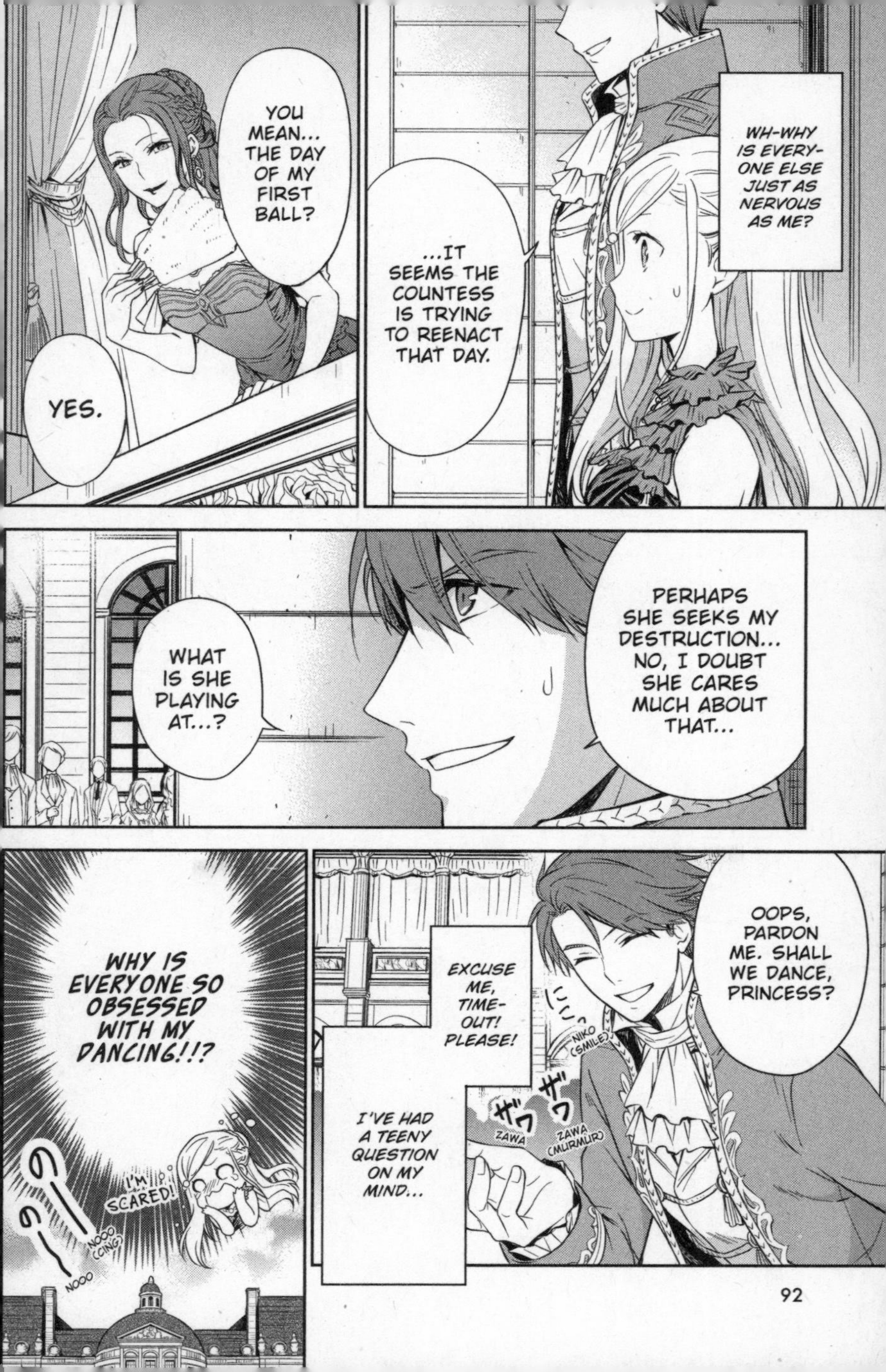
WH-WHY IS EVERYONE ELSE JUST AS NERVOUS AS ME?
...IT SEEMS THE COUNTESS IS TRYING TO REENACT THAT DAY.
YOU MEAN... THE DAY OF MY FIRST BALL?
YES.
PERHAPS SHE SEEKS MY DESTRUCTION... NO, I DOUBT SHE CARES MUCH ABOUT THAT...
WHAT IS SHE PLAYING AT...?
OOPS, PARDON ME. SHALL WE DANCE, PRINCESS?
NIKO (SMILE)
ZAWA (MURMUR)
ZAWA
EXCUSE ME, TIME-OUT! PLEASE!
I'VE HAD A TEENY QUESTION ON MY MIND...
WHY IS EVERYONE SO OBSESSED WITH MY DANCING!!?
I'M SCARED!
NOOO (CING)
NOOO

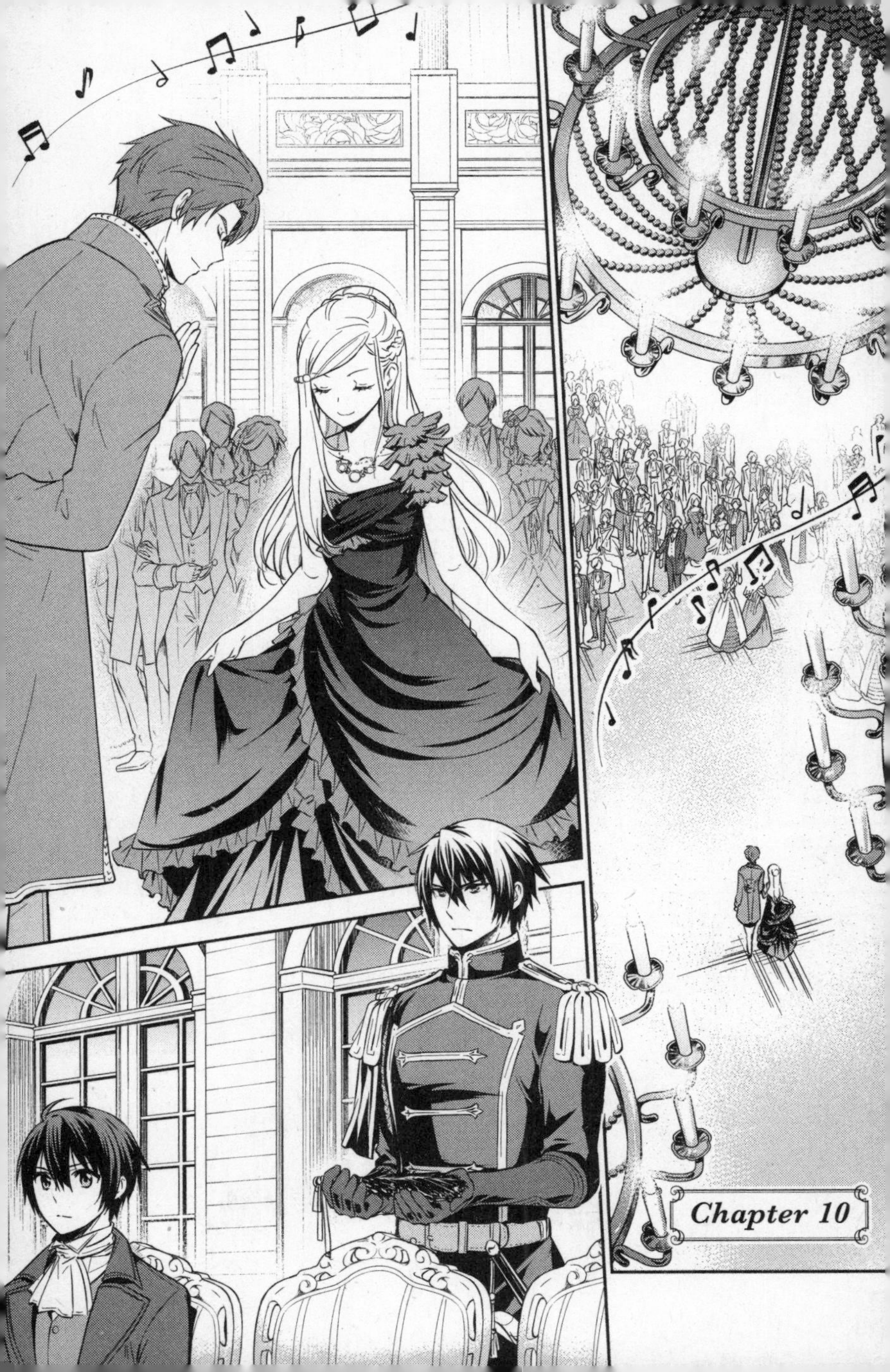
Chapter 10

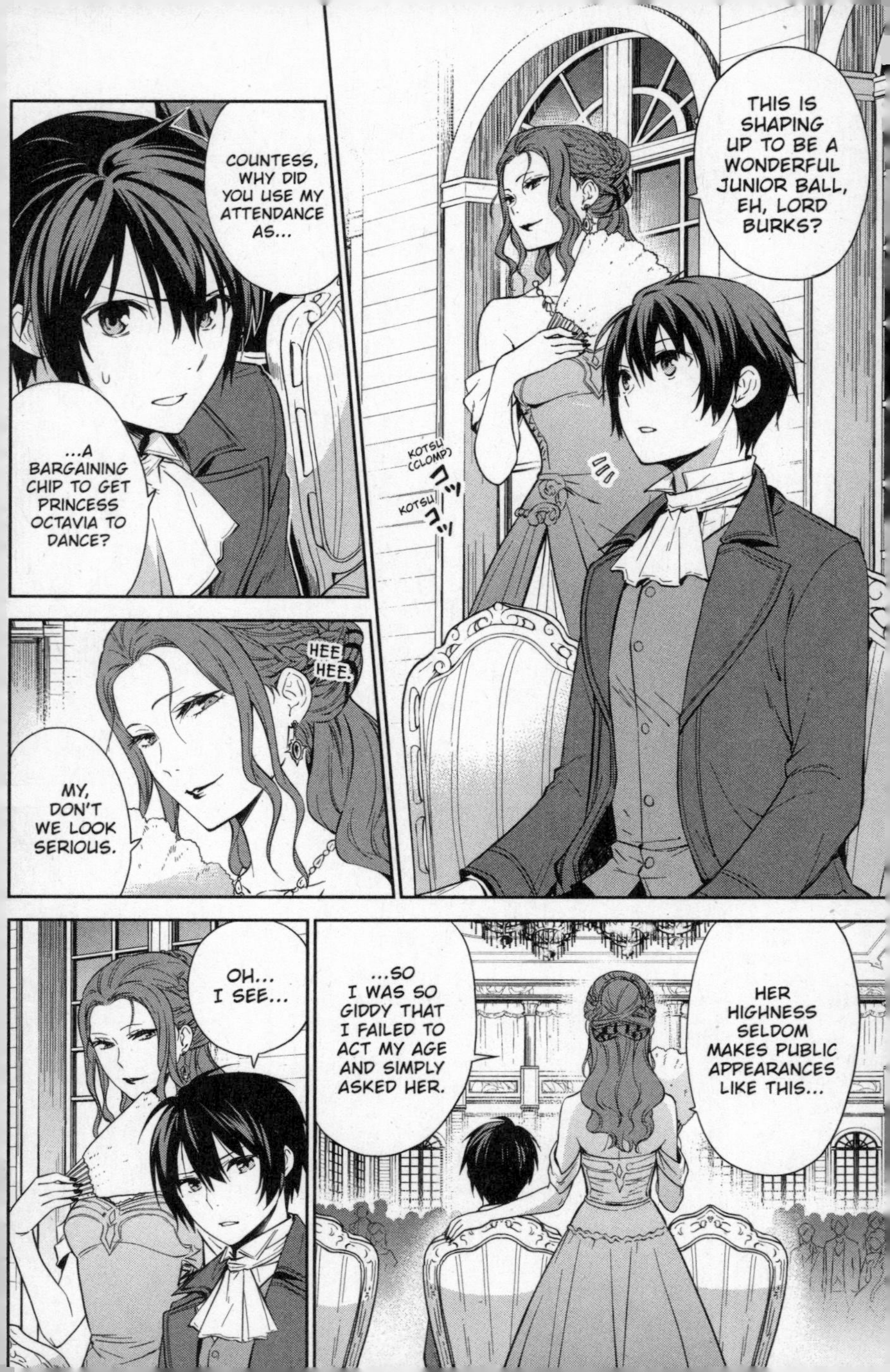
THIS IS SHAPING UP TO BE A WONDERFUL JUNIOR BALL, EH, LORD BURKS?
KOTSU (CLOMP) コッ
KOTSU コッ
COUNTESS, WHY DID YOU USE MY ATTENDANCE AS...
...A BARGAINING CHIP TO GET PRINCESS OCTAVIA TO DANCE?
HEE HEE.
MY, DON'T WE LOOK SERIOUS.
HER HIGHNESS SELDOM MAKES PUBLIC APPEARANCES LIKE THIS...
...SO I WAS SO GIDDY THAT I FAILED TO ACT MY AGE AND SIMPLY ASKED HER.
OH... I SEE...

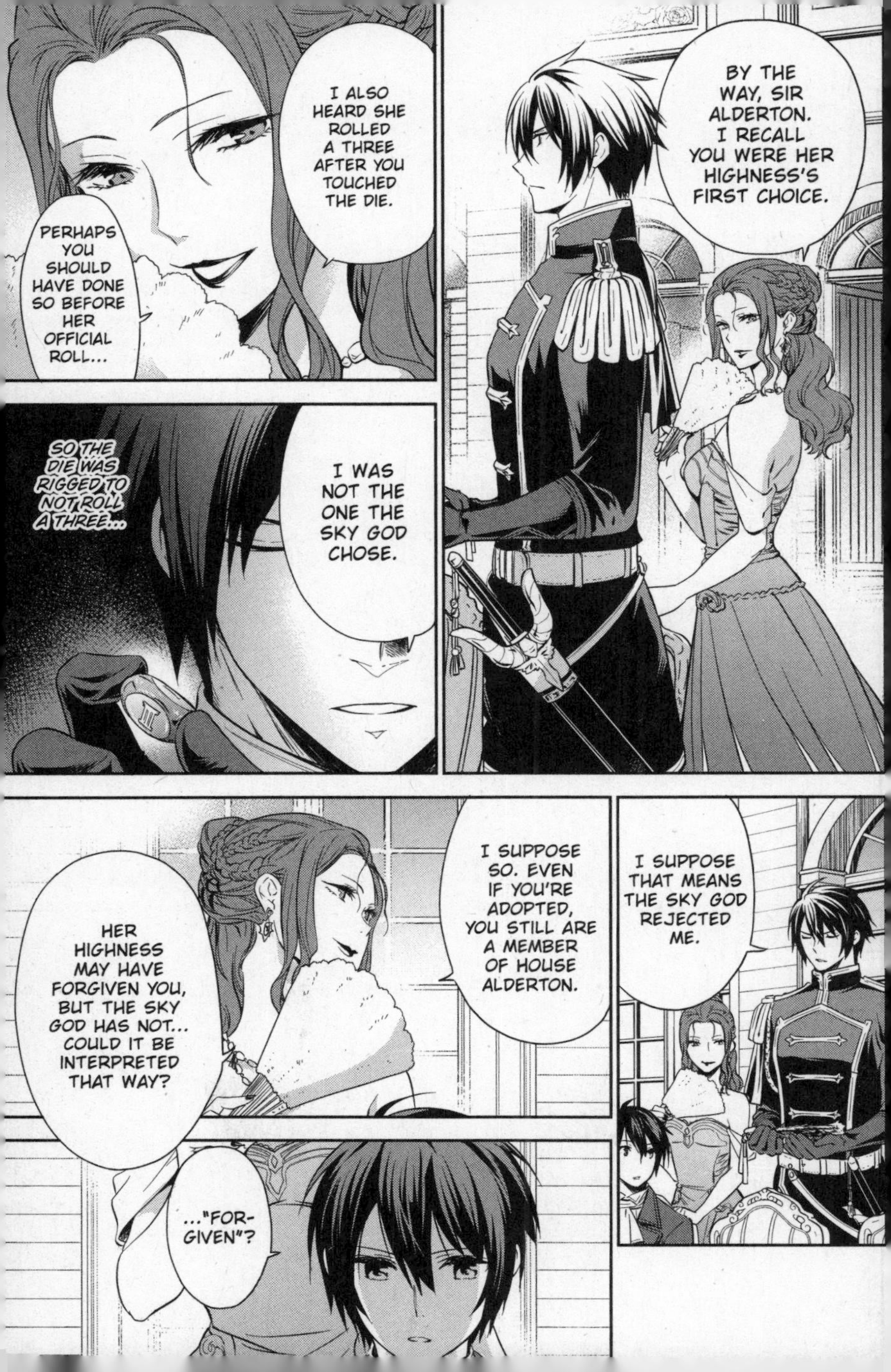
BY THE WAY, SIR ALDERTON. I RECALL YOU WERE HER HIGHNESS'S FIRST CHOICE.
I ALSO HEARD SHE ROLLED A THREE AFTER YOU TOUCHED THE DIE.
PERHAPS YOU SHOULD HAVE DONE SO BEFORE HER OFFICIAL ROLL...
I WAS NOT THE ONE THE SKY GOD CHOSE.
SO THE DIE WAS RIGGED TO NOT ROLL A THREE...
I SUPPOSE THAT MEANS THE SKY GOD REJECTED ME.
I SUPPOSE SO. EVEN IF YOU'RE ADOPTED, YOU STILL ARE A MEMBER OF HOUSE ALDERTON.
HER HIGHNESS MAY HAVE FORGIVEN YOU, BUT THE SKY GOD HAS NOT... COULD IT BE INTERPRETED THAT WAY?
..."FOR-GIVEN"?

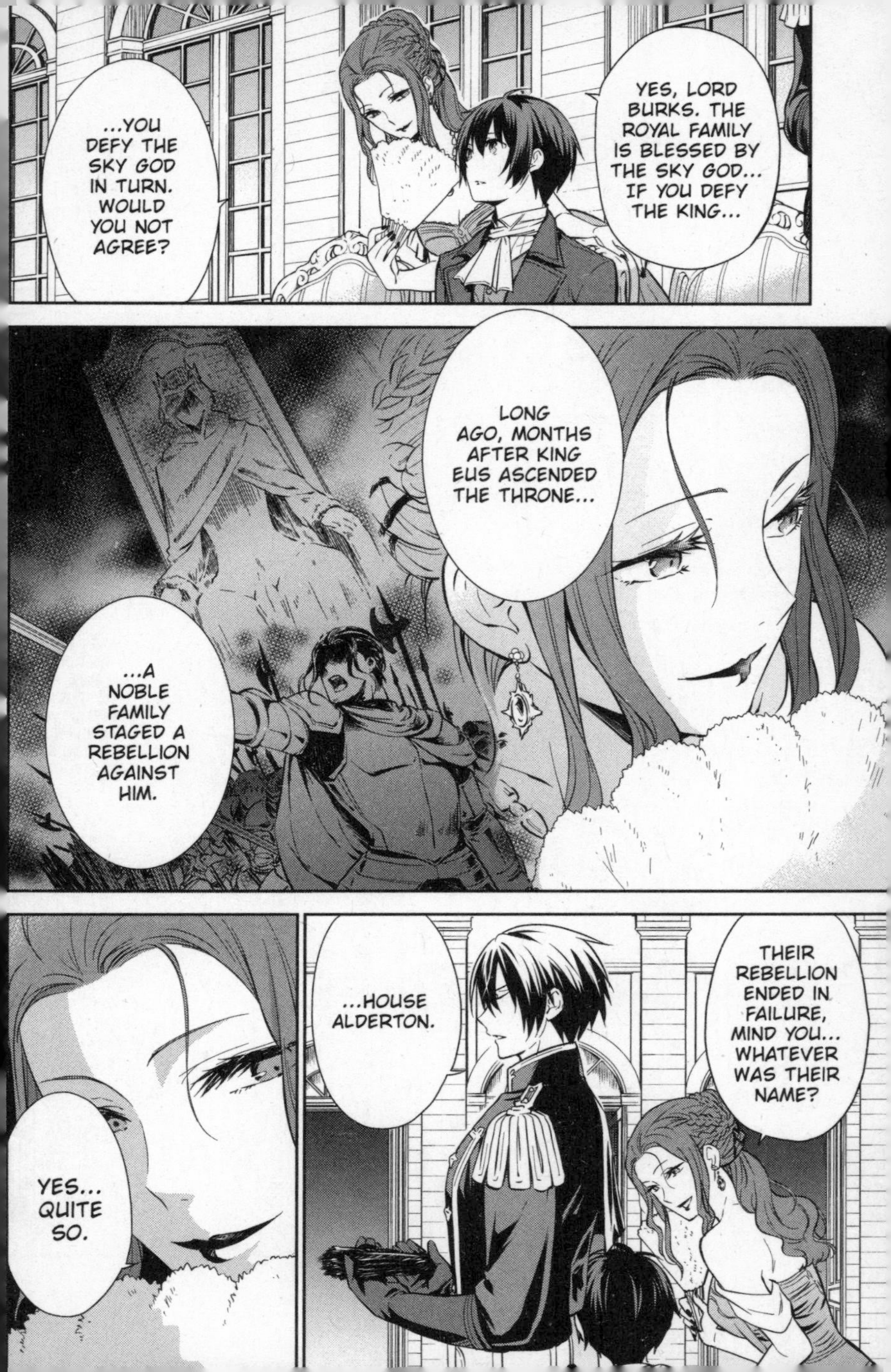
YES, LORD BURKS. THE ROYAL FAMILY IS BLESSED BY THE SKY GOD... IF YOU DEFY THE KING...
...YOU DEFY THE SKY GOD IN TURN. WOULD YOU NOT AGREE?
LONG AGO, MONTHS AFTER KING EUS ASCENDED THE THRONE...
...A NOBLE FAMILY STAGED A REBELLION AGAINST HIM.
THEIR REBELLION ENDED IN FAILURE, MIND YOU... WHATEVER WAS THEIR NAME?
...HOUSE ALDERTON.
YES... QUITE SO.

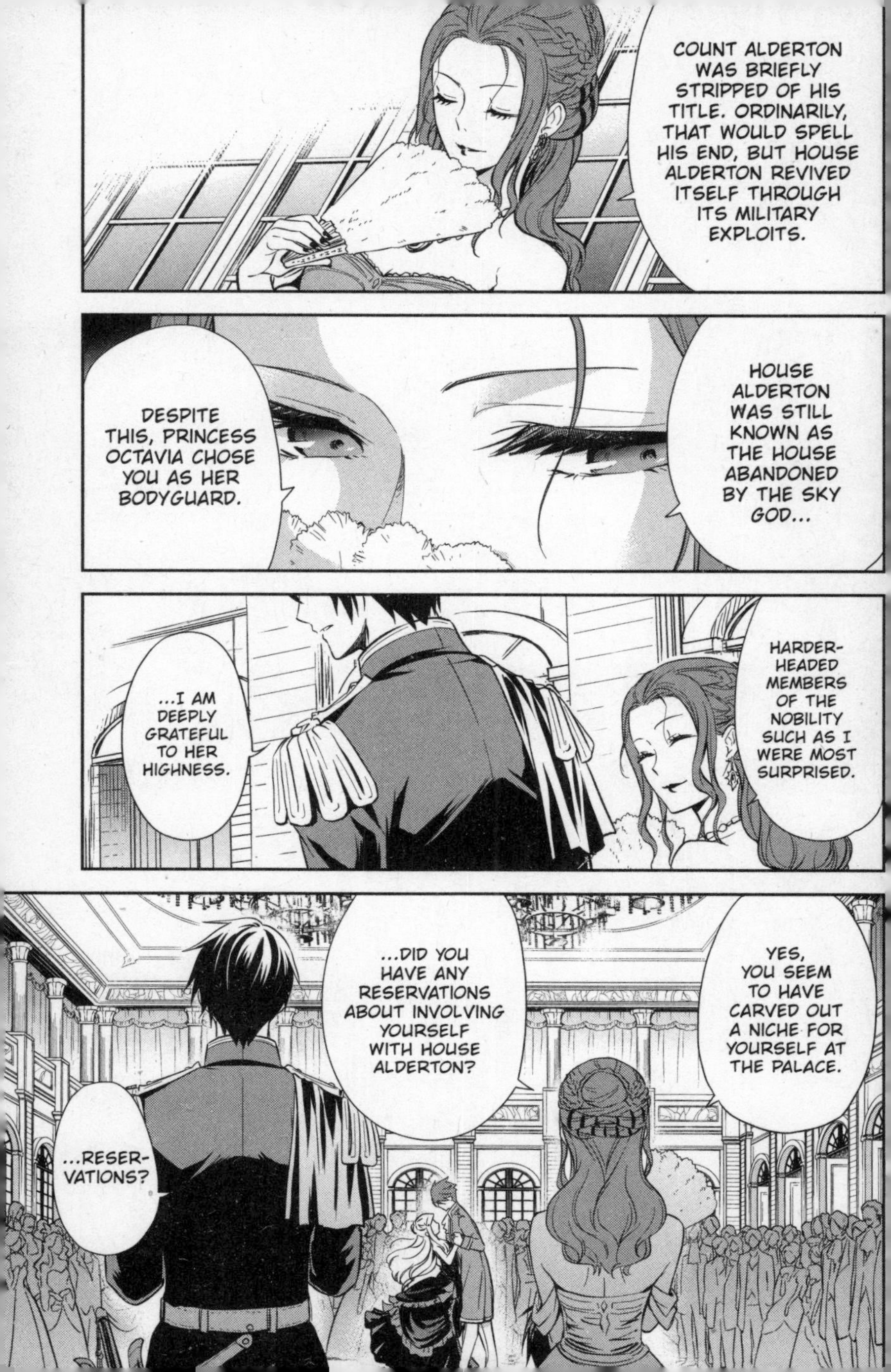
COUNT ALDERTON WAS BRIEFLY STRIPPED OF HIS TITLE. ORDINARILY, THAT WOULD SPELL HIS END, BUT HOUSE ALDERTON REVIVED ITSELF THROUGH ITS MILITARY EXPLOITS.
HOUSE ALDERTON WAS STILL KNOWN AS THE HOUSE ABANDONED BY THE SKY GOD...
DESPITE THIS, PRINCESS OCTAVIA CHOSE YOU AS HER BODYGUARD.
HARDER-HEADED MEMBERS OF THE NOBILITY SUCH AS I WERE MOST SURPRISED.
...I AM DEEPLY GRATEFUL TO HER HIGHNESS.
YES, YOU SEEM TO HAVE CARVED OUT A NICHE FOR YOURSELF AT THE PALACE.
...DID YOU HAVE ANY RESERVATIONS ABOUT INVOLVING YOURSELF WITH HOUSE ALDERTON?
...RESER-VATIONS?

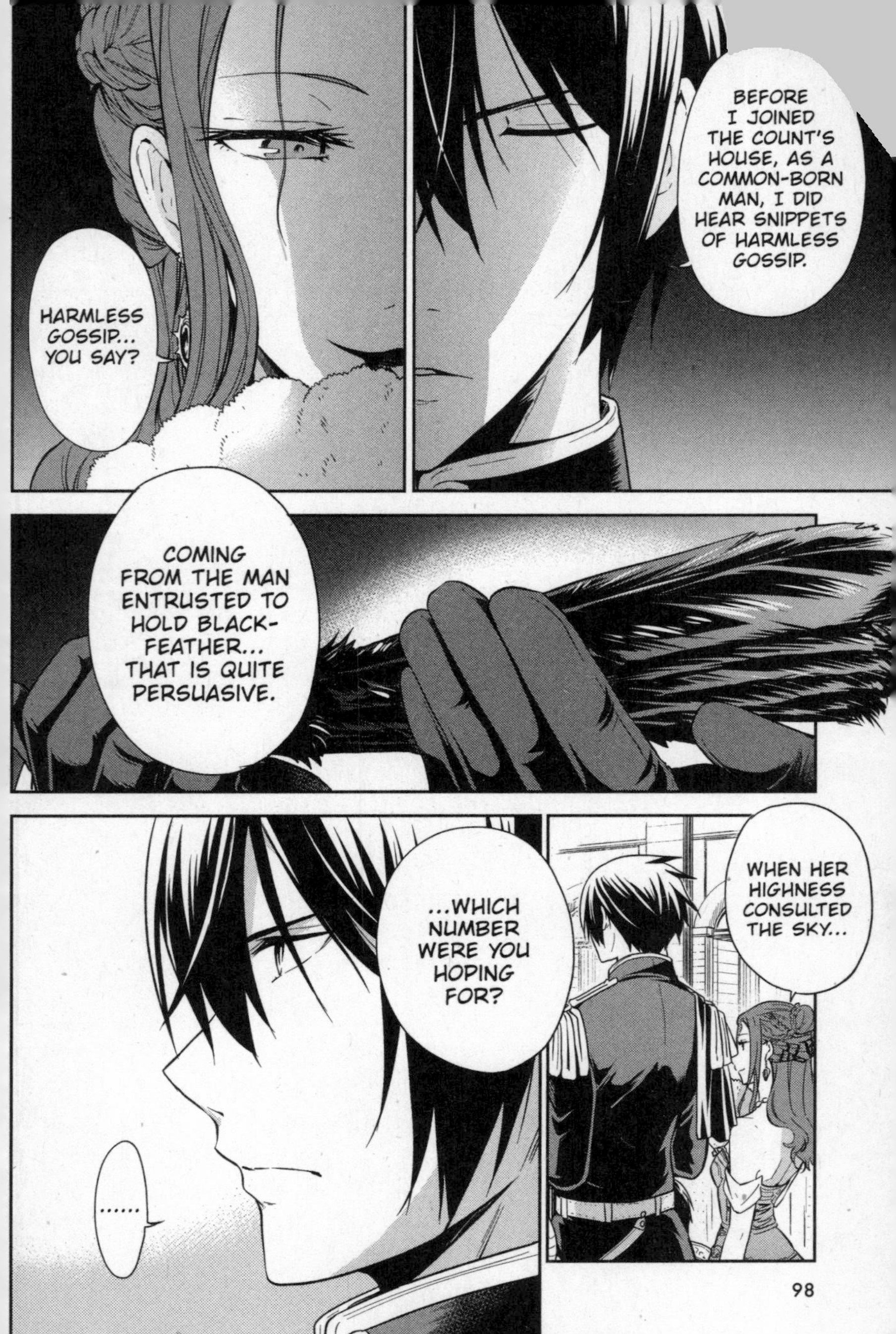
BEFORE I JOINED THE COUNT'S HOUSE, AS A COMMON-BORN MAN, I DID HEAR SNIPPETS OF HARMLESS GOSSIP.
HARMLESS GOSSIP... YOU SAY?
COMING FROM THE MAN ENTRUSTED TO HOLD BLACK-FEATHER... THAT IS QUITE PERSUASIVE.
WHEN HER HIGHNESS CONSULTED THE SKY...
...WHICH NUMBER WERE YOU HOPING FOR?
......

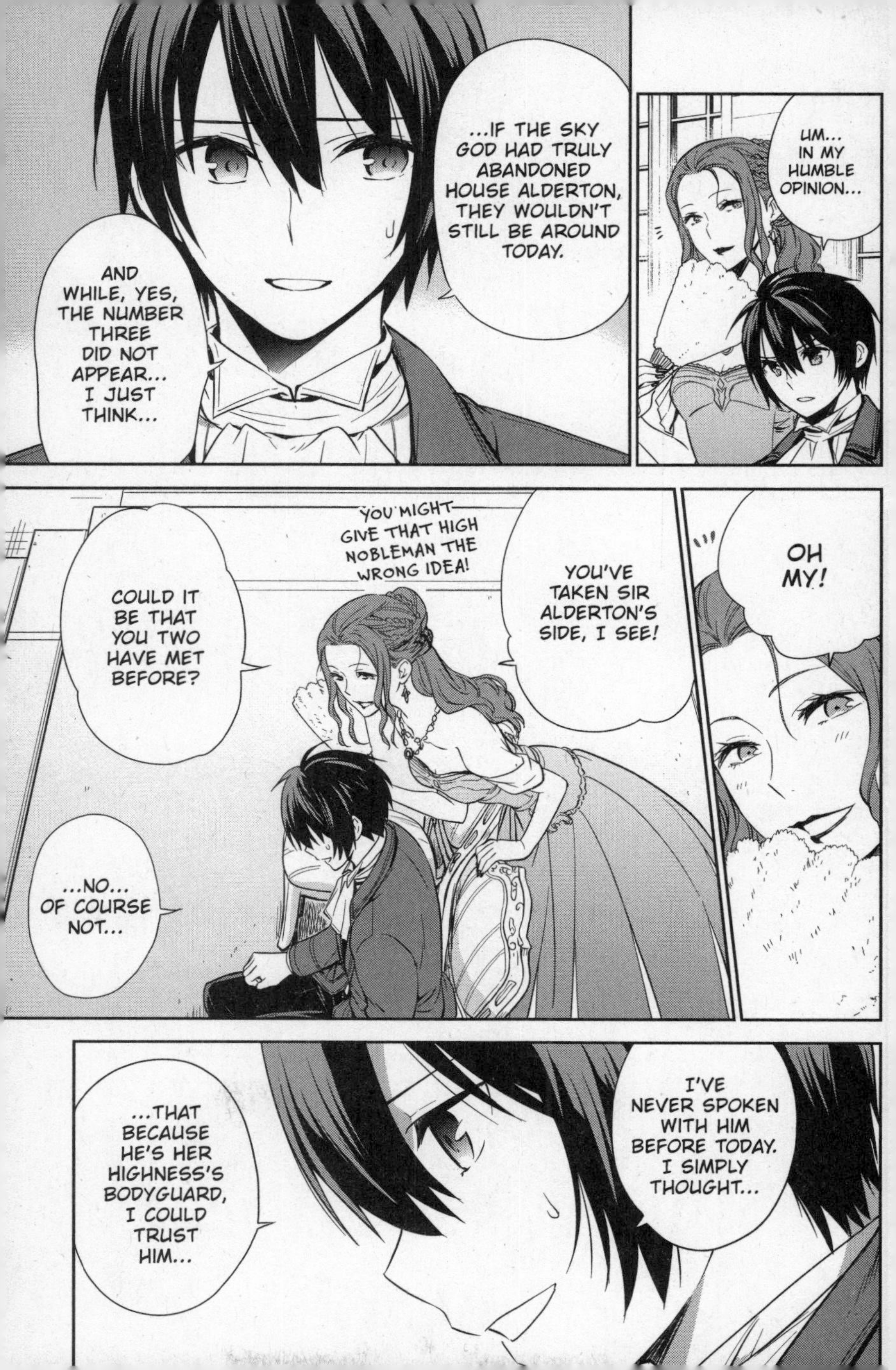
UM... IN MY HUMBLE OPINION...
...IF THE SKY GOD HAD TRULY ABANDONED HOUSE ALDERTON, THEY WOULDN'T STILL BE AROUND TODAY.
AND WHILE, YES, THE NUMBER THREE DID NOT APPEAR... I JUST THINK...
OH MY!
YOU'VE TAKEN SIR ALDERTON'S SIDE, I SEE!
YOU MIGHT GIVE THAT HIGH NOBLEMAN THE WRONG IDEA!
COULD IT BE THAT YOU TWO HAVE MET BEFORE?
...NO... OF COURSE NOT...
I'VE NEVER SPOKEN WITH HIM BEFORE TODAY. I SIMPLY THOUGHT...
...THAT BECAUSE HE'S HER HIGHNESS'S BODYGUARD, I COULD TRUST HIM...

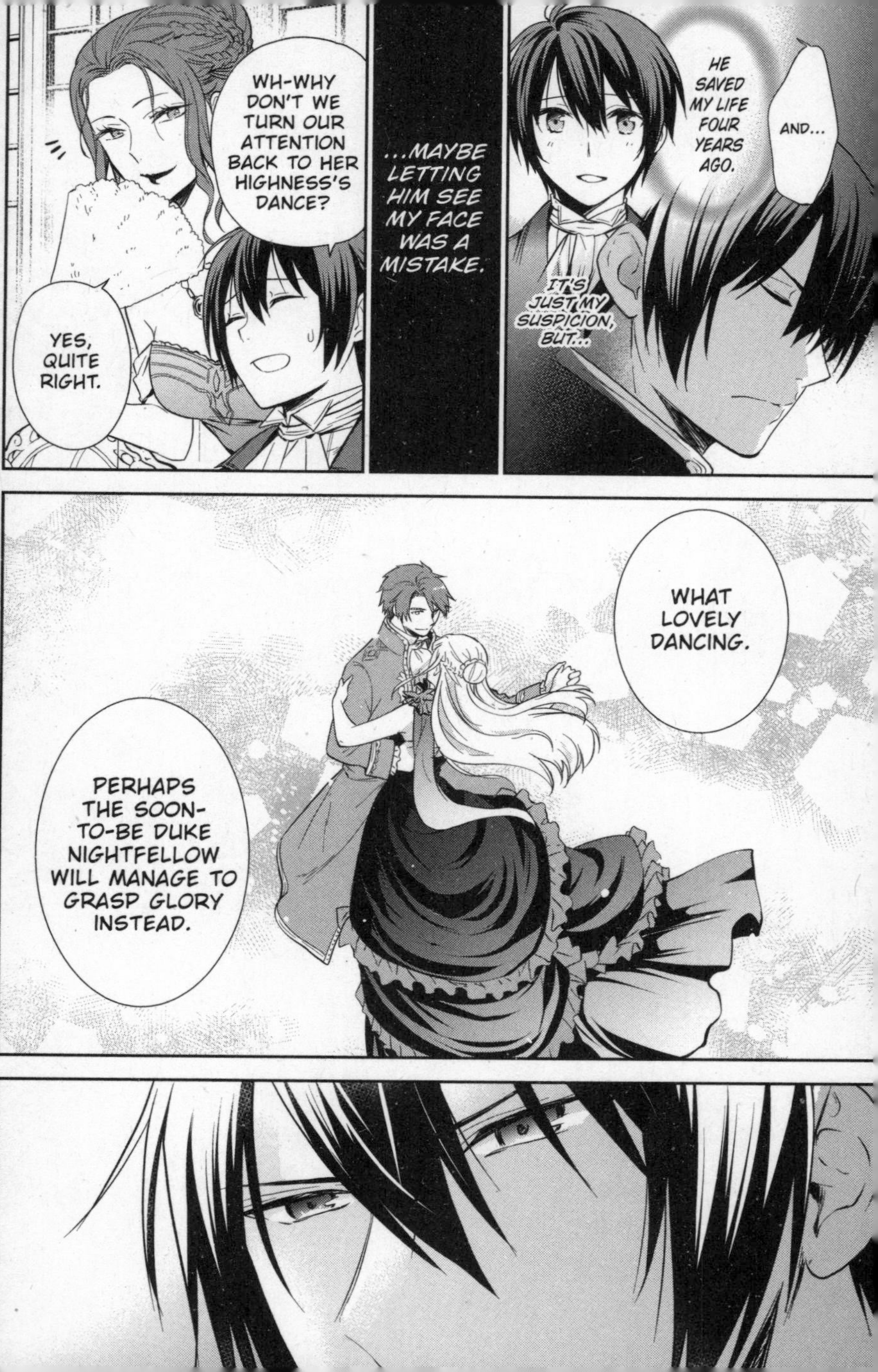
HE SAVED MY LIFE FOUR YEARS AGO.
AND...
IT'S JUST MY SUSPICION, BUT...
...MAYBE LETTING HIM SEE MY FACE WAS A MISTAKE.
WH-WHY DON'T WE TURN OUR ATTENTION BACK TO HER HIGHNESS'S DANCE?
YES, QUITE RIGHT.
WHAT LOVELY DANCING.
PERHAPS THE SOON-TO-BE DUKE NIGHTFELLOW WILL MANAGE TO GRASP GLORY INSTEAD.

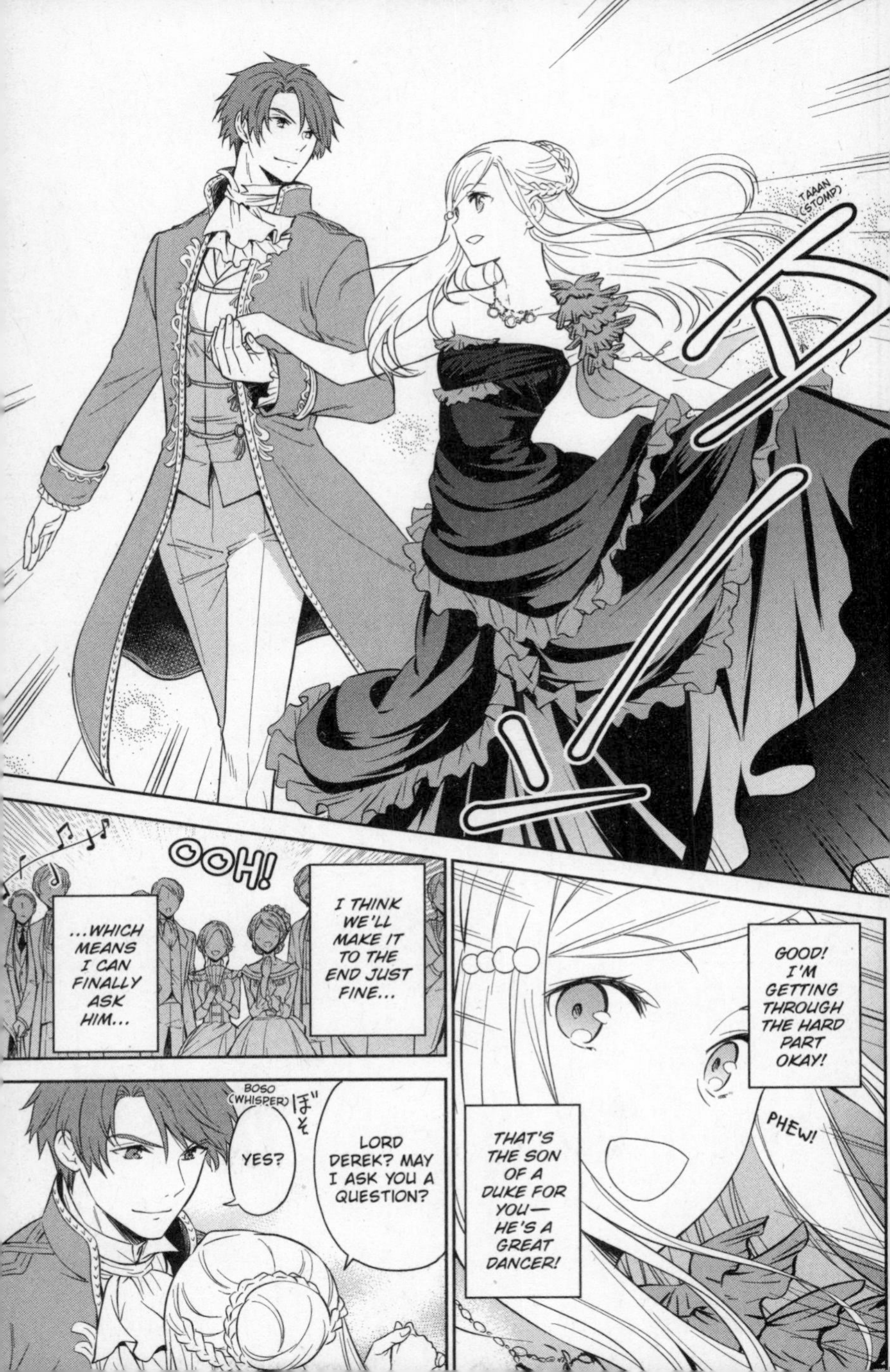
TAAAN (STOMP)
GOOD! I'M GETTING THROUGH THE HARD PART OKAY!
PHEW!
THAT'S THE SON OF A DUKE FOR YOU— HE'S A GREAT DANCER!
I THINK WE'LL MAKE IT TO THE END JUST FINE...
OOH!
...WHICH MEANS I CAN FINALLY ASK HIM...
LORD DEREK? MAY I ASK YOU A QUESTION?
ぼそ
BOSO (WHISPER)
YES?

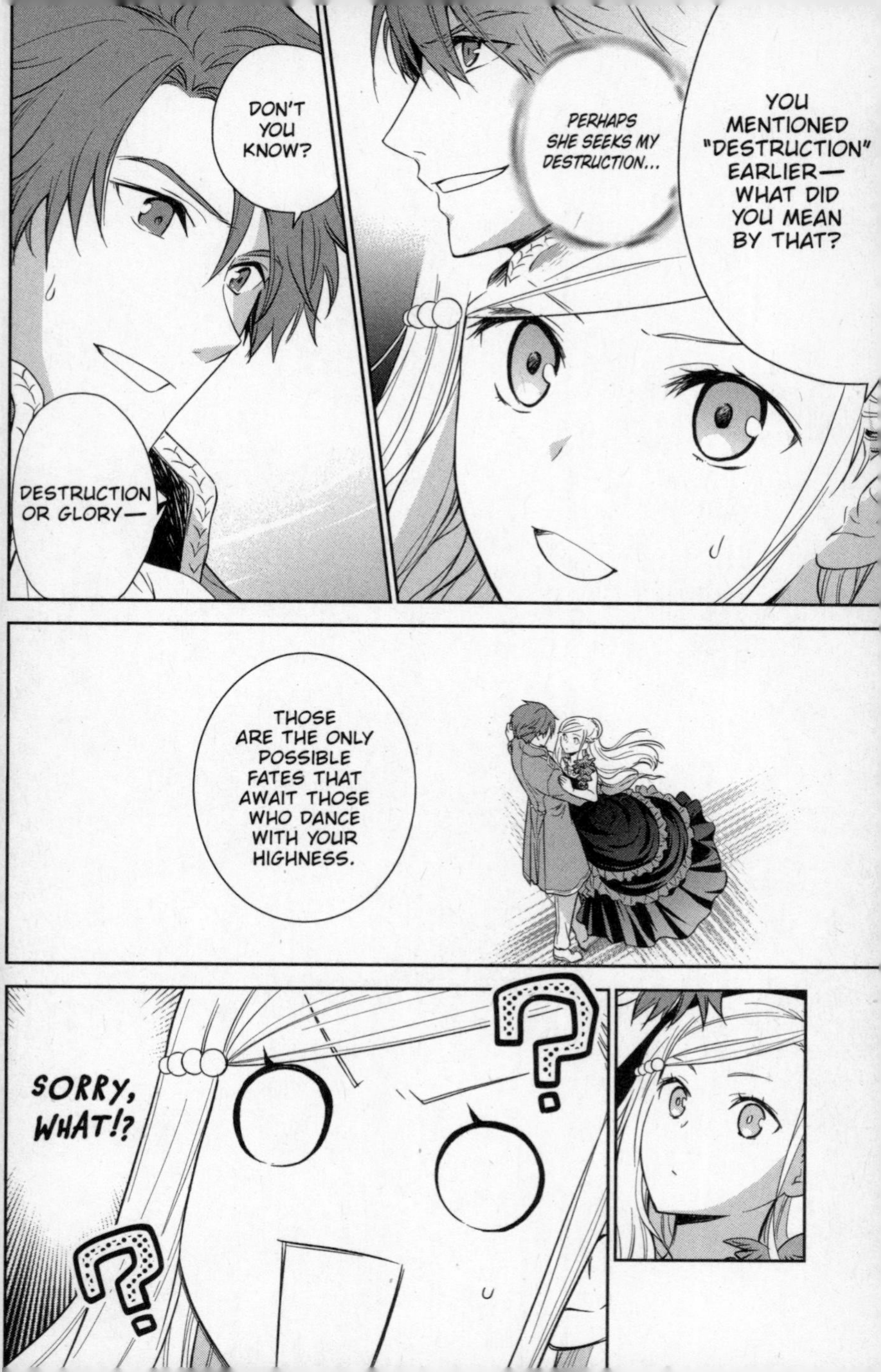
YOU MENTIONED "DESTRUCTION" EARLIER— WHAT DID YOU MEAN BY THAT?
PERHAPS SHE SEEKS MY DESTRUCTION...
DON'T YOU KNOW?
DESTRUCTION OR GLORY—
THOSE ARE THE ONLY POSSIBLE FATES THAT AWAIT THOSE WHO DANCE WITH YOUR HIGHNESS.
?
SORRY, WHAT!?
?

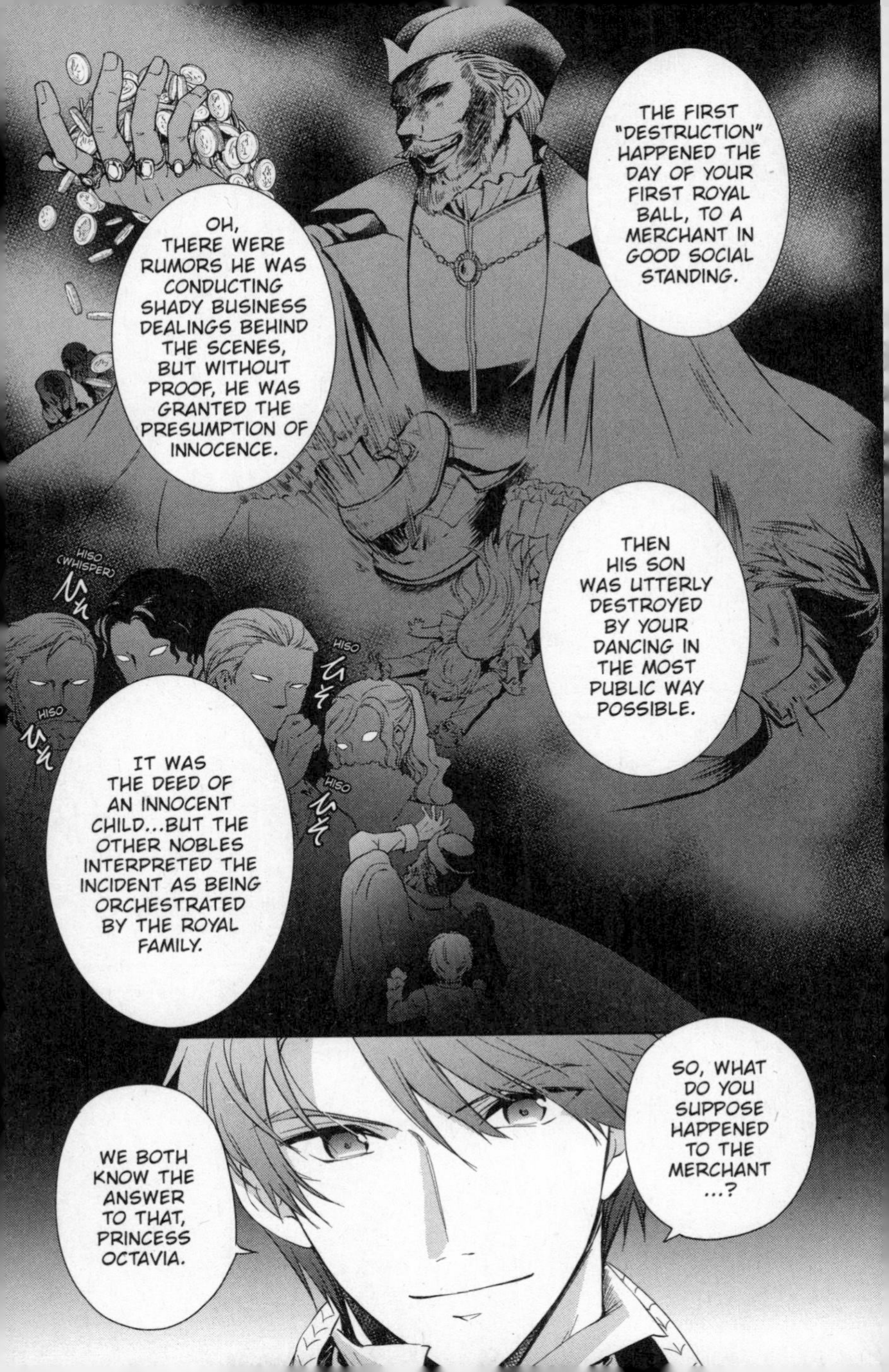
THE FIRST "DESTRUCTION" HAPPENED THE DAY OF YOUR FIRST ROYAL BALL, TO A MERCHANT IN GOOD SOCIAL STANDING.
OH, THERE WERE RUMORS HE WAS CONDUCTING SHADY BUSINESS DEALINGS BEHIND THE SCENES, BUT WITHOUT PROOF, HE WAS GRANTED THE PRESUMPTION OF INNOCENCE.
THEN HIS SON WAS UTTERLY DESTROYED BY YOUR DANCING IN THE MOST PUBLIC WAY POSSIBLE.
HISO
HISO (WHISPER)
HISO
HISO
IT WAS THE DEED OF AN INNOCENT CHILD...BUT THE OTHER NOBLES INTERPRETED THE INCIDENT AS BEING ORCHESTRATED BY THE ROYAL FAMILY.
SO, WHAT DO YOU SUPPOSE HAPPENED TO THE MERCHANT ...?
WE BOTH KNOW THE ANSWER TO THAT, PRINCESS OCTAVIA.

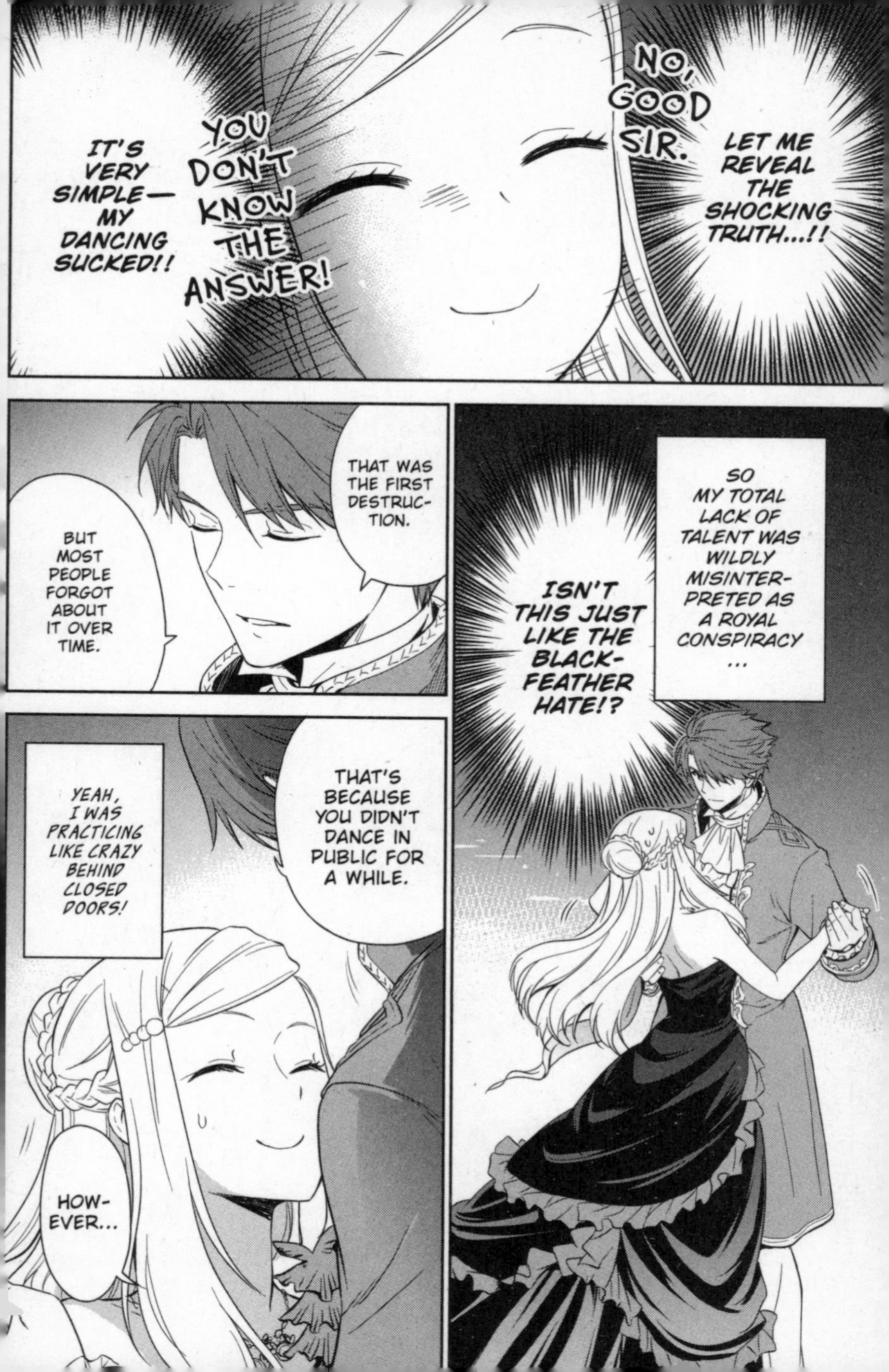
NO, GOOD SIR.
LET ME REVEAL THE SHOCKING TRUTH...!!
YOU DON'T KNOW THE ANSWER!
IT'S VERY SIMPLE—MY DANCING SUCKED!!
SO MY TOTAL LACK OF TALENT WAS WILDLY MISINTER-PRETED AS A ROYAL CONSPIRACY ...
ISN'T THIS JUST LIKE THE BLACK-FEATHER HATE!?
THAT WAS THE FIRST DESTRUC-TION.
BUT MOST PEOPLE FORGOT ABOUT IT OVER TIME.
THAT'S BECAUSE YOU DIDN'T DANCE IN PUBLIC FOR A WHILE.
YEAH, I WAS PRACTICING LIKE CRAZY BEHIND CLOSED DOORS!
HOW-EVER...

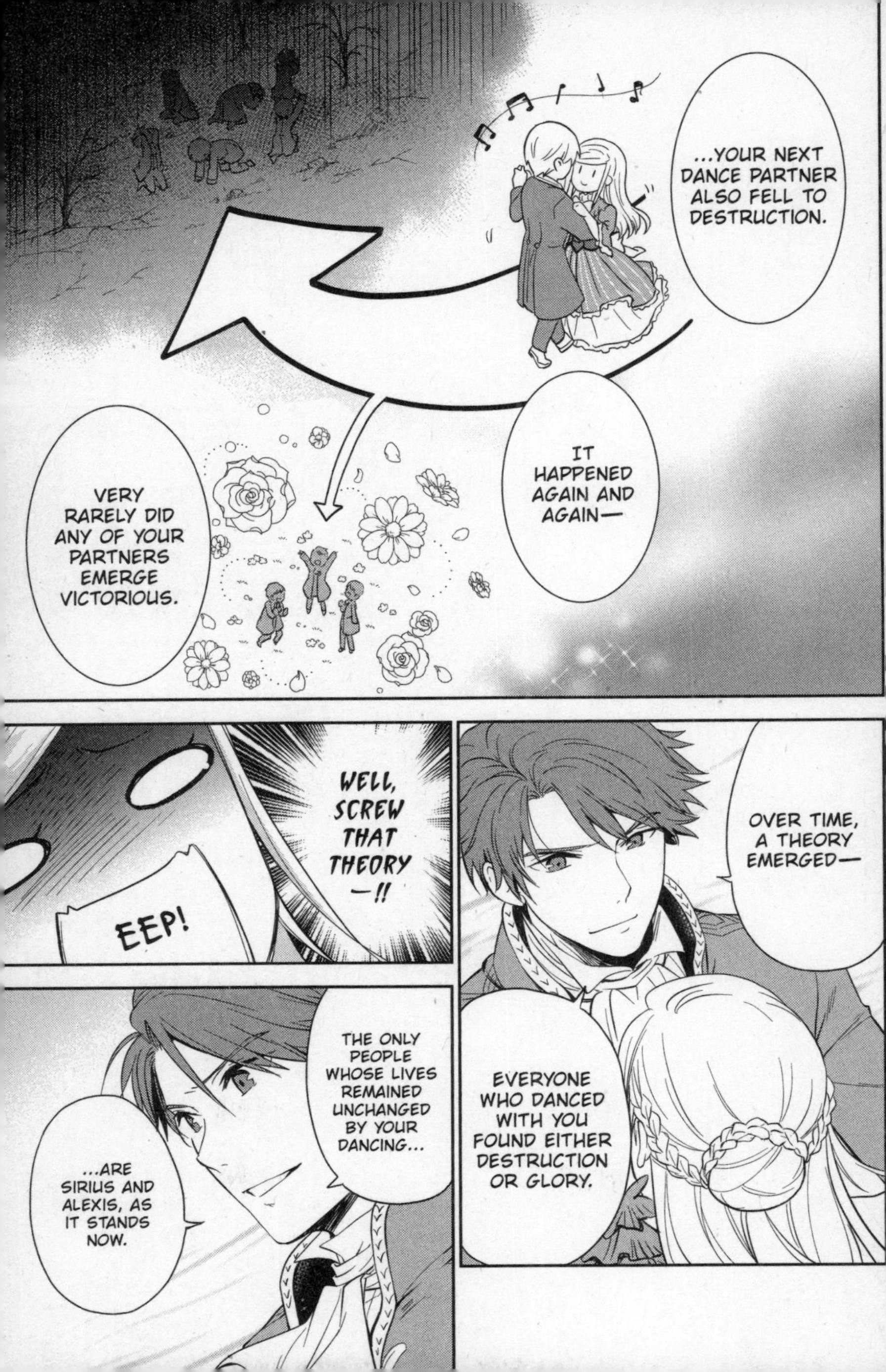
...YOUR NEXT DANCE PARTNER ALSO FELL TO DESTRUCTION.
IT HAPPENED AGAIN AND AGAIN—
VERY RARELY DID ANY OF YOUR PARTNERS EMERGE VICTORIOUS.
OVER TIME, A THEORY EMERGED—
EVERYONE WHO DANCED WITH YOU FOUND EITHER DESTRUCTION OR GLORY.
WELL, SCREW THAT THEORY—!!
EEP!
THE ONLY PEOPLE WHOSE LIVES REMAINED UNCHANGED BY YOUR DANCING...
...ARE SIRIUS AND ALEXIS, AS IT STANDS NOW.

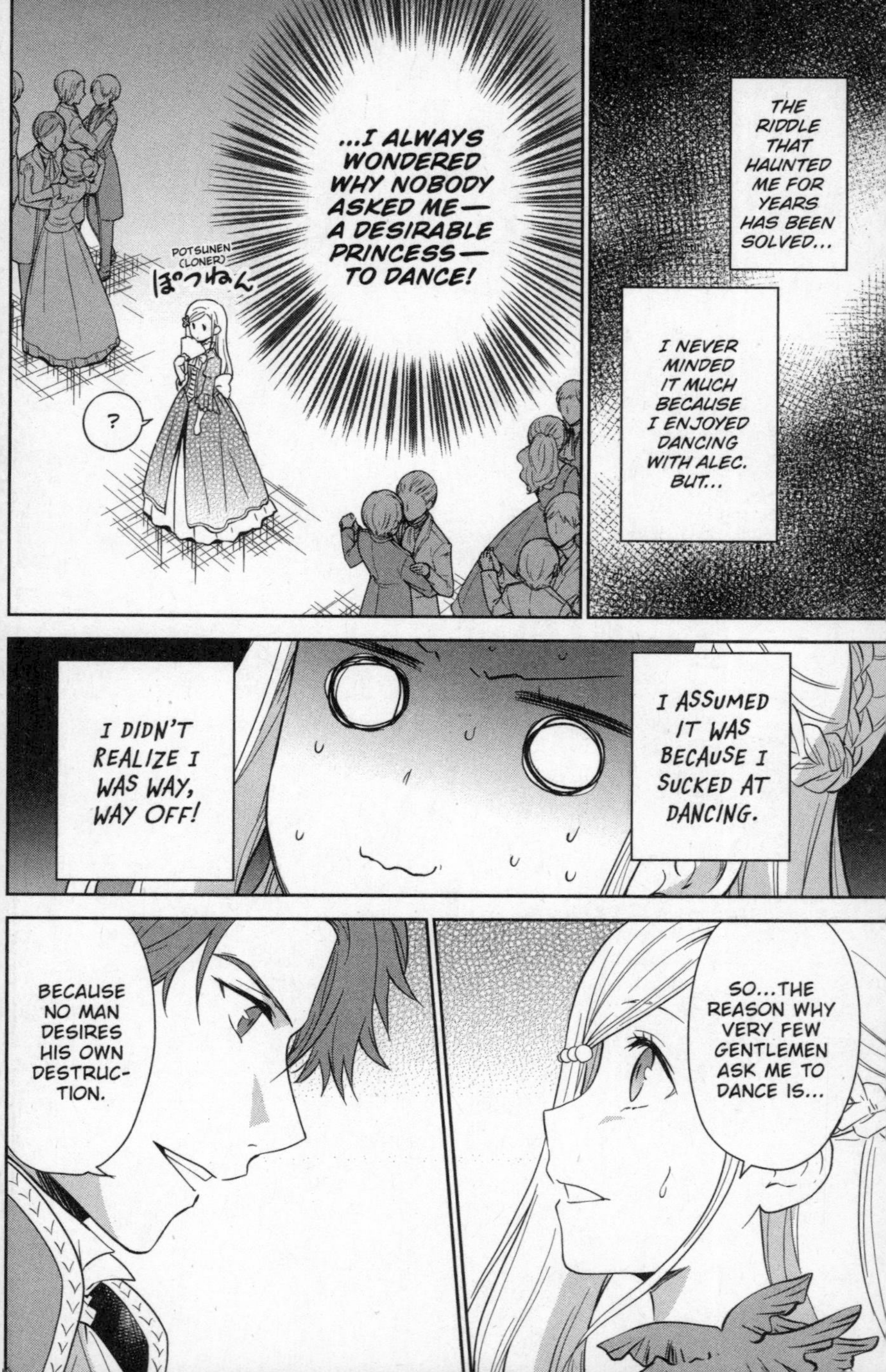
THE RIDDLE THAT HAUNTED ME FOR YEARS HAS BEEN SOLVED...
I NEVER MINDED IT MUCH BECAUSE I ENJOYED DANCING WITH ALEC. BUT...
...I ALWAYS WONDERED WHY NOBODY ASKED ME—A DESIRABLE PRINCESS—TO DANCE!
ぽつねん
POTSUNEN (LONER)
?
I ASSUMED IT WAS BECAUSE I SUCKED AT DANCING.
I DIDN'T REALIZE I WAS WAY, WAY OFF!
SO...THE REASON WHY VERY FEW GENTLEMEN ASK ME TO DANCE IS...
BECAUSE NO MAN DESIRES HIS OWN DESTRUC-TION.

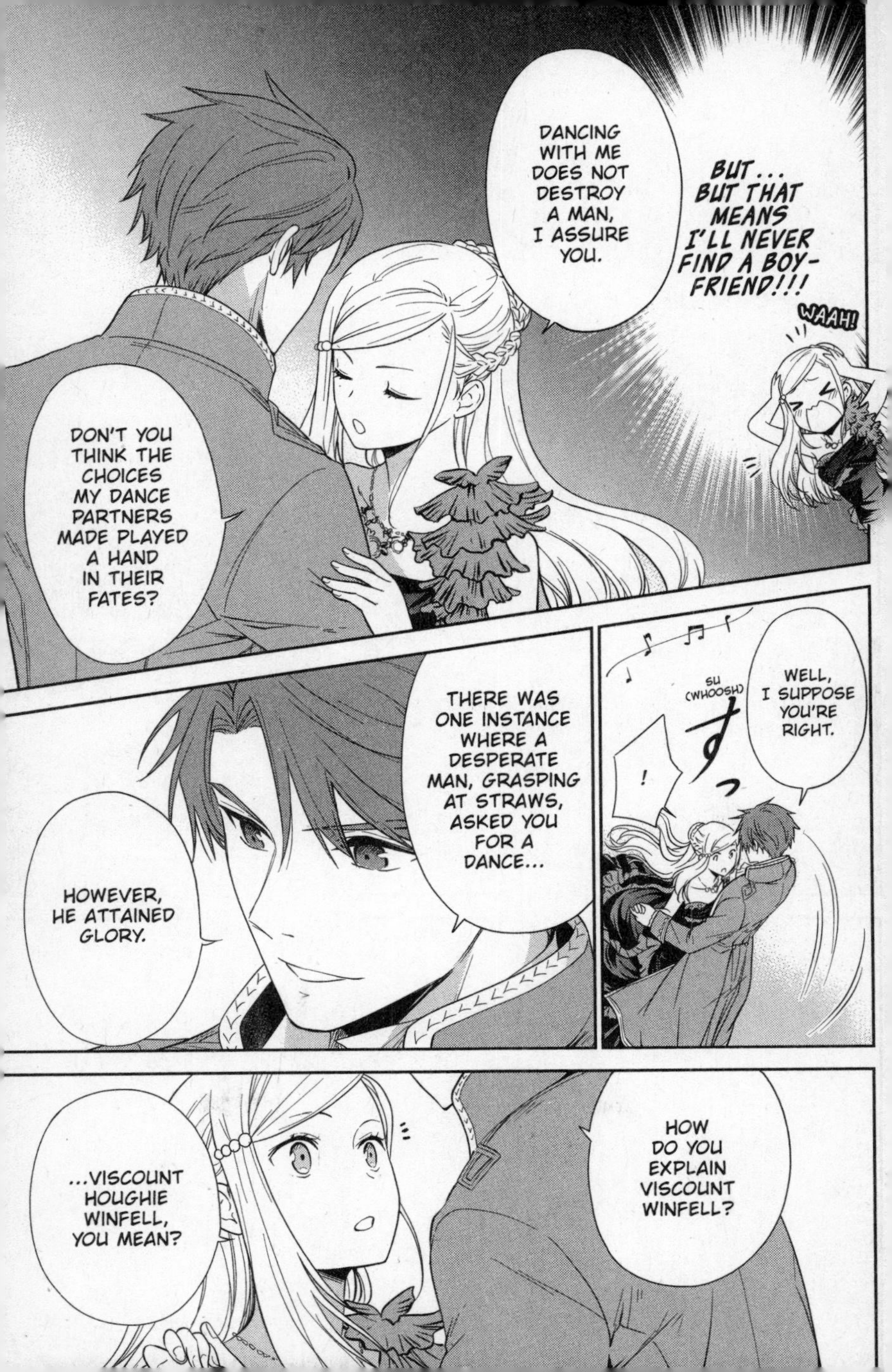
DON'T YOU THINK THE CHOICES MY DANCE PARTNERS MADE PLAYED A HAND IN THEIR FATES?
DANCING WITH ME DOES NOT DESTROY A MAN, I ASSURE YOU.
BUT ... BUT THAT MEANS I'LL NEVER FIND A BOY-FRIEND!!!
WAAH!
WELL, I SUPPOSE YOU'RE RIGHT.
SU (WHOOSH)
!
THERE WAS ONE INSTANCE WHERE A DESPERATE MAN, GRASPING AT STRAWS, ASKED YOU FOR A DANCE...
HOWEVER, HE ATTAINED GLORY.
HOW DO YOU EXPLAIN VISCOUNT WINFELL?
...VISCOUNT HOUGHIE WINFELL, YOU MEAN?

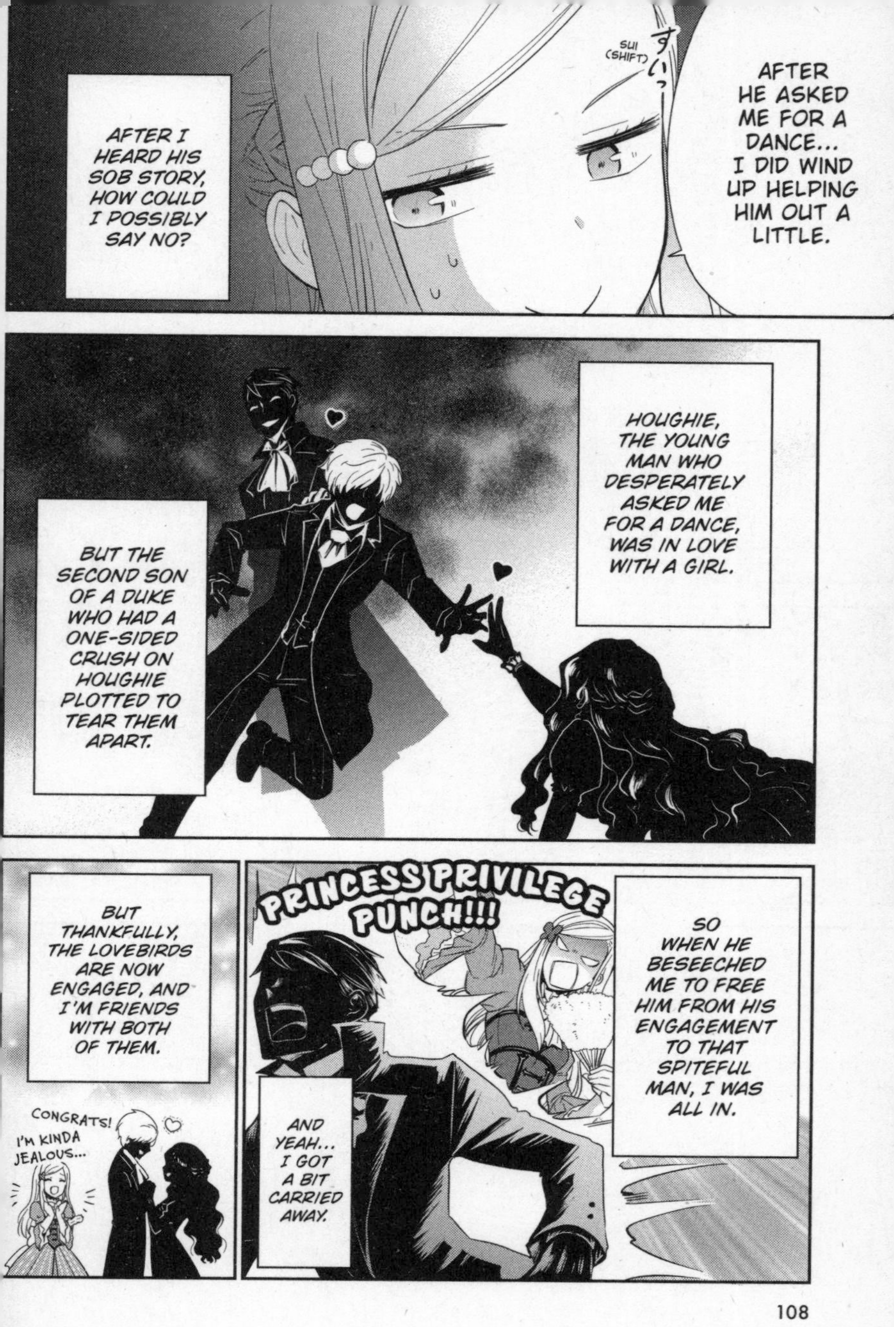
AFTER HE ASKED ME FOR A DANCE... I DID WIND UP HELPING HIM OUT A LITTLE.
SUI (SHIFT)
AFTER I HEARD HIS SOB STORY, HOW COULD I POSSIBLY SAY NO?
HOUGHIE, THE YOUNG MAN WHO DESPERATELY ASKED ME FOR A DANCE, WAS IN LOVE WITH A GIRL.
BUT THE SECOND SON OF A DUKE WHO HAD A ONE-SIDED CRUSH ON HOUGHIE PLOTTED TO TEAR THEM APART.
SO WHEN HE BESEECHED ME TO FREE HIM FROM HIS ENGAGEMENT TO THAT SPITEFUL MAN, I WAS ALL IN.
PRINCESS PRIVILEGE PUNCH!!!
AND YEAH... I GOT A BIT CARRIED AWAY.
BUT THANKFULLY, THE LOVEBIRDS ARE NOW ENGAGED, AND I'M FRIENDS WITH BOTH OF THEM.
CONGRATS!
I'M KINDA JEALOUS...

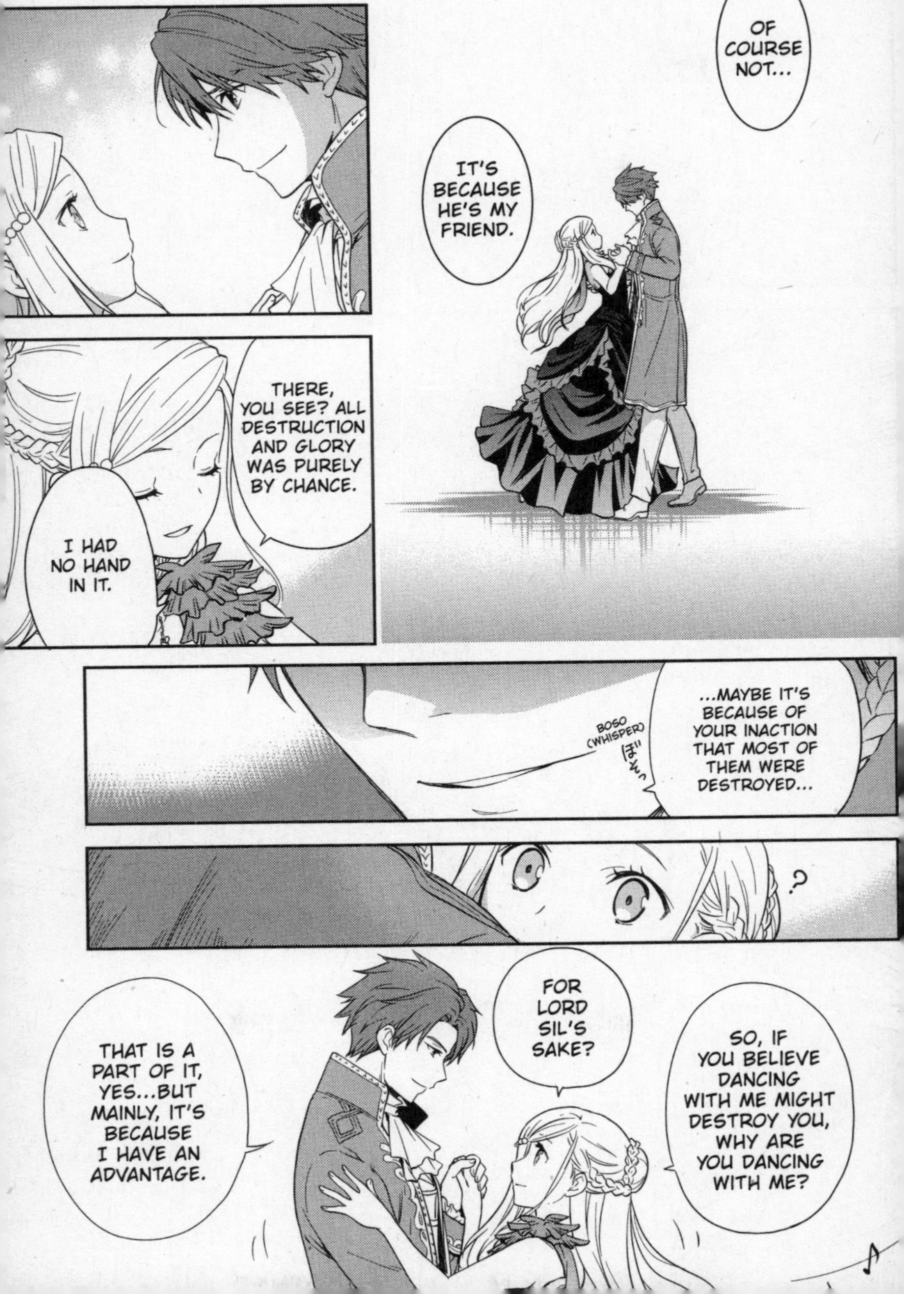
OF COURSE NOT...
IT'S BECAUSE HE'S MY FRIEND.
THERE, YOU SEE? ALL DESTRUCTION AND GLORY WAS PURELY BY CHANCE.
I HAD NO HAND IN IT.
...MAYBE IT'S BECAUSE OF YOUR INACTION THAT MOST OF THEM WERE DESTROYED...
BOSO (WHISPER)
ぼそっ
?
SO, IF YOU BELIEVE DANCING WITH ME MIGHT DESTROY YOU, WHY ARE YOU DANCING WITH ME?
FOR LORD SIL'S SAKE?
THAT IS A PART OF IT, YES...BUT MAINLY, IT'S BECAUSE I HAVE AN ADVANTAGE.

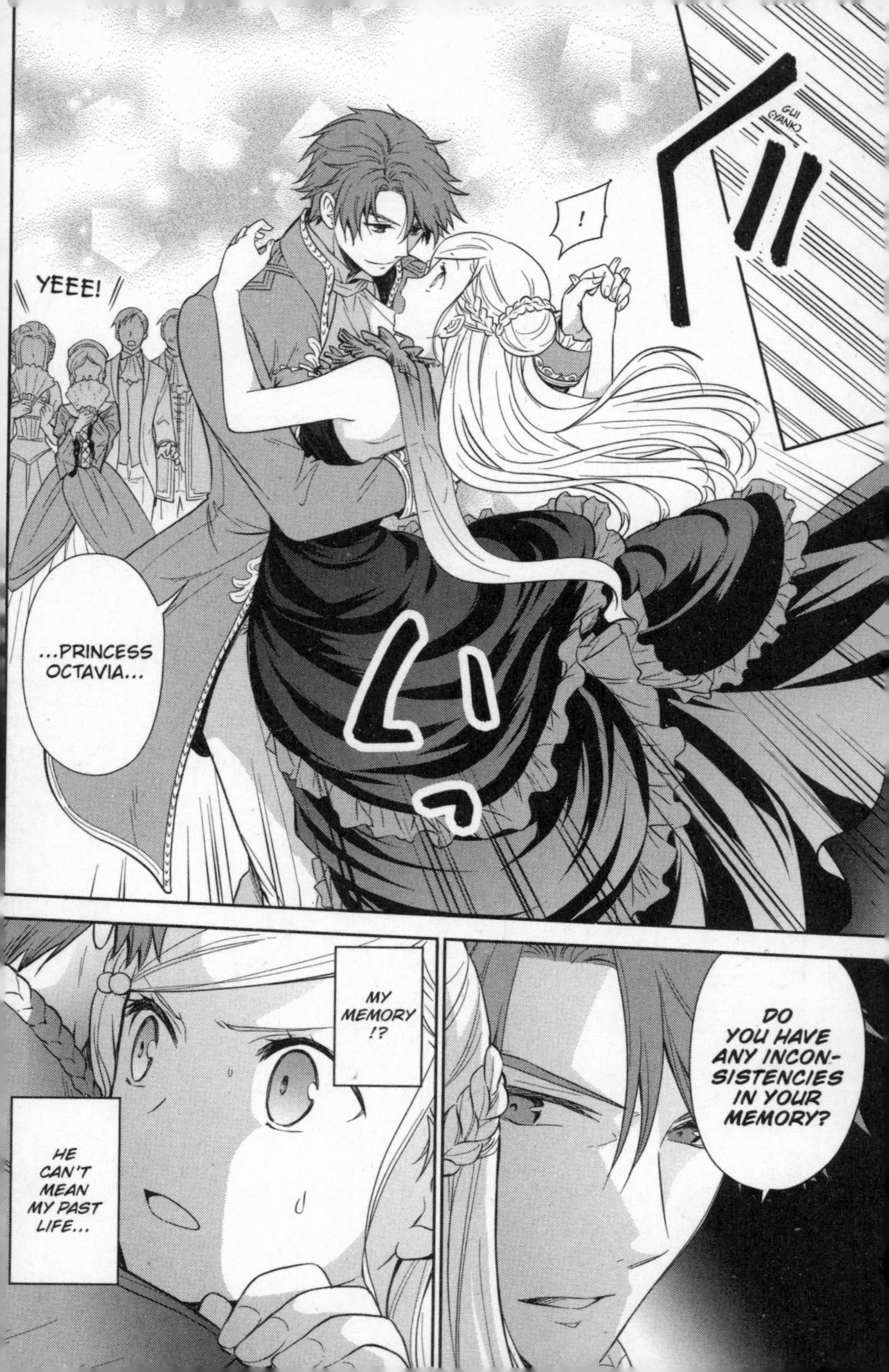
GUI (YANK)
!
YEEE!
...PRINCESS OCTAVIA...
DO YOU HAVE ANY INCONSISTENCIES IN YOUR MEMORY?
MY MEMORY!?
HE CAN'T MEAN MY PAST LIFE...

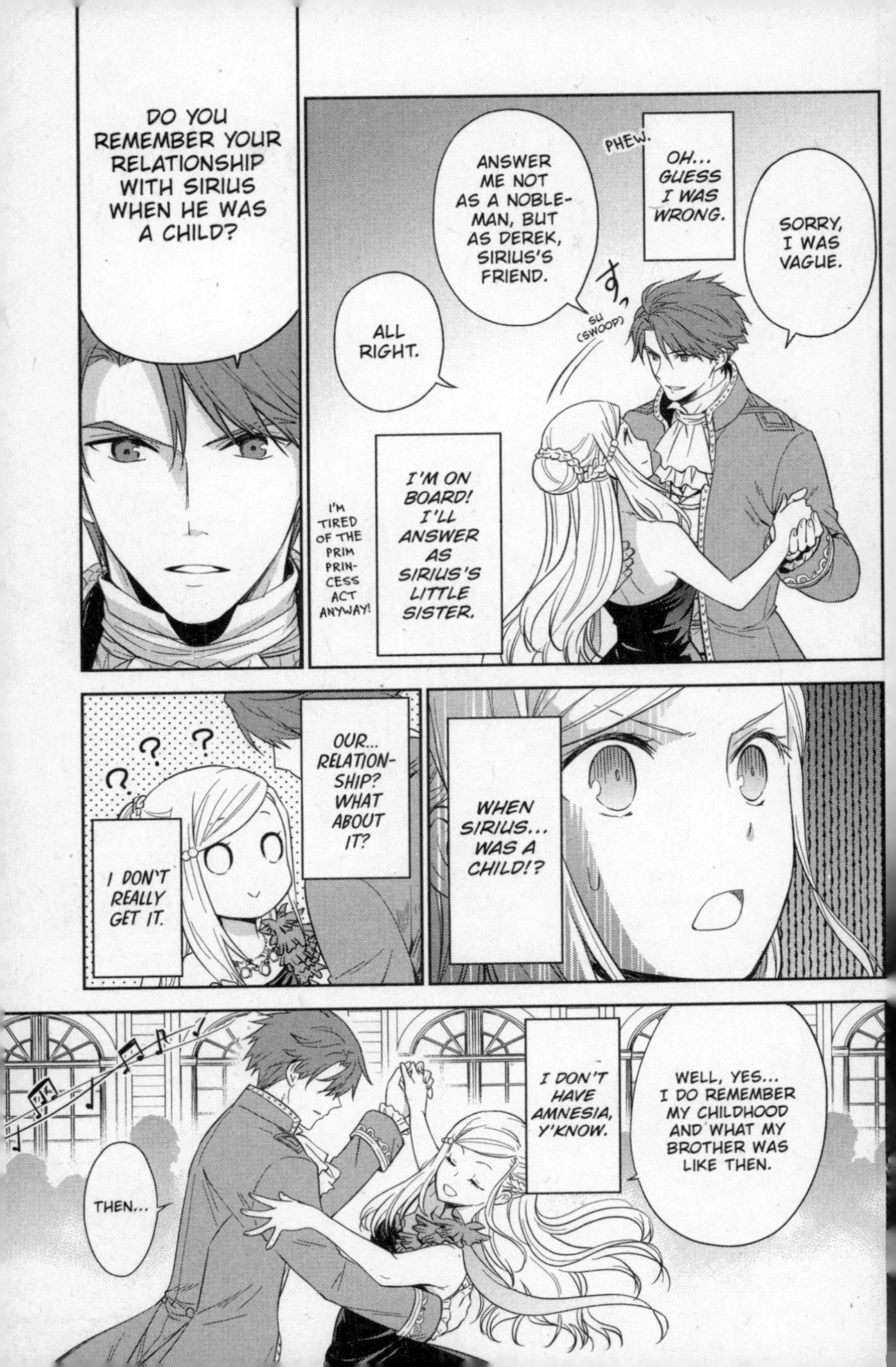
SORRY, I WAS VAGUE.
OH... GUESS I WAS WRONG.
PHEW.
ANSWER ME NOT AS A NOBLEMAN, BUT AS DEREK, SIRIUS'S FRIEND.
す
SU (SWOOP)
ALL RIGHT.
I'M ON BOARD! I'LL ANSWER AS SIRIUS'S LITTLE SISTER.
I'M TIRED OF THE PRIM PRINCESS ACT ANYWAY!
DO YOU REMEMBER YOUR RELATIONSHIP WITH SIRIUS WHEN HE WAS A CHILD?
WHEN SIRIUS... WAS A CHILD!?
OUR... RELATIONSHIP? WHAT ABOUT IT?
I DON'T REALLY GET IT.
WELL, YES... I DO REMEMBER MY CHILDHOOD AND WHAT MY BROTHER WAS LIKE THEN.
I DON'T HAVE AMNESIA, Y'KNOW.
THEN...

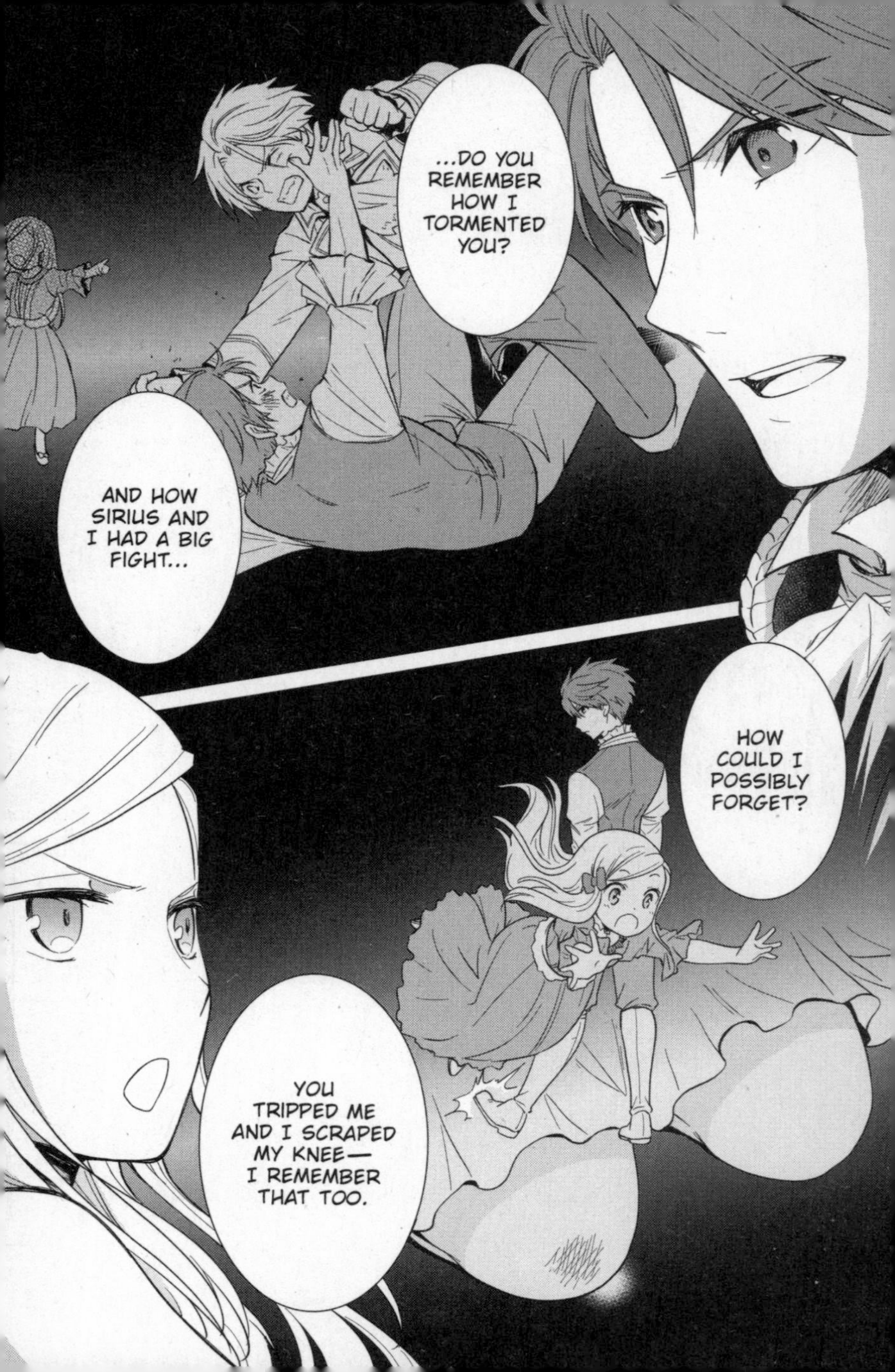
...DO YOU REMEMBER HOW I TORMENTED YOU?
AND HOW SIRIUS AND I HAD A BIG FIGHT...
HOW COULD I POSSIBLY FORGET?
YOU TRIPPED ME AND I SCRAPED MY KNEE— I REMEMBER THAT TOO.

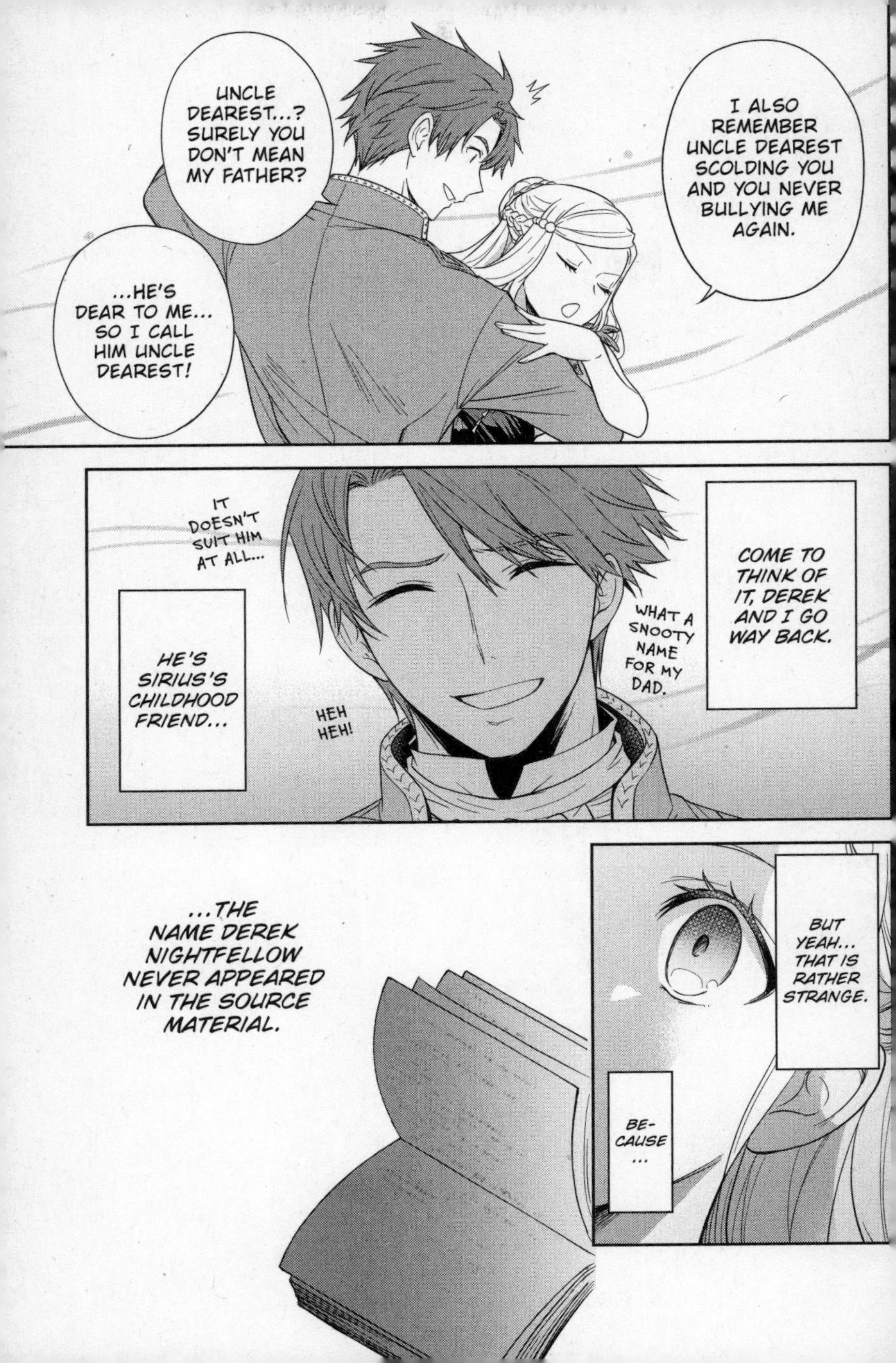

I ALSO REMEMBER UNCLE DEAREST SCOLDING YOU AND YOU NEVER BULLYING ME AGAIN.
UNCLE DEAREST...? SURELY YOU DON'T MEAN MY FATHER?
...HE'S DEAR TO ME... SO I CALL HIM UNCLE DEAREST!
COME TO THINK OF IT, DEREK AND I GO WAY BACK.
WHAT A SNOOTY NAME FOR MY DAD.
IT DOESN'T SUIT HIM AT ALL...
HEH HEH!
HE'S SIRIUS'S CHILDHOOD FRIEND...
BUT YEAH... THAT IS RATHER STRANGE.
BE-CAUSE ...
...THE NAME DEREK NIGHTFELLOW NEVER APPEARED IN THE SOURCE MATERIAL.

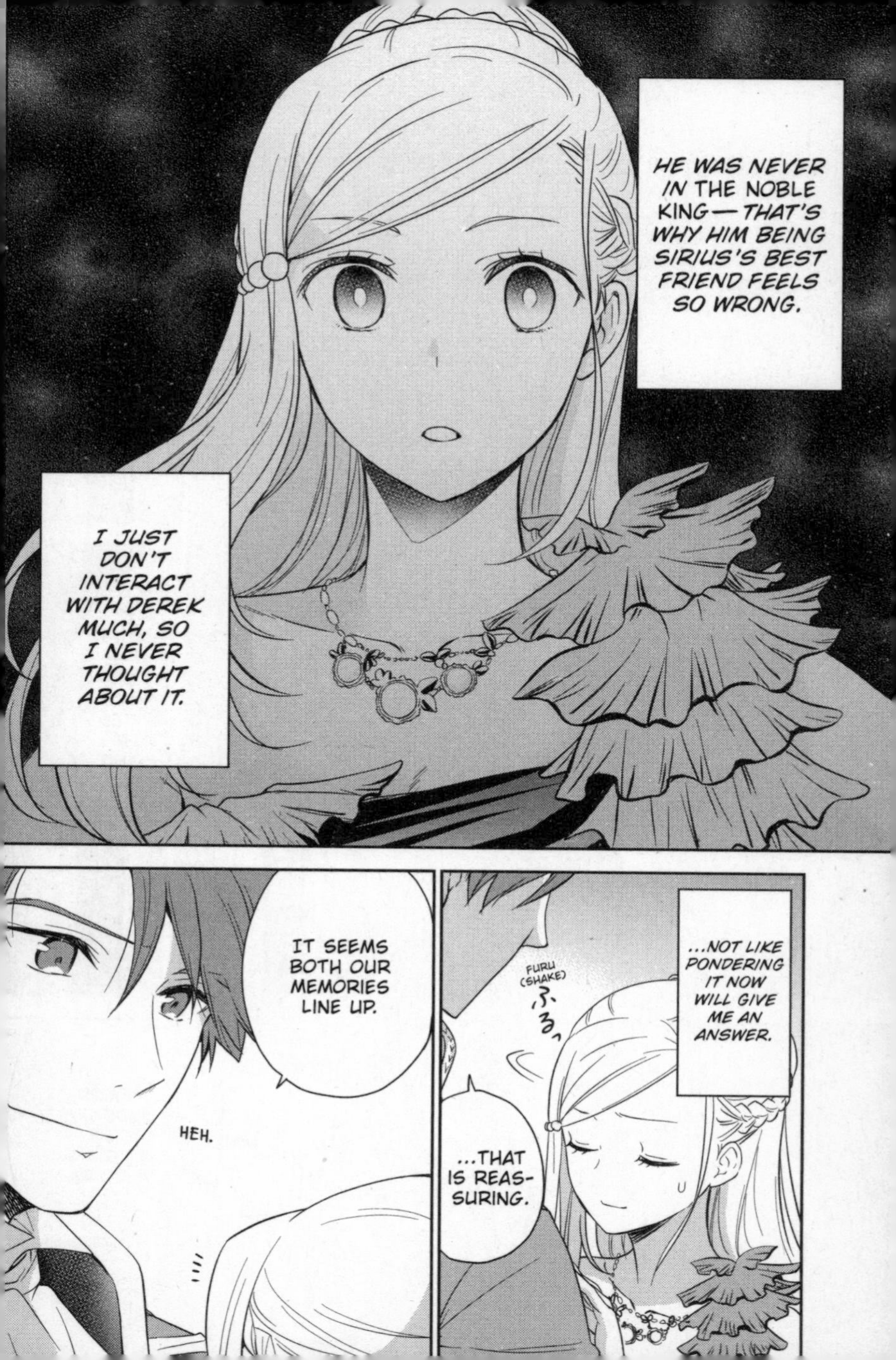
HE WAS NEVER IN THE NOBLE KING—THAT'S WHY HIM BEING SIRIUS'S BEST FRIEND FEELS SO WRONG.
I JUST DON'T INTERACT WITH DEREK MUCH, SO I NEVER THOUGHT ABOUT IT.
...NOT LIKE PONDERING IT NOW WILL GIVE ME AN ANSWER.
FURU (SHAKE)
ふる
...THAT IS REAS-SURING.
IT SEEMS BOTH OUR MEMORIES LINE UP.
HEH.

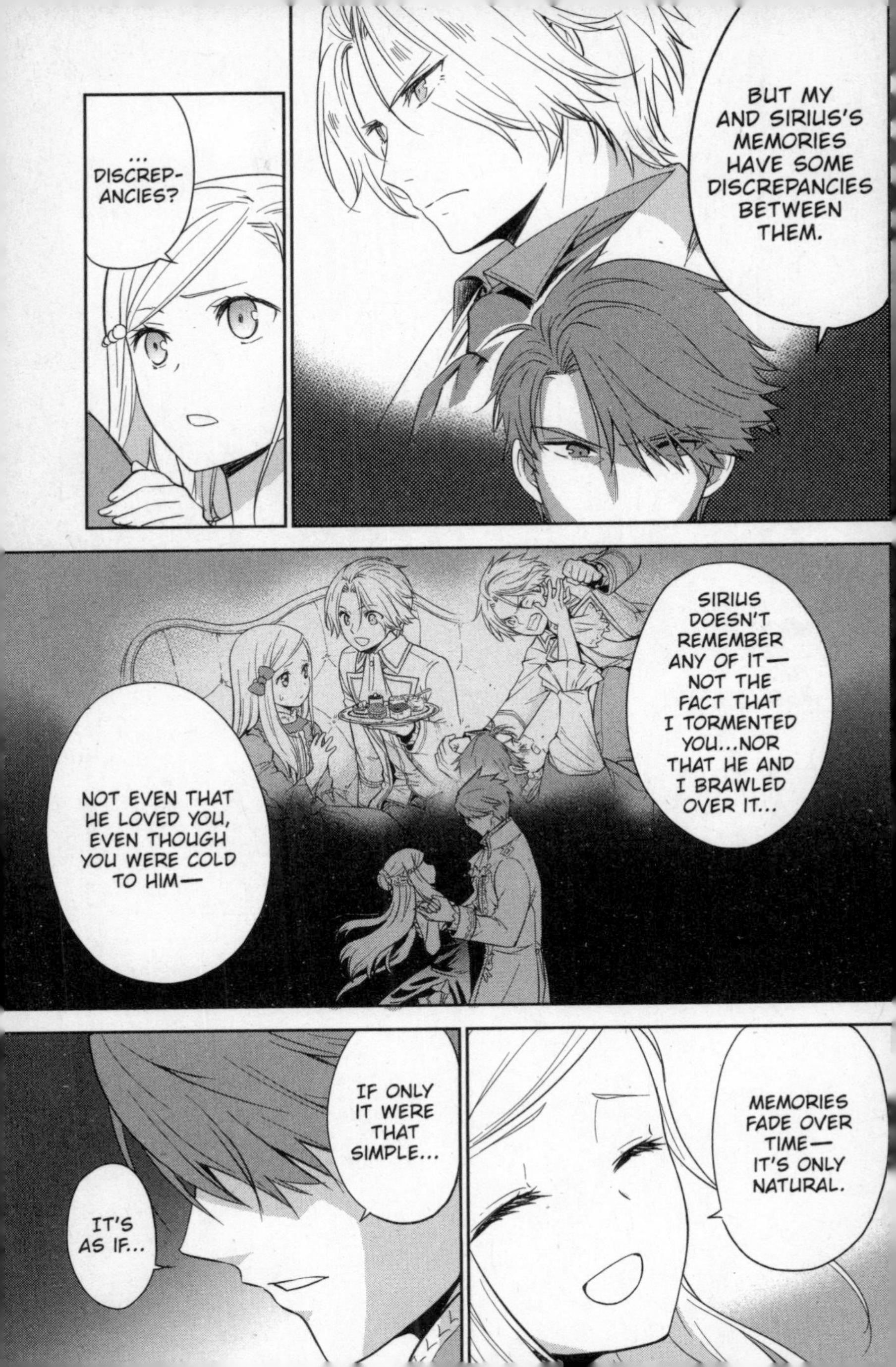
BUT MY AND SIRIUS'S MEMORIES HAVE SOME DISCREPANCIES BETWEEN THEM.
...DISCREP-ANCIES?
SIRIUS DOESN'T REMEMBER ANY OF IT— NOT THE FACT THAT I TORMENTED YOU...NOR THAT HE AND I BRAWLED OVER IT...
NOT EVEN THAT HE LOVED YOU, EVEN THOUGH YOU WERE COLD TO HIM—
MEMORIES FADE OVER TIME— IT'S ONLY NATURAL.
IF ONLY IT WERE THAT SIMPLE...
IT'S AS IF...

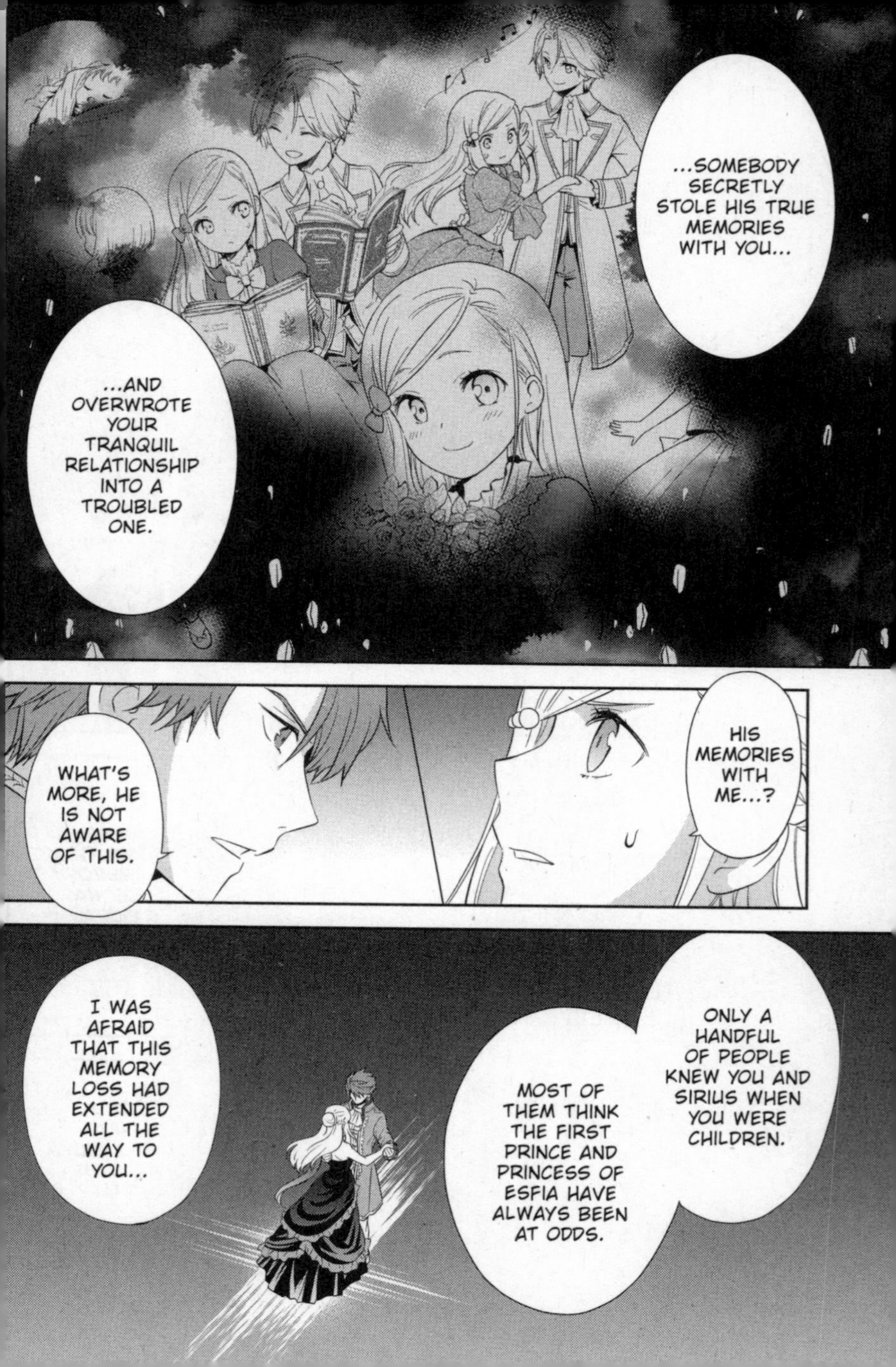
...SOMEBODY SECRETLY STOLE HIS TRUE MEMORIES WITH YOU...
...AND OVERWROTE YOUR TRANQUIL RELATIONSHIP INTO A TROUBLED ONE.
HIS MEMORIES WITH ME...?
WHAT'S MORE, HE IS NOT AWARE OF THIS.
ONLY A HANDFUL OF PEOPLE KNEW YOU AND SIRIUS WHEN YOU WERE CHILDREN.
MOST OF THEM THINK THE FIRST PRINCE AND PRINCESS OF ESFIA HAVE ALWAYS BEEN AT ODDS.
I WAS AFRAID THAT THIS MEMORY LOSS HAD EXTENDED ALL THE WAY TO YOU...

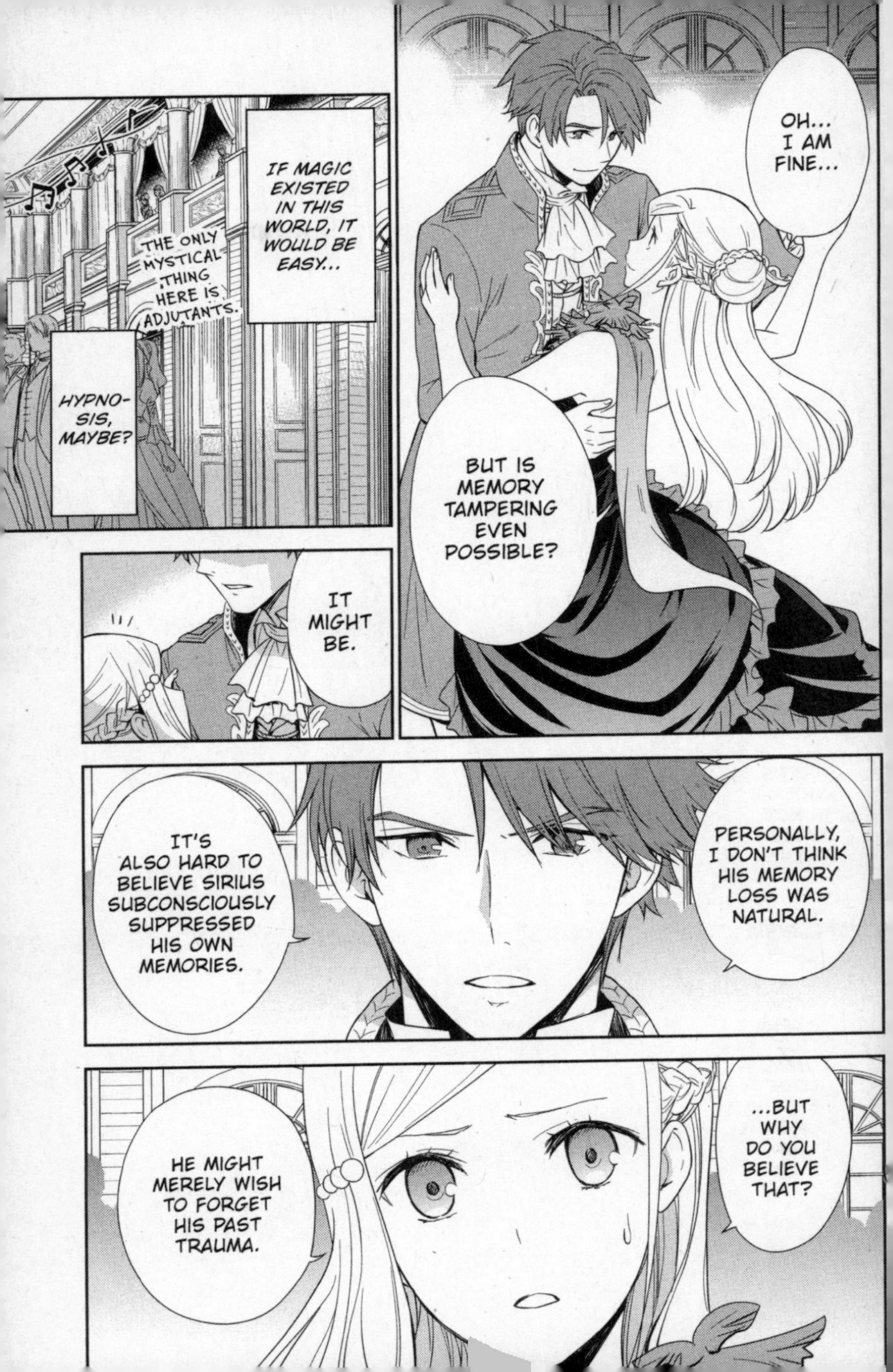
OH... I AM FINE...
BUT IS MEMORY TAMPERING EVEN POSSIBLE?
IF MAGIC EXISTED IN THIS WORLD, IT WOULD BE EASY...
THE ONLY MYSTICAL THING HERE IS ADJUTANTS.
HYPNOSIS, MAYBE?
IT MIGHT BE.
PERSONALLY, I DON'T THINK HIS MEMORY LOSS WAS NATURAL.
IT'S ALSO HARD TO BELIEVE SIRIUS SUBCONSCIOUSLY SUPPRESSED HIS OWN MEMORIES.
...BUT WHY DO YOU BELIEVE THAT?
HE MIGHT MERELY WISH TO FORGET HIS PAST TRAUMA.

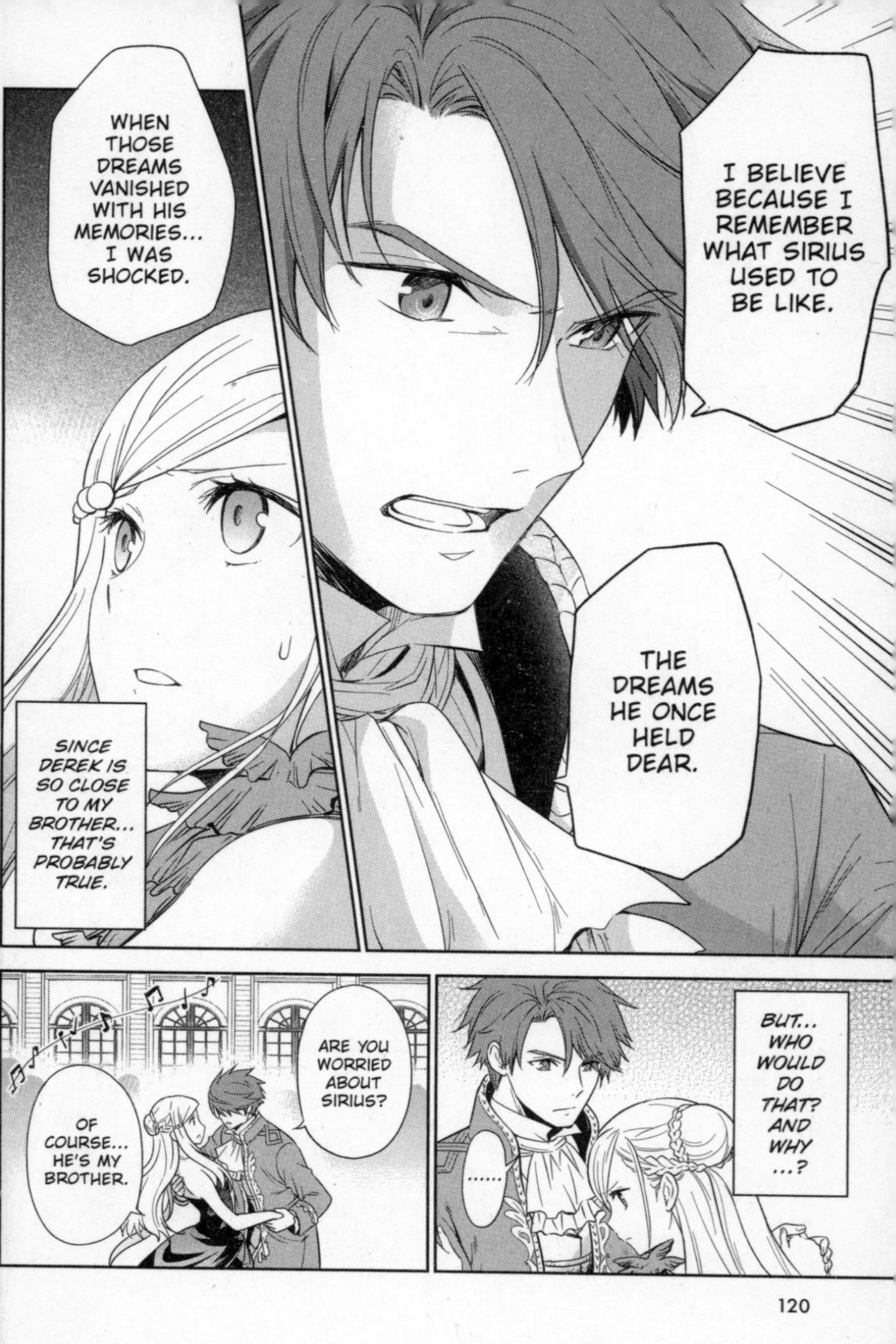
I BELIEVE BECAUSE I REMEMBER WHAT SIRIUS USED TO BE LIKE.
THE DREAMS HE ONCE HELD DEAR.
WHEN THOSE DREAMS VANISHED WITH HIS MEMORIES... I WAS SHOCKED.
SINCE DEREK IS SO CLOSE TO MY BROTHER... THAT'S PROBABLY TRUE.
BUT... WHO WOULD DO THAT? AND WHY ...?
......
ARE YOU WORRIED ABOUT SIRIUS?
OF COURSE... HE'S MY BROTHER.

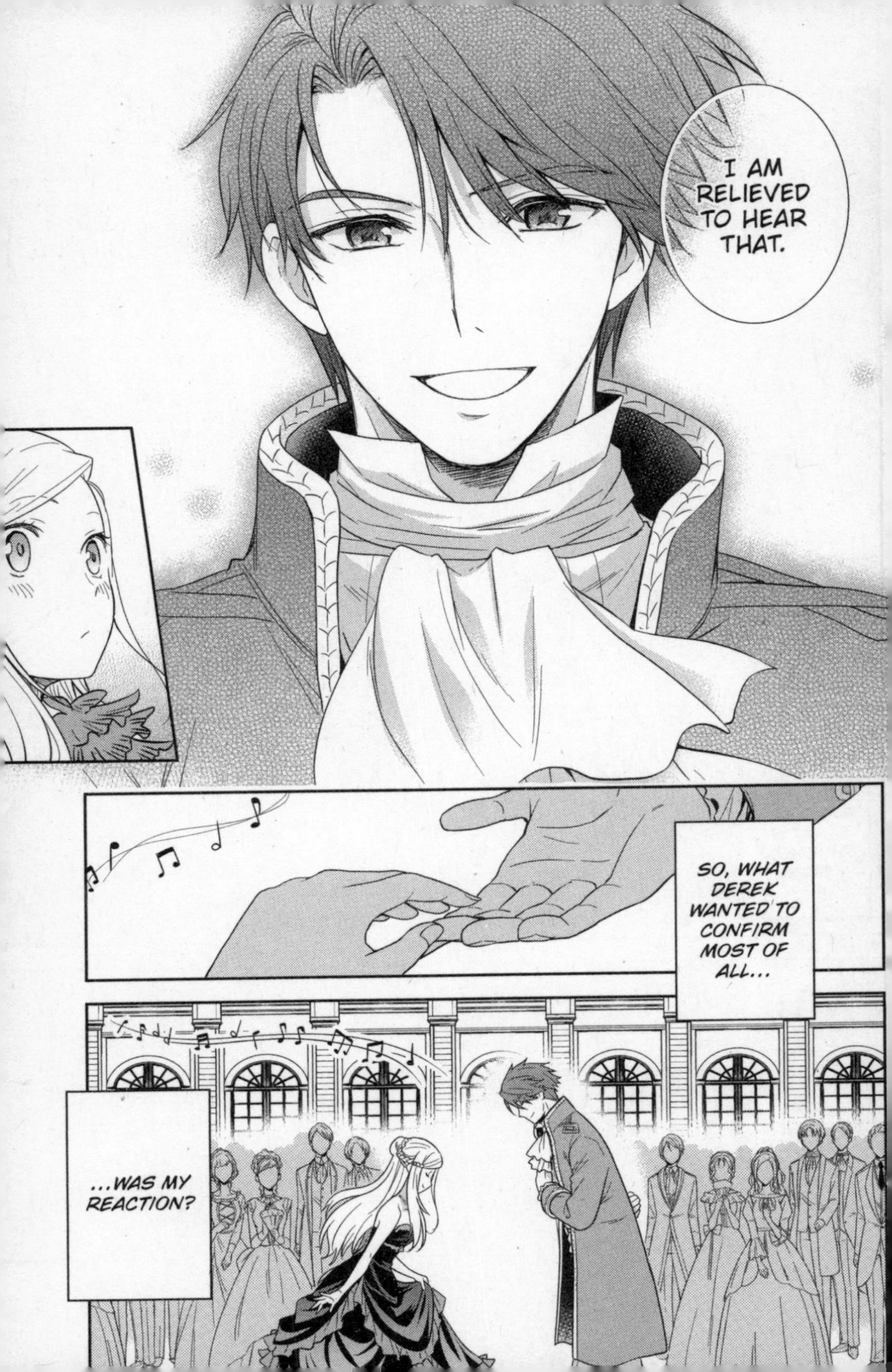
I AM RELIEVED TO HEAR THAT.
SO, WHAT DEREK WANTED TO CONFIRM MOST OF ALL...
...WAS MY REACTION?

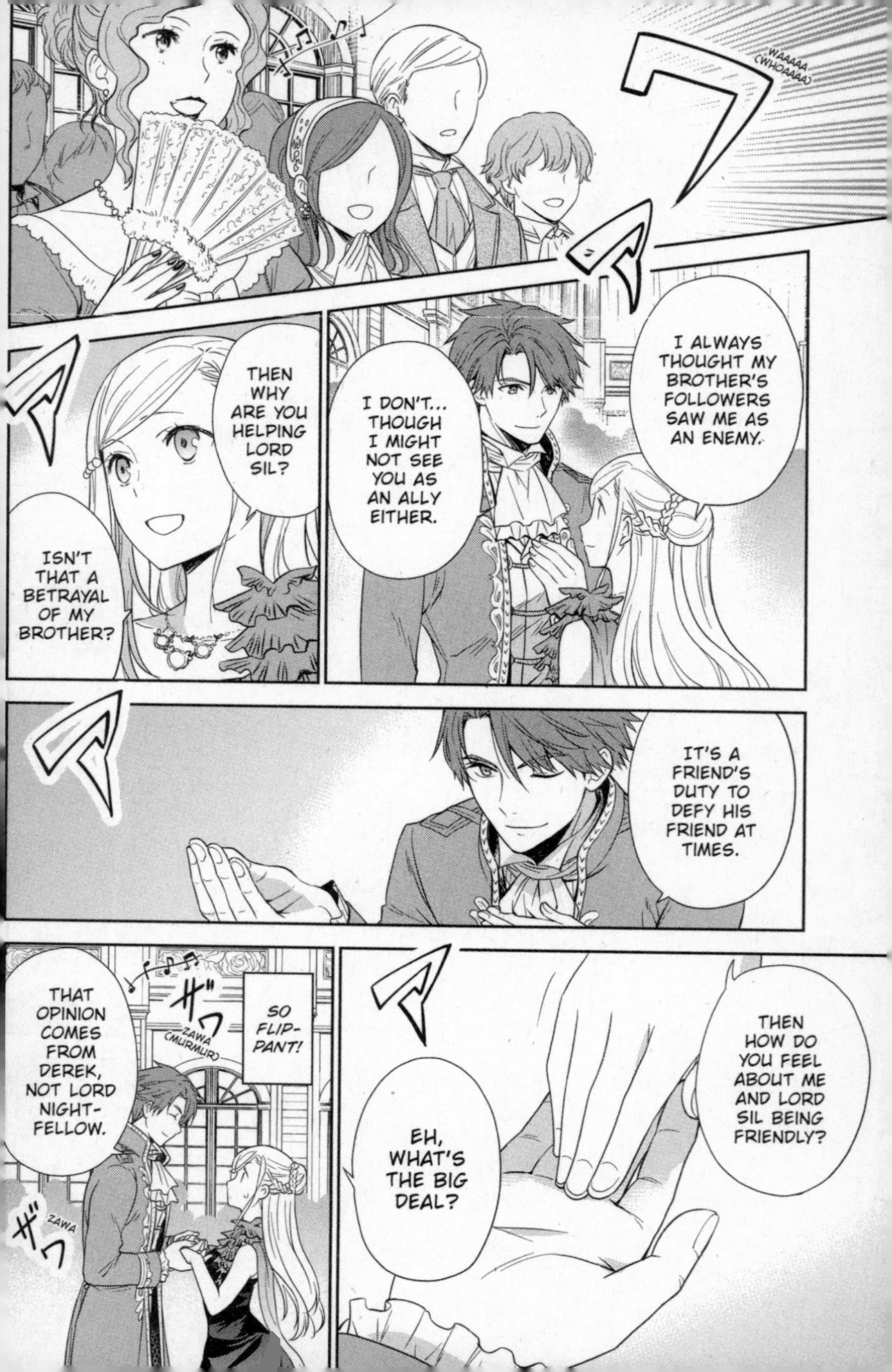
WAAAAA (WHOAAAA)
I ALWAYS THOUGHT MY BROTHER'S FOLLOWERS SAW ME AS AN ENEMY.
I DON'T... THOUGH I MIGHT NOT SEE YOU AS AN ALLY EITHER.
THEN WHY ARE YOU HELPING LORD SIL?
ISN'T THAT A BETRAYAL OF MY BROTHER?
IT'S A FRIEND'S DUTY TO DEFY HIS FRIEND AT TIMES.
THEN HOW DO YOU FEEL ABOUT ME AND LORD SIL BEING FRIENDLY?
EH, WHAT'S THE BIG DEAL?
SO FLIP-PANT!
ZAWA (MURMUR)
THAT OPINION COMES FROM DEREK, NOT LORD NIGHT-FELLOW.
ZAWA

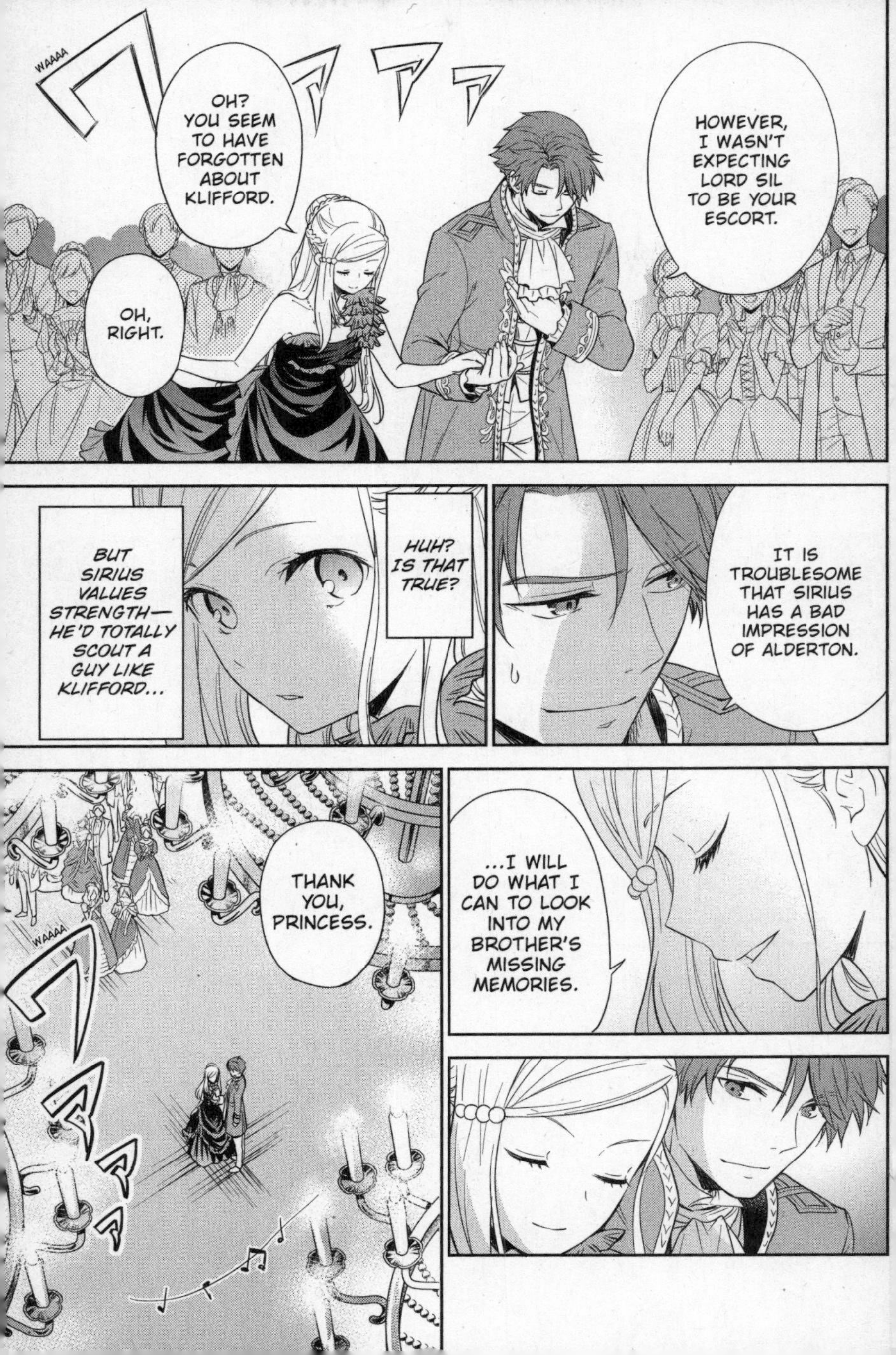
HOWEVER, I WASN'T EXPECTING LORD SIL TO BE YOUR ESCORT.
WAAAA
OH? YOU SEEM TO HAVE FORGOTTEN ABOUT KLIFFORD.
OH, RIGHT.
IT IS TROUBLESOME THAT SIRIUS HAS A BAD IMPRESSION OF ALDERTON.
HUH? IS THAT TRUE?
BUT SIRIUS VALUES STRENGTH— HE'D TOTALLY SCOUT A GUY LIKE KLIFFORD...
...I WILL DO WHAT I CAN TO LOOK INTO MY BROTHER'S MISSING MEMORIES.
THANK YOU, PRINCESS.
WAAAA

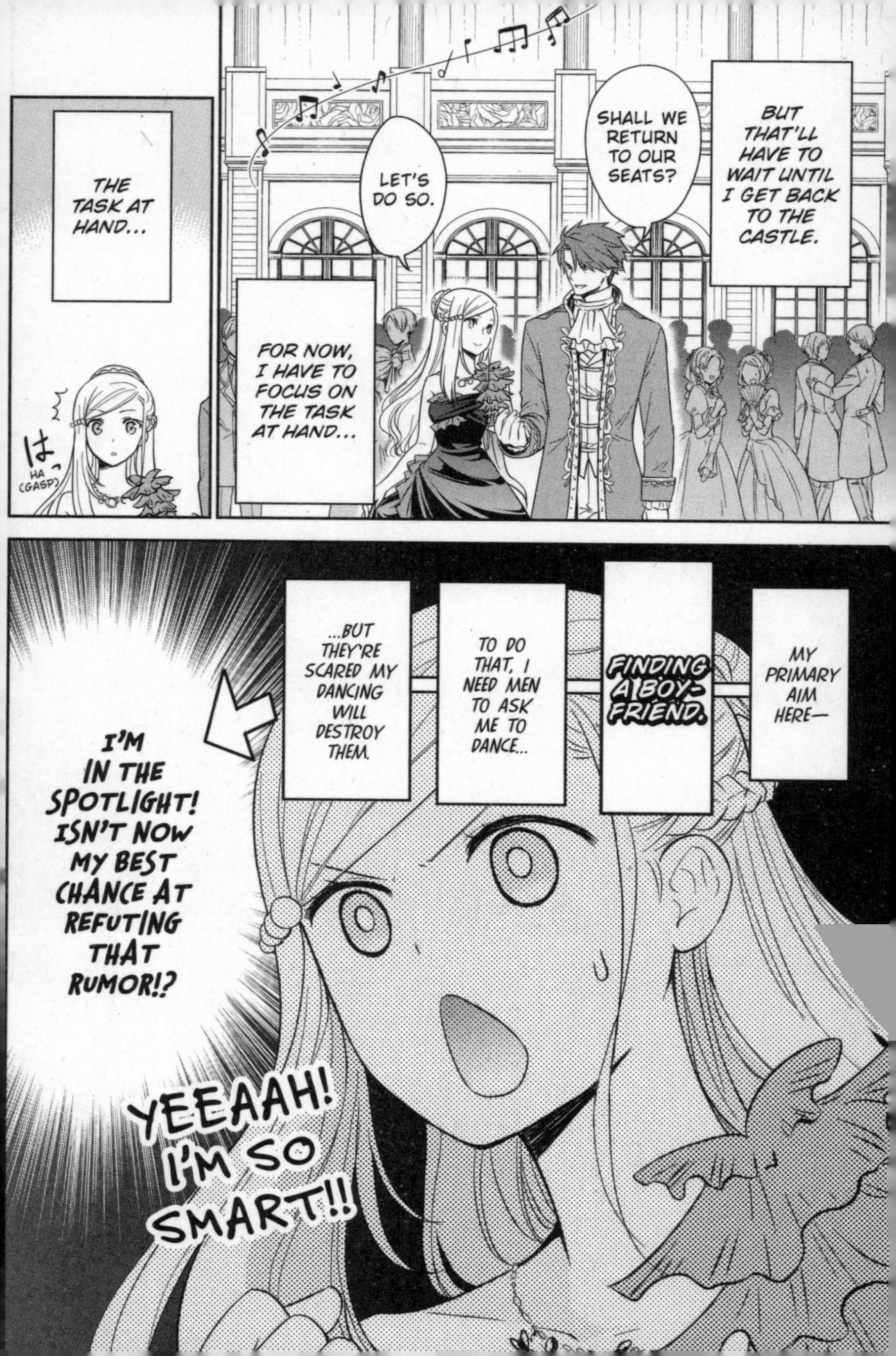

BUT THAT'LL HAVE TO WAIT UNTIL I GET BACK TO THE CASTLE.
SHALL WE RETURN TO OUR SEATS?
LET'S DO SO.
FOR NOW, I HAVE TO FOCUS ON THE TASK AT HAND...
THE TASK AT HAND...
は
HA (GASP)
MY PRIMARY AIM HERE—
FINDING A BOY-FRIEND.
TO DO THAT, I NEED MEN TO ASK ME TO DANCE...
...BUT THEY'RE SCARED MY DANCING WILL DESTROY THEM.
I'M IN THE SPOTLIGHT! ISN'T NOW MY BEST CHANCE AT REFUTING THAT RUMOR!?
YEEAAH! I'M SO SMART!!

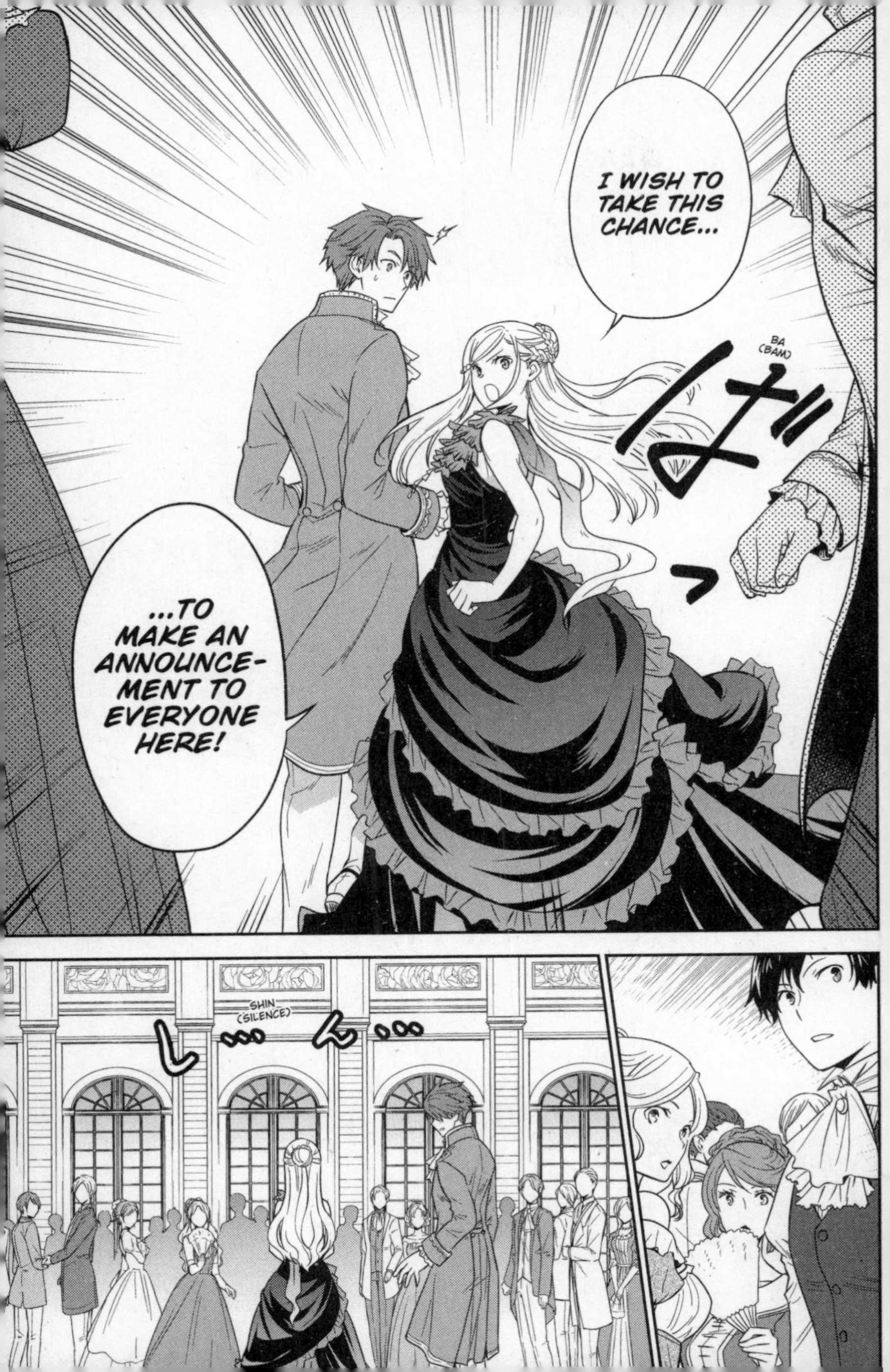

I WISH TO TAKE THIS CHANCE...
BA (BAM)
...TO MAKE AN ANNOUNCE-MENT TO EVERYONE HERE!
SHIN (SILENCE)

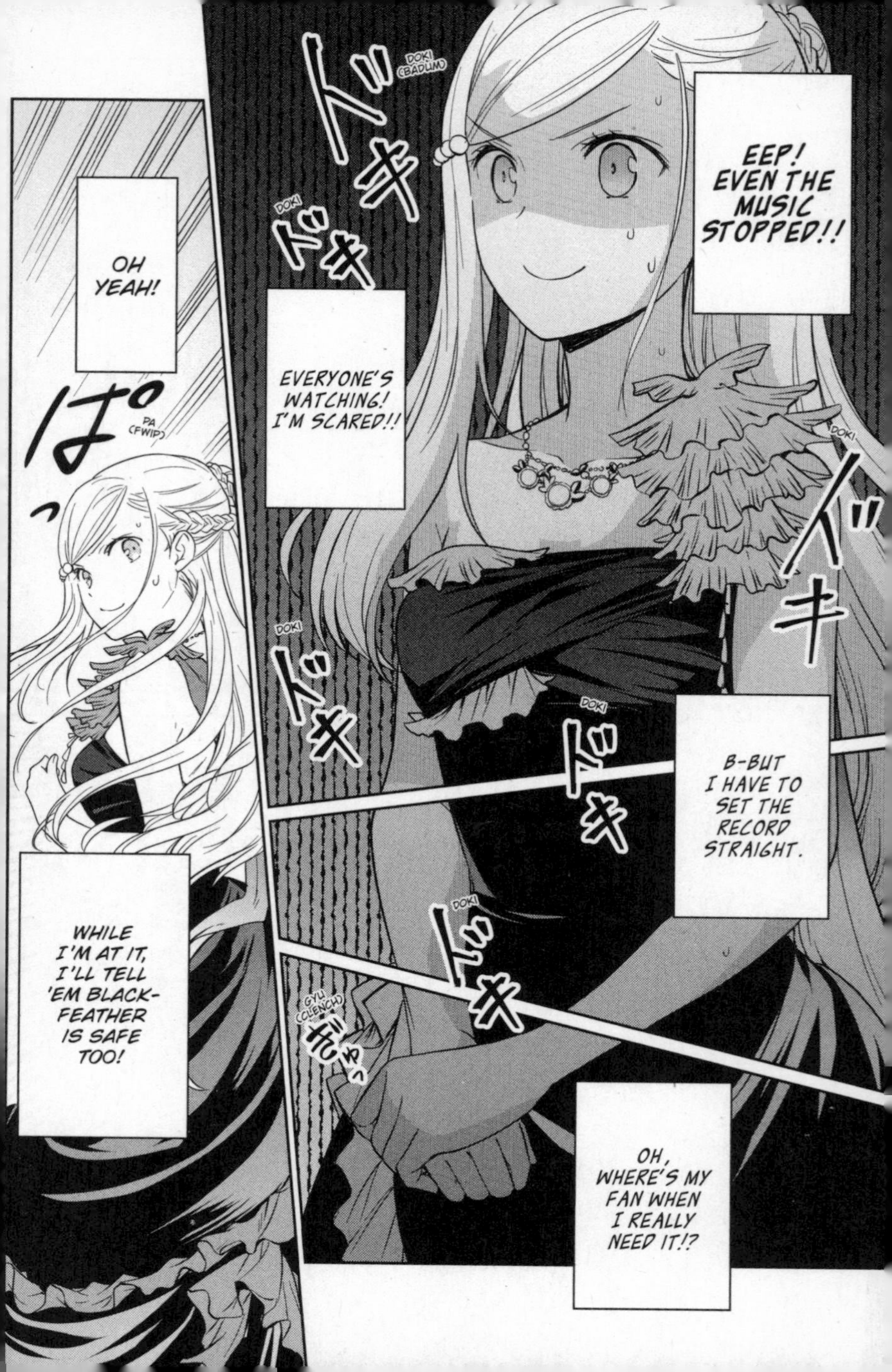
EEP! EVEN THE MUSIC STOPPED!!
ドキ
DOKI (BADUM)
ドキ
DOKI
EVERYONE'S WATCHING! I'M SCARED!!
ドキ
DOKI
ドキ
DOKI
ドキ
DOKI
B-BUT I HAVE TO SET THE RECORD STRAIGHT.
ドキ
DOKI
ぎゅっ
GYU (CLENCH)
OH, WHERE'S MY FAN WHEN I REALLY NEED IT!?
OH YEAH!
ぱっ
PA (FWIP)
WHILE I'M AT IT, I'LL TELL 'EM BLACK-FEATHER IS SAFE TOO!

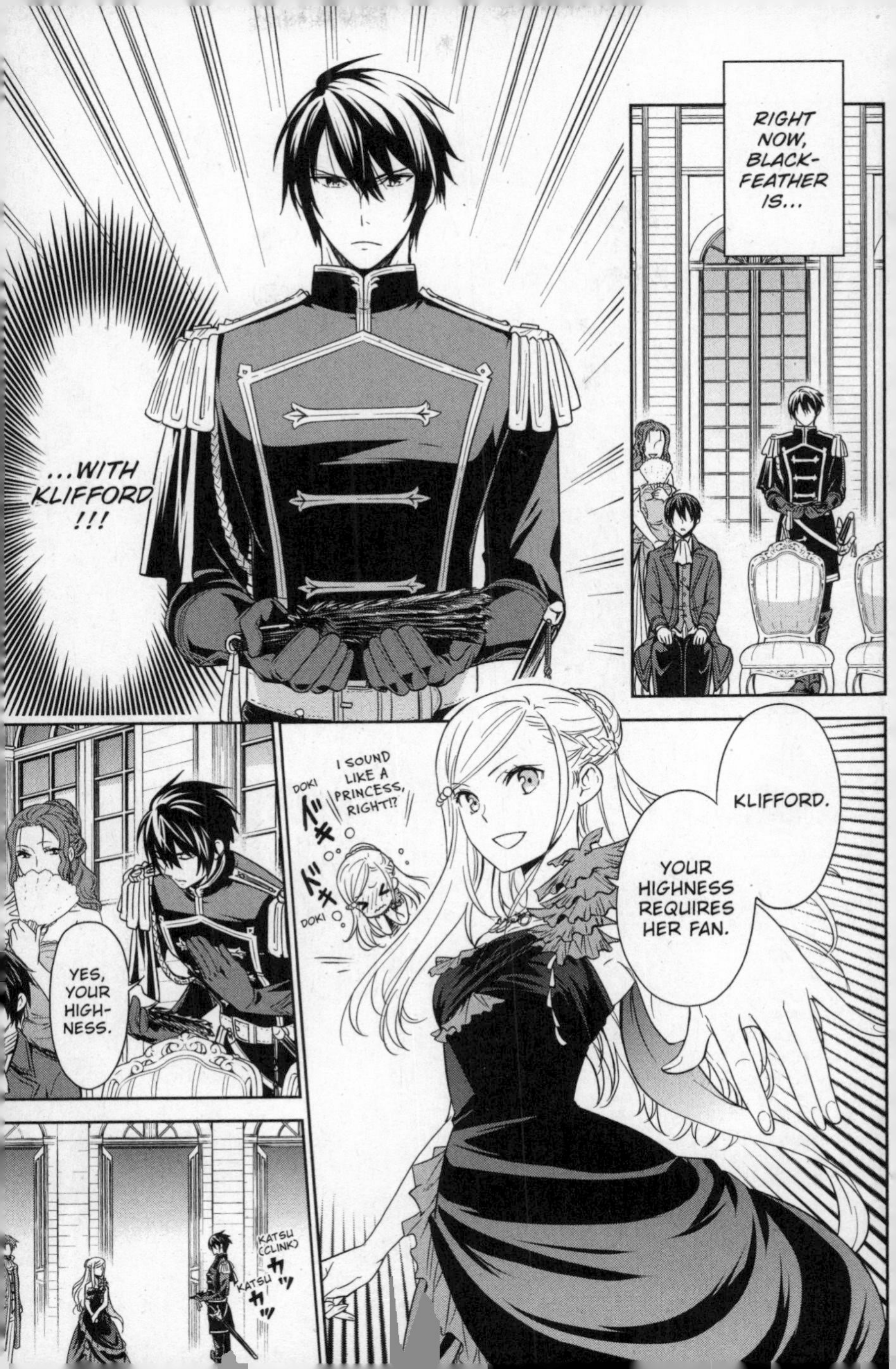

RIGHT NOW, BLACK-FEATHER IS...
...WITH KLIFFORD!!!
KLIFFORD.
YOUR HIGHNESS REQUIRES HER FAN.
I SOUND LIKE A PRINCESS, RIGHT!?
DOKI
DOKI
YES, YOUR HIGH-NESS.
KATSU (CLINK)
KATSU

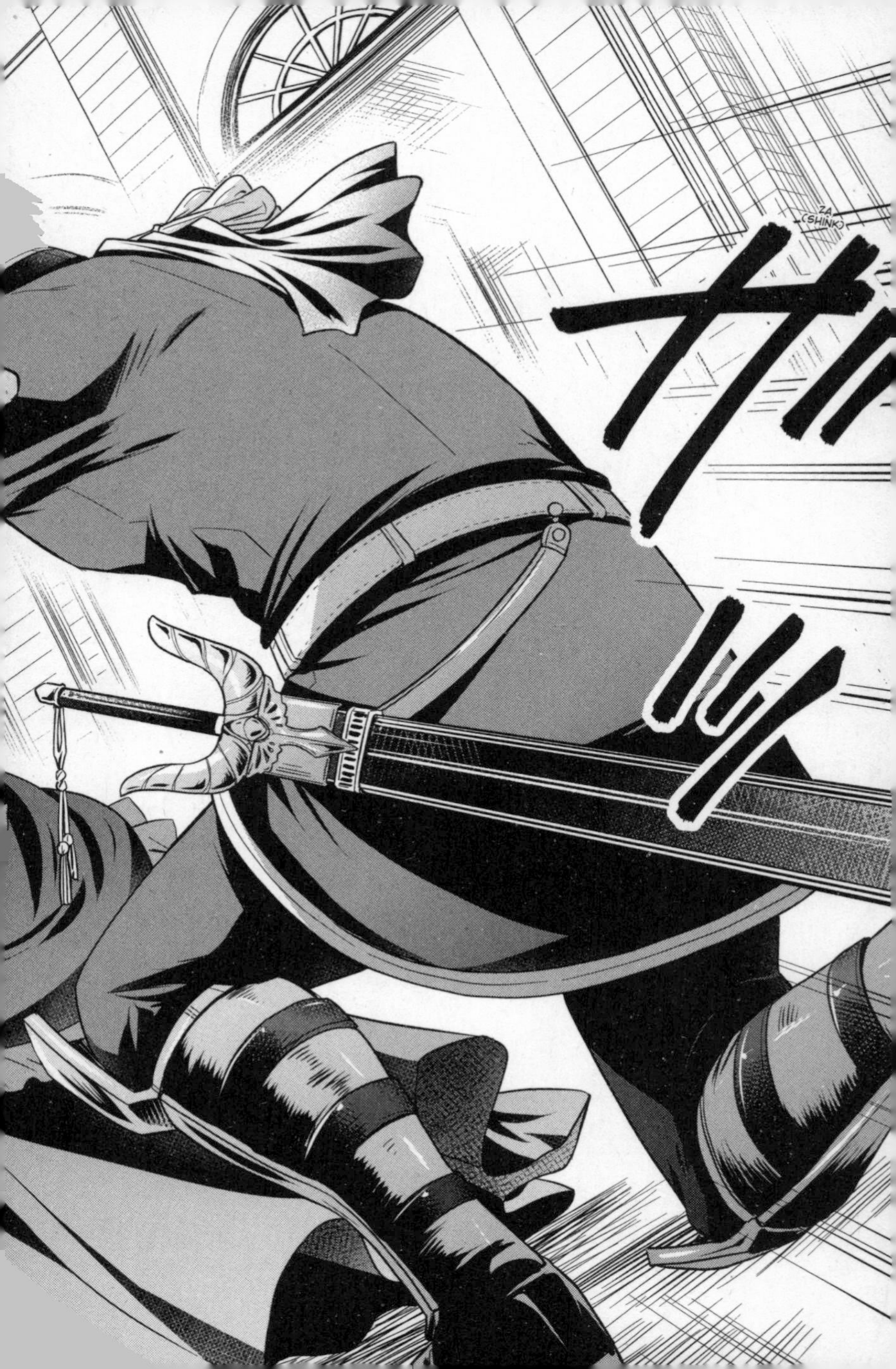
ZA
(SHINK)

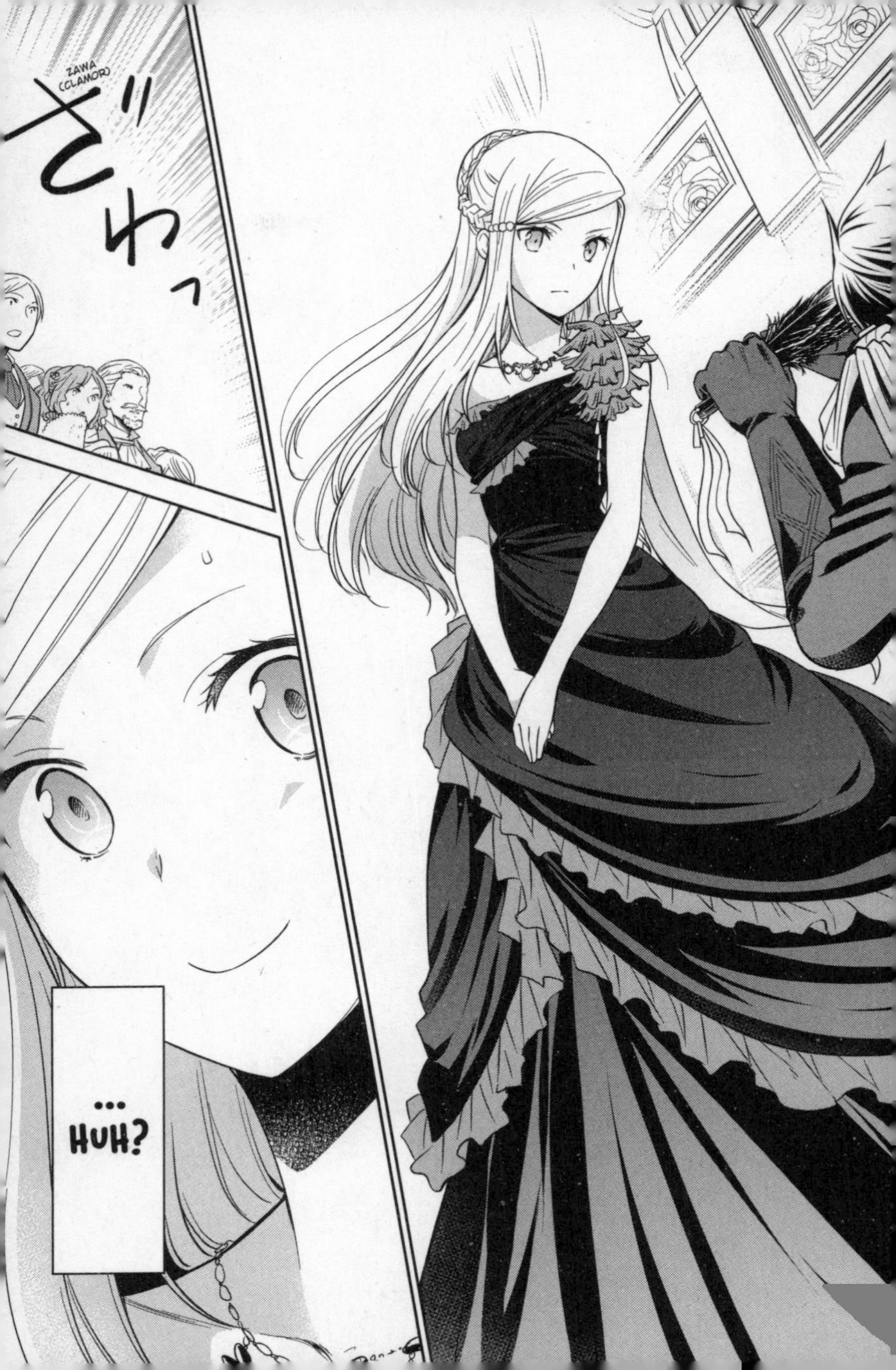
ZAWA (CLAMOR)
ざわっ
... HUH?

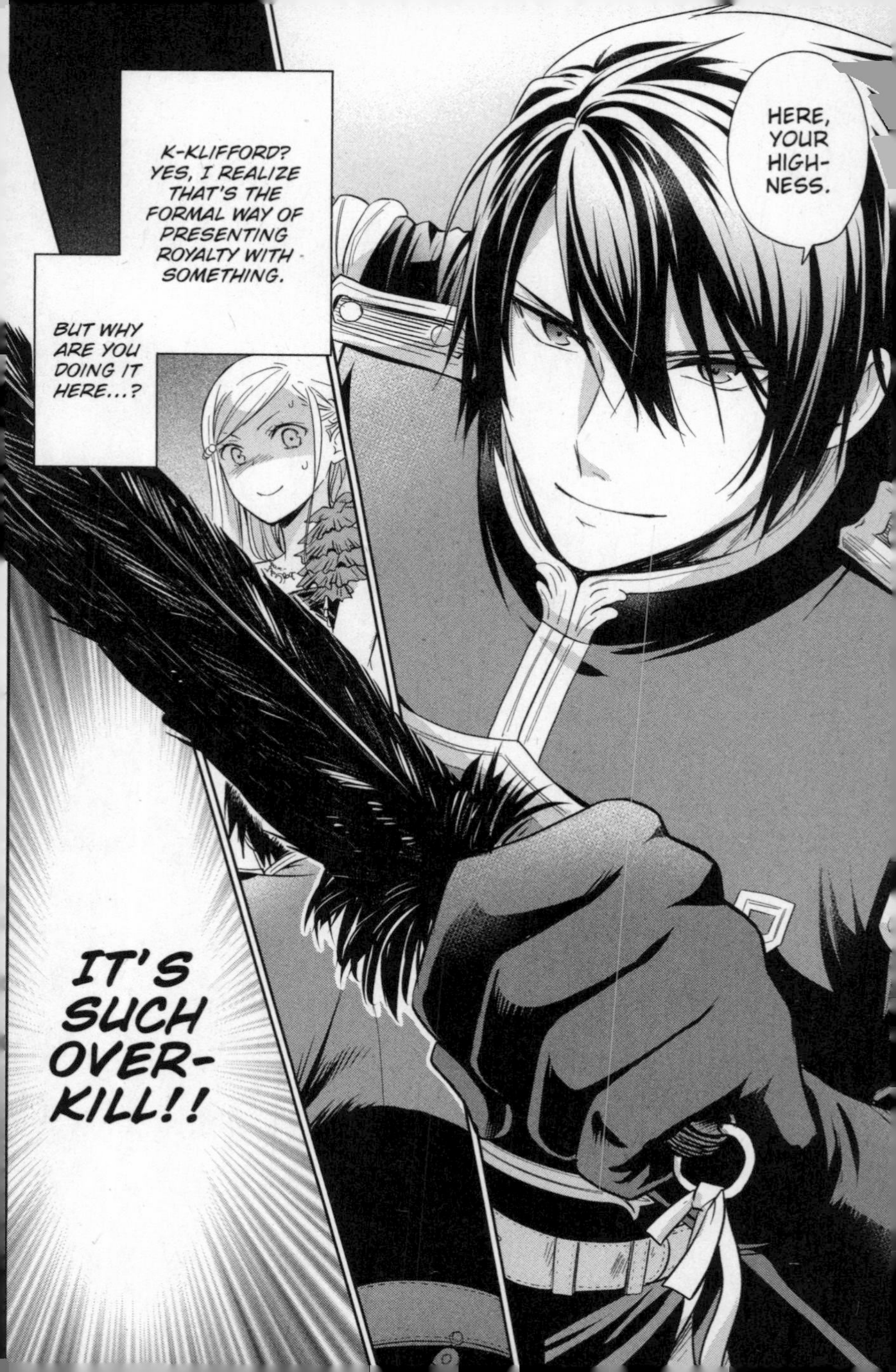
HERE, YOUR HIGH- NESS.
K-KLIFFORD? YES, I REALIZE THAT'S THE FORMAL WAY OF PRESENTING ROYALTY WITH SOMETHING.
BUT WHY ARE YOU DOING IT HERE...?
IT'S SUCH OVER- KILL!!

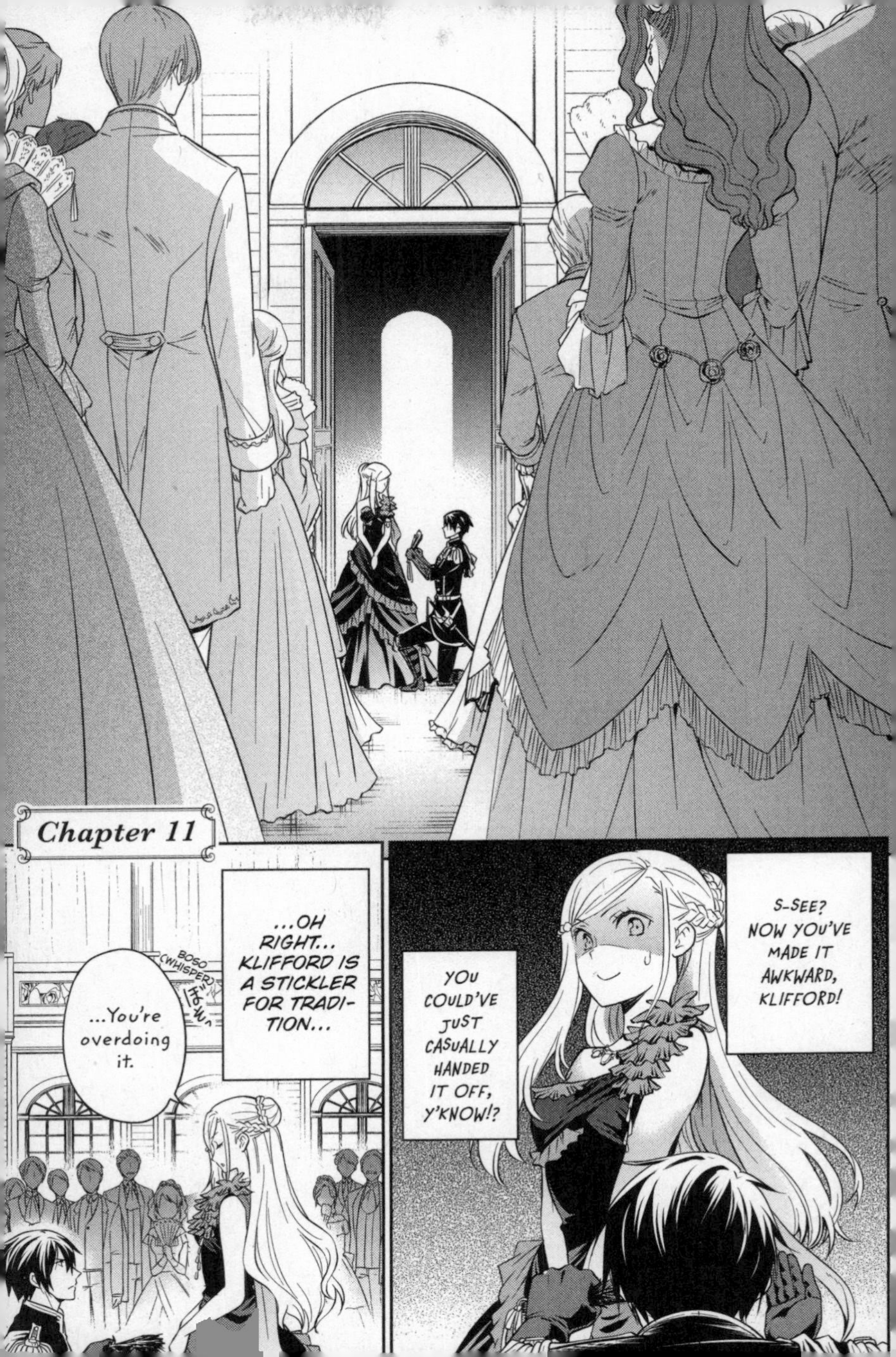
Chapter 11
S-SEE? NOW YOU'VE MADE IT AWKWARD, KLIFFORD!
YOU COULD'VE JUST CASUALLY HANDED IT OFF, Y'KNOW!?
...OH RIGHT... KLIFFORD IS A STICKLER FOR TRADITION...
BOSO (WHISPER)
...You're overdoing it.

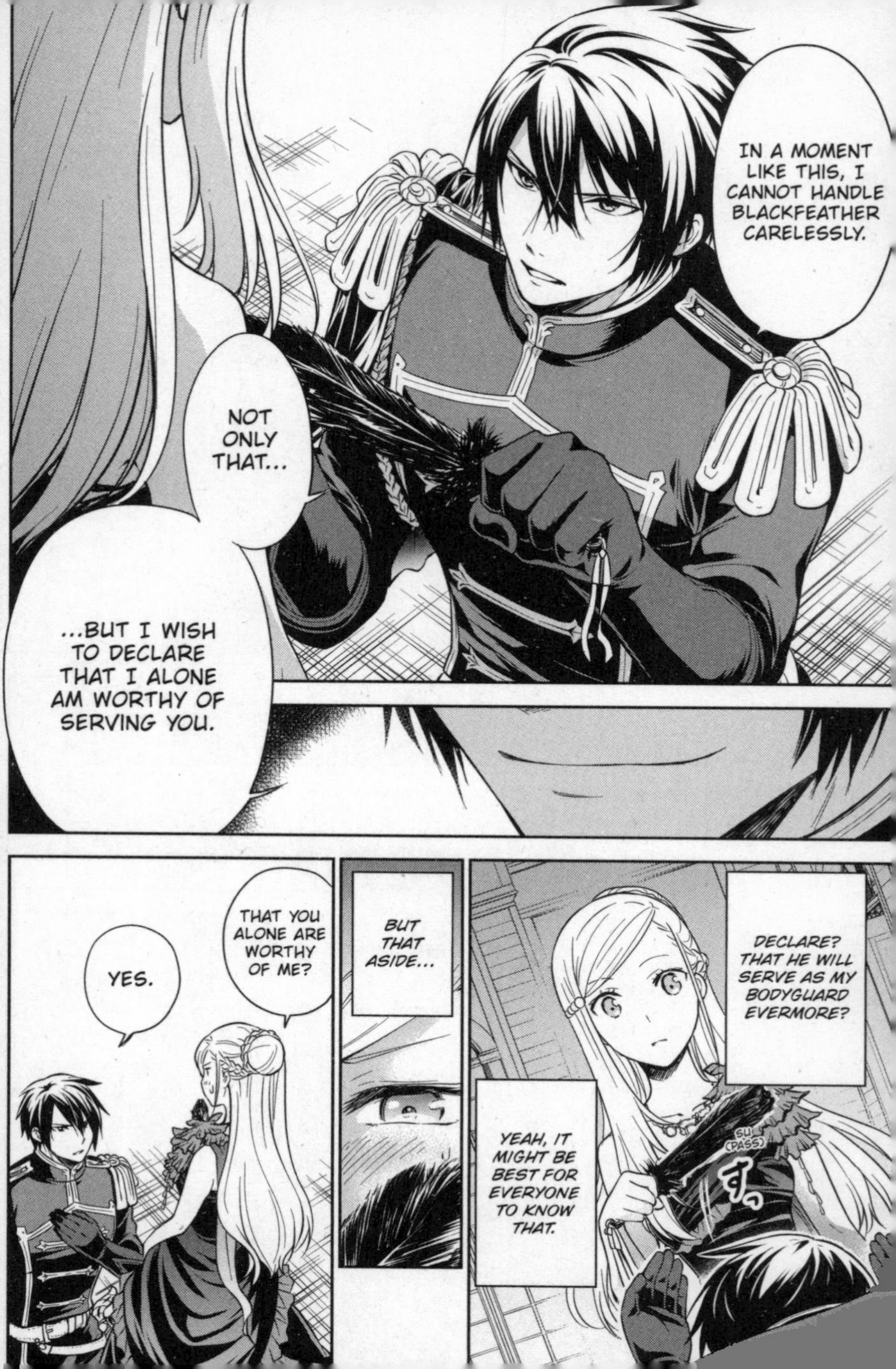

IN A MOMENT LIKE THIS, I CANNOT HANDLE BLACKFEATHER CARELESSLY.
NOT ONLY THAT...
...BUT I WISH TO DECLARE THAT I ALONE AM WORTHY OF SERVING YOU.
DECLARE? THAT HE WILL SERVE AS MY BODYGUARD EVERMORE?
SU (PASS)
すっ
YEAH, IT MIGHT BE BEST FOR EVERYONE TO KNOW THAT.
BUT THAT ASIDE...
THAT YOU ALONE ARE WORTHY OF ME?
YES.

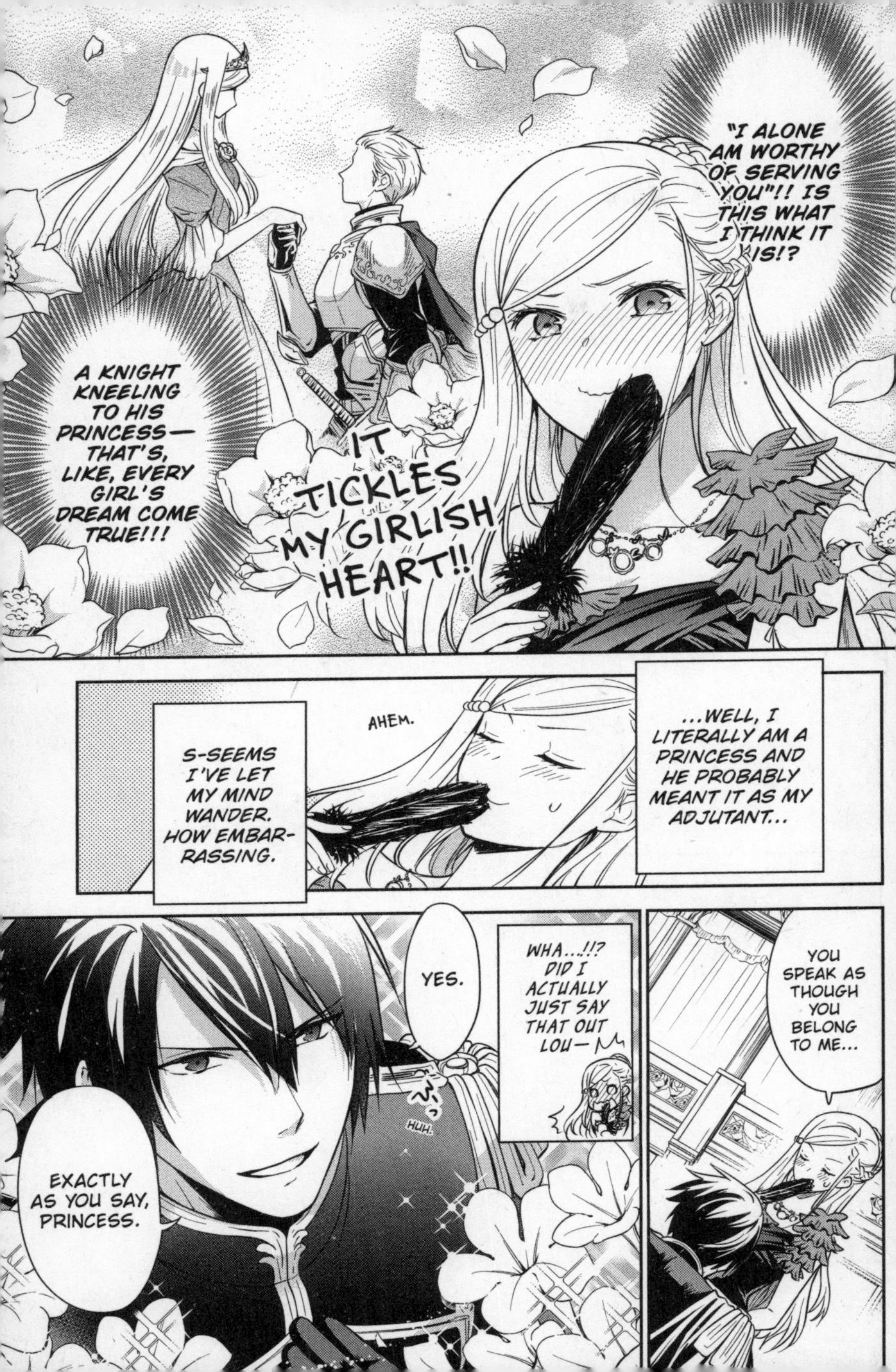
"I ALONE AM WORTHY OF SERVING YOU"!! IS THIS WHAT I THINK IT IS!?
A KNIGHT KNEELING TO HIS PRINCESS—THAT'S, LIKE, EVERY GIRL'S DREAM COME TRUE!!!
IT TICKLES MY GIRLISH HEART!!
...WELL, I LITERALLY AM A PRINCESS AND HE PROBABLY MEANT IT AS MY ADJUTANT...
AHEM.
S-SEEMS I'VE LET MY MIND WANDER. HOW EMBARRASSING.
YOU SPEAK AS THOUGH YOU BELONG TO ME...
WHA...!!? DID I ACTUALLY JUST SAY THAT OUT LOU—
YES.
HUH.
EXACTLY AS YOU SAY, PRINCESS.

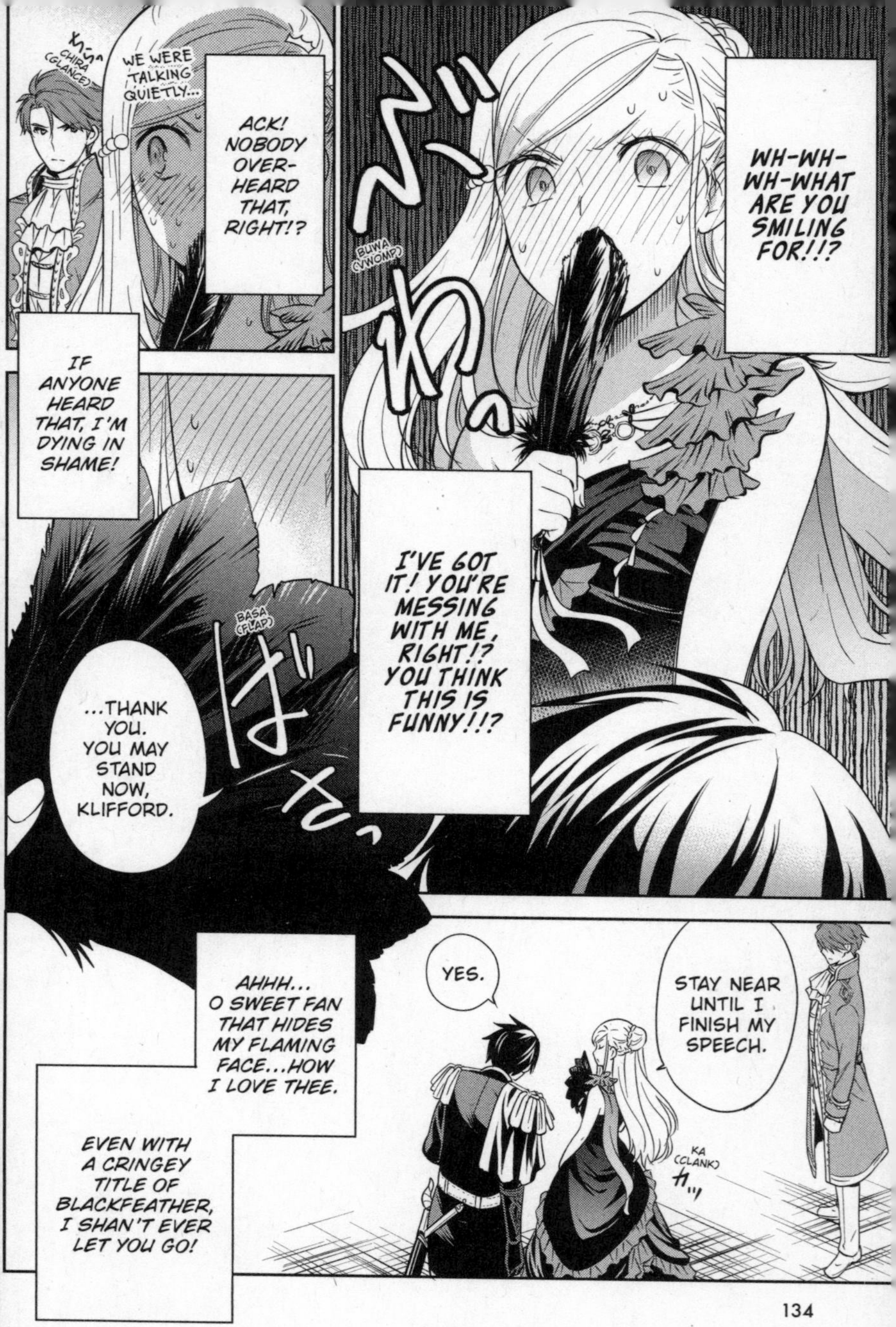
WH-WH-WH-WHAT ARE YOU SMILING FOR!!?
BUWA (VWOMP)
I'VE GOT IT! YOU'RE MESSING WITH ME, RIGHT!? YOU THINK THIS IS FUNNY!!?
CHIRA (GLANCE)
WE WERE TALKING QUIETLY...
ACK! NOBODY OVER-HEARD THAT, RIGHT!?
IF ANYONE HEARD THAT, I'M DYING IN SHAME!
BASA (FLAP)
...THANK YOU. YOU MAY STAND NOW, KLIFFORD.
STAY NEAR UNTIL I FINISH MY SPEECH.
YES.
KA (CLANK)
AHHH... O SWEET FAN THAT HIDES MY FLAMING FACE...HOW I LOVE THEE.
EVEN WITH A CRINGEY TITLE OF BLACKFEATHER, I SHAN'T EVER LET YOU GO!

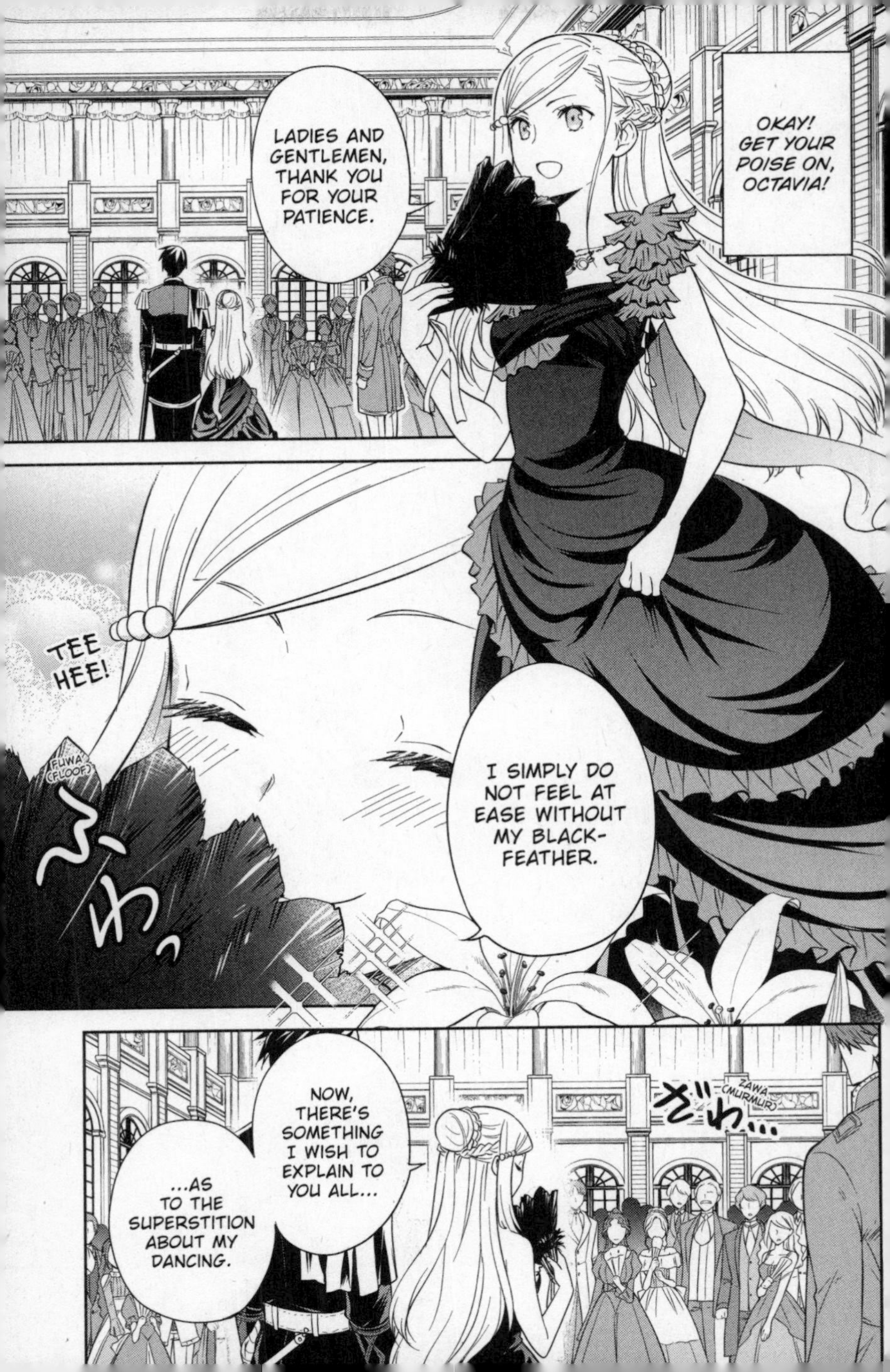
OKAY! GET YOUR POISE ON, OCTAVIA!
LADIES AND GENTLEMEN, THANK YOU FOR YOUR PATIENCE.
I SIMPLY DO NOT FEEL AT EASE WITHOUT MY BLACK-FEATHER.
TEE HEE!
FUWA (FLOOF)
ZAWA (MURMUR)
NOW, THERE'S SOMETHING I WISH TO EXPLAIN TO YOU ALL...
...AS TO THE SUPERSTITION ABOUT MY DANCING.

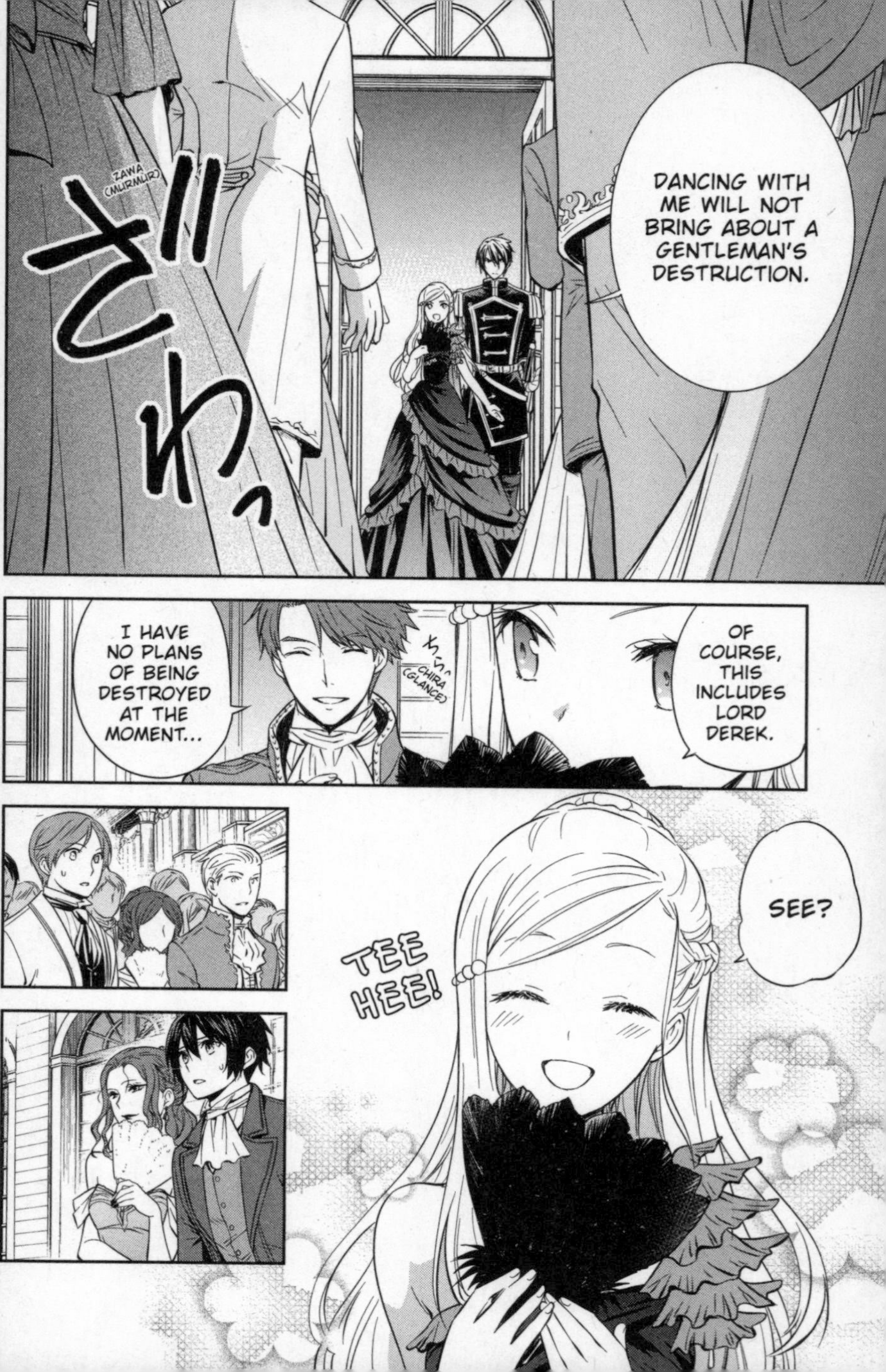

DANCING WITH ME WILL NOT BRING ABOUT A GENTLEMAN'S DESTRUCTION.
ざわっ
ZAWA (MURMUR)
OF COURSE, THIS INCLUDES LORD DEREK.
ちら
CHIRA (GLANCE)
I HAVE NO PLANS OF BEING DESTROYED AT THE MOMENT...
SEE?
TEE HEE!

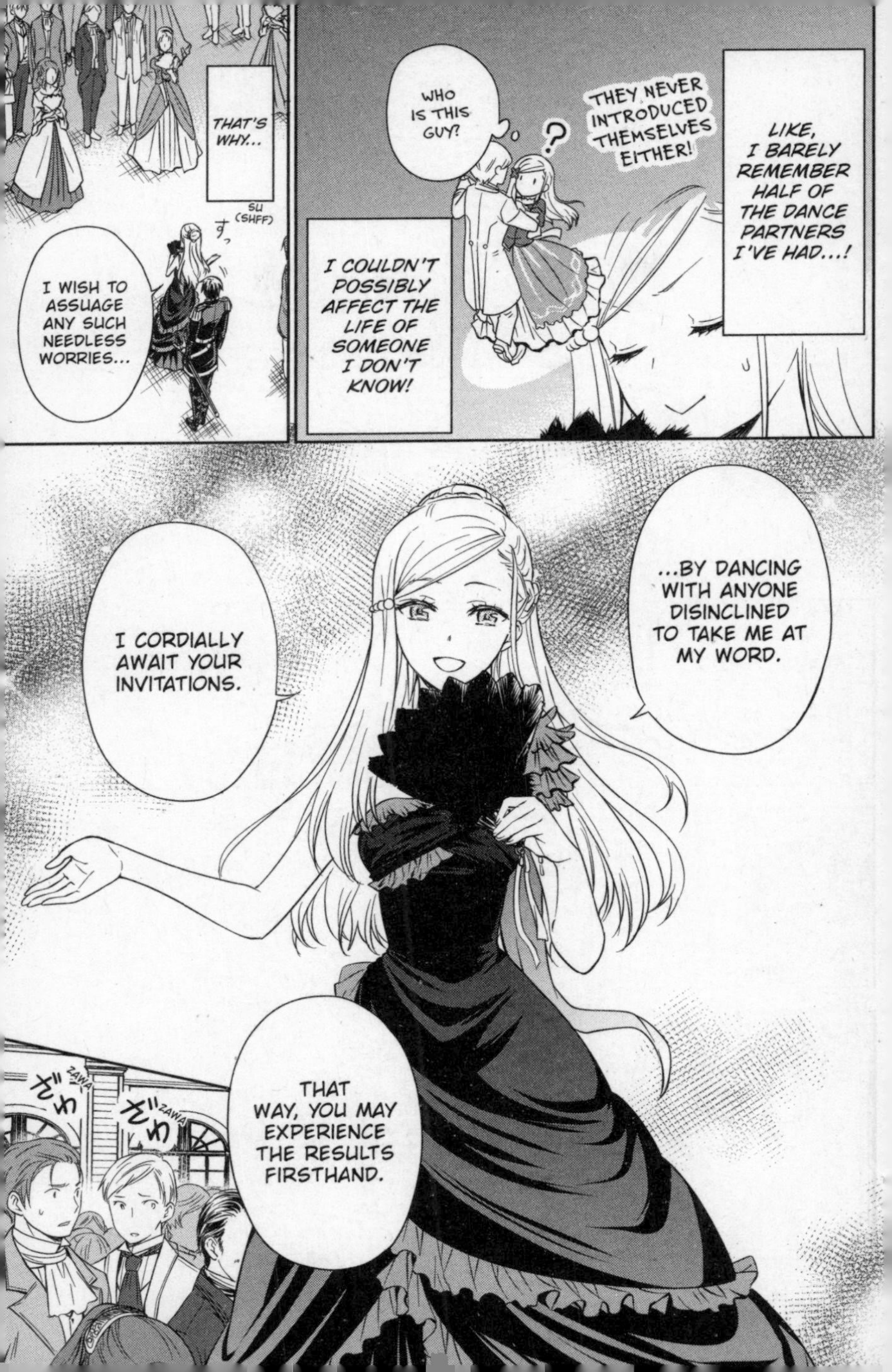
LIKE, I BARELY REMEMBER HALF OF THE DANCE PARTNERS I'VE HAD...!
THEY NEVER INTRODUCED THEMSELVES EITHER!
WHO IS THIS GUY?
?
I COULDN'T POSSIBLY AFFECT THE LIFE OF SOMEONE I DON'T KNOW!
THAT'S WHY...
すっ
SU (SHFF)
I WISH TO ASSUAGE ANY SUCH NEEDLESS WORRIES...
...BY DANCING WITH ANYONE DISINCLINED TO TAKE ME AT MY WORD.
I CORDIALLY AWAIT YOUR INVITATIONS.
THAT WAY, YOU MAY EXPERIENCE THE RESULTS FIRSTHAND.
ざわ ZAWA
ざわ ZAWA

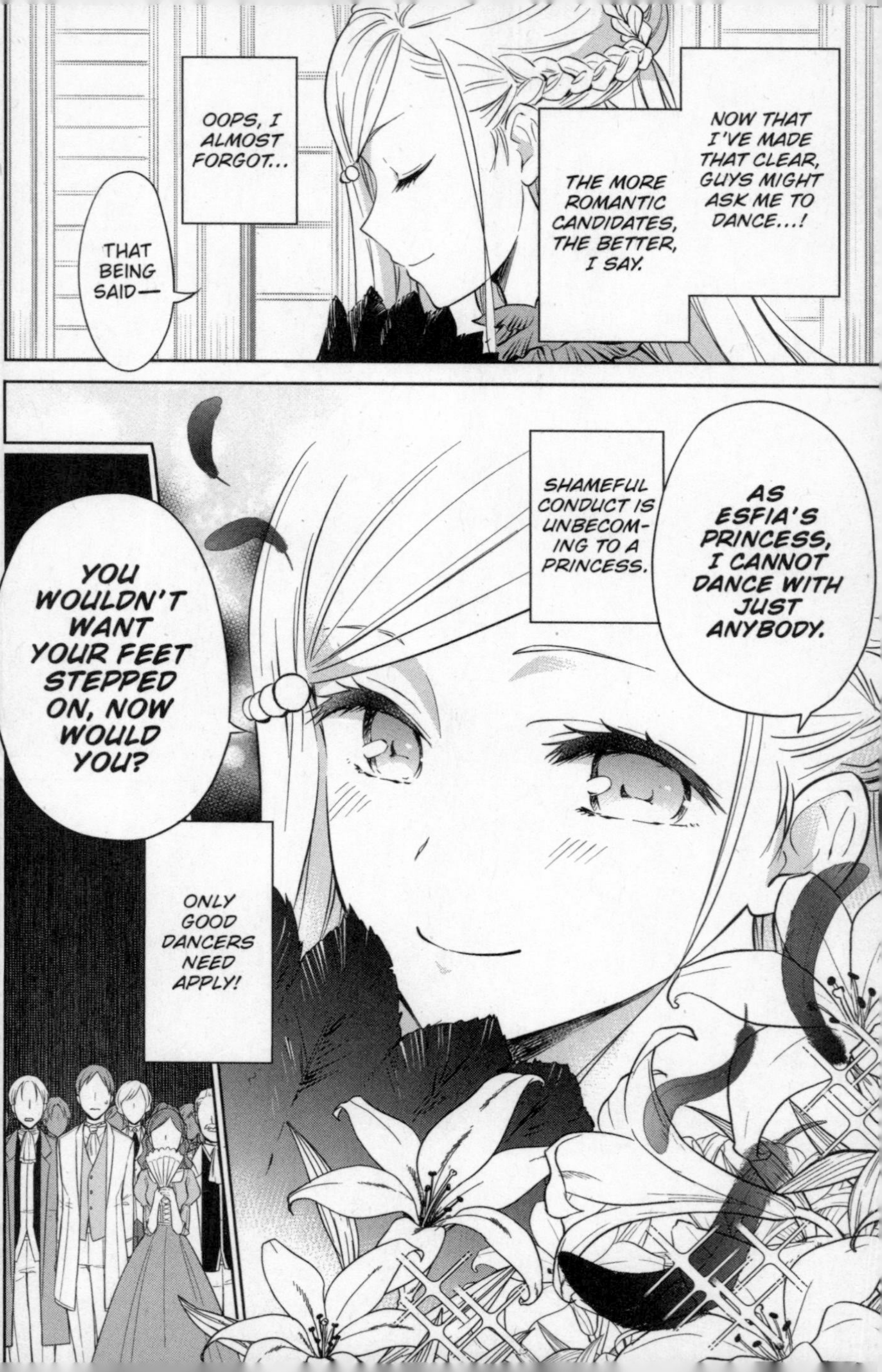
NOW THAT I'VE MADE THAT CLEAR, GUYS MIGHT ASK ME TO DANCE...!
THE MORE ROMANTIC CANDIDATES, THE BETTER, I SAY.
OOPS, I ALMOST FORGOT...
THAT BEING SAID—
AS ESFIA'S PRINCESS, I CANNOT DANCE WITH JUST ANYBODY.
SHAMEFUL CONDUCT IS UNBECOMING TO A PRINCESS.
YOU WOULDN'T WANT YOUR FEET STEPPED ON, NOW WOULD YOU?
ONLY GOOD DANCERS NEED APPLY!

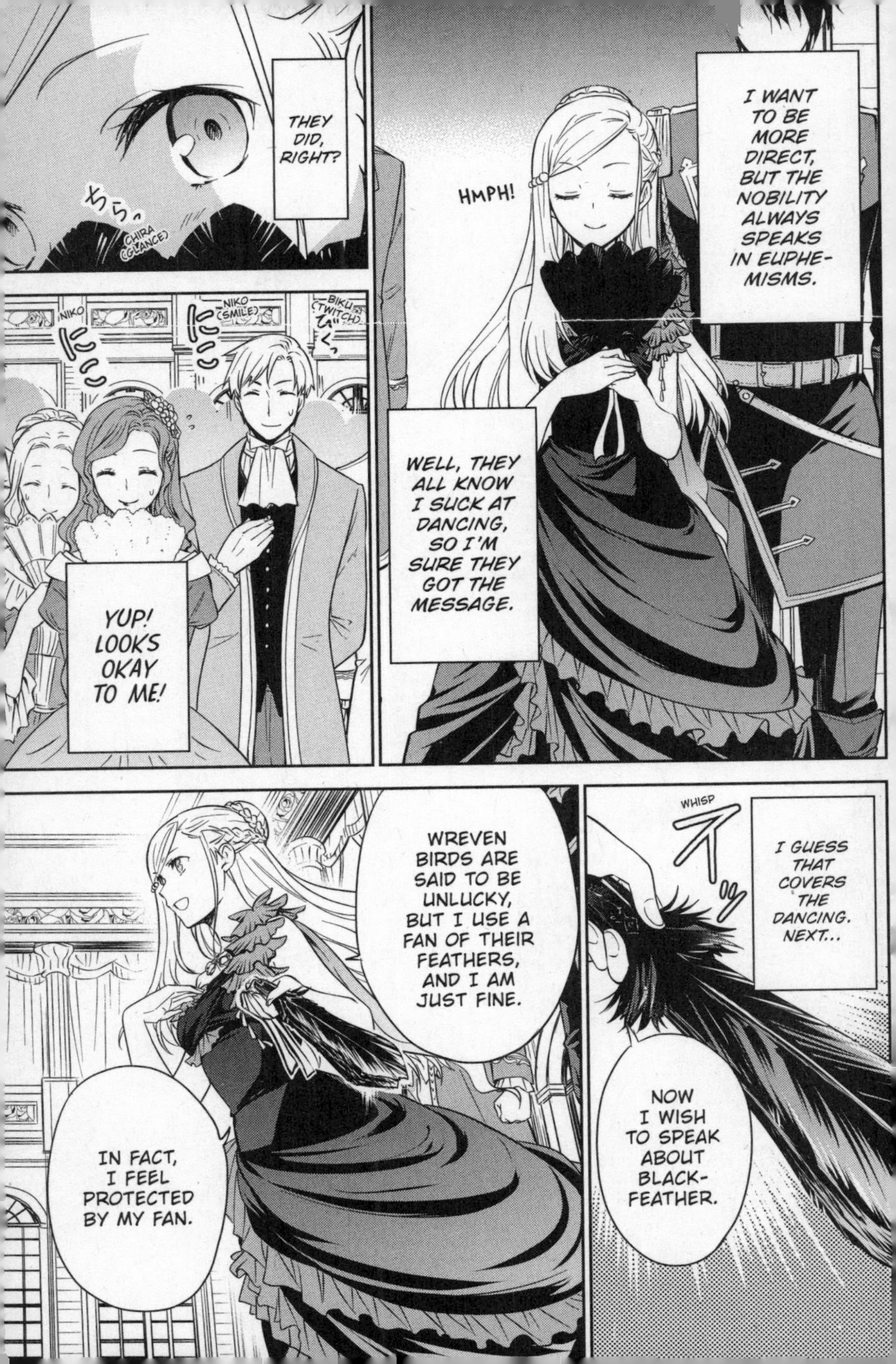
I WANT TO BE MORE DIRECT, BUT THE NOBILITY ALWAYS SPEAKS IN EUPHE- MISMS.
HMPH!
WELL, THEY ALL KNOW I SUCK AT DANCING, SO I'M SURE THEY GOT THE MESSAGE.
THEY DID, RIGHT?
CHIRA (GLANCE)
BIKU (TWITCH)
NIKO (SMILE)
NIKO
YUP! LOOKS OKAY TO ME!
WHISP
I GUESS THAT COVERS THE DANCING. NEXT...
NOW I WISH TO SPEAK ABOUT BLACK- FEATHER.
WREVEN BIRDS ARE SAID TO BE UNLUCKY, BUT I USE A FAN OF THEIR FEATHERS, AND I AM JUST FINE.
IN FACT, I FEEL PROTECTED BY MY FAN.

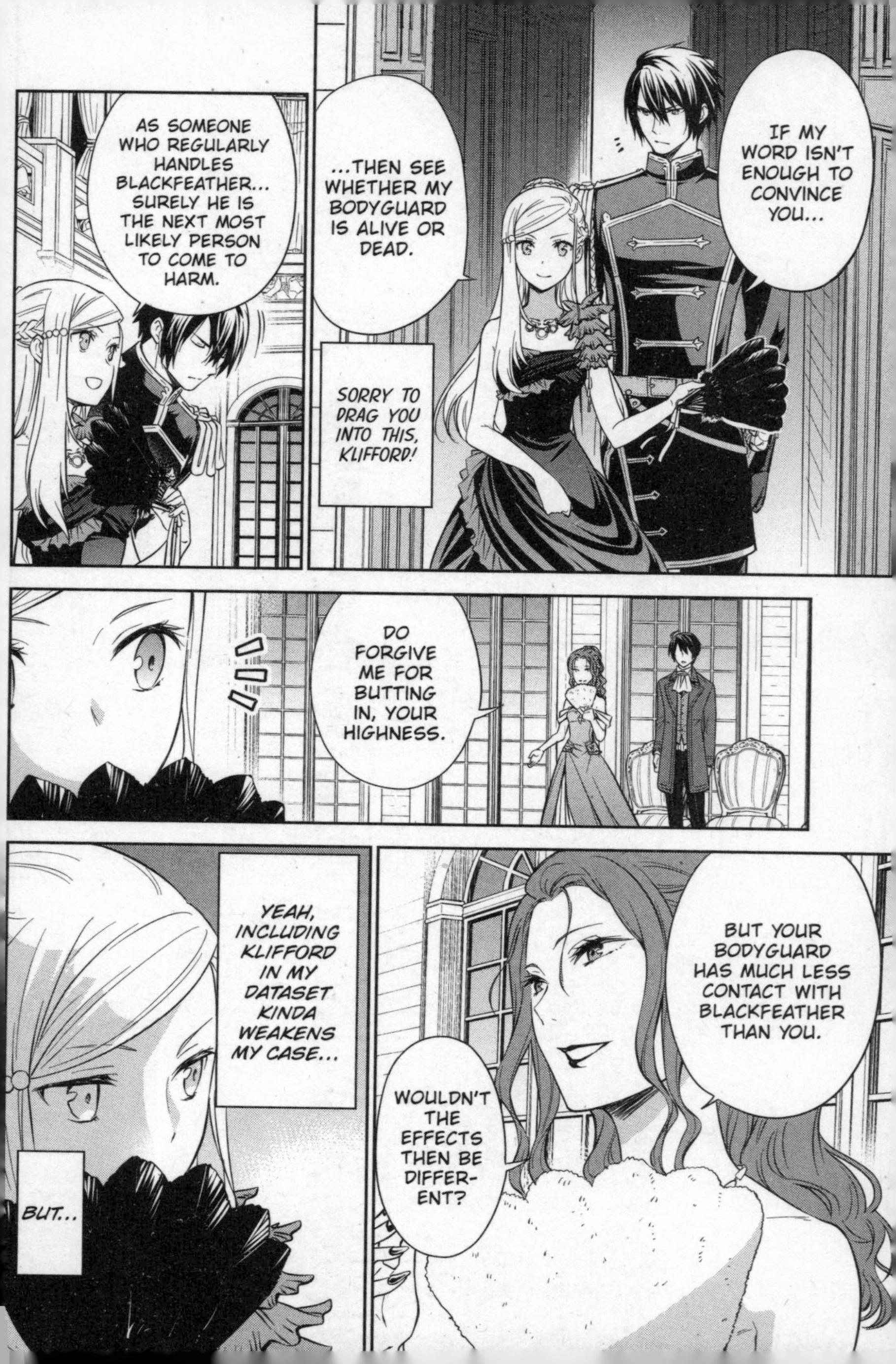

IF MY WORD ISN'T ENOUGH TO CONVINCE YOU...
...THEN SEE WHETHER MY BODYGUARD IS ALIVE OR DEAD.
SORRY TO DRAG YOU INTO THIS, KLIFFORD!
AS SOMEONE WHO REGULARLY HANDLES BLACKFEATHER... SURELY HE IS THE NEXT MOST LIKELY PERSON TO COME TO HARM.
DO FORGIVE ME FOR BUTTING IN, YOUR HIGHNESS.
BUT YOUR BODYGUARD HAS MUCH LESS CONTACT WITH BLACKFEATHER THAN YOU.
WOULDN'T THE EFFECTS THEN BE DIFFER-ENT?
YEAH, INCLUDING KLIFFORD IN MY DATASET KINDA WEAKENS MY CASE...
BUT...

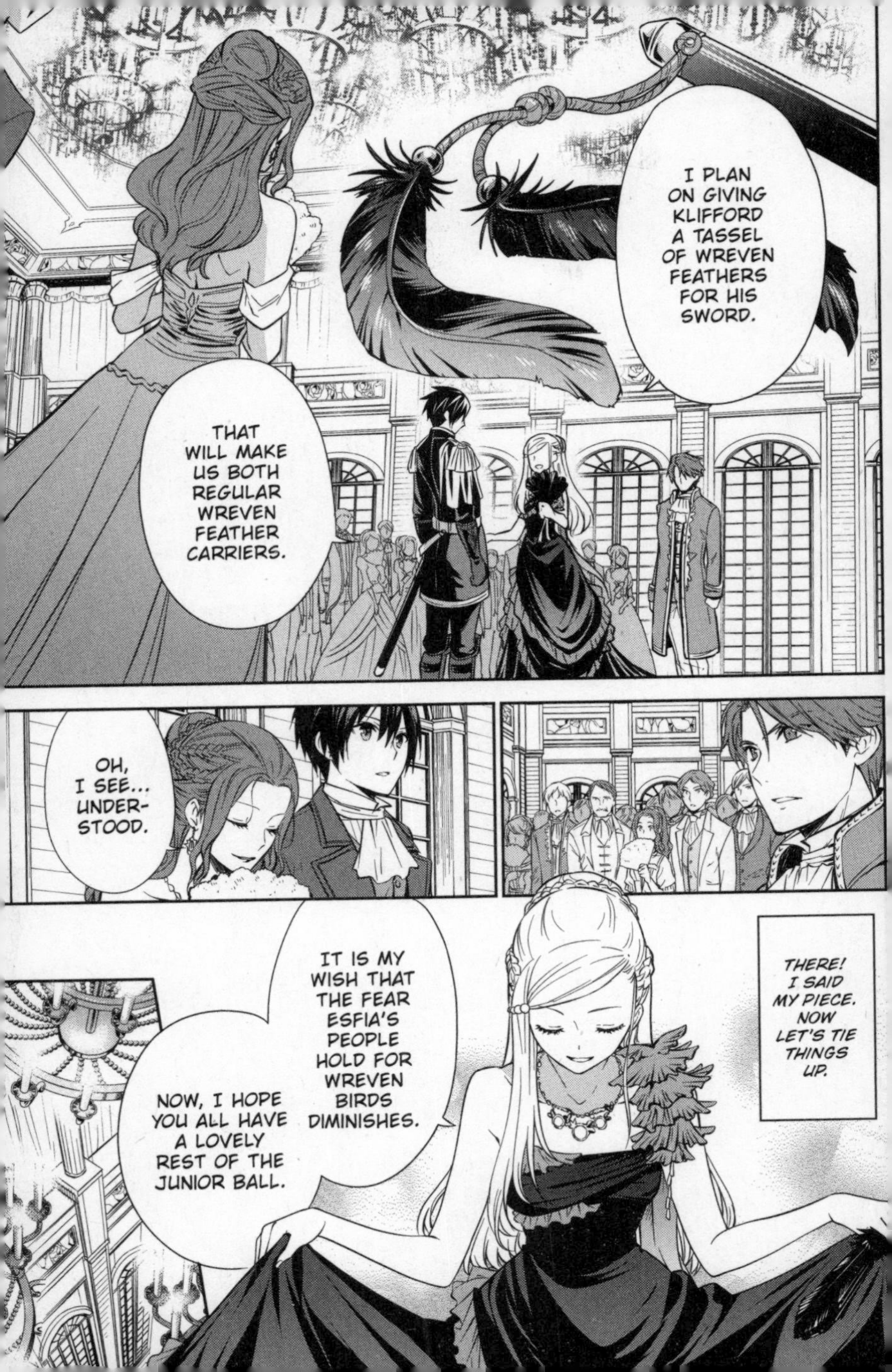
I PLAN ON GIVING KLIFFORD A TASSEL OF WREVEN FEATHERS FOR HIS SWORD.
THAT WILL MAKE US BOTH REGULAR WREVEN FEATHER CARRIERS.
OH, I SEE... UNDER-STOOD.
THERE! I SAID MY PIECE. NOW LET'S TIE THINGS UP.
IT IS MY WISH THAT THE FEAR ESFIA'S PEOPLE HOLD FOR WREVEN BIRDS DIMINISHES.
NOW, I HOPE YOU ALL HAVE A LOVELY REST OF THE JUNIOR BALL.

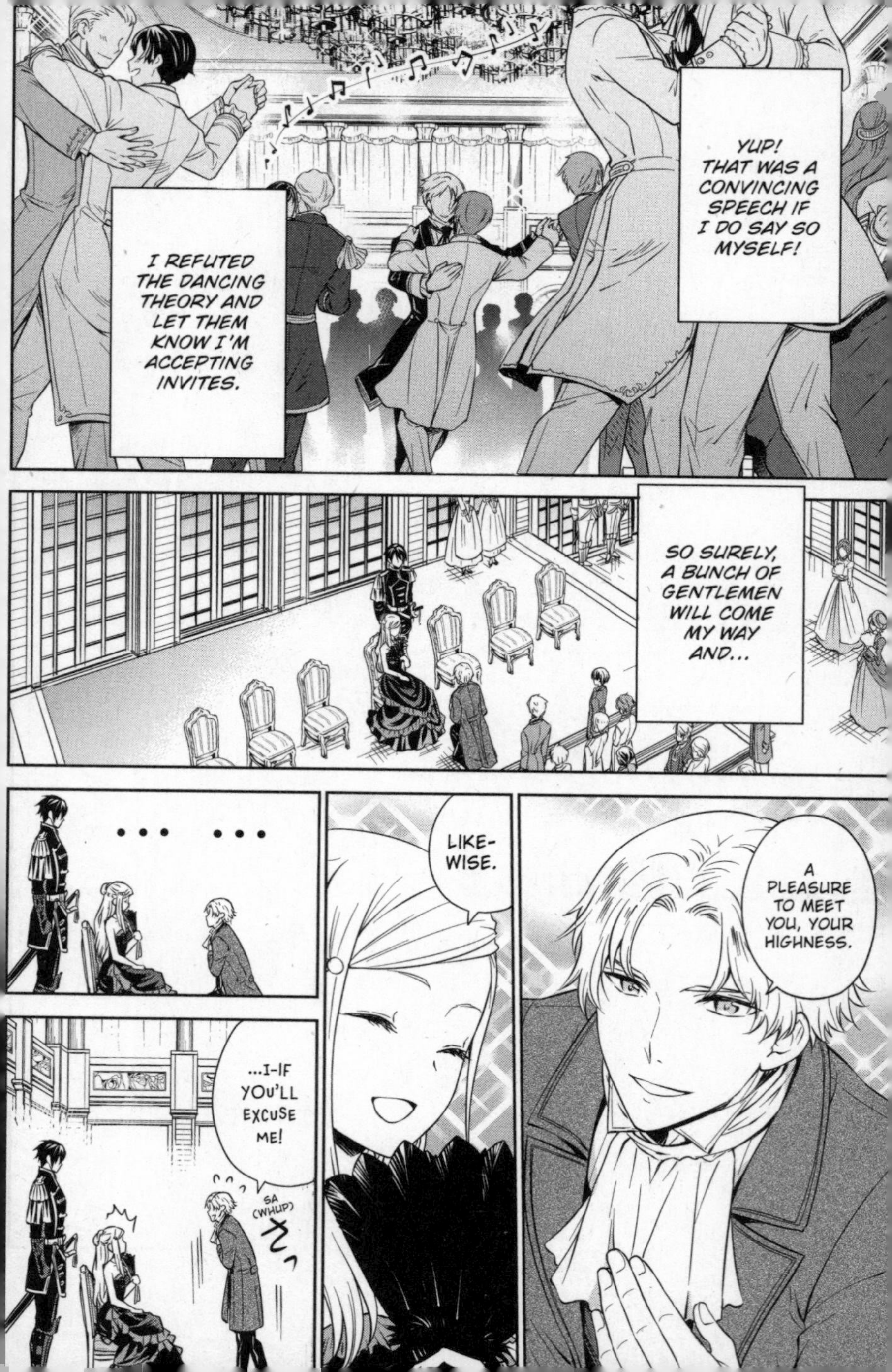
YUP! THAT WAS A CONVINCING SPEECH IF I DO SAY SO MYSELF!
I REFUTED THE DANCING THEORY AND LET THEM KNOW I'M ACCEPTING INVITES.
SO SURELY, A BUNCH OF GENTLEMEN WILL COME MY WAY AND...
A PLEASURE TO MEET YOU, YOUR HIGHNESS.
LIKE-WISE.
... ...
...I-IF YOU'LL EXCUSE ME!
SA (WHUP)

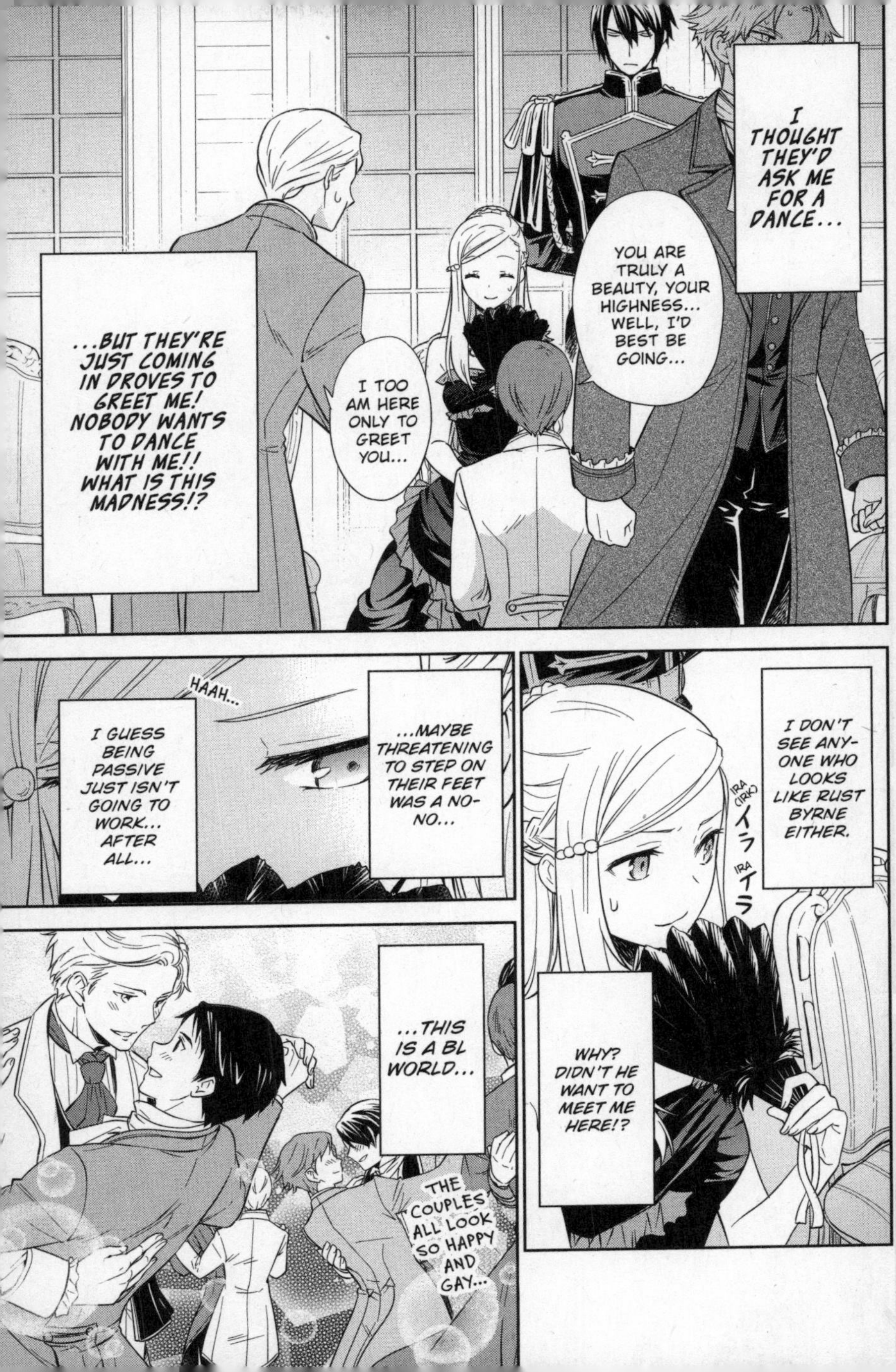
I THOUGHT THEY'D ASK ME FOR A DANCE...
YOU ARE TRULY A BEAUTY, YOUR HIGHNESS... WELL, I'D BEST BE GOING...
I TOO AM HERE ONLY TO GREET YOU...
...BUT THEY'RE JUST COMING IN DROVES TO GREET ME! NOBODY WANTS TO DANCE WITH ME!! WHAT IS THIS MADNESS!?
I DON'T SEE ANY-ONE WHO LOOKS LIKE RUST BYRNE EITHER.
IRA (IRK) イラ
IRA イラ
WHY? DIDN'T HE WANT TO MEET ME HERE!?
...MAYBE THREATENING TO STEP ON THEIR FEET WAS A NO-NO...
HAAH...
I GUESS BEING PASSIVE JUST ISN'T GOING TO WORK... AFTER ALL...
...THIS IS A BL WORLD...
THE COUPLES ALL LOOK SO HAPPY AND GAY...

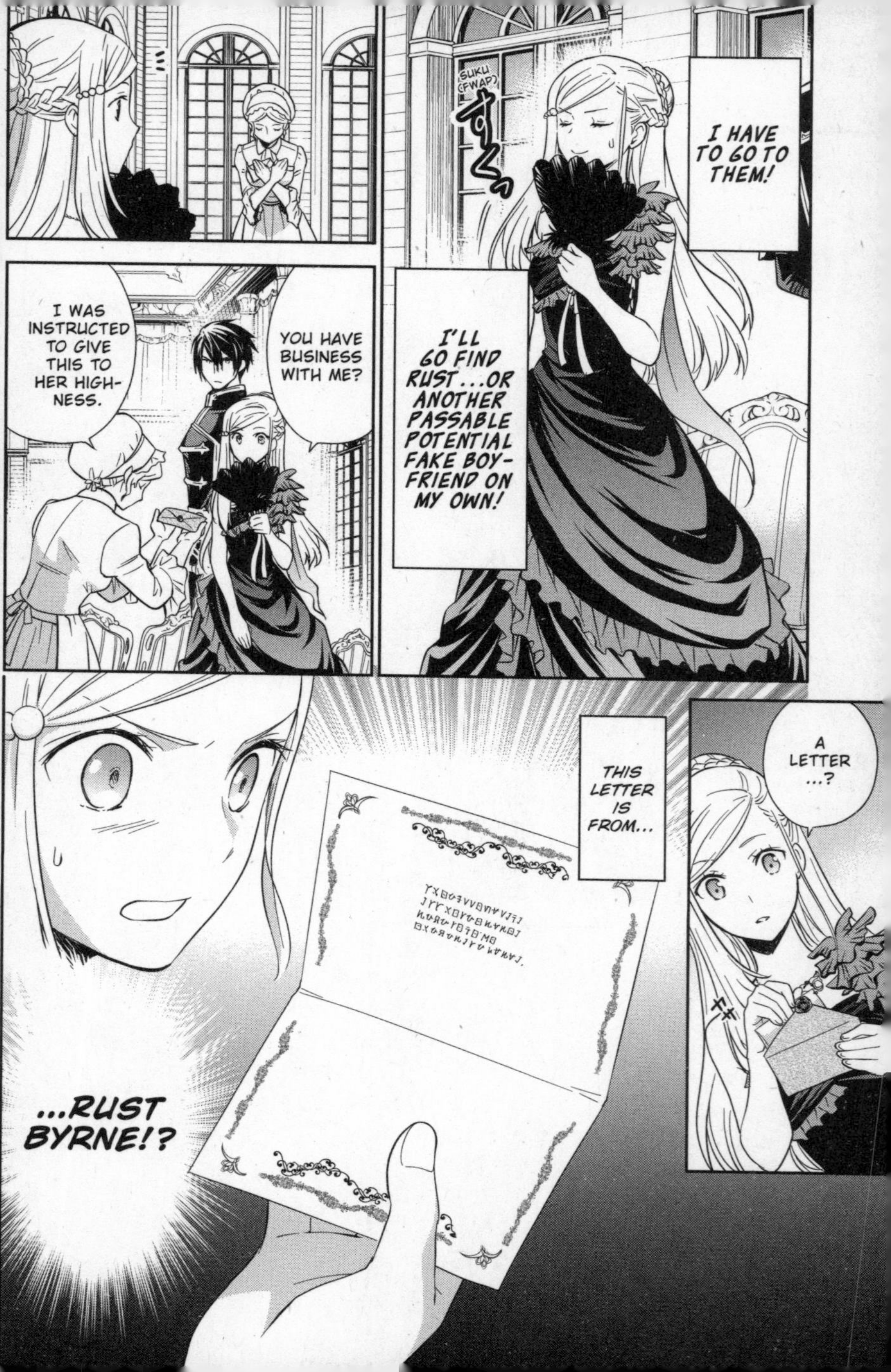
I HAVE TO GO TO THEM!
SUKU (FWAP)
I'LL GO FIND RUST...OR ANOTHER PASSABLE POTENTIAL FAKE BOY-FRIEND ON MY OWN!
YOU HAVE BUSINESS WITH ME?
I WAS INSTRUCTED TO GIVE THIS TO HER HIGH-NESS.
A LETTER ...?
THIS LETTER IS FROM...
...RUST BYRNE!?

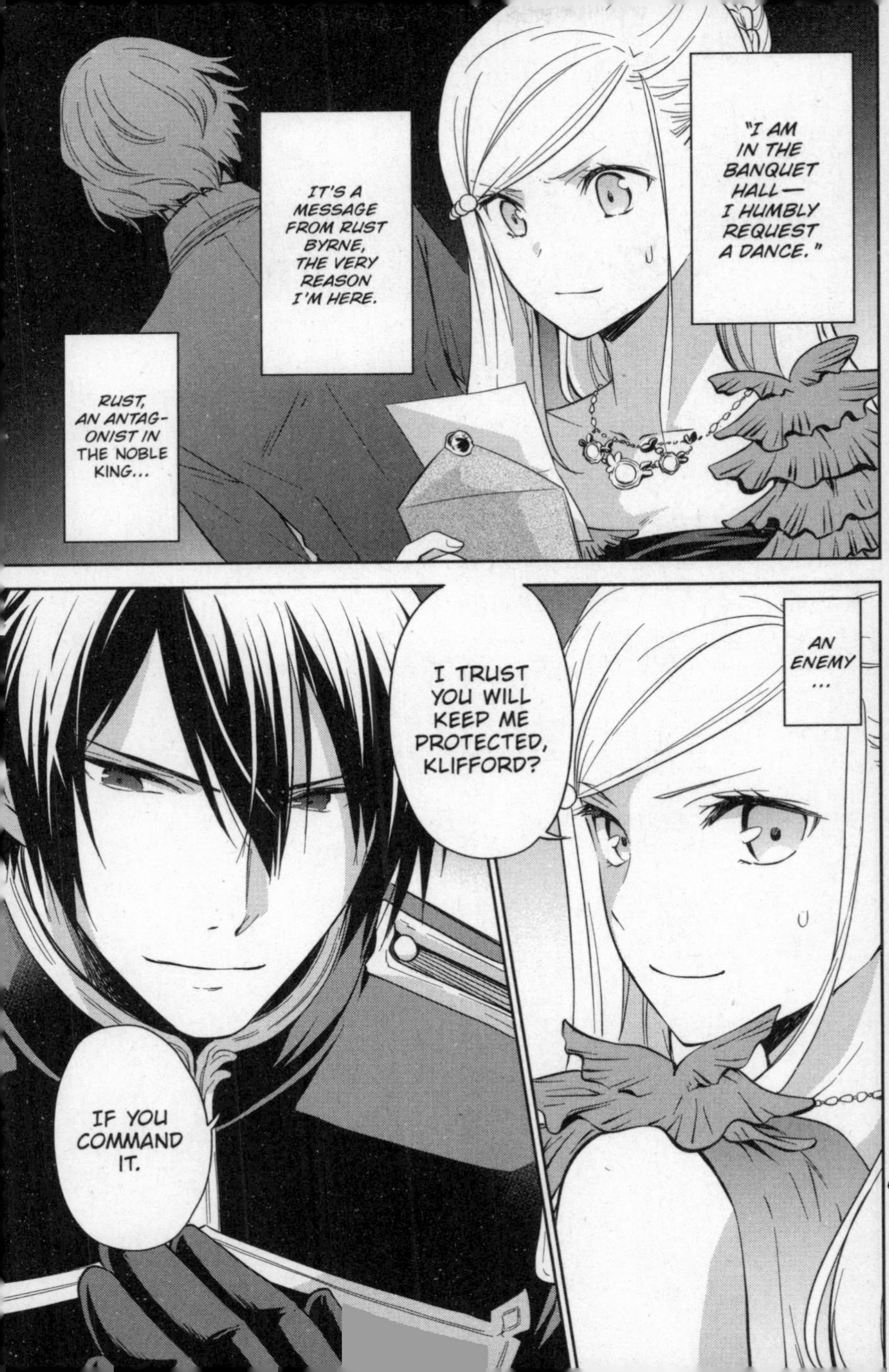
"I AM IN THE BANQUET HALL— I HUMBLY REQUEST A DANCE."
IT'S A MESSAGE FROM RUST BYRNE, THE VERY REASON I'M HERE.
RUST, AN ANTAG-ONIST IN THE NOBLE KING...
AN ENEMY...
I TRUST YOU WILL KEEP ME PROTECTED, KLIFFORD?
IF YOU COMMAND IT.

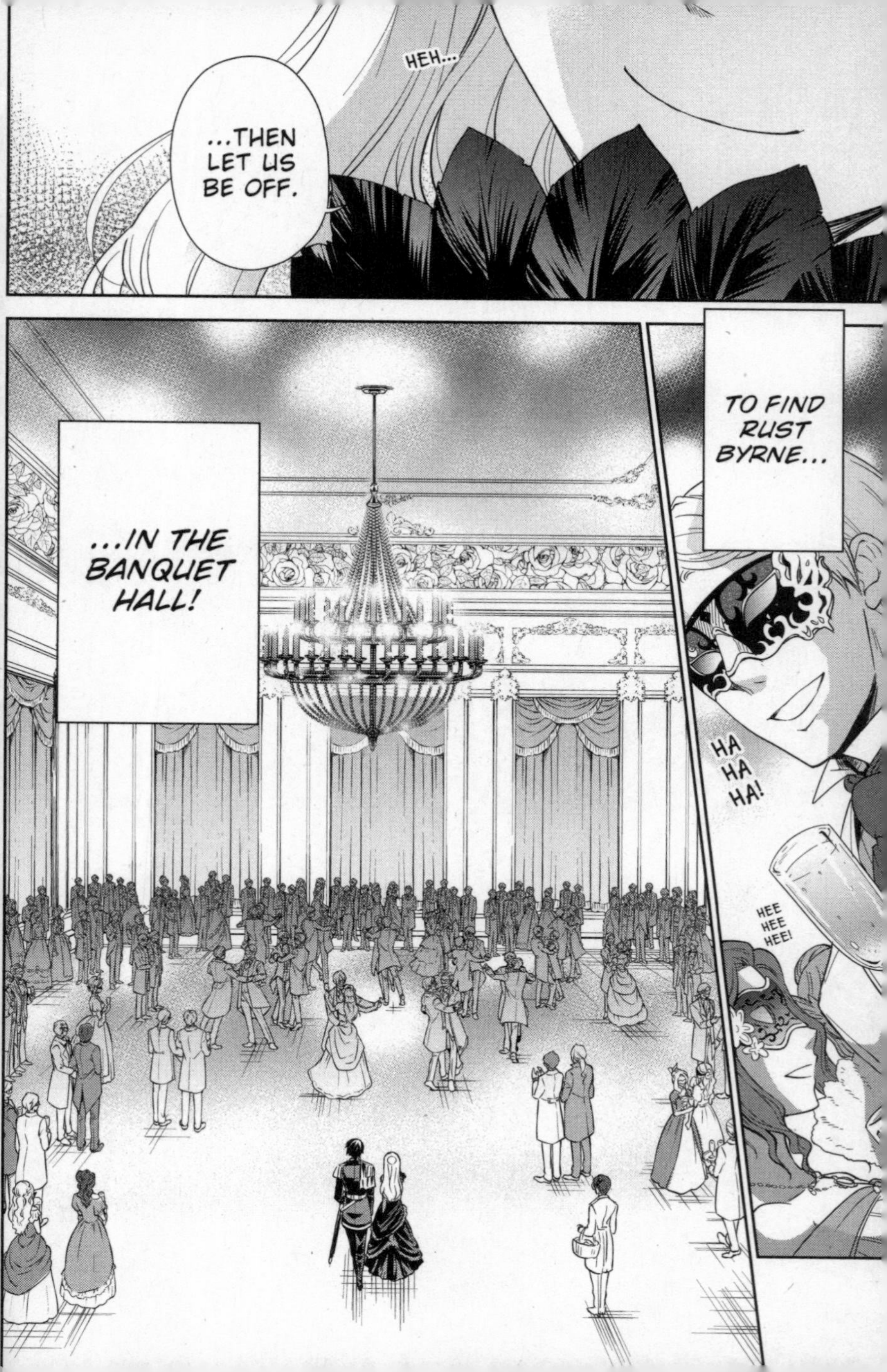
HEH...
...THEN LET US BE OFF.
TO FIND RUST BYRNE...
HA HA HA!
HEE HEE HEE!
...IN THE BANQUET HALL!

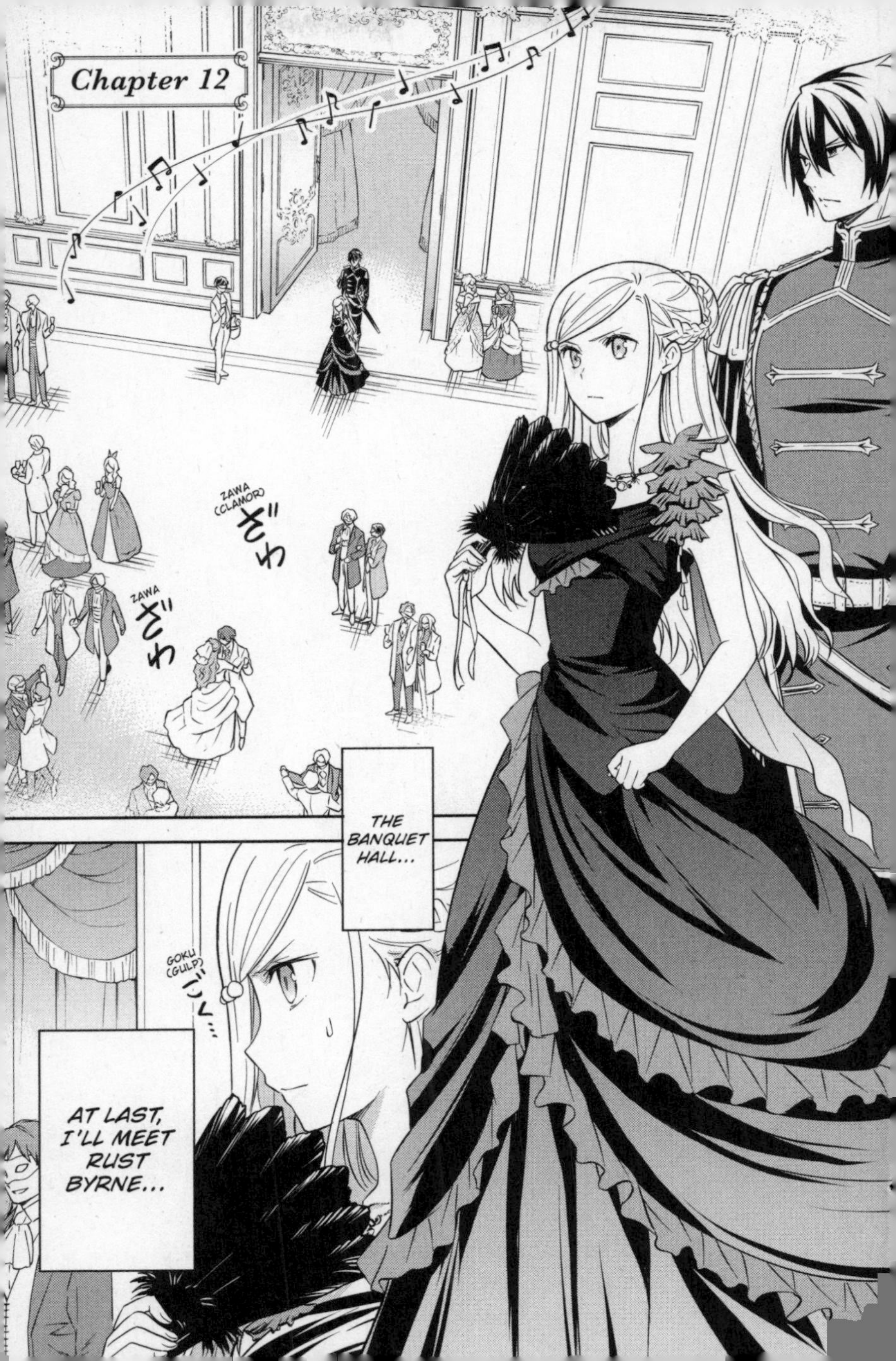
THE BANQUET HALL...
Chapter 12
ZAWA (CLAMOR) ざわ
ZAWA ざわ
GOKU (GULP) ごく...
AT LAST, I'LL MEET RUST BYRNE...

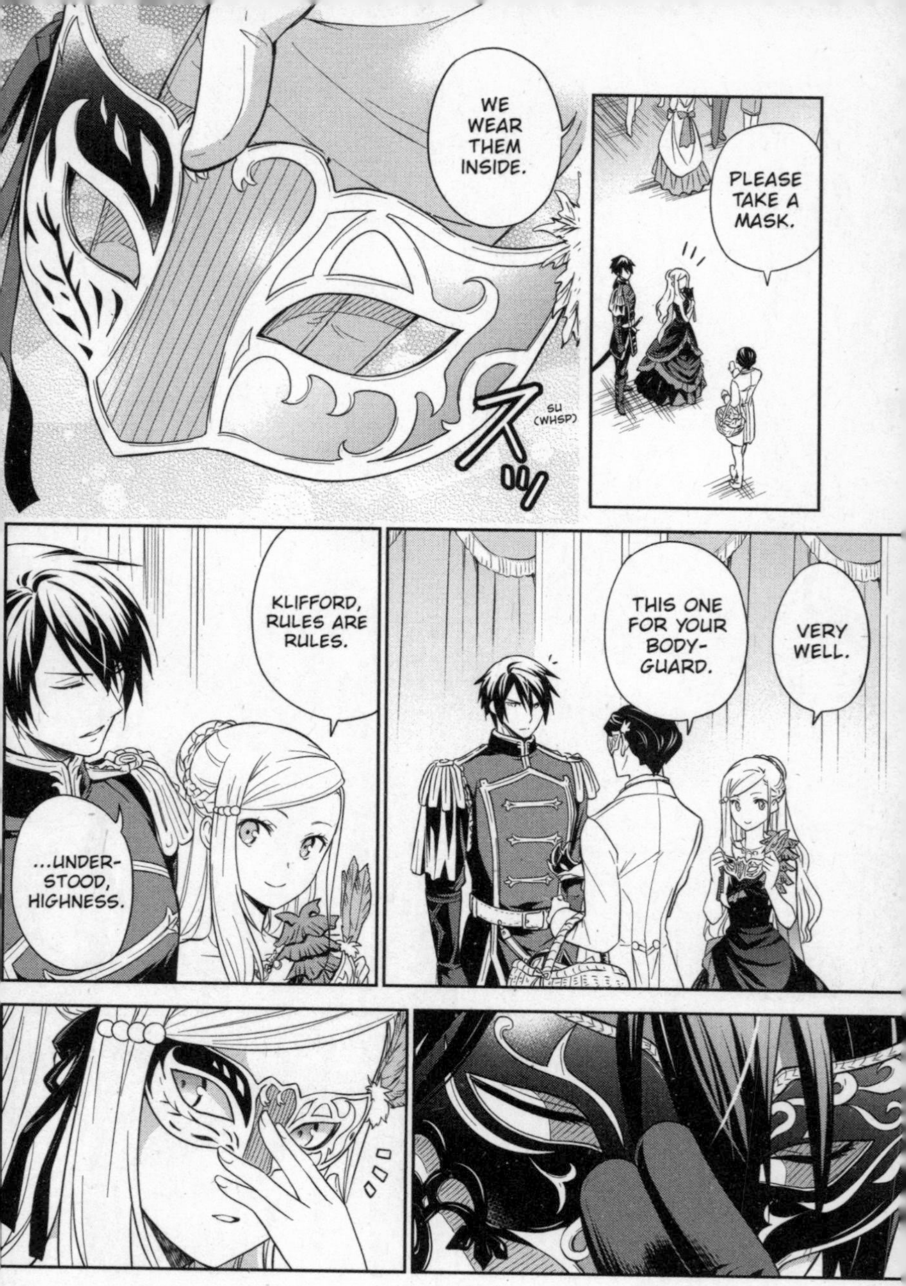
PLEASE TAKE A MASK.
WE WEAR THEM INSIDE.
SU (WHSP)
VERY WELL.
THIS ONE FOR YOUR BODY-GUARD.
KLIFFORD, RULES ARE RULES.
...UNDER-STOOD, HIGHNESS.

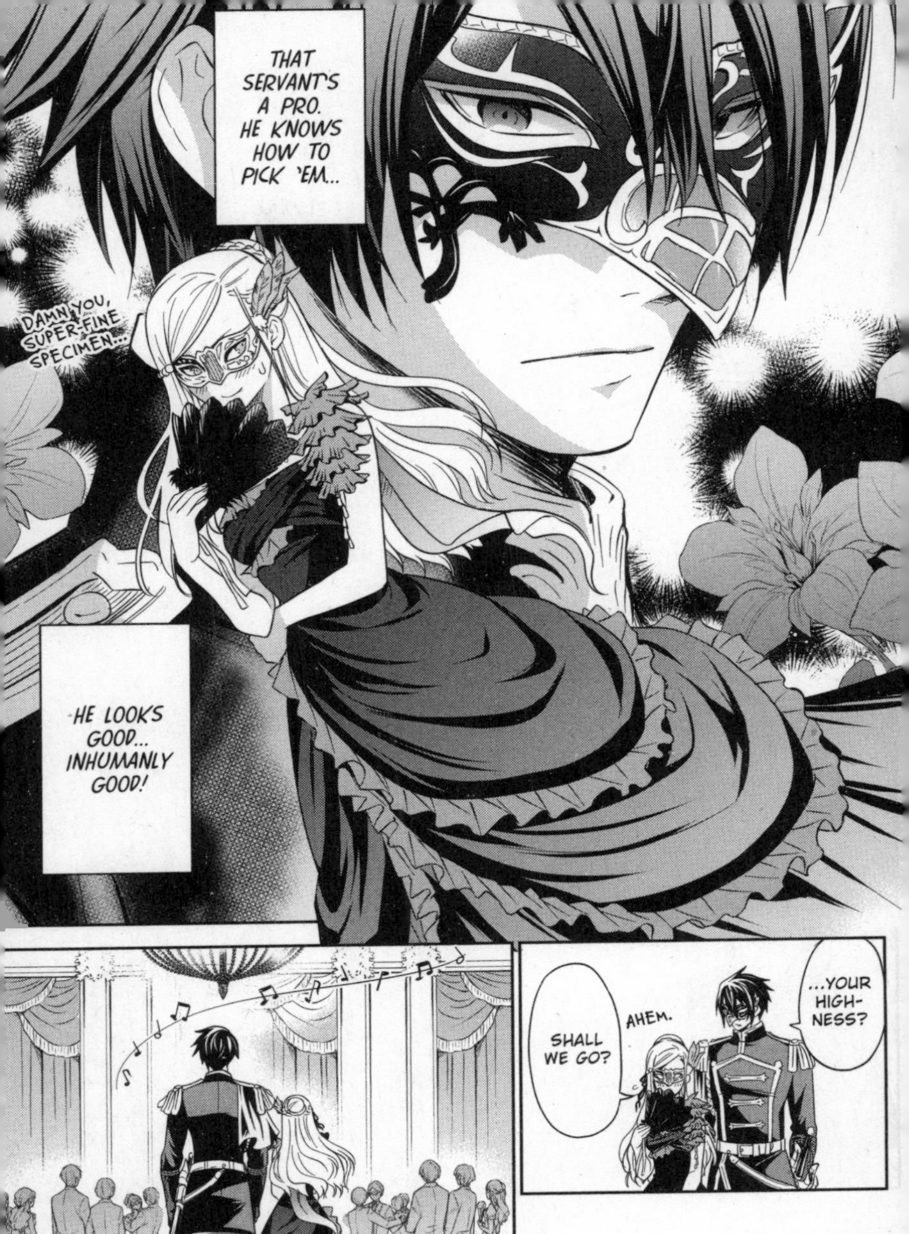
THAT SERVANT'S A PRO. HE KNOWS HOW TO PICK 'EM...
DAMN YOU, SUPER-FINE SPECIMEN...
HE LOOKS GOOD... INHUMANLY GOOD!
...YOUR HIGH-NESS?
AHEM.
SHALL WE GO?

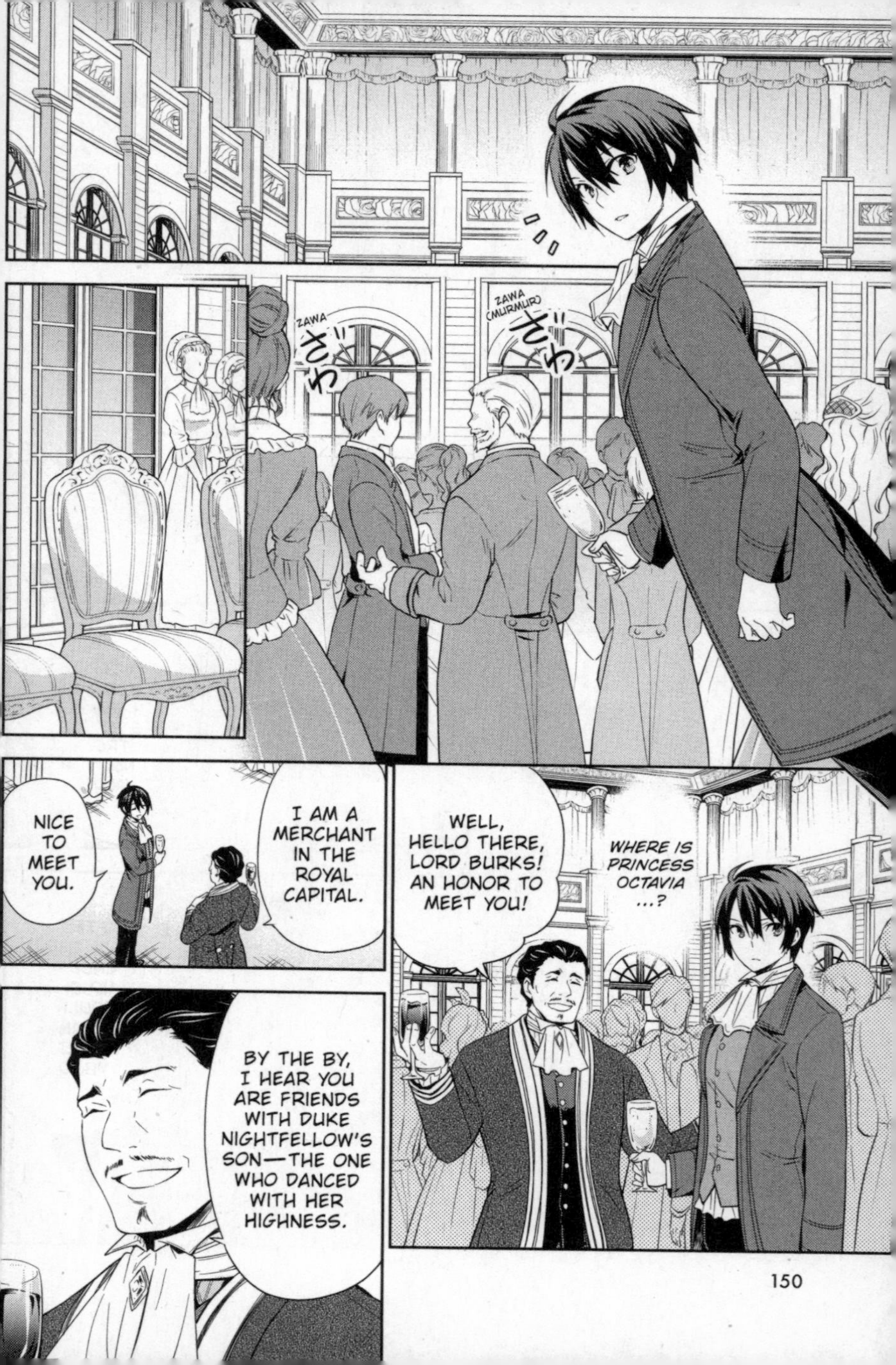
ZAWA (MURMUR)
ざわ
ZAWA
ざわ
WHERE IS PRINCESS OCTAVIA ...?
WELL, HELLO THERE, LORD BURKS! AN HONOR TO MEET YOU!
I AM A MERCHANT IN THE ROYAL CAPITAL.
NICE TO MEET YOU.
BY THE BY, I HEAR YOU ARE FRIENDS WITH DUKE NIGHTFELLOW'S SON—THE ONE WHO DANCED WITH HER HIGHNESS.

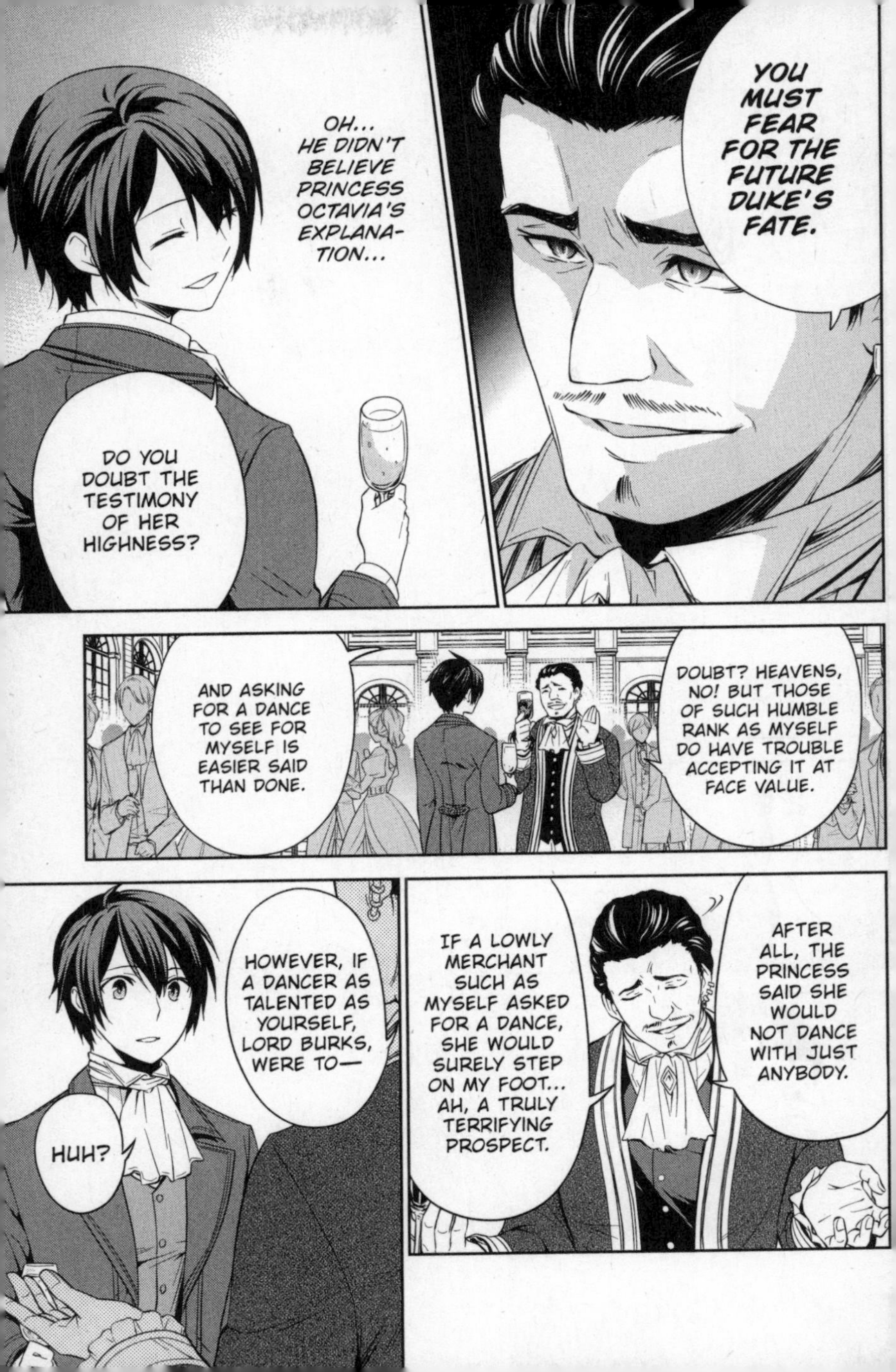
YOU MUST FEAR FOR THE FUTURE DUKE'S FATE.
OH... HE DIDN'T BELIEVE PRINCESS OCTAVIA'S EXPLANATION...
DO YOU DOUBT THE TESTIMONY OF HER HIGHNESS?
DOUBT? HEAVENS, NO! BUT THOSE OF SUCH HUMBLE RANK AS MYSELF DO HAVE TROUBLE ACCEPTING IT AT FACE VALUE.
AND ASKING FOR A DANCE TO SEE FOR MYSELF IS EASIER SAID THAN DONE.
AFTER ALL, THE PRINCESS SAID SHE WOULD NOT DANCE WITH JUST ANYBODY.
IF A LOWLY MERCHANT SUCH AS MYSELF ASKED FOR A DANCE, SHE WOULD SURELY STEP ON MY FOOT... AH, A TRULY TERRIFYING PROSPECT.
HOWEVER, IF A DANCER AS TALENTED AS YOURSELF, LORD BURKS, WERE TO—
HUH?

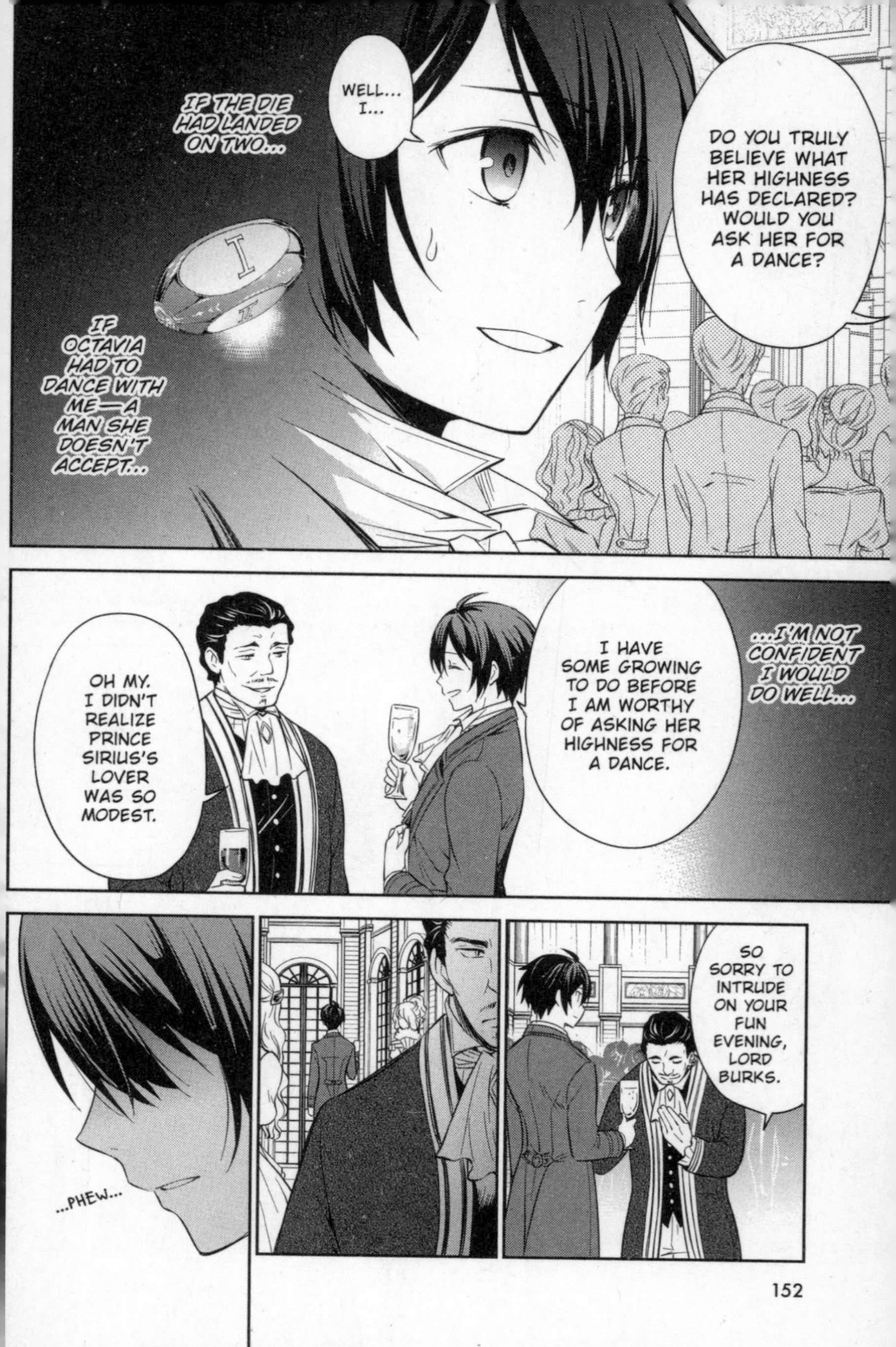
DO YOU TRULY BELIEVE WHAT HER HIGHNESS HAS DECLARED? WOULD YOU ASK HER FOR A DANCE?
WELL... I...
IF THE DIE HAD LANDED ON TWO...
IF OCTAVIA HAD TO DANCE WITH ME—A MAN SHE DOESN'T ACCEPT...
...I'M NOT CONFIDENT I WOULD DO WELL...
I HAVE SOME GROWING TO DO BEFORE I AM WORTHY OF ASKING HER HIGHNESS FOR A DANCE.
OH MY. I DIDN'T REALIZE PRINCE SIRIUS'S LOVER WAS SO MODEST.
SO SORRY TO INTRUDE ON YOUR FUN EVENING, LORD BURKS.
...PHEW...

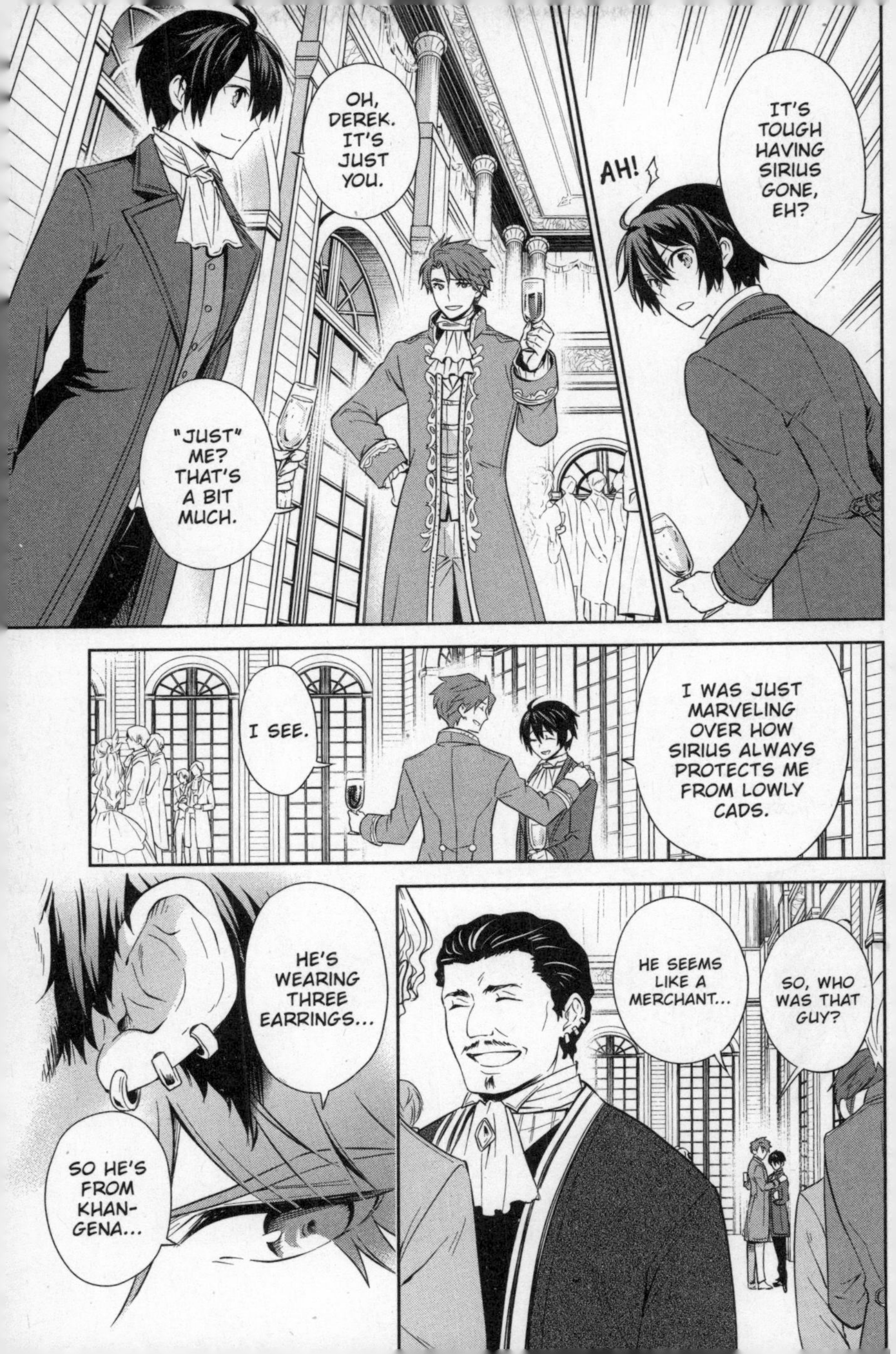
IT'S TOUGH HAVING SIRIUS GONE, EH?
AH!
OH, DEREK. IT'S JUST YOU.
"JUST" ME? THAT'S A BIT MUCH.
I WAS JUST MARVELING OVER HOW SIRIUS ALWAYS PROTECTS ME FROM LOWLY CADS.
I SEE.
SO, WHO WAS THAT GUY?
HE SEEMS LIKE A MERCHANT...
HE'S WEARING THREE EARRINGS...
SO HE'S FROM KHAN-GENA...

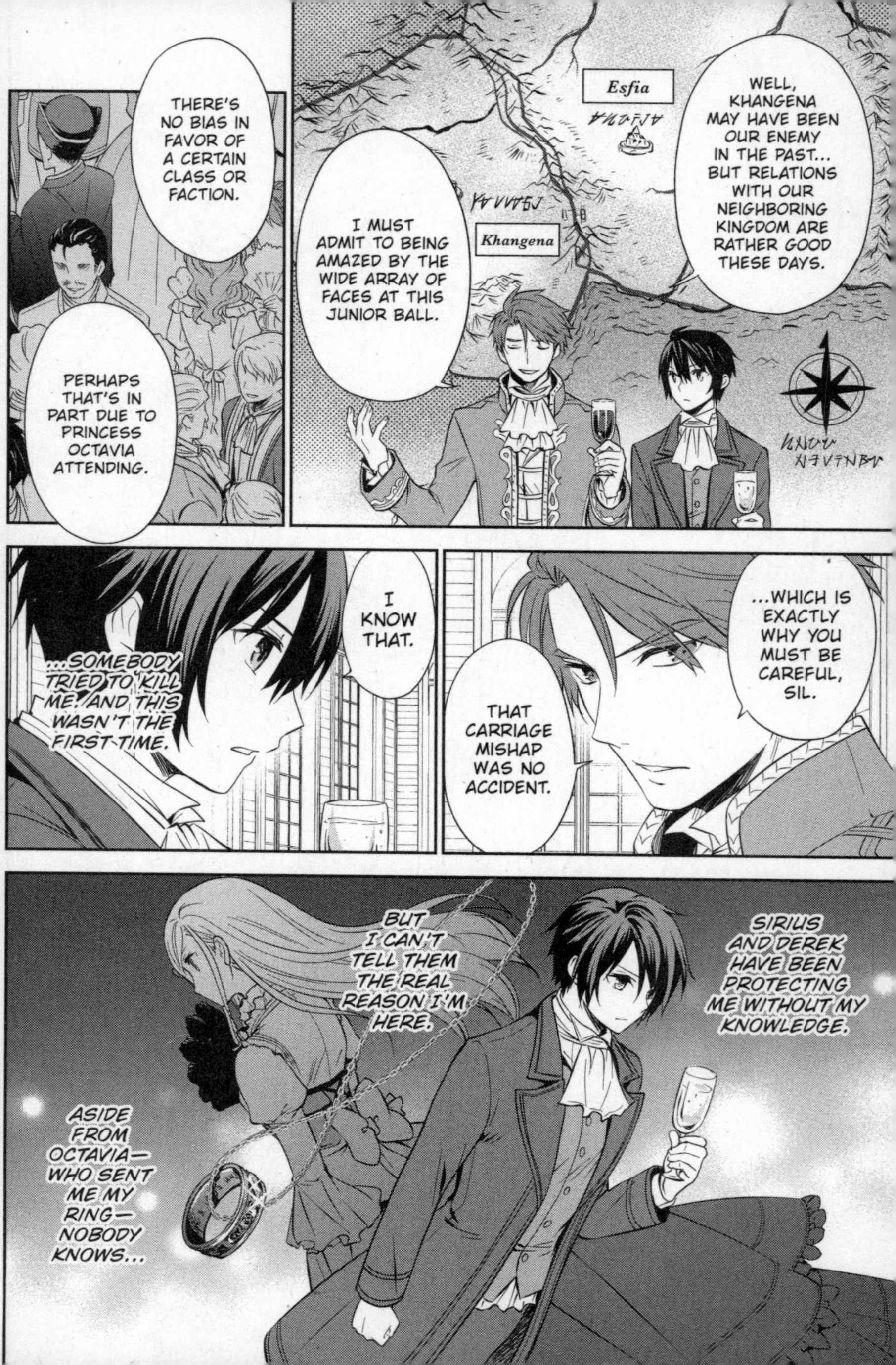
Esfia
Khangena
WELL, KHANGENA MAY HAVE BEEN OUR ENEMY IN THE PAST... BUT RELATIONS WITH OUR NEIGHBORING KINGDOM ARE RATHER GOOD THESE DAYS.
I MUST ADMIT TO BEING AMAZED BY THE WIDE ARRAY OF FACES AT THIS JUNIOR BALL.
THERE'S NO BIAS IN FAVOR OF A CERTAIN CLASS OR FACTION.
PERHAPS THAT'S IN PART DUE TO PRINCESS OCTAVIA ATTENDING.
...WHICH IS EXACTLY WHY YOU MUST BE CAREFUL, SIL.
THAT CARRIAGE MISHAP WAS NO ACCIDENT.
I KNOW THAT.
...SOMEBODY TRIED TO KILL ME. AND THIS WASN'T THE FIRST TIME.
SIRIUS AND DEREK HAVE BEEN PROTECTING ME WITHOUT MY KNOWLEDGE.
BUT I CAN'T TELL THEM THE REAL REASON I'M HERE.
ASIDE FROM OCTAVIA—WHO SENT ME MY RING—NOBODY KNOWS...

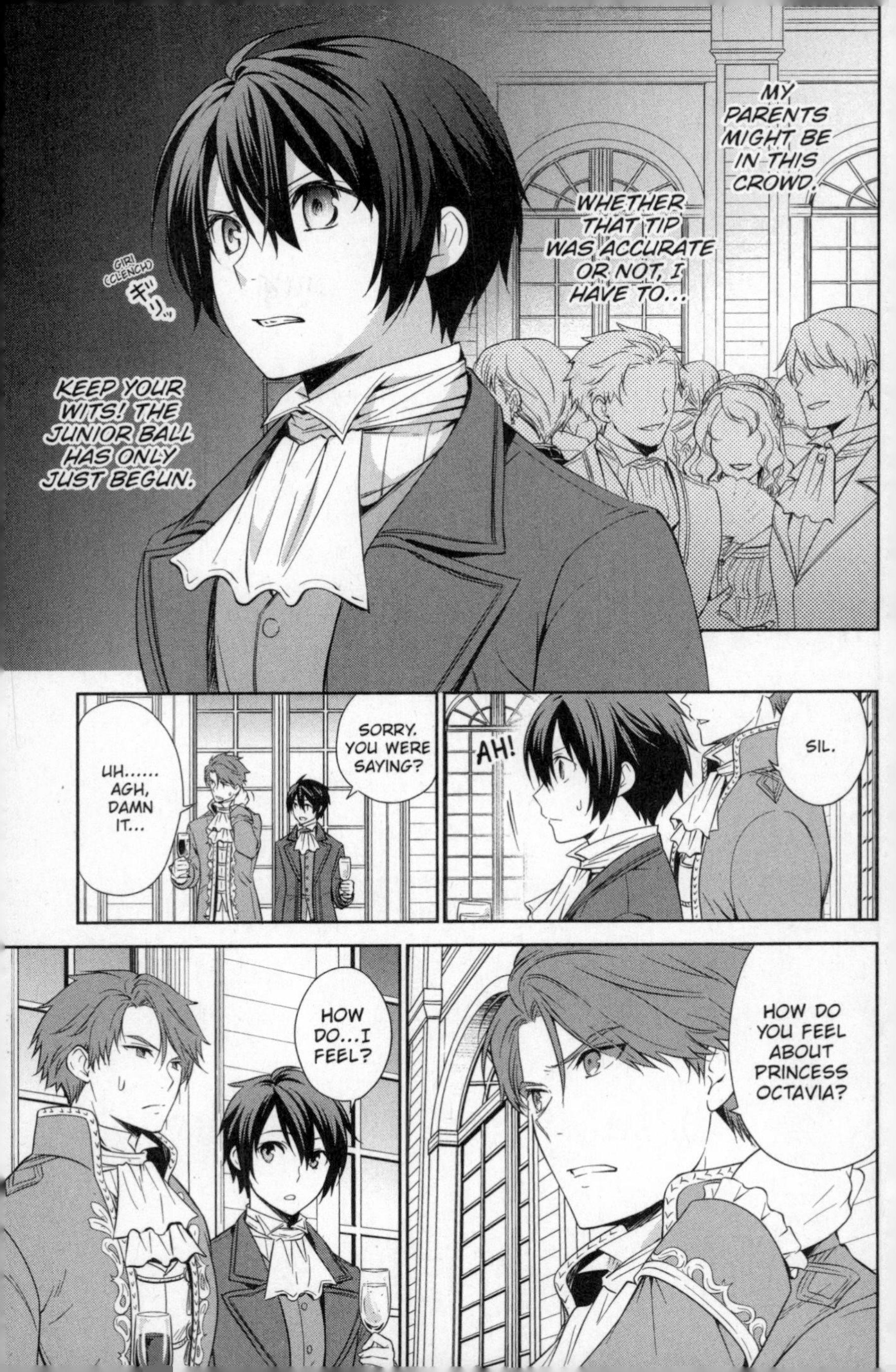
MY PARENTS MIGHT BE IN THIS CROWD.
WHETHER THAT TIP WAS ACCURATE OR NOT, I HAVE TO...
GIRI (CLENCH)
ギリッ
KEEP YOUR WITS! THE JUNIOR BALL HAS ONLY JUST BEGUN.
SIL.
AH!
SORRY. YOU WERE SAYING?
UH...... AGH, DAMN IT...
HOW DO YOU FEEL ABOUT PRINCESS OCTAVIA?
HOW DO...I FEEL?

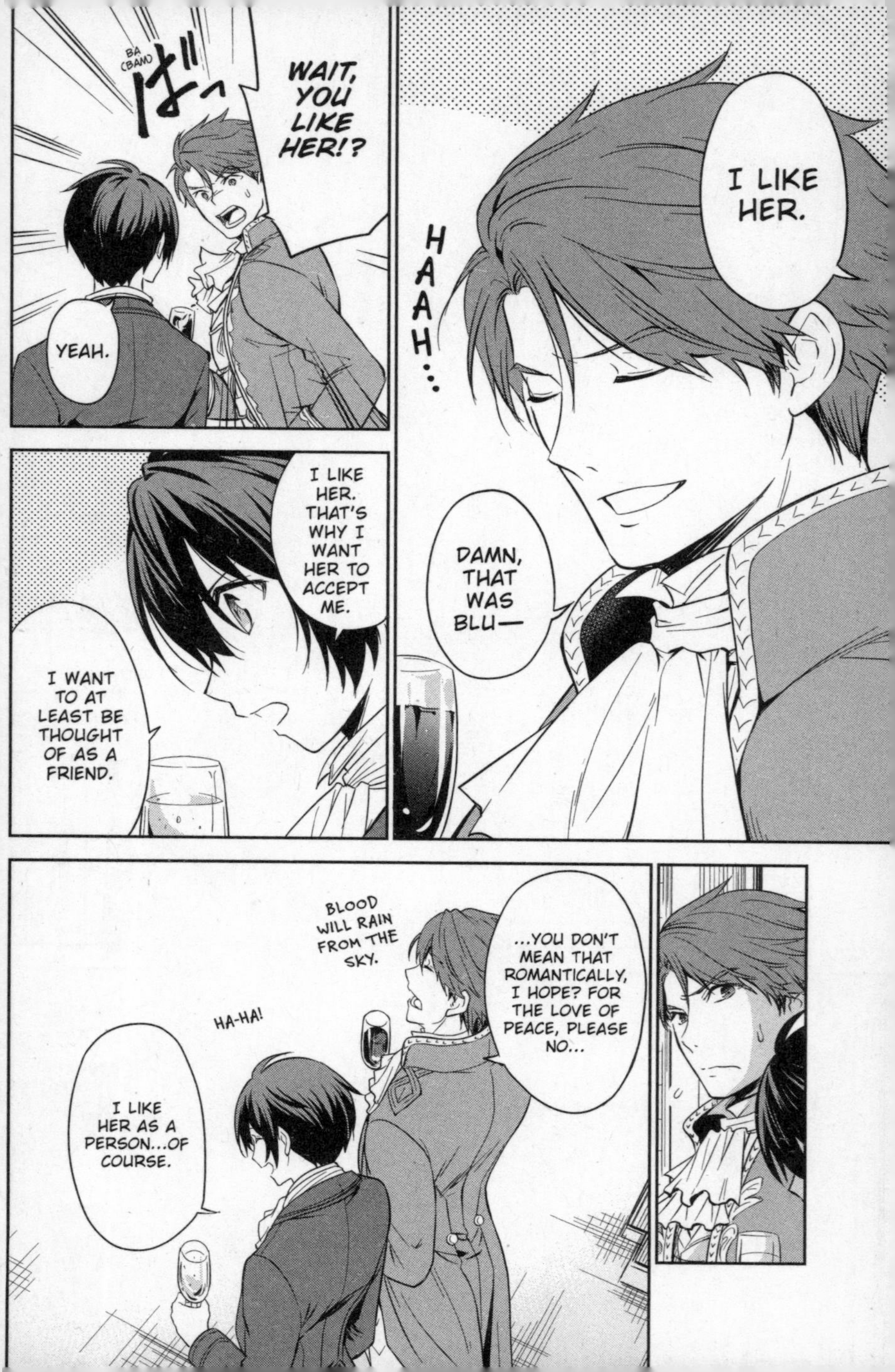
I LIKE HER.
HAAAH...
DAMN, THAT WAS BLU—
BA (BAM) ばっ
WAIT, YOU LIKE HER!?
YEAH.
I LIKE HER. THAT'S WHY I WANT HER TO ACCEPT ME.
I WANT TO AT LEAST BE THOUGHT OF AS A FRIEND.
...YOU DON'T MEAN THAT ROMANTICALLY, I HOPE? FOR THE LOVE OF PEACE, PLEASE NO...
BLOOD WILL RAIN FROM THE SKY.
HA-HA!
I LIKE HER AS A PERSON...OF COURSE.

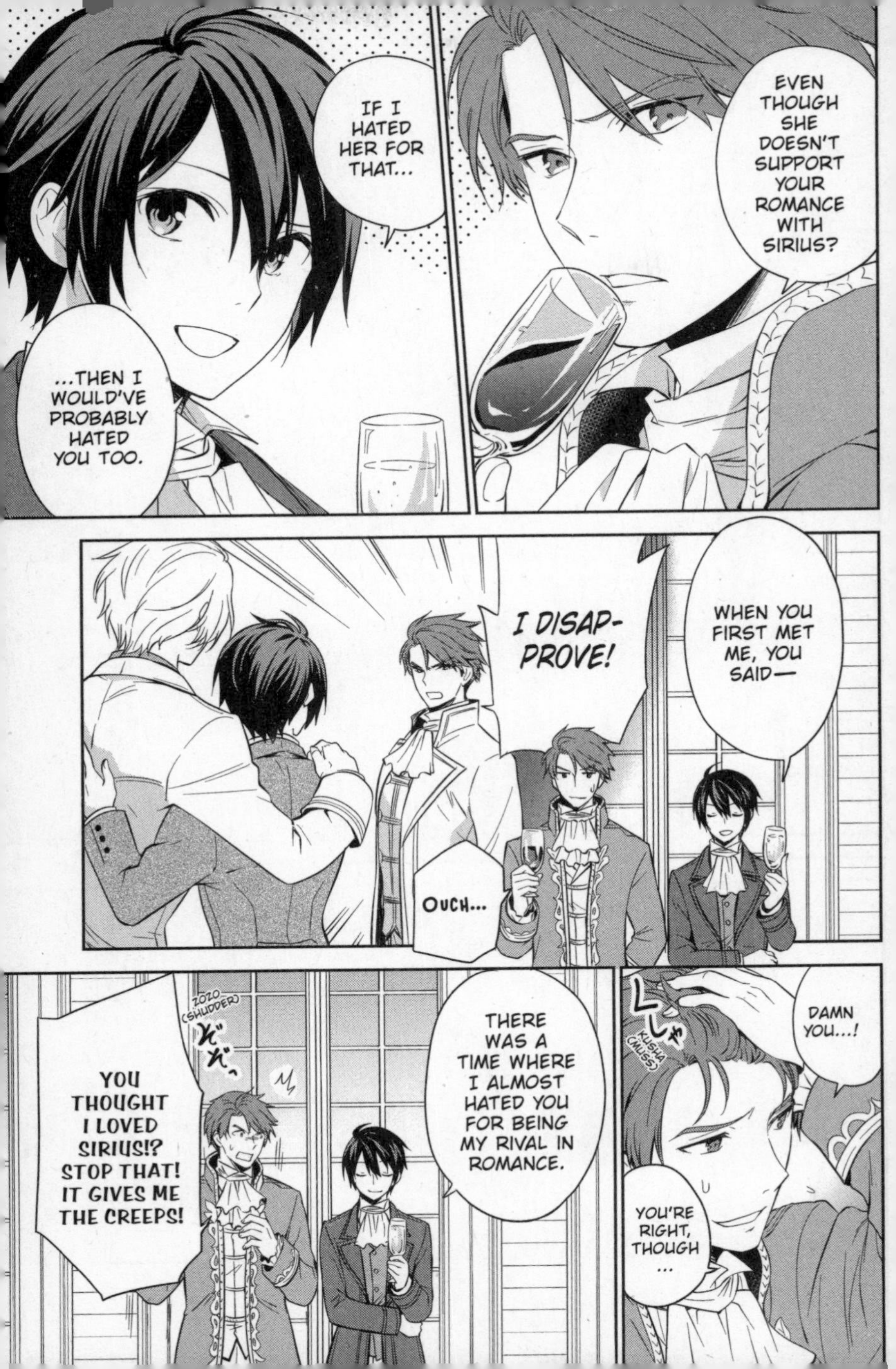
EVEN THOUGH SHE DOESN'T SUPPORT YOUR ROMANCE WITH SIRIUS?
IF I HATED HER FOR THAT...
...THEN I WOULD'VE PROBABLY HATED YOU TOO.
WHEN YOU FIRST MET ME, YOU SAID—
I DISAP-PROVE!
OUCH...
DAMN YOU...!
KUSHA (MUSS)
YOU'RE RIGHT, THOUGH ...
THERE WAS A TIME WHERE I ALMOST HATED YOU FOR BEING MY RIVAL IN ROMANCE.
ZOZO (SHUDDER)
YOU THOUGHT I LOVED SIRIUS!? STOP THAT! IT GIVES ME THE CREEPS!

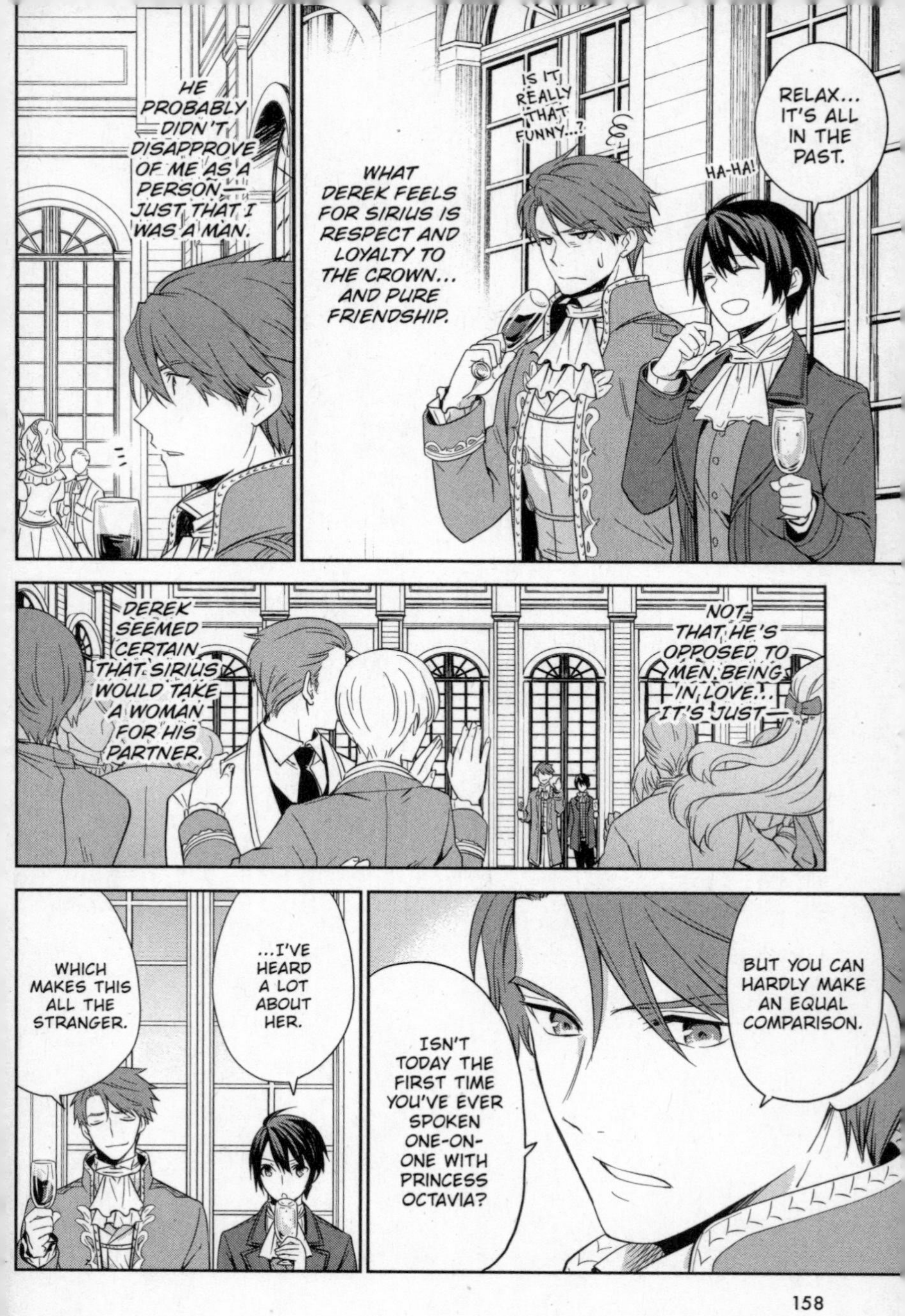
RELAX... IT'S ALL IN THE PAST.
HA-HA!
IS IT REALLY THAT FUNNY...?
WHAT DEREK FEELS FOR SIRIUS IS RESPECT AND LOYALTY TO THE CROWN... AND PURE FRIENDSHIP.
HE PROBABLY DIDN'T DISAPPROVE OF ME AS A PERSON—JUST THAT I WAS A MAN.
NOT THAT HE'S OPPOSED TO MEN BEING IN LOVE... IT'S JUST—
DEREK SEEMED CERTAIN THAT SIRIUS WOULD TAKE A WOMAN FOR HIS PARTNER.
BUT YOU CAN HARDLY MAKE AN EQUAL COMPARISON.
ISN'T TODAY THE FIRST TIME YOU'VE EVER SPOKEN ONE-ON-ONE WITH PRINCESS OCTAVIA?
...I'VE HEARD A LOT ABOUT HER.
WHICH MAKES THIS ALL THE STRANGER.

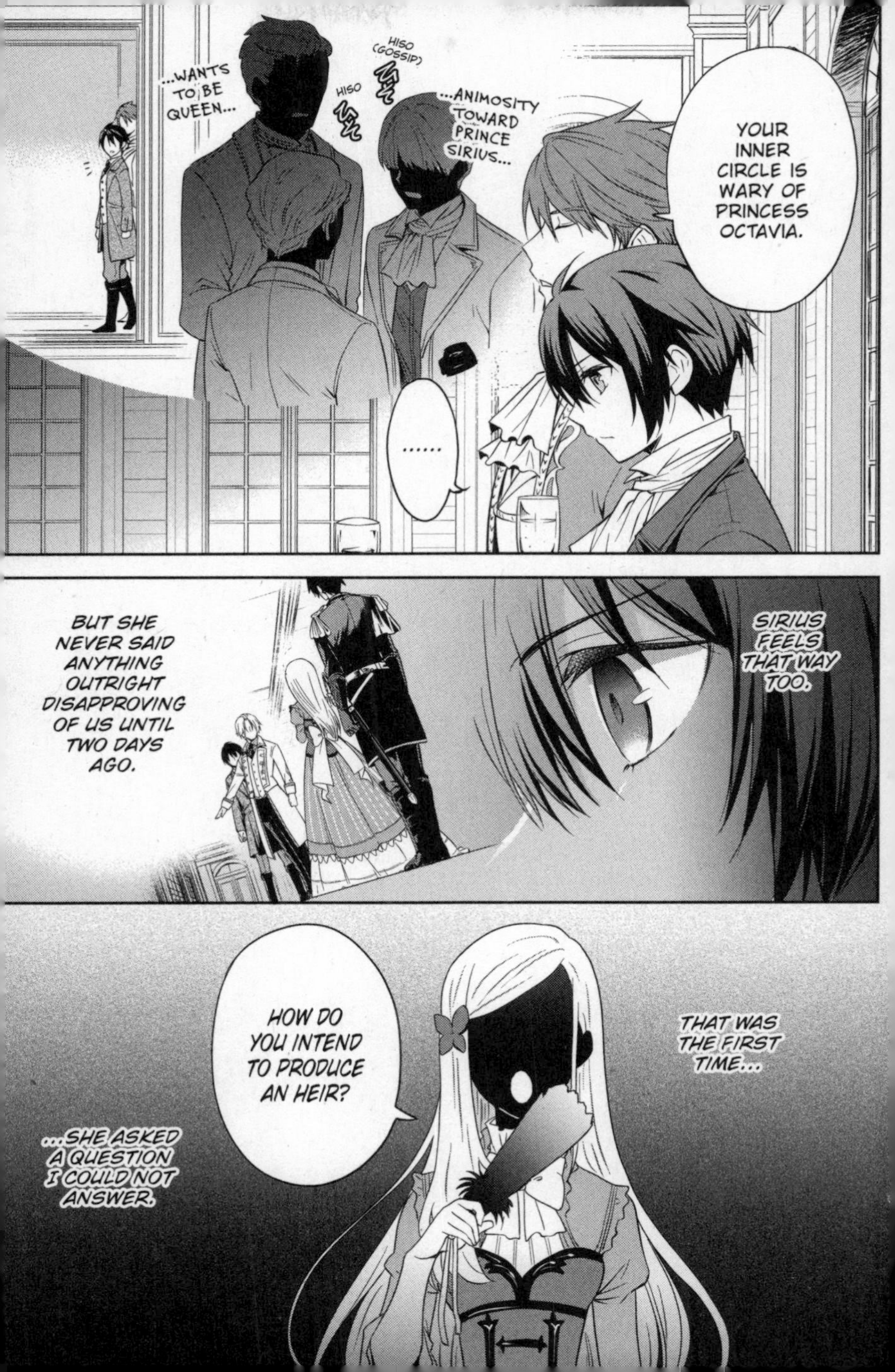
YOUR INNER CIRCLE IS WARY OF PRINCESS OCTAVIA.
...ANIMOSITY TOWARD PRINCE SIRIUS...
HISO (GOSSIP)
HISO
...WANTS TO BE QUEEN...
......
SIRIUS FEELS THAT WAY TOO.
BUT SHE NEVER SAID ANYTHING OUTRIGHT DISAPPROVING OF US UNTIL TWO DAYS AGO.
THAT WAS THE FIRST TIME...
HOW DO YOU INTEND TO PRODUCE AN HEIR?
...SHE ASKED A QUESTION I COULD NOT ANSWER.

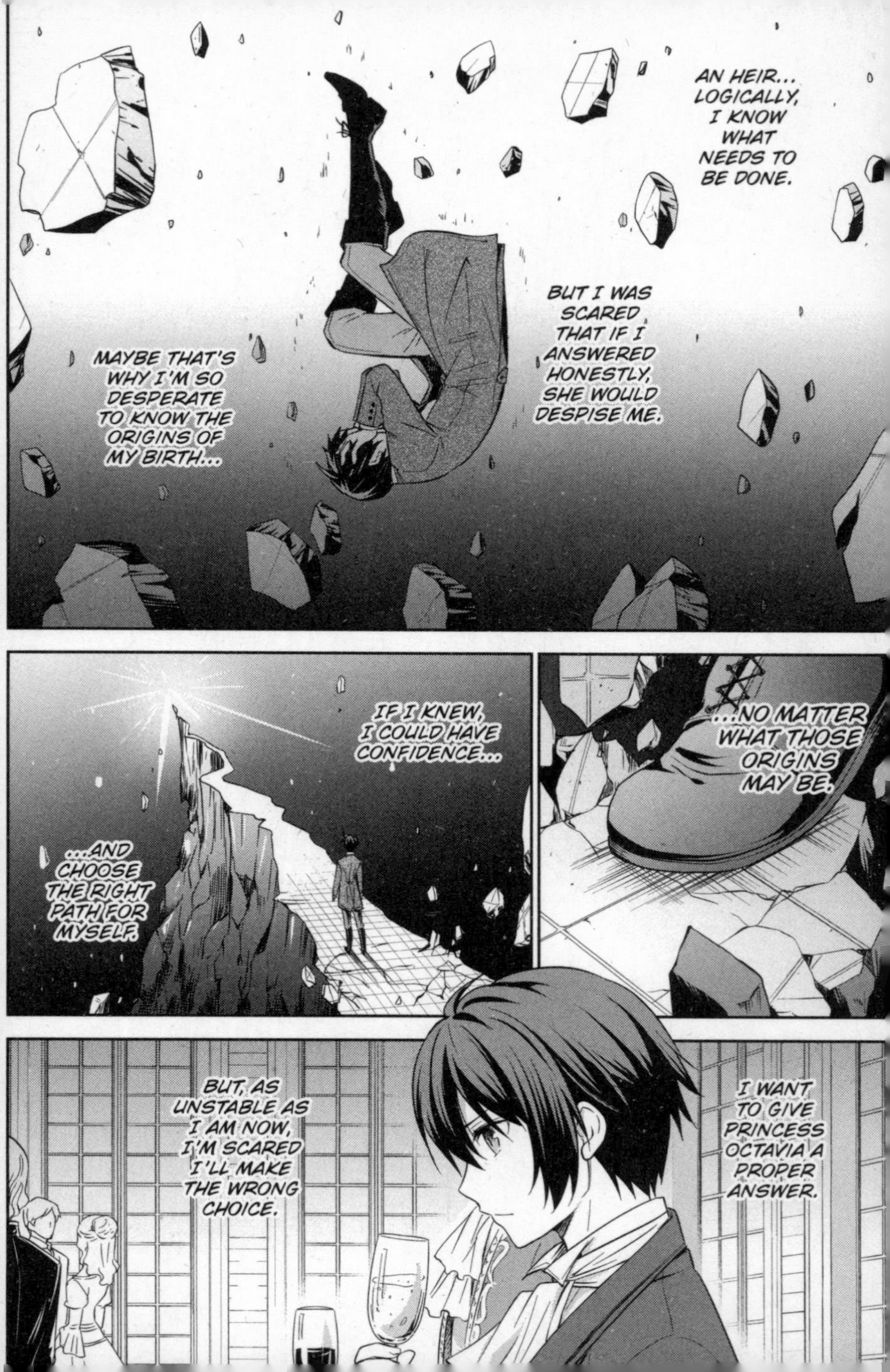

AN HEIR... LOGICALLY, I KNOW WHAT NEEDS TO BE DONE.
BUT I WAS SCARED THAT IF I ANSWERED HONESTLY, SHE WOULD DESPISE ME.
MAYBE THAT'S WHY I'M SO DESPERATE TO KNOW THE ORIGINS OF MY BIRTH...
IF I KNEW, I COULD HAVE CONFIDENCE...
...AND CHOOSE THE RIGHT PATH FOR MYSELF.
...NO MATTER WHAT THOSE ORIGINS MAY BE.
I WANT TO GIVE PRINCESS OCTAVIA A PROPER ANSWER.
BUT, AS UNSTABLE AS I AM NOW, I'M SCARED I'LL MAKE THE WRONG CHOICE.

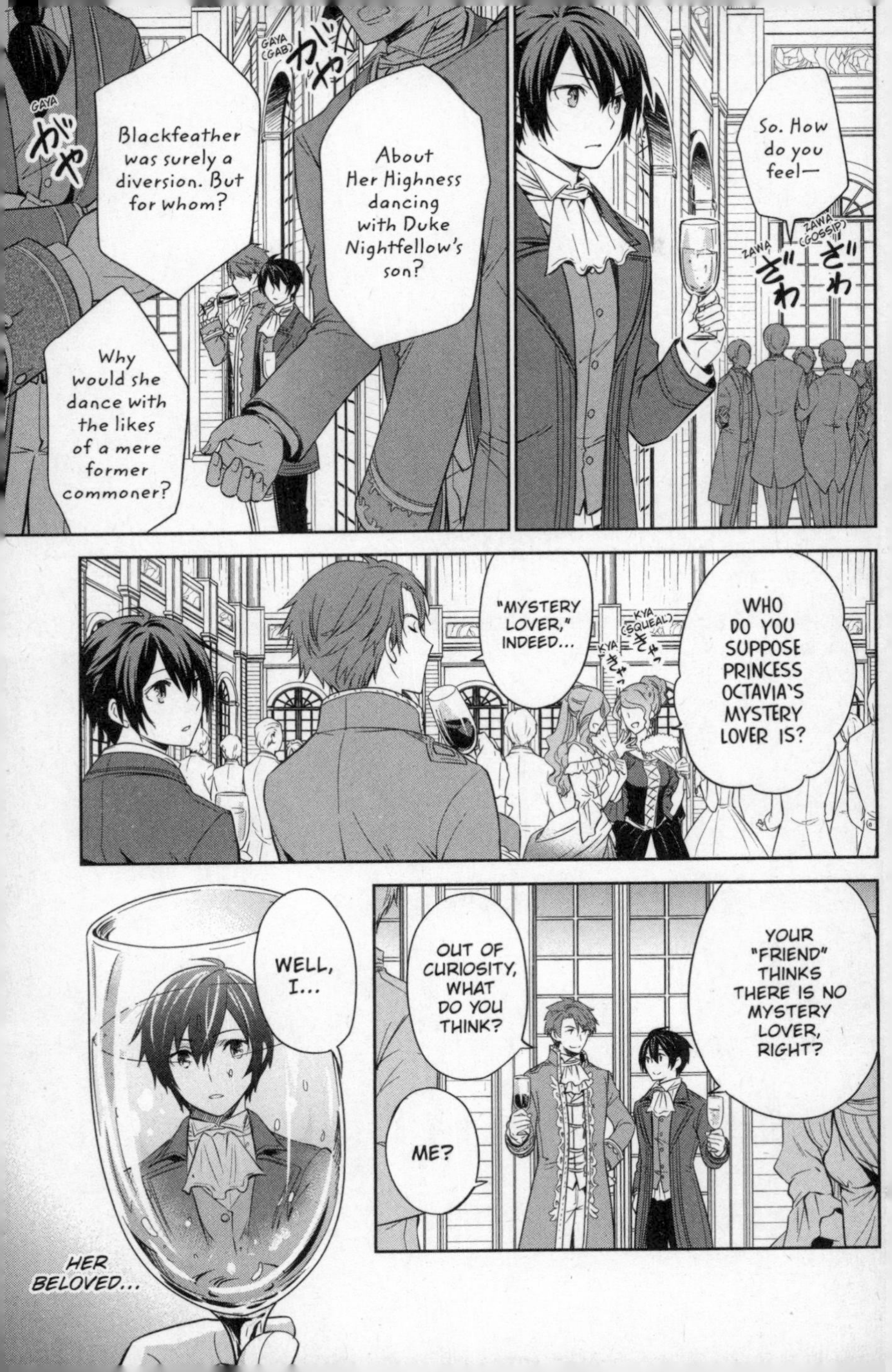
So. How do you feel—
ZAWA (GOSSIP)
ざわ
ZAWA
ざわ
GAYA (GAB)
がや
About Her Highness dancing with Duke Nightfellow's son?
Blackfeather was surely a diversion. But for whom?
GAYA
がや
Why would she dance with the likes of a mere former commoner?
WHO DO YOU SUPPOSE PRINCESS OCTAVIA'S MYSTERY LOVER IS?
KYA (SQUEAL)
きゃっ
KYA
きゃっ
"MYSTERY LOVER," INDEED...
YOUR "FRIEND" THINKS THERE IS NO MYSTERY LOVER, RIGHT?
OUT OF CURIOSITY, WHAT DO YOU THINK?
ME?
WELL, I...
HER BELOVED...

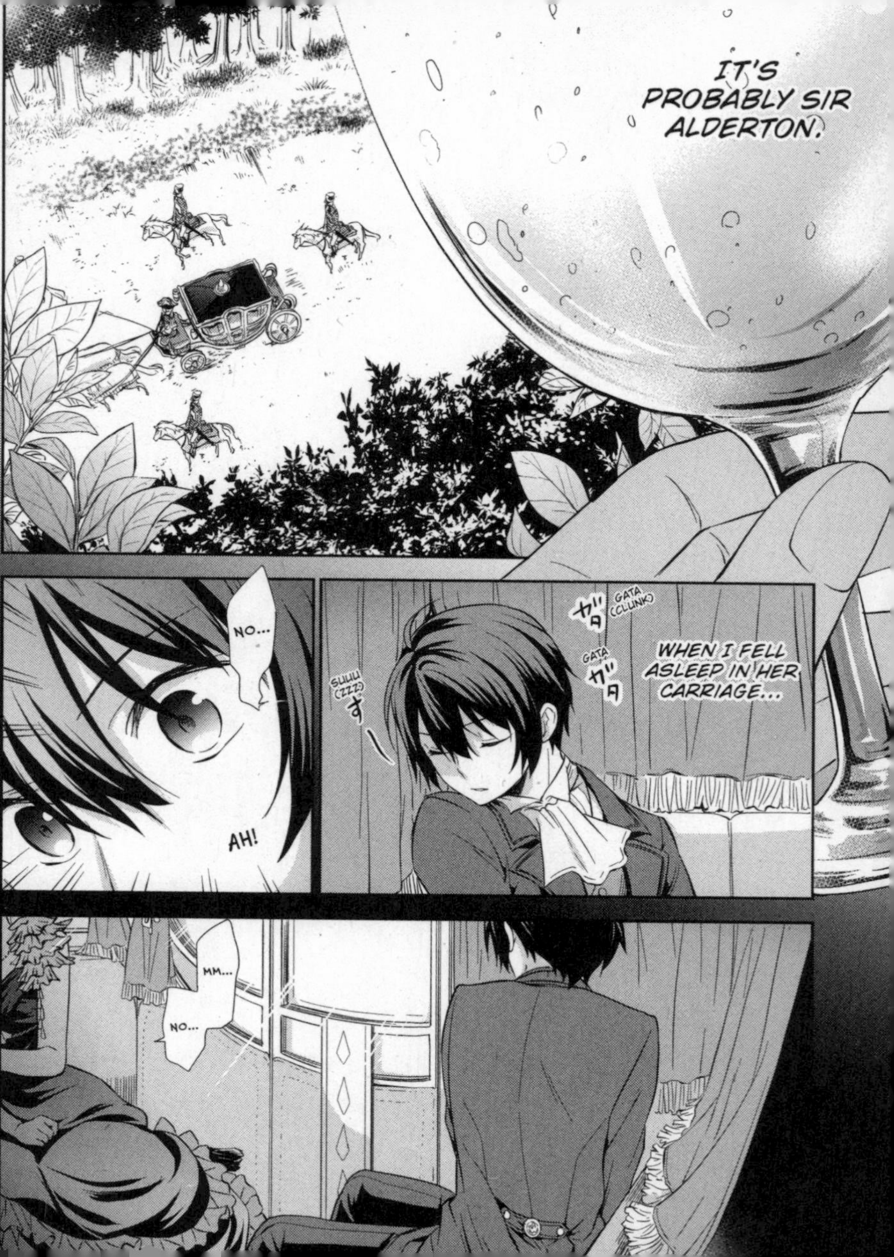
IT'S PROBABLY SIR ALDERTON.
ガタ GATA (CLLINK)
ガタ GATA
WHEN I FELL ASLEEP IN HER CARRIAGE...
すー SUUU (ZZZ)
NO...
AH!
MM...
NO...

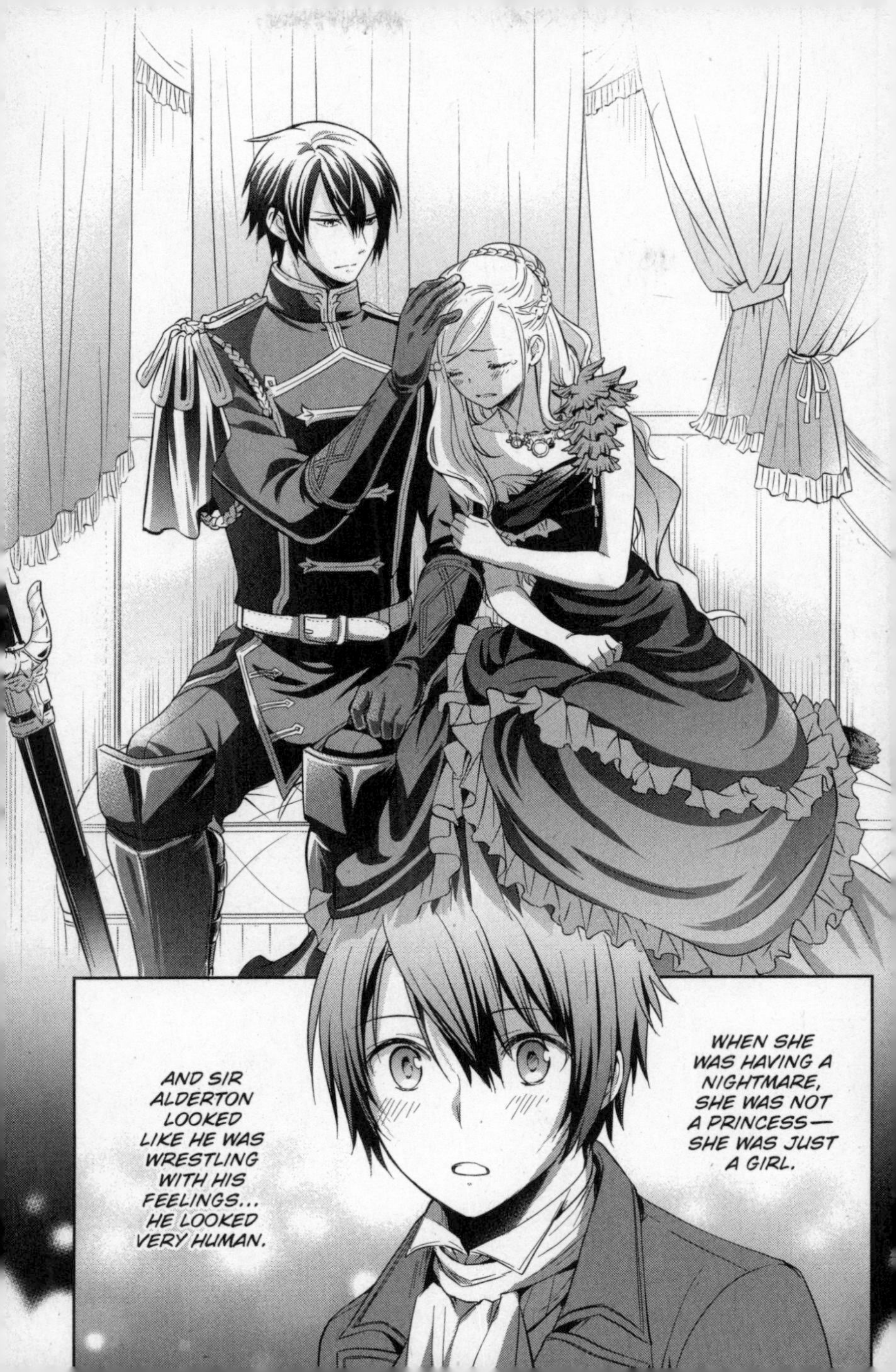
WHEN SHE WAS HAVING A NIGHTMARE, SHE WAS NOT A PRINCESS— SHE WAS JUST A GIRL.
AND SIR ALDERTON LOOKED LIKE HE WAS WRESTLING WITH HIS FEELINGS... HE LOOKED VERY HUMAN.

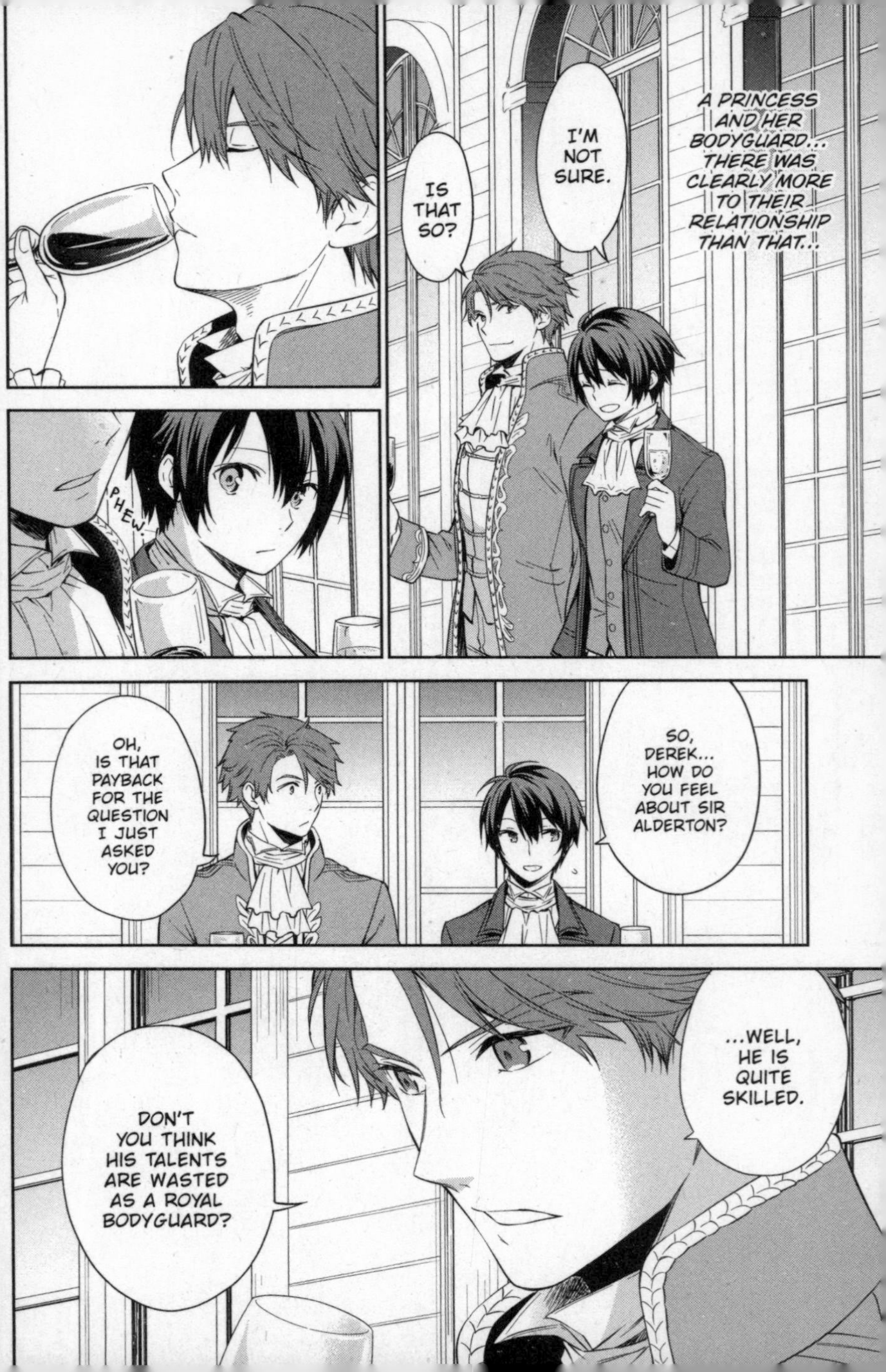
A PRINCESS AND HER BODYGUARD... THERE WAS CLEARLY MORE TO THEIR RELATIONSHIP THAN THAT...
I'M NOT SURE.
IS THAT SO?
PHEW.
SO, DEREK... HOW DO YOU FEEL ABOUT SIR ALDERTON?
OH, IS THAT PAYBACK FOR THE QUESTION I JUST ASKED YOU?
...WELL, HE IS QUITE SKILLED.
DON'T YOU THINK HIS TALENTS ARE WASTED AS A ROYAL BODYGUARD?

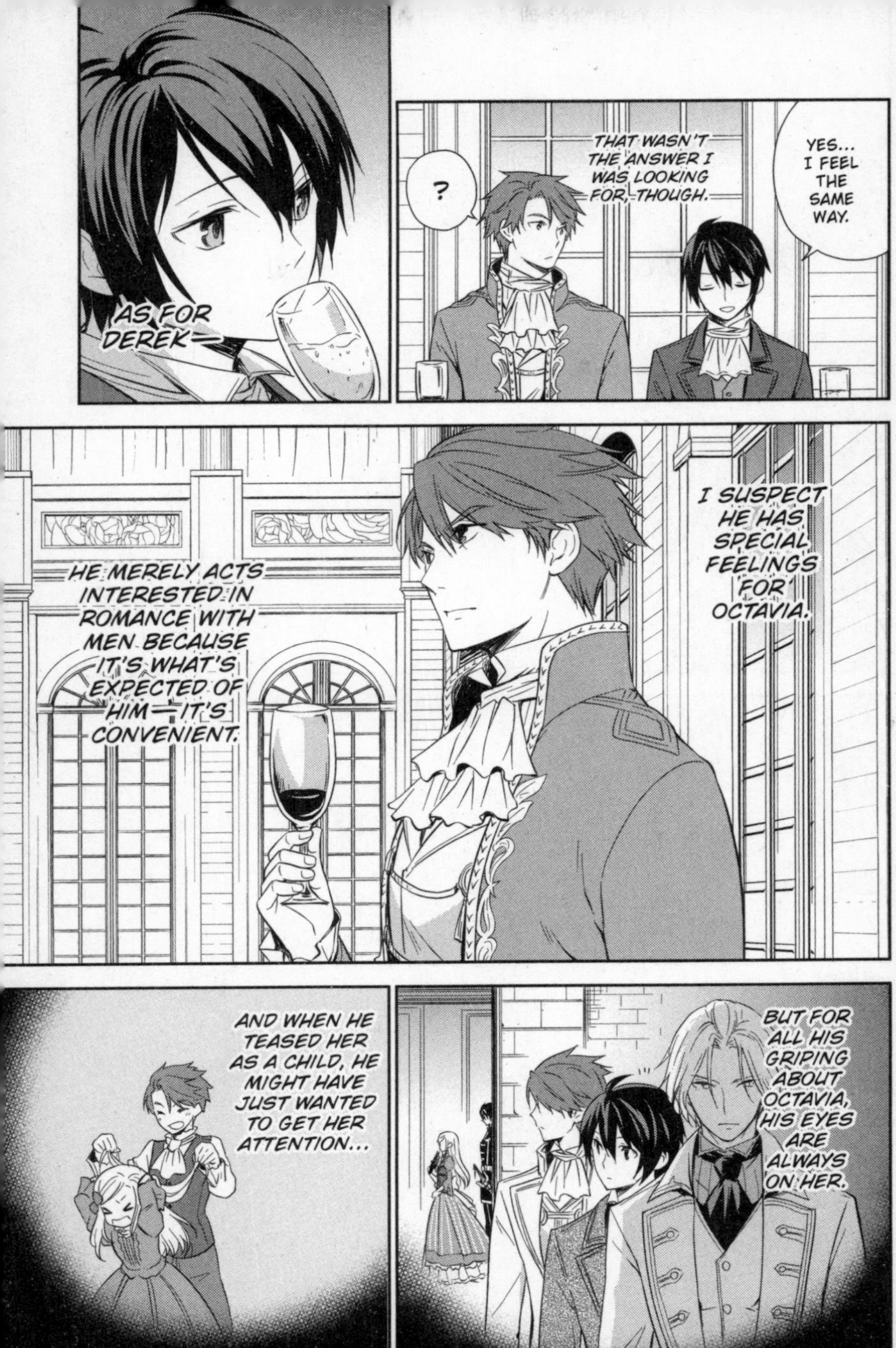
YES... I FEEL THE SAME WAY.
THAT WASN'T THE ANSWER I WAS LOOKING FOR, THOUGH.
?
AS FOR DEREK—
I SUSPECT HE HAS SPECIAL FEELINGS FOR OCTAVIA.
HE MERELY ACTS INTERESTED IN ROMANCE WITH MEN BECAUSE IT'S WHAT'S EXPECTED OF HIM—IT'S CONVENIENT.
BUT FOR ALL HIS GRIPING ABOUT OCTAVIA, HIS EYES ARE ALWAYS ON HER.
AND WHEN HE TEASED HER AS A CHILD, HE MIGHT HAVE JUST WANTED TO GET HER ATTENTION...

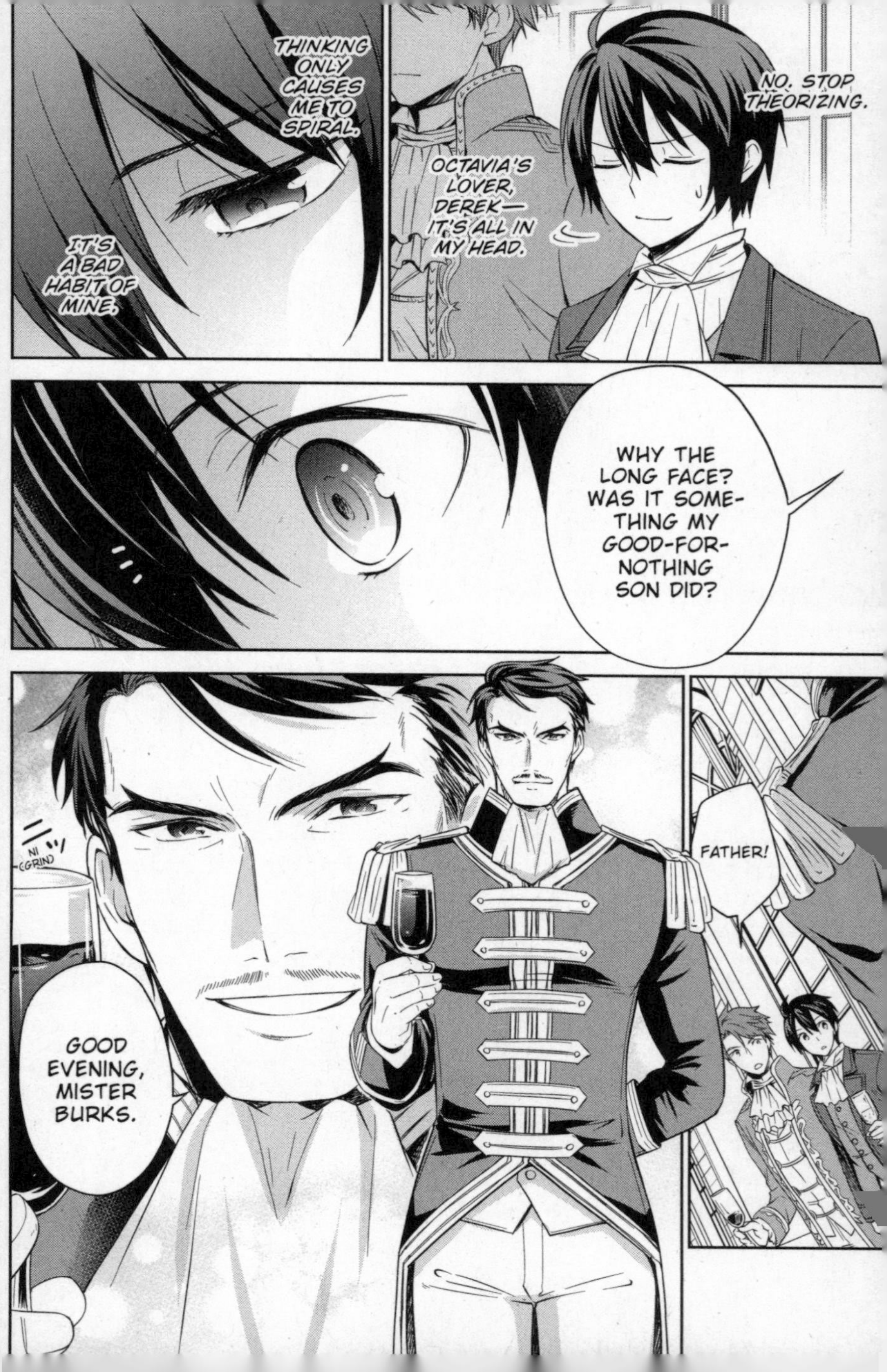
NO. STOP THEORIZING.
OCTAVIA'S LOVER, DEREK—IT'S ALL IN MY HEAD.
THINKING ONLY CAUSES ME TO SPIRAL.
IT'S A BAD HABIT OF MINE.
WHY THE LONG FACE? WAS IT SOME-THING MY GOOD-FOR-NOTHING SON DID?
FATHER!
NI (GRIN)
GOOD EVENING, MISTER BURKS.

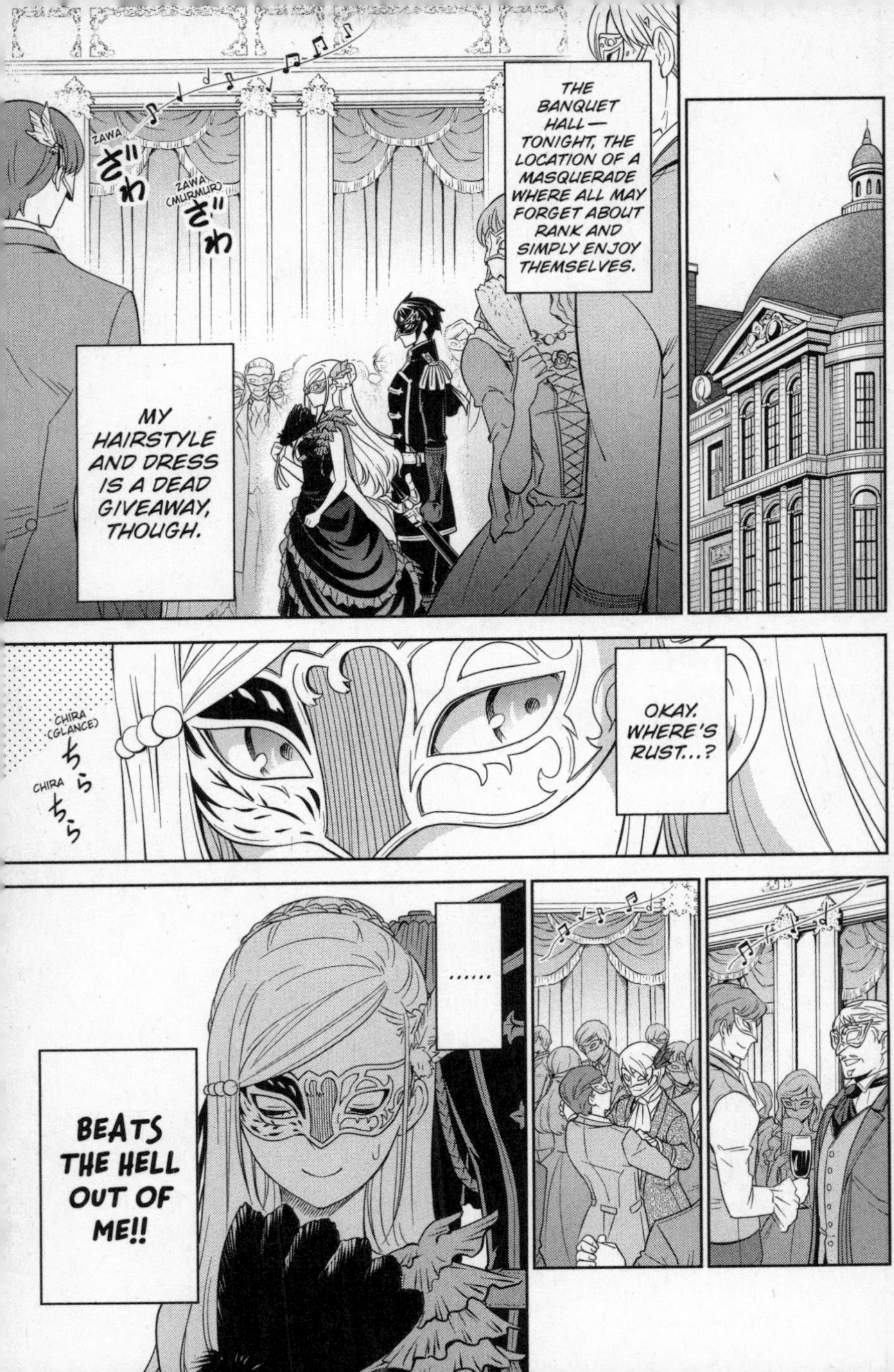
THE BANQUET HALL—TONIGHT, THE LOCATION OF A MASQUERADE WHERE ALL MAY FORGET ABOUT RANK AND SIMPLY ENJOY THEMSELVES.
ZAWA ざわ
ZAWA (MURMUR) ざわ
MY HAIRSTYLE AND DRESS IS A DEAD GIVEAWAY, THOUGH.
OKAY. WHERE'S RUST...?
CHIRA (GLANCE) ちら
CHIRA ちら
......
BEATS THE HELL OUT OF ME!!

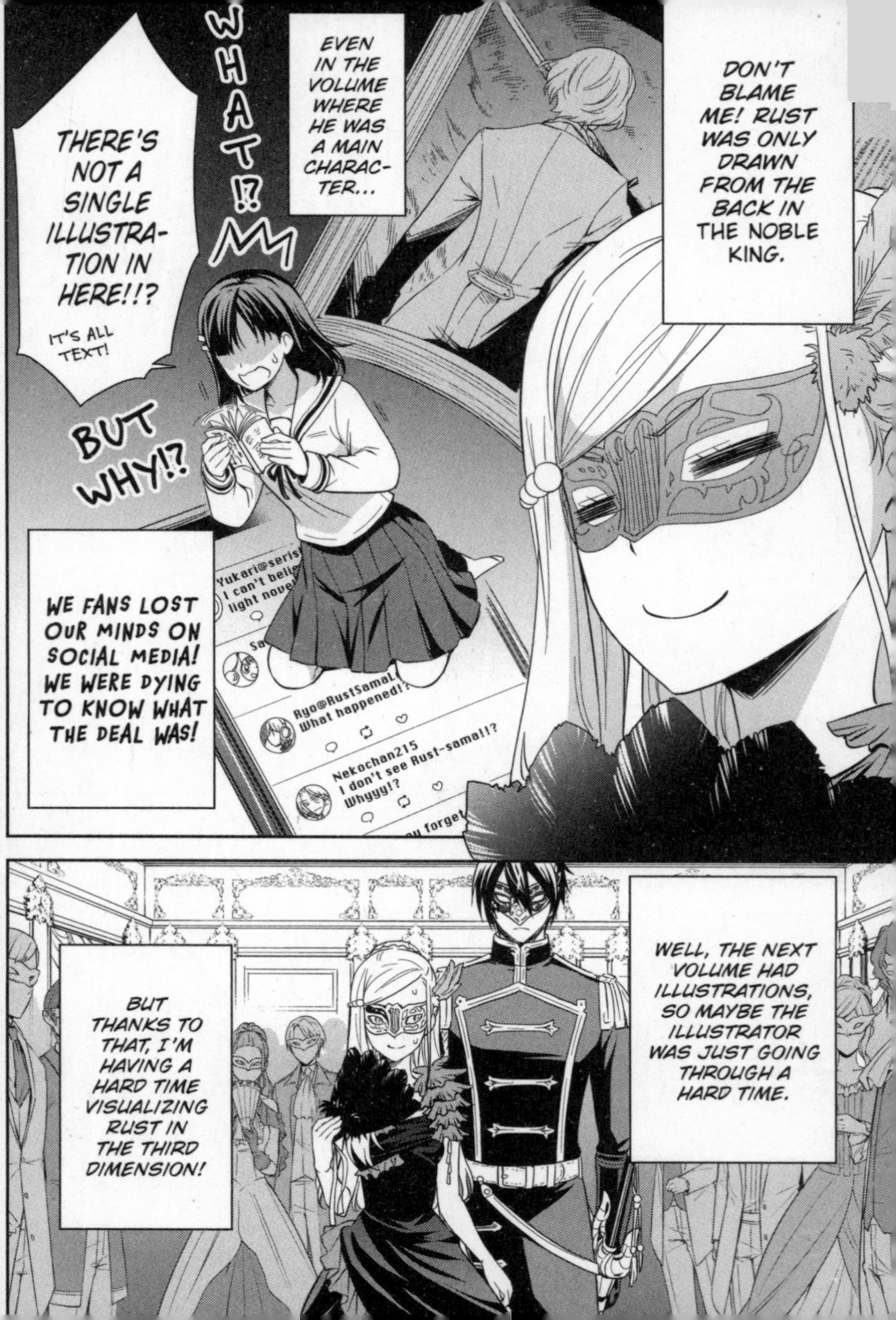
DON'T BLAME ME! RUST WAS ONLY DRAWN FROM THE BACK IN THE NOBLE KING.
EVEN IN THE VOLUME WHERE HE WAS A MAIN CHARAC-TER...
WHAT!?
THERE'S NOT A SINGLE ILLUSTRA-TION IN HERE!!?
IT'S ALL TEXT!
BUT WHY!?
WE FANS LOST OUR MINDS ON SOCIAL MEDIA! WE WERE DYING TO KNOW WHAT THE DEAL WAS!
What happened!?
Nekochan215
I don't see Rust-sama!!?
Whyyy!?
WELL, THE NEXT VOLUME HAD ILLUSTRATIONS, SO MAYBE THE ILLUSTRATOR WAS JUST GOING THROUGH A HARD TIME.
BUT THANKS TO THAT, I'M HAVING A HARD TIME VISUALIZING RUST IN THE THIRD DIMENSION!

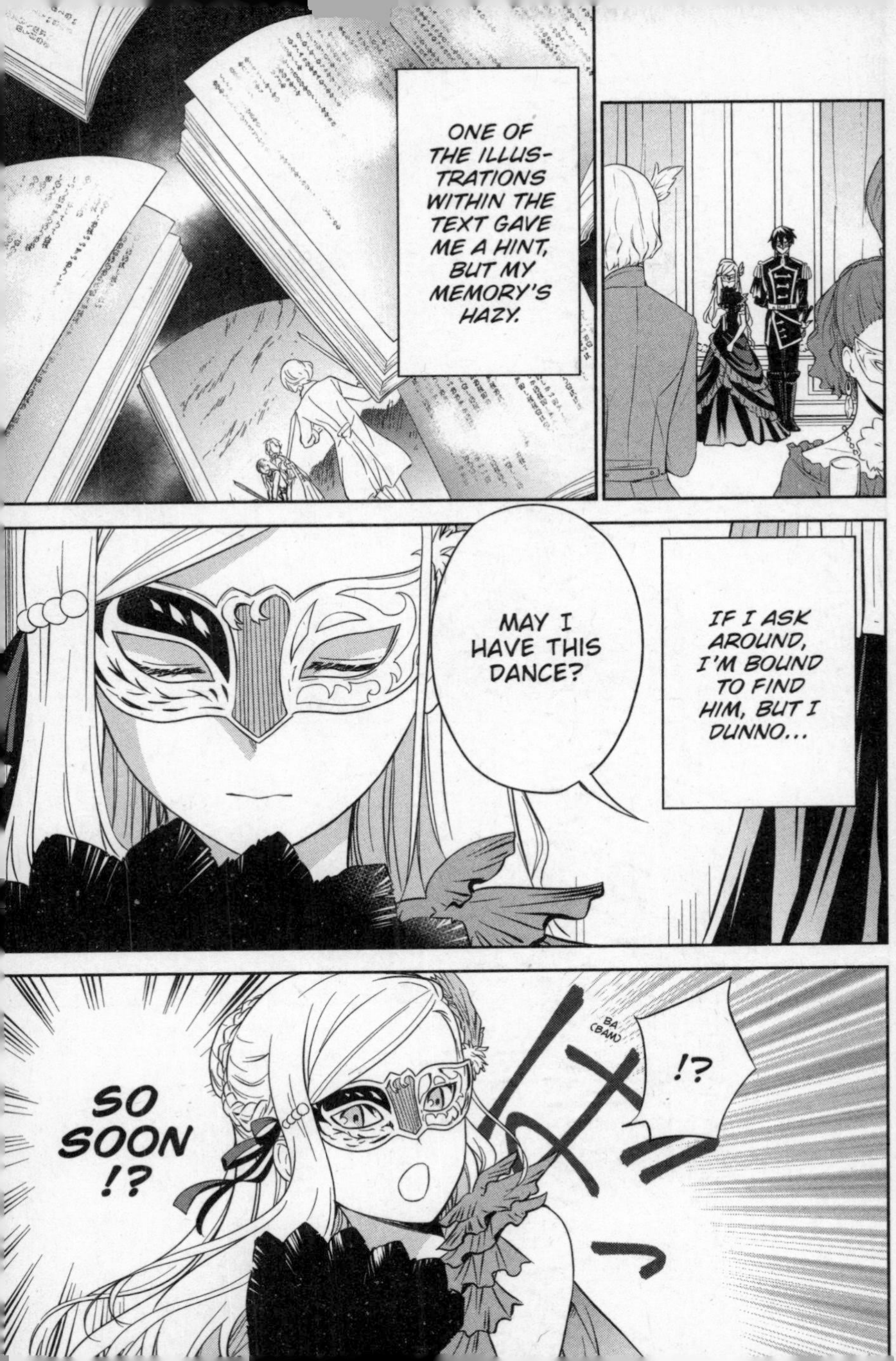
ONE OF THE ILLUS-TRATIONS WITHIN THE TEXT GAVE ME A HINT, BUT MY MEMORY'S HAZY.
IF I ASK AROUND, I'M BOUND TO FIND HIM, BUT I DUNNO...
MAY I HAVE THIS DANCE?
BA (BAM)
!?
SO SOON !?

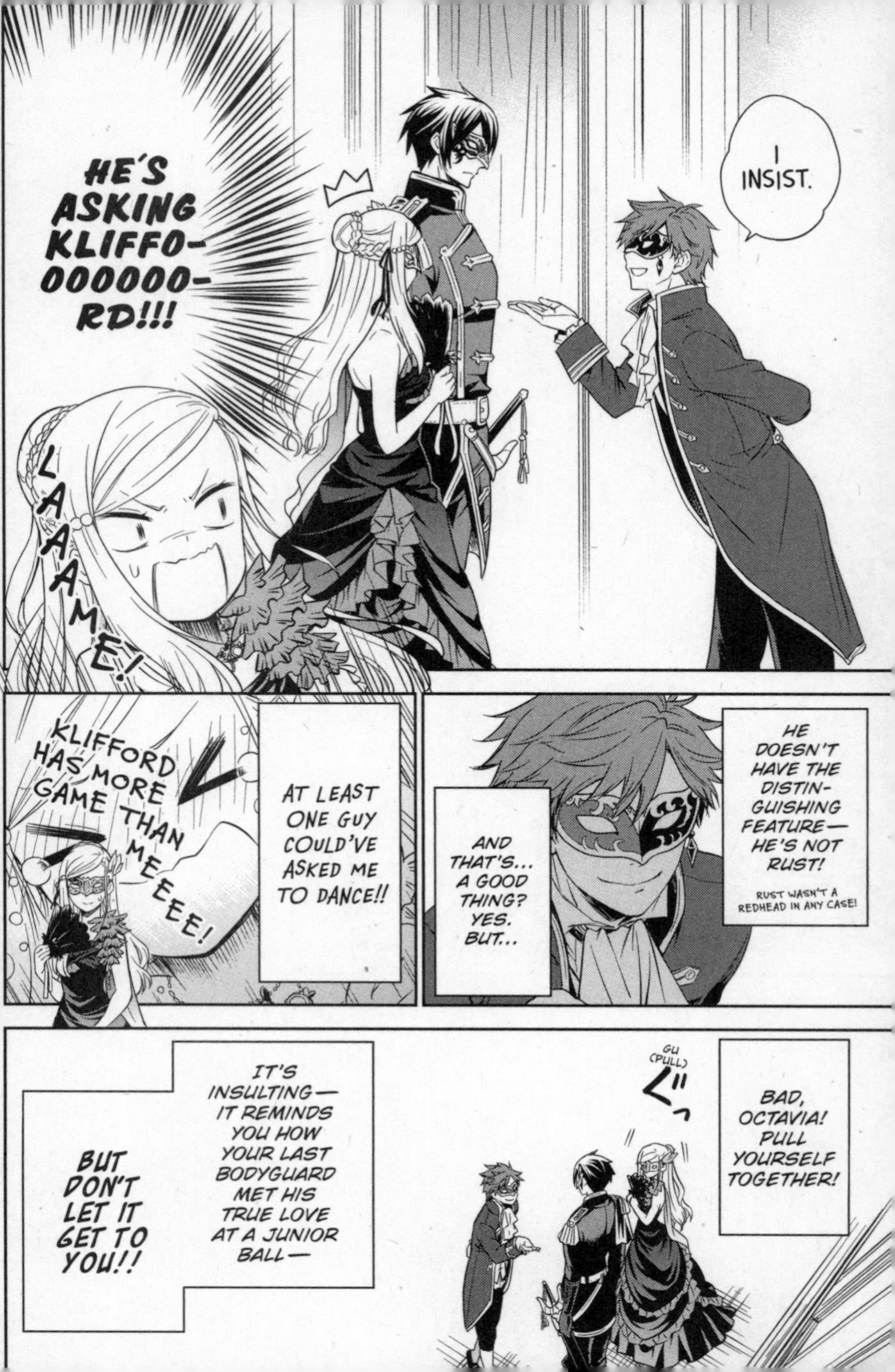
I INSIST.
HE'S ASKING KLIFFO-OOOOOOO-RD!!!
LAAAAME!
HE DOESN'T HAVE THE DISTIN-GUISHING FEATURE—HE'S NOT RUST!
RUST WASN'T A REDHEAD IN ANY CASE!
AND THAT'S... A GOOD THING? YES. BUT...
AT LEAST ONE GUY COULD'VE ASKED ME TO DANCE!!
KLIFFORD HAS MORE GAME THAN MEEEEE!
BAD, OCTAVIA! PULL YOURSELF TOGETHER!
GU (PULL)
ぐっ
IT'S INSULTING—IT REMINDS YOU HOW YOUR LAST BODYGUARD MET HIS TRUE LOVE AT A JUNIOR BALL—
BUT DON'T LET IT GET TO YOU!!

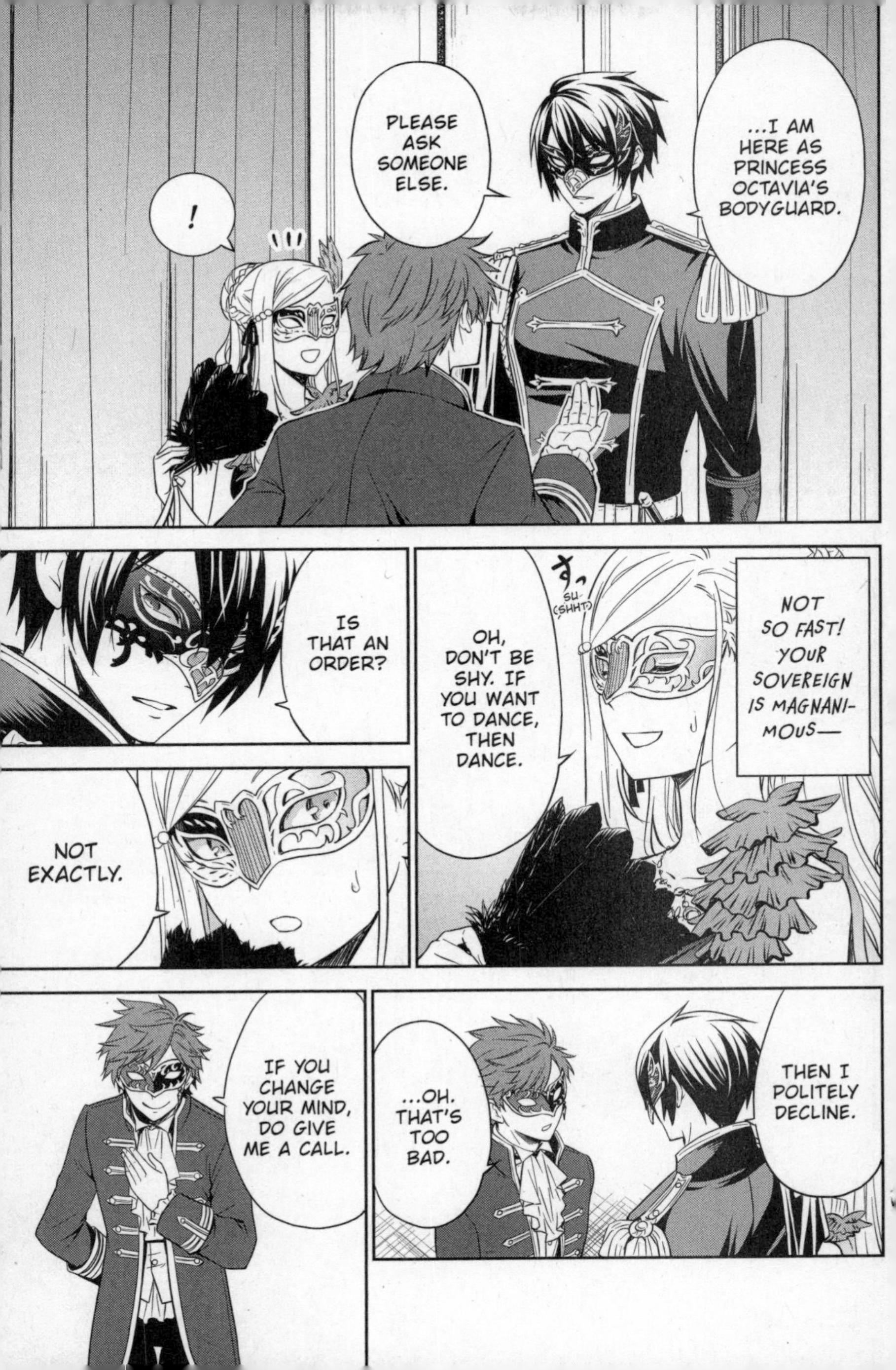
...I AM HERE AS PRINCESS OCTAVIA'S BODYGUARD.
PLEASE ASK SOMEONE ELSE.
!
NOT SO FAST! YOUR SOVEREIGN IS MAGNANIMOUS—
すっ
SU- (SHHT)
OH, DON'T BE SHY. IF YOU WANT TO DANCE, THEN DANCE.
IS THAT AN ORDER?
NOT EXACTLY.
THEN I POLITELY DECLINE.
...OH. THAT'S TOO BAD.
IF YOU CHANGE YOUR MIND, DO GIVE ME A CALL.

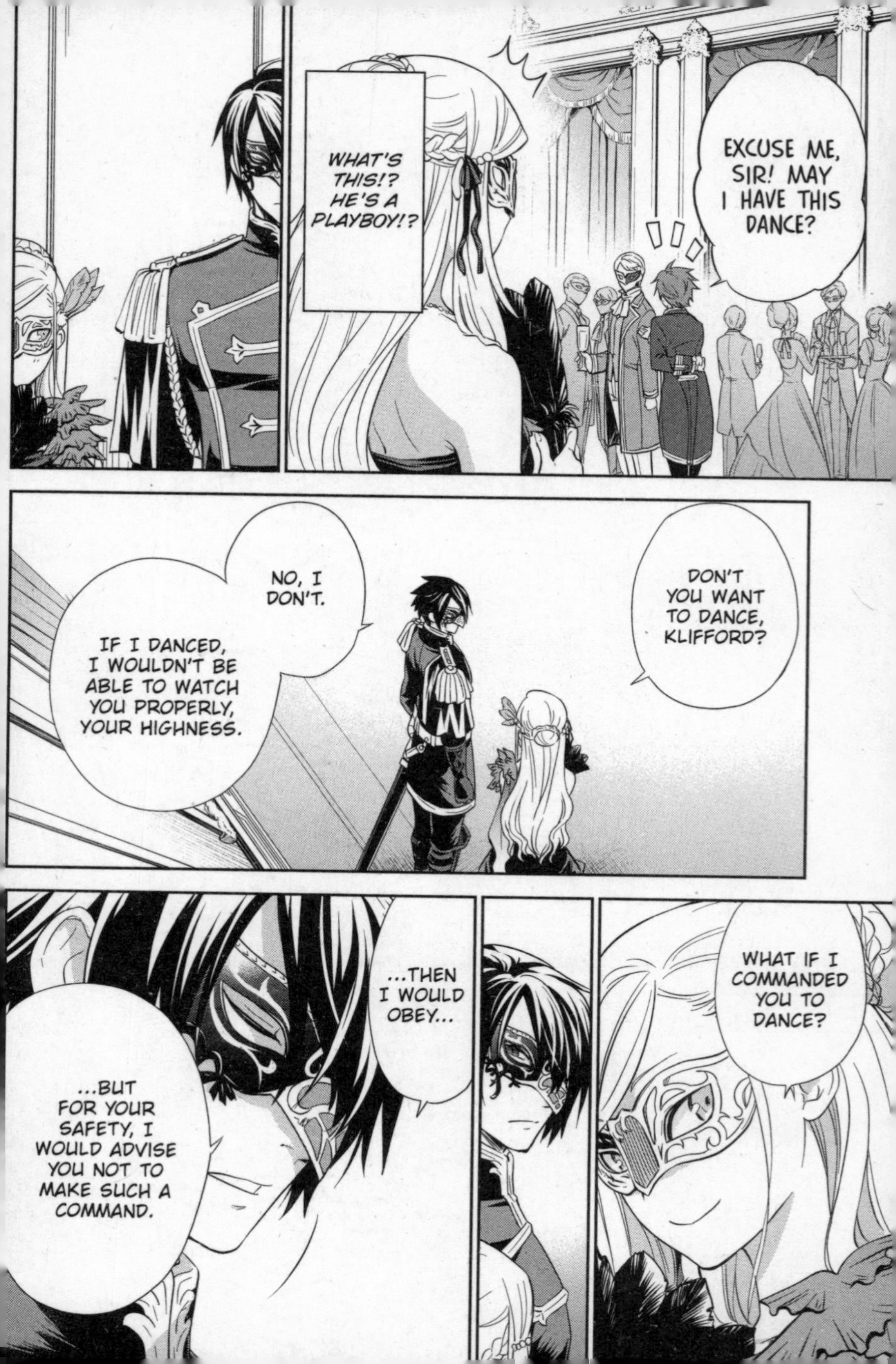
EXCUSE ME, SIR! MAY I HAVE THIS DANCE?
WHAT'S THIS!? HE'S A PLAYBOY!?
DON'T YOU WANT TO DANCE, KLIFFORD?
NO, I DON'T.
IF I DANCED, I WOULDN'T BE ABLE TO WATCH YOU PROPERLY, YOUR HIGHNESS.
WHAT IF I COMMANDED YOU TO DANCE?
...THEN I WOULD OBEY...
...BUT FOR YOUR SAFETY, I WOULD ADVISE YOU NOT TO MAKE SUCH A COMMAND.

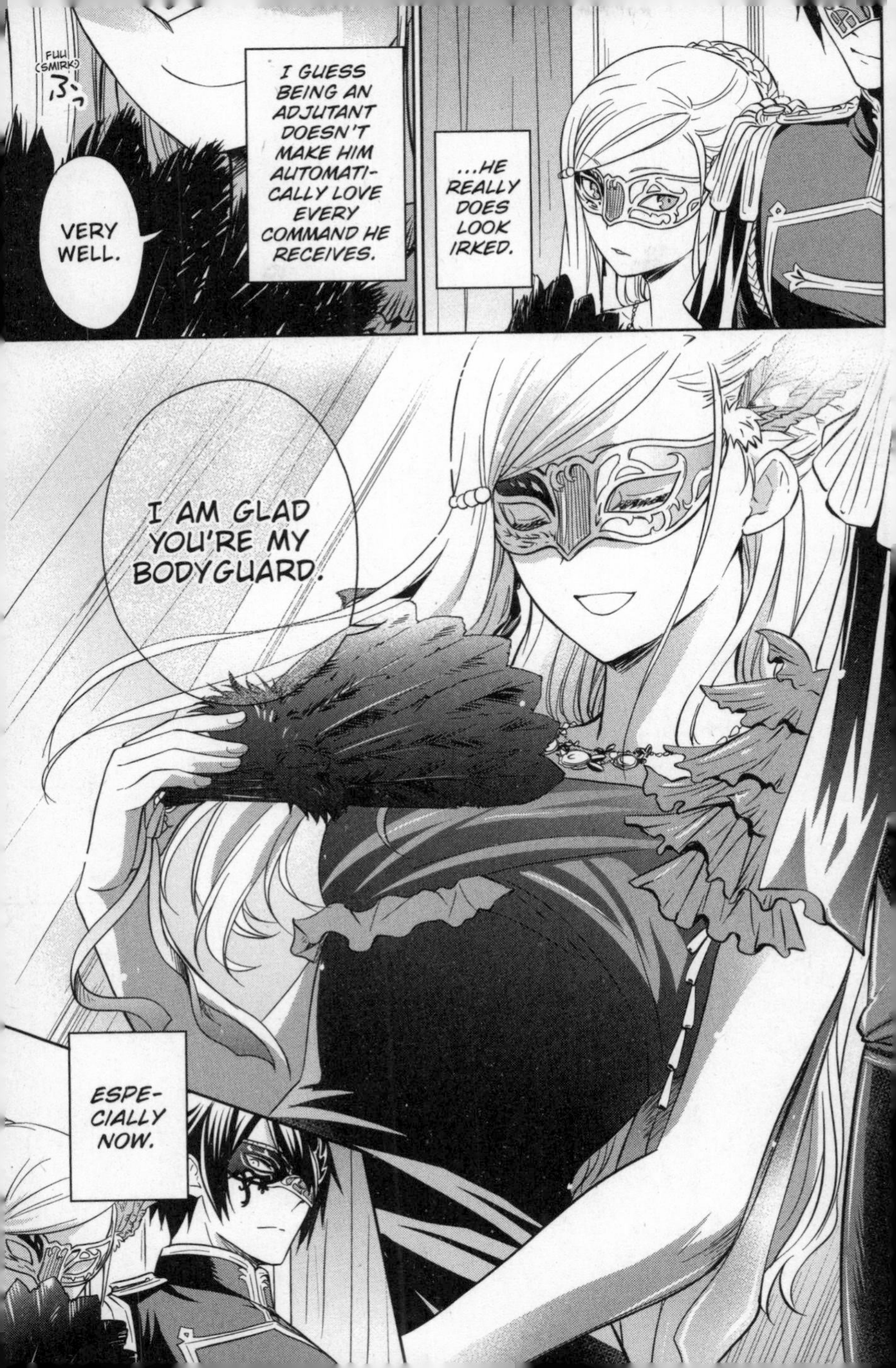
...HE REALLY DOES LOOK IRKED.
I GUESS BEING AN ADJUTANT DOESN'T MAKE HIM AUTOMATICALLY LOVE EVERY COMMAND HE RECEIVES.
FUU (SMIRK) ふっ
VERY WELL.
I AM GLAD YOU'RE MY BODYGUARD.
ESPECIALLY NOW.

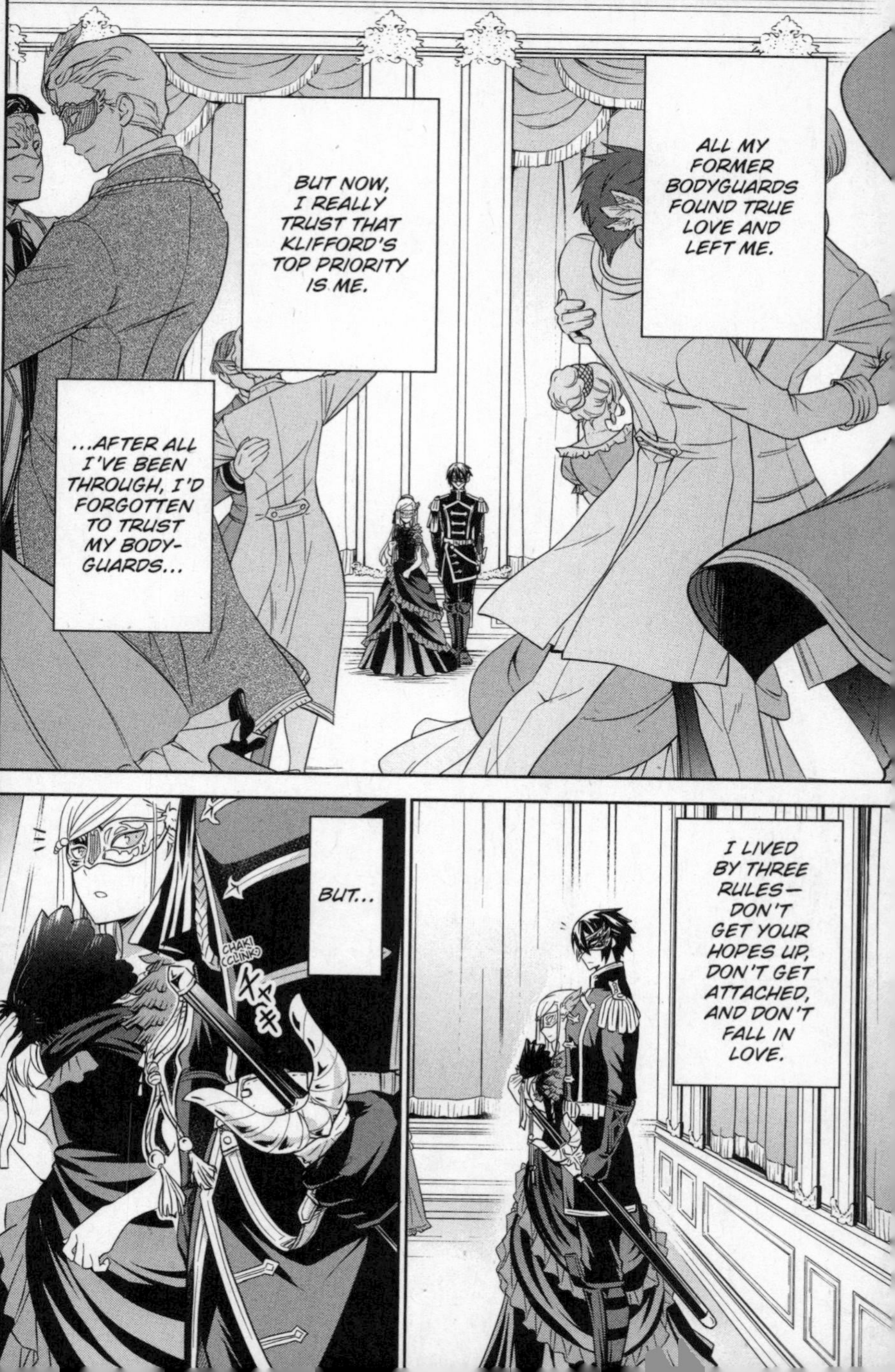
ALL MY FORMER BODYGUARDS FOUND TRUE LOVE AND LEFT ME.
BUT NOW, I REALLY TRUST THAT KLIFFORD'S TOP PRIORITY IS ME.
...AFTER ALL I'VE BEEN THROUGH, I'D FORGOTTEN TO TRUST MY BODY-GUARDS...
I LIVED BY THREE RULES—DON'T GET YOUR HOPES UP, DON'T GET ATTACHED, AND DON'T FALL IN LOVE.
BUT...
CHAKI (CLINK)

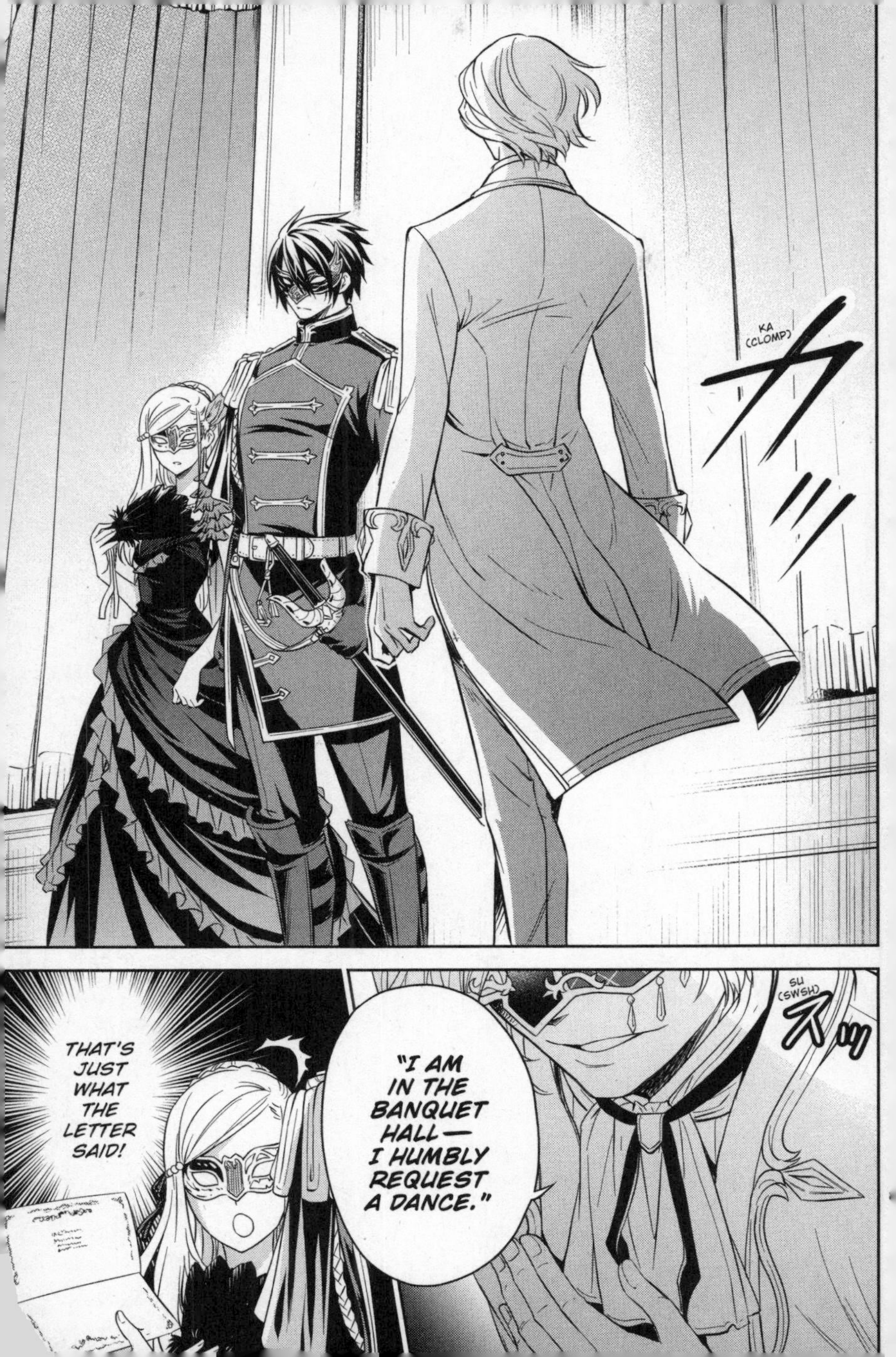
KA (CLOMP)
SU (SWSH)
"I AM IN THE BANQUET HALL— I HUMBLY REQUEST A DANCE."
THAT'S JUST WHAT THE LETTER SAID!

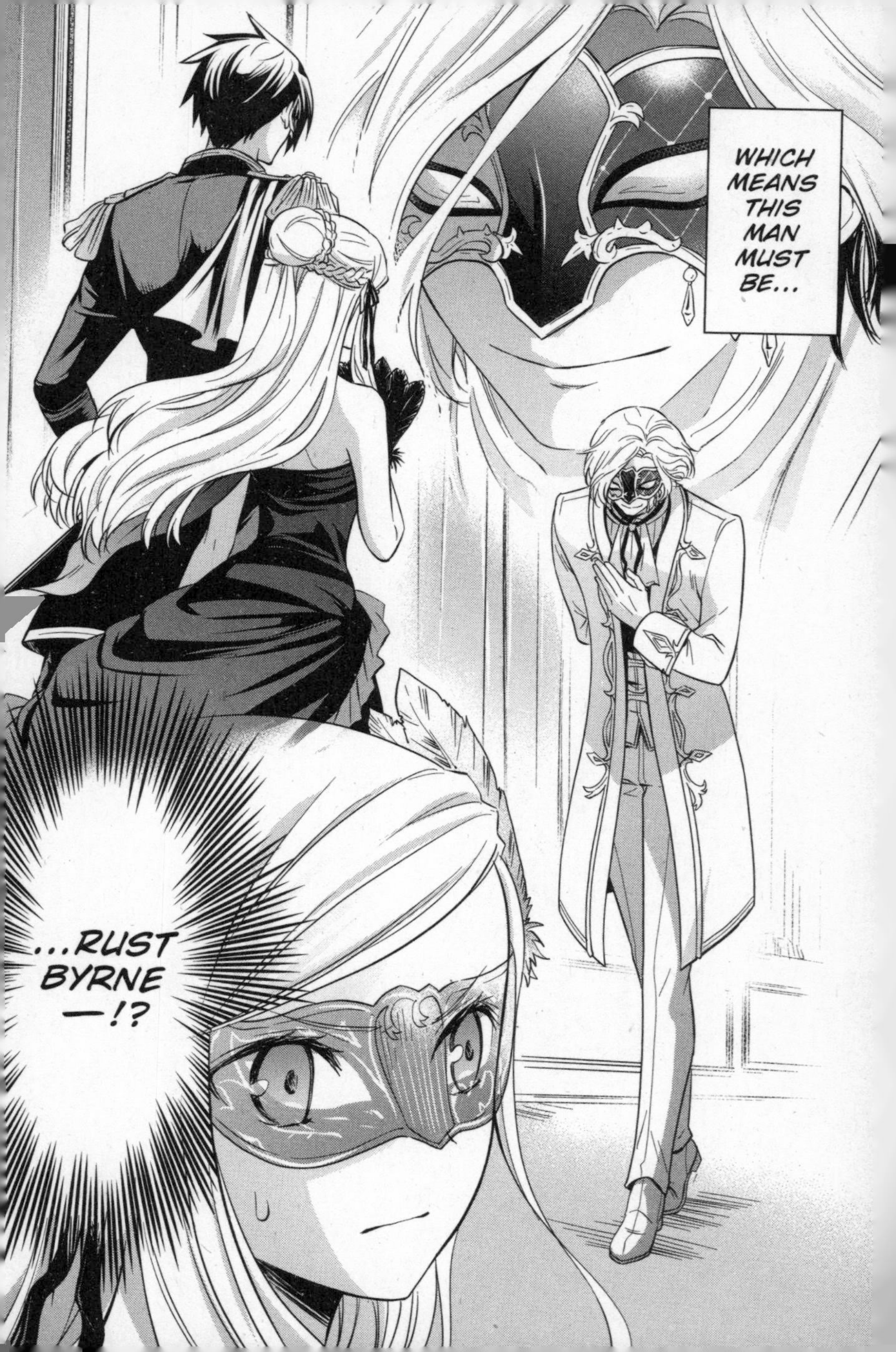
WHICH MEANS THIS MAN MUST BE...
...RUST BYRNE—!?